Professional Communication

PRECISION EXAMS

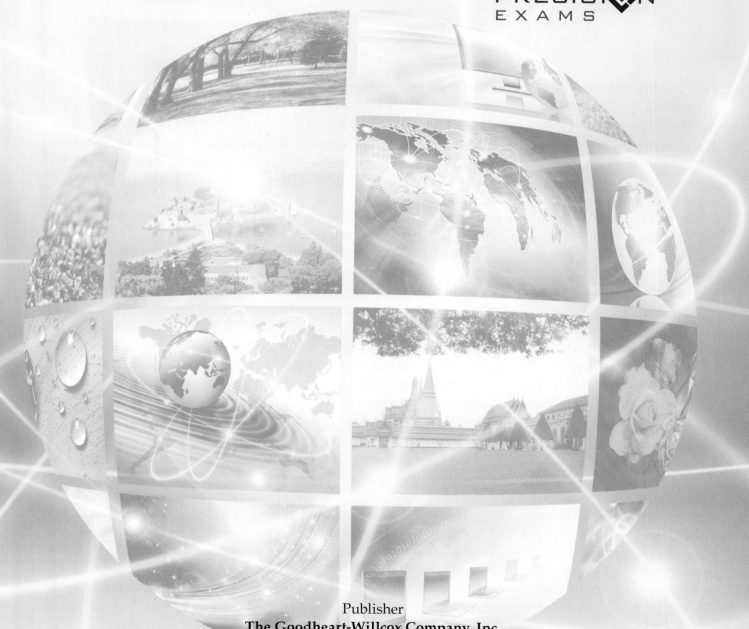

Publisher
The Goodheart-Willcox Company, Inc.
Tinley Park, Illinois
www.g-w.com

Introduction

As you prepare for college and career, an important key to success will be your communication skills. Individuals who understand how to incorporate written, verbal, visual, and digital communication to create clear messages take the first step toward personal success. By studying *Professional Communication*, you will have an opportunity to develop your skills and become career ready.

Each chapter is designed with you in mind. The topics are presented in a manner that is easy to read and understand. Numerous illustrations and photos enhance the concepts for clear understanding. Opportunities to evaluate what you have learned, as well as apply the concepts, help assure that you grasp the topics that have been presented.

As you progress through *Professional Communication*, you will learn how communication impacts your life now and how it will influence your future. Topics such as digital citizenship and grammar basics will help sharpen your skills and prepare you for college and career. Learning how to apply the writing process to create clear and concise messages will lead you to develop sought-after professional skills that are needed in the workplace. Other relevant topics, such as making presentations and interviewing skills, will prepare you to become an effective contributor in the 21st century.

Professional Communication provides an opportunity for you to maximize and refine your talents. As you explore and discover communication in this text, you will learn life-long skills that will follow you wherever your interests may lead.

Contributors

Goodheart-Willcox Publisher would like to thank the following educators who contributed to the development of *Professional Communication*.

Diane Wuthrich
Communications Specialist
Katy Independent School District
Katy, Texas

Beth Thomson Huse
Professional Communications and Business
  English Teacher
Lindale High School
Lindale, Texas

Al Marks
Business and Animation Teacher
Grand Prairie Independent School District
Grand Prairie, Texas

Dana Murphy
Literacy Coach
Midlothian School District 143
Midlothian, Illinois

H. Roger Fulk
Professor Emeritus
Wright State University
Dayton, Ohio

Reviewers

Goodheart-Willcox Publisher would also like to thank the following instructors and professionals who reviewed selected manuscript chapters and provided input for the development of *Professional Communication*.

Nancy Bowers
Instructor/Lecturer
Department of English
Northern Kentucky University
Highland Heights, Kentucky

Gregory A. Cardino
Fine Arts Department Chairperson
Mainland High School
Daytona Beach, Florida

Bob Crossen
General Assignment Reporter
Campbell Publications
Jerseyville, Illinois

Don Dunlap
Business Instructor
Patrick Henry High School
Stockbridge, Georgia

Cynthia Fillpot
CTE Teacher, International Business
  Academy Lead
Mark Keppel High School
Alhambra, California

Dawn Fischer
Career and Technical Education Teacher
Taylor High School
Taylor, Texas

Randy Hamm
English and Journalism Teacher (Retired)
East Bakersfield High School
Bakersfield, California

Connie Hampton
CTE Instructional Leader
Woodrow Wilson High School
Portsmouth, Virginia

Mike Harlen
Business Education Teacher
Brookland-Cayce High School
Cayce, South Carolina

Chris Kaminksi
Digital Media Teacher
Fairview Park City Schools
Fairview Park, Ohio

Gerri M. Kimble
Business Teacher
Hoover City Schools
Hoover, Alabama

James H. Miller
Journalism and Communication
  Department Chair
duPont Manual High School
Louisville, Kentucky

Renee Monteith
Business and Marketing Teacher,
  DECA Advisor
Clover High School
Clover, South Carolina

Julie Pritchett
Professional Communications Teacher
Irving High School
Irving, Texas

Lauren Pellegrino
Business Technologies Instructor
Wake Technical Community College
Raleigh, North Carolina

Deborah M. Rice, M.Ed.
Family and Consumer Science Teacher
Southwest Independent School District
Southwest High School
San Antonio, Texas

Joy Smith
Curriculum Consultant
Business, Finance, and Marketing
Tennessee Department of Education
Nashville, Tennessee

Precision Exams Certification

Goodheart-Willcox is pleased to partner with Precision Exams by correlating *Professional Communication* to the Standards, Objectives, and Indicators for Precision Exams Business Communication I and Business Communication II exams. Precision Exams were created in concert with industry and subject matter experts to match real-world job skills and marketplace demands. Students who pass the exam and performance portion of the exam can earn a Career Skills Certification ™. To see how *Professional Communication* correlates to the Precision Exam Standards, please visit www.g-w.com/professional-communication-2017 and click on the Correlations tab. For more information on Precision Exams, please visit www.precisionexams.com.

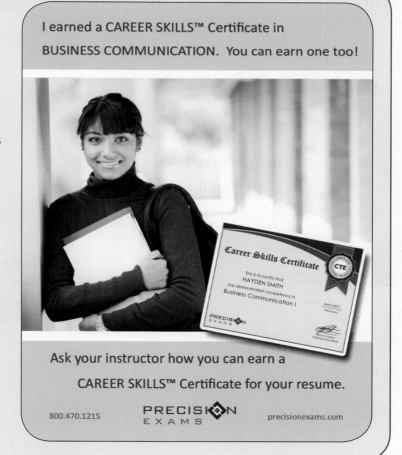

I earned a CAREER SKILLS™ Certificate in BUSINESS COMMUNICATION. You can earn one too!

Ask your instructor how you can earn a CAREER SKILLS™ Certificate for your resume.

800.470.1215   PRECISION EXAMS   precisionexams.com

Contents in Brief

Expanded Table of Contents vii

Features

Case Study

Exploring Communication Careers

Green

Ethics

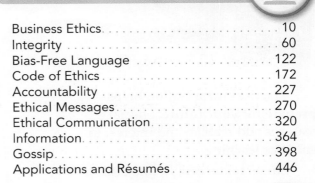

Business Protocol

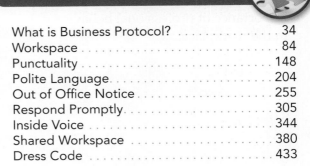

Prepare for Your Future

As you prepare for college and career, an important key to success will be your communication skills. Learning how to apply written, verbal, visual, and digital communication skills to communicate is the first step toward personal success. By studying *Professional Communication*, you will have an opportunity to learn about the communication process and how to make it work for you.

It is all about getting ready for college and career. College and career readiness activities address literacy skills to help prepare you for the real world.

- English/Language Arts standards for reading, writing, speaking, and listening are incorporated in **Reading Prep** activities, as well as in end-of-chapter applications.

- **Exploring Communication Careers** features present information about potential career opportunities in the Arts, A/V Technology & Communication career cluster. By studying these, you can explore career possibilities for your future.

- **Portfolio Development** activities provide guidance to create a personal portfolio for use when exploring volunteer, education and training, and career opportunities.

Practical information helps prepare for your future. Special features add realism and interest to enhance learning.

- **Ethics** offers insight into ethical issues with which you will be confronted in the workplace.

- **Business Protocol** illustrates the importance of professional behavior in the workplace.

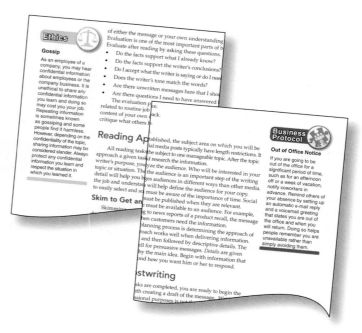

Amplify Your Learning

Content is presented in an easy-to-comprehend and relevant format. Activities relate everyday learning to enable you to experience real-life communication situations and challenges.

- Each chapter opens with a **pretest**. The pretest will help you evaluate your prior knowledge of the chapter content.

- Each chapter concludes with a **posttest**. The posttest will help you evaluate what you have learned after studying the chapter

- A **Case Study** in the chapter opener presents a communication situation that challenges you to answer thought-provoking questions about real-world scenarios.

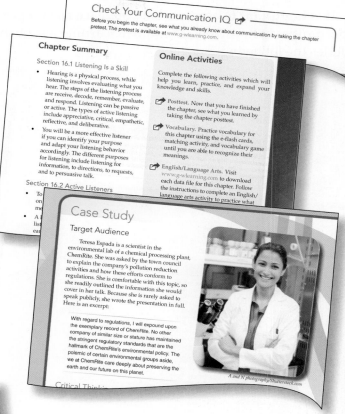

A and N photography/Shutterstock.com

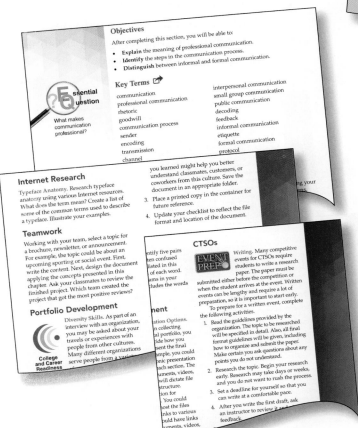

- The **Essential Question** at the beginning of each section will engage you as you uncover the important points presented in the content.

- Research skills are critical for success in college and career. **Internet Research** activities at the end of each chapter provide opportunities to put them to work.

- **Event Prep** presents information to use when preparing for competitive activities in career and technical student organization (CTSO) competitions.

Copyright Goodheart-Willcox Co., Inc.

xiii

Assess Your Progress

It is important to assess what you learn as you progress through the textbook. Multiple opportunities are provided to confirm learning as you explore the content. *Formative assessment* includes the following:

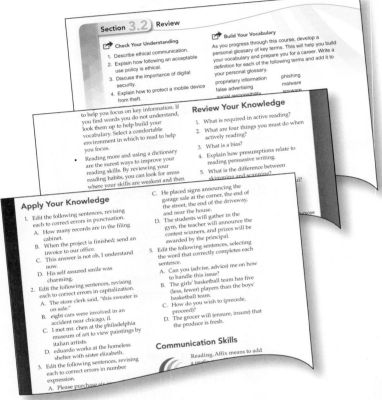

- **Check Your Understanding** questions at the end of each major section of the chapter provide an opportunity to review what you have learned before moving on to additional content.

- **Build Your Vocabulary** activities review the key terms presented in each major section. By completing these activities, you will be able to demonstrate your understanding of communication terms

- **Review Your Knowledge** activities cover basic concepts presented in the chapter so you can evaluate your understanding of the material.

- **Apply Your Knowledge** activities challenge you to relate what you learned in the chapter with your own ideas, experiences, and goals.

- **Communication Skills** activities provide ways for you to demonstrate the literacy and career readiness skills you have mastered.

- **Teamwork** activities encourage a collaborative experience to help you learn to interact with other students in a productive manner.

G-W Learning Companion Website

Technology is an important part of your world. So, it should be part of your everyday learning experiences. G-W Learning for *Professional Communication* is a study reference that contains activity files, vocabulary exercises, interactive quizzes, and more.

Visit www.g-wlearning.com/communication/.

G-W Learning provides you with opportunities for hands-on interactivity so you can study on the go. Look for the activity icon in the text next to the following activities:

- **Communication videos** at the beginning of each unit bring the content to life and illustrate how professional communication skills are used in the real world.

- Chapter **pretests** and **posttests** allow you to assess what you know before you begin the chapter as well as evaluate what you have learned at the completion of your study.

- **E-flash cards** and **matching activities** for every key term in each chapter will reinforce vocabulary learned in the text and enable you to study on the go.

- **English/Language Arts activity files** are downloadable hands-on activities that provide opportunities to apply reading, writing, speaking, and listening skills to prepare you for college and career.

Goodheart-Willcox QR Codes

This Goodheart-Willcox product contains QR codes*, or quick response codes. These codes can be scanned with smartphone bar code reader to access communication videos. For more information on using QR codes and a recommended QR code reader, visit G-W Learning.

www.g-wlearning.com

An Internet connection is required to access the QR code destinations. Data-transfer rates may apply. Check with your Internet service provider for information on your data-transfer rates.

G-W Integrated Learning Solution

The G-W Integrated Learning Solution offers easy-to-use resources for both students and instructors. Digital and blended learning content can be accessed through any Internet-enabled device such as a computer, smartphone, or tablet. Students spend more time learning, and instructors spend less time administering.

G-W Learning Companion Website/ Student Textbook

The G-W Learning companion website is a study reference that contains e-flash cards, vocabulary exercises, interactive quizzes, and more! Accessible from any digital device, the G-W Learning companion website complements the textbook and is available to the student at no charge. Visit www.g-wlearning.com.

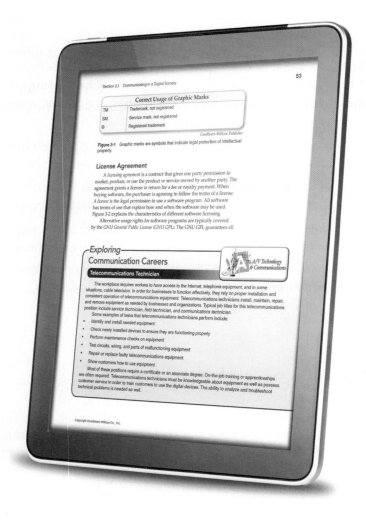

Online Learning Suite

Available as a classroom subscription, the Online Learning Suite provides the foundation of instruction and learning for digital and blended classrooms. An easy-to-manage shared classroom subscription makes it a hassle-free solution for both students and instructors. An online student text and workbook, along with rich supplemental content, brings digital learning to the classroom. All instructional materials are found on a convenient online bookshelf and accessible at home, at school, or on the go.

Online Learning Suite/Student Textbook Bundle

Looking for a blended solution? Goodheart-Willcox offers the Online Learning Suite bundled with the printed text in one easy-to-access package. Students have the flexibility to use the print version, the Online Learning Suite, or a combination of both components to meet their individual learning style. The convenient packaging makes managing and accessing content easy and efficient.

Online Instructor Resources

Online Instructor Resources provide all the support needed to make preparation and classroom instruction easier than ever. Available in one accessible location, support materials include Answer Keys, Lesson Plans, Instructor Presentations for PowerPoint®, ExamView® Assessment Suite, and more! Online Instructor Resources are available as a subscription and can be accessed at school or at home.

G-W Integrated Learning Solution

For the Student:
Student Textbook (print)

Student Workbook (print)

G-W Learning Companion Website (free)

Online Learning Suite (subscription)

Online Learning Suite/Student Textbook
  Bundle

For the Instructor:
Instructor's Presentations for PowerPoint® (CD)

ExamView® Assessment Suite (CD)

Instructor Resources (CD)

Online Instructor Resources (subscription)

Unit

1

Communication for a Digital Society

Professional Communication

Why It Matters

Communication is of vital importance to every business. Employees who understand and apply the communication process can contribute to a more productive and successful workplace.

Employers seek individuals who are well spoken, possess good writing skills, and demonstrate effectiveness when interacting with others one-on-one and in groups. People with excellent technology skills and the professionalism to use those skills appropriately in our digital society are essential to workplace success.

Good communication skills are not developed overnight. Hard work, patience, and focus can make you a professional communicator.

Chapters

Chapter 1   Professional Communication

Chapter 2   Communicating in the Workplace

Chapter 3   Digital Citizenship

While studying, look for the activity icon for:

- Pretests and posttests
- Vocabulary terms with e-flash cards and matching activities
- Videos
- Self-assessment

Video

Before you begin this unit, scan the QR code to view a video about professional communication. If you do not have a smartphone, visit www.g-wlearning.com.

wavebreakmedia/Shutterstock.com

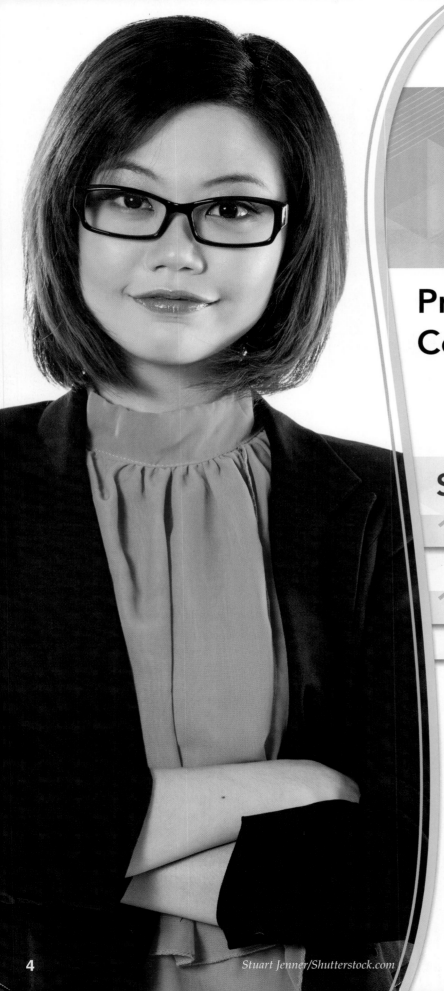

1

Professional Communication

Sections

1.1 Introduction to Professional Communication

1.2 Communicating Effectively

College and Career Readiness

Reading Prep. As you read this chapter, determine the point of view or purpose of the author. What aspects of the text help to establish this purpose or point of view?

Check Your Communication IQ ➦

Before you begin the chapter, see what you already know about communication by taking the chapter pretest. The pretest is available at www.g-wlearning.com.

Case Study

Nonverbal Messages

The weekly budget meeting at Leading Edge Productions is routine: same day, time, place, and participants. Charlie Burrows makes it a habit to arrive at every meeting ten minutes late. On Friday, as Charlie walked in, Hannah Rankowski stopped presenting and sneered momentarily before turning back to the board and continuing with her presentation. Charlie ignored Hannah's nonverbal communication signals and went to his place at the meeting table and took a seat. A few moments later, Charlie started checking e-mails on his cell phone.

lightwavemedia/Shutterstock.com

Critical Thinking

1. What message is Charlie sending by arriving late to budget meetings and not paying attention to the speaker?

2. How important were the nonverbal messages the speaker was sending Charlie?

Introduction to Professional Communication

Objectives

After completing this section, you will be able to:

- **Explain** the meaning of professional communication.
- **Identify** the steps in the communication process.
- **Distinguish** between informal and formal communication.

Key Terms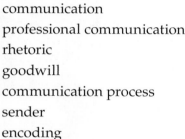

communication	interpersonal communication
professional communication	small group communication
rhetoric	public communication
goodwill	decoding
communication process	feedback
sender	informal communication
encoding	etiquette
transmission	formal communication
channel	protocol
receiver	peer

?Essential Question

What makes communication professional?

Professional Communication

What does communication mean to you? Sending an e-mail? Using your cell phone? **Communication** is the process of using words, sounds, signs, or actions to exchange information or express thoughts. Communication skills affect your basic ability to understand others, establish positive relationships, and perform in most situations. Being able to communicate skillfully, therefore, is essential to your ability to succeed in your career.

Communication that is associated with technology or business can be described as professional communication. **Professional communication** incorporates written, verbal, visual, and digital communication to provide factual information that is usable in the workplace. Professional communication focuses on using technology to create and distribute information. It *does not* focus on creative writing techniques. Instead, professional communication uses visuals such as charts, design elements, and illustrations to convey data. The language is simple and descriptive.

All communication has a purpose. When people communicate, there is a specific reason for doing so. Identifying the purpose of communication is also known as the *intent*. The purpose of professional communication will usually fall into one of these categories.

- *Inform.* A message that informs is one that provides information or education. For example, a nutrition label on a product conveys a message that informs the consumer. A major goal of professional communication is to inform.

- *Persuade.* A message that persuades is one that attempts to change the behavior of the receiver. A car advertisement is an example of a message that attempts to persuade the receiver of the information to buy a car. Professional communication attempts to persuade and change behavior through messages such as an advertisement or a brochure.

- *Instruct.* A message that instructs others is one that attempts to provide direction or guidance. If you send an e-mail to your department directing them to attend a meeting, you are sending a message to instruct others. Professional communication focuses on influencing the audience by providing guidance such as directions in a technical document or manual. It uses graphics to help readability and visuals to provide appeal.

- *Make a request.* Many messages that you send during a day take the form of a request. A message that makes a request is one that asks a question about information or asks for an action to occur. Sending an e-mail to your supervisor to request to use your vacation time is an example.

- *Respond to a request.* Alternatively to making a request, there will be times that you must respond to a request that has been made of you. You are responding to a request when a customer asks you to suggest the right product for his or her needs and you make a recommendation.

Rido/Shutterstock.com

Communication involves written, verbal, and nonverbal messages.

Rhetoric is an important part of professional communication. **Rhetoric** is the study of writing or speaking as a way of communicating information or persuading an individual. Professional communication focuses on improving the ability of writers and speakers to inform, persuade, or instruct the audience to respond in a certain manner.

Professional communication encourages goodwill. **Goodwill** is the advantage an individual or an organization has due to its good reputation; it cannot be bought. It is the positive opinions that a business creates. The goal is to encourage better communication between people in the workplace and those outside of the workplace.

Communication Process

Before you begin to study the skills that will make you a better writer, speaker, listener, and reader, it is a good idea to explore the broader concept of the communication process. The **communication process** is a series of actions on the part of the sender and the receiver of a message and the path the message follows. The six elements of the process are the sender, message, channel, receiver, translation, and feedback, as shown in Figure 1-1.

Sender

The person who has a message to communicate is called the **sender**. The sender begins the communication process. First, the sender decides there is a need to relay information to the receiver.

Intrapersonal communication is the conversation a person has with one's self. Sometimes known as *self-talk*, this is how most individuals sort through the information they want to convey. Next, the information is assembled and takes the form of a message.

Message

The sender decides which format the message will take. The sender might choose to use written words, spoken words, pictures, or other visuals such as a YouTube video. **Encoding** is the process of turning the idea for

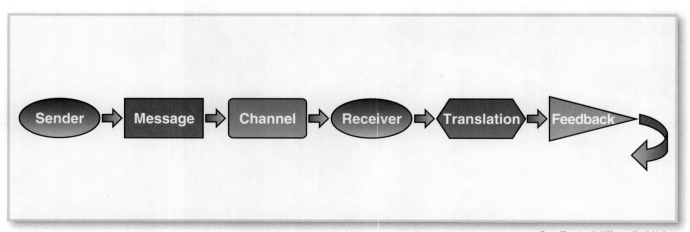

Goodheart-Willcox Publisher

Figure 1-1   Each of the six parts of the communication process is important.

a message into symbols that can be communicated. Most people convert their messages into a language of written or spoken words or symbols the receiver can understand. In order for the message to be understood, both the sender and the receiver must be able to interpret the words or symbols.

Channel

Once the message is encoded, it is ready to be sent. The act of sending a message is called **transmission**. The **channel** is how the message is transmitted such as face-to-face conversation, telephone, text, or any other vehicle that is appropriate for the situation.

The sender decides the best channel through which to send the message. Factors that influence how a message is transmitted include:

- need for security or confidentiality
- importance of having a written record of the information
- need for the receiver to have the information immediately
- proximity, which is how close you are to the receiver
- number of people receiving the message
- level of formality necessary
- expectations of the receiver

Analyzing these factors can help you select the appropriate channel for your message.

Receiver

The **receiver** is the person who reads, hears, or sees the message. The receiver is also known as the *audience*. The receiver can be any number of people, from one coworker to the thousands of people who see a television commercial. **Interpersonal communication** is communication that occurs between the sender and one other person. **Small group communication** is communication that occurs with 3 to 20 people. **Public communication** is communicating with a group larger than 20 people.

The receiver has a responsibility to the sender because communication is a two-

Monkey Business Images/Shutterstock.com

There are many different communication channels, from a letter or e-mail to a face-to-face conversation.

way process. How do you feel when you send an e-mail to which you never receive a response? Paying attention to the sender is a matter of courtesy and necessity and is essential to the communication process.

Translation

Once the receiver receives the message, it will be decoded. **Decoding** is the translation of a message into terms that the receiver can understand. It occurs in the receiver's mind. Decoding is usually seen as the process of understanding a message. The message is not technically received if the receiver does not understand what has been read.

Feedback

Feedback is the receiver's response to the sender and concludes the communication process. Providing feedback to a sender is a crucial step in the process. This tells the sender if the receiver understood the message as it was intended. If the sender does not receive feedback to be sure the message was understood, the communication process has failed.

Informal and Formal Communication

Communication management is the planning and execution of professional communication within an organization. It involves awareness of the appropriate channels for communication as well as which individuals need specific information. Before communication occurs, decisions must be made to determine the level of formality that is necessary. Communication in the workplace may be informal or formal.

Informal communication is casual sharing of information with no customs or rules of etiquette involved. **Etiquette** is the art of using good manners in any situation. Reporting hierarchy is not important in informal communication. People from various levels, divisions, and positions interact with each other in a casual way. Informal communication could be text messaging, telephone calls, or just talking in the hallway. Informal communication is necessary to build teamwork and cooperation within an organization. However, it may or may not be a dependable source of facts.

Formal communication is sharing of information that conforms to specific protocol. **Protocol** is a set of customs or rules of etiquette. Formal communication typically takes place in letters, e-mails, presentations, or other messages that are planned and put into words. Written documents are generally used when it is necessary to record information for future reference. They may be used for internal or external communication.

By applying communication management skills and following business protocol, identifying standards for communication choices can become routine. For example, it may not be appropriate for a manager to bypass the vice president about an issue and go straight to the CEO. Formal communication usually happens according to level within an organization. It flows in three directions, as shown in Figure 1-2.

- *Upward communication* is the flow of information from lower levels of an organization to those people in higher levels.
- *Lateral communication* is communication that takes place between peers. **Peers** are persons of equal standing or work position.
- *Downward communication* is the flow of information from higher levels of an organization to those people in lower levels.

Business Ethics

Ethics is a set of rules that define what is right and wrong. Ethics helps people make good decisions in both their personal and professional lives. *Business ethics* is a set of rules that help define appropriate behavior in the business setting.

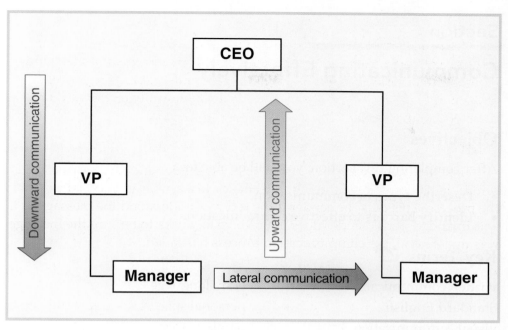

Figure 1-2   Communication within a business flows in one of three ways.

Section Review

Check Your Understanding

1. What is the purpose of professional communication?
2. List the elements of the communication process.
3. Explain the role of a channel in the communication process.
4. Explain the difference between formal and informal communication.
5. Explain how to identify standards for making appropriate communication choices in the workplace.

Build Your Vocabulary

As you progress through this course, develop a personal glossary of key terms. This will help you build your vocabulary and prepare you for a career. Write a definition for each of the following terms and add it to your personal glossary.

communication	interpersonal communication
professional communication	small group communication
rhetoric	public communication
goodwill	decoding
communication process	feedback
sender	informal communication
encoding	etiquette
transmission	formal communication
channel	protocol
receiver	peer

Communicating Effectively

Objectives

After completing this section, you will be able to:

- **Describe** types of communication.
- **Identify** barriers to effective communication.

Key Terms 📤

written communication	body language
Standard English	personal space
visual communication	paralanguage
verbal communication	barrier
nonverbal communication	sending barrier
context	receiving barrier

?Essential Question

How does the *way* in which you communicate affect *what* you communicate?

Types of Communication

The communication process is taken for granted most of the time. You would not be able to get through the day if you stopped to plan and analyze the impact of every communication you have. On the other hand, there are many times when you do stop to think and prepare before you communicate. Most people have a natural sense for when planning and preparation are critical to what is said and how it is stated.

Why do you communicate? In a typical day, you might:

- write an e-mail explaining a new company policy
- call a colleague to say congratulations on a job well done
- create a sales message to persuade customers to buy your product
- design a digital media presentation for a meeting
- send a text message to a friend

If you were to chart your daily activities, you would find that you spend most of your time communicating. Communication skills affect your basic ability to understand others, establish positive relationships, and perform in most situations.

Written and Visual Communication

Written communication is recording words through writing to communicate. Written communication is used to record and convey information of varying levels of importance. It can have an enormous impact on how a business functions. Business communication represents you and your company.

Professional writing requires use of Standard English. **Standard English** refers to English language usage that follows accepted rules for spelling, grammar, and punctuation. This is true of all documents including digital communication.

Words are the tools of all written communication. How well you use these tools affects the success of your messages. When you send messages, you select language and construct sentences in a way that will achieve your purpose. It is necessary to stop and think before writing, whether it is a document, a blog, or an e-mail. Every written communication creates a record that can be recalled in the future.

Professional communication applies visual communication as a tool. **Visual communication** is using visual aids or graphics to communicate an idea or concept. It may or may not accompany written communication. Visuals add clarity, understanding, and interest to attract and maintain the attention of the audience. Visuals are described in Chapter 12.

Verbal Communication

Verbal communication is speaking words to communicate. It is also known as *oral communication*. In the course of a workday, most people spend at least some portion of time talking with coworkers, supervisors, managers, or customers. This communication involves a variety of situations, such as conversations about work tasks, asking and answering questions, making requests, giving information, and participating in meetings. Professional communicators learn to speak fluently and with confidence.

Words are the tools of verbal communication. You must plan and organize your thoughts to select the appropriate words for the message. This might be as simple as thinking before you speak. It could also be as elaborate as outlining a presentation and practicing several times before you deliver it. Planning always involves thinking about who will receive the message and what you want to accomplish. Making notes before a phone call, having an agenda for a meeting, or researching information in advance are all methods that can be used to prepare before talking to people at work. Planning helps you clearly focus on your purpose so that you can choose the appropriate language and channel. It also saves time because you are less likely to need to repeat a message or have a second meeting to clarify.

Monkey Business Images/Shutterstock.com

Verbal communication involves speaking words to transmit a message.

Nonverbal Communication

Nonverbal communication is an action, behavior, or attitude that sends a message to the receiver. Some nonverbal messages are subtle. Others involve behavior that sends loud messages in spite of what you might say. For example, if you visit a client's office and leave your coat on while standing near the door, the client is going to receive the message that you are in a hurry to leave.

Nonverbal communication is often used in conjunction with verbal communication. Nonverbal communication can be so strong that it overwhelms the verbal message. For example, if you tell a coworker you are not busy but keep scrolling through your mailbox, the message sent is that you *are* busy.

Nonverbal messages may not always be clear. Most nonverbal messages must be considered in the context in which they occur. **Context** is the environment or setting in which something occurs or is communicated. It is the situation that surrounds a word, action, or idea and helps clarify meaning. For example, a smile can mean a person finds your statement funny or it could mean he or she does not believe you. Context is used to determine what the nonverbal message actually means.

Body Language

Body language is nonverbal messages sent through gestures, facial expressions, posture, and other body actions. If you smile, sneer, raise an eyebrow, shrug your shoulders, nod in agreement, cross your arms, or clench your teeth, you are communicating just as if you are talking. The receiver picks up on these cues and they become an important part of your message. This is why being aware of body language is an essential professional skill. In the business environment, you must be aware of the nonverbal messages you send and receive. Otherwise, you run the risk of sending the wrong message or feedback.

 Green   Environmental Protection Agency

The United States Environmental Protection Agency (EPA) is a government organization with a mission to protect human health and the environment. The EPA is a rich resource of information on environmental issues, such as pollution, climate change, protecting wildlife, and hazardous waste disposal.

The EPA also publishes information on environmental regulations by business sector. It is important for businesses to do their part to protect the environment. Every type of business must follow laws enforced by the EPA. Visit www.epa.gov to learn more about what individuals and businesses can do to preserve the Earth.

Additionally, businesses can go above and beyond what is legally required. Green businesses lead by example and educate their employees on sustainable business practices. Through sustainability training, employees learn the importance of *going green* at work and the best practices to reduce waste and lower energy consumption.

Have you ever had a facial expression betray your emotions no matter how hard you tried to hide them? This type of nonverbal message is not only unintentional, it is often uncontrollable. In fact, sending nonverbal messages without realizing it is quite common.

Eye Contact

In American culture, *eye contact* is an important form of body language. Appropriate eye contact means looking directly at the other person while engaged in conversation, but not staring too intently. Staring may make the other person uncomfortable. In some cultures, it may be considered rude to make eye contact when speaking or listening. In other cultures, eye contact is expected.

Most people have a natural tendency to look directly at the person with whom they are engaged in conversation. What if someone approaches you while you are in the middle of doing something, such as dialing a telephone or reading an e-mail? If you do not stop what you are doing and make eye contact, you are saying, "Please go away, I'm too busy to talk to you now."

A distracted listener may allow his or her eyes to roam the room, not realizing that the speaker interprets the wandering eyes as disinterest or disdain. Being more self-aware is the only way to prevent these kinds of unintended messages.

Eye contact is a meaningful form of body language in every culture.

Andrey_Popov/Shutterstock.com

Touch

Touch is another form of body language that sends strong messages. *Haptics communication* refers to nonverbal communication that occurs through touch. A firm handshake, along with eye contact and a smile, sends an important message when you are introduced to someone new. These gestures convey openness and confidence. Open and confident body language in professional situations helps you create an impression of someone who is competent and trustworthy.

In the workplace, a handshake is about the only form of touch that is acceptable. Any other form of physical contact must be within the boundaries of correctness. These boundaries vary, depending on the nature of the business and the culture. For example, a dentist must touch your face in order to complete an examination. However, if you work in an office and somebody touched your face, you would be offended, if not very upset. In general, do not engage in any physical contact other than what is required of your work.

Personal Space

Personal space is the physical space between two individuals. It is another aspect of body language. How close to someone do you stand or sit? The personal-space boundary becomes apparent when someone gets too close. Be aware that cultural background may be a factor in defining the personal-space boundary. Americans tend to keep a slightly greater distance between themselves and others than do people from certain cultures. Consider this when interacting with people in diverse settings.

Exploring
Communication Careers

Graphic Designer

Print and online advertising rely to some extent on graphic images to catch the eye of potential customers. The job of a graphic designer is to create illustrative elements that present goods or services in an appealing manner for packaging, logos, brochures, and other items that represent the business. Typical job titles for this visual arts position also include *graphic artist*, *creative director*, *design director*, and *desktop publisher*.

Some examples of tasks that graphic designers perform include:

- Consult with the client to determine design.
- Create designs and layouts for product packaging and company logos.
- Use graphic design software to generate layouts.
- Design the arrangement of illustrations and text.
- Prepare final layouts for printing or production.

Graphic designers need a solid knowledge of layout principles and design concepts, as well as artistic ability. They must also be familiar with design, illustration, photo editing, and layout software. Many graphic design jobs require a bachelor degree, but talented and experienced designers may be hired without a four-year degree.

How you identify your personal space and the judgment you apply to the space of others varies depending on your social upbringing and community norms. When you enter a professional environment, be aware that the workplace has its own unwritten rules of social and community behavior. Noticing and adapting to them will help you to communicate with comfort and assure that those receiving your message are comfortable.

Behavior

Nonverbal messages can compete with verbal messages and can even negate them. This is true of body language. It is also true when it comes to your behavior. If you say one thing and do another, your verbal messages are likely to be ignored. For example, a supervisor who asks workers to stay late but who does not do the same will probably find few staff members willing to work late. As the saying goes, actions speak louder than words. In this example, the supervisor is saying, "the work isn't as important as I said it was."

When first entering the workforce, it is important to take behavioral cues from others with more experience, but do not make the mistake of emulating poor habits. For example, suppose the starting time is 9:00 a.m. and you are allotted one hour for lunch. But, several employees arrive a little later than nine and take a little longer than an hour for lunch. Do not follow this behavior. Arriving on time and limiting your lunch to the allotted one hour lets your boss know that you are dependable and willing to follow the rules.

Attitude

Paralanguage is the attitude you project with the tone and pitch of your voice. It is reflected in speech as a sharp or soft tone, raising or lowering of the voice, speaking quickly or slowly, and the general quality of the voice. Paralanguage is nonverbal communication that reflects the speaker's true attitude, so it is important to be aware of it. When the content of your message is contradicted by the attitude with which you are communicating, your message will be received accordingly. If you say you are not angry but you raise your voice, the receiver will know you really are angry.

Whenever you are speaking, remember that the tone, pitch, quality of voice, and rate of speaking convey emotions that will be judged by the receiver, regardless of the content of the message. If you get critical feedback from others about any of these voice qualities, be sure to take it seriously. The voice is not just a vehicle for the message; it is part of the message. As a communicator, you should be sensitive to the influence of paralanguage on the interpretation of your message by the receiver. When your voice complements the message, there is a greater chance that your words will be received as you intended.

Barriers to Effective Communication

The six steps in the communication process can create potential barriers at the sender's end of the process, at the receiver's end, or both. A **barrier** is anything that prevents clear, effective communication. Barriers may occur in written, verbal, and nonverbal communication.

Sending Barriers

A **sending barrier** can occur when the sender says or does something that causes the receiver to stop listening. This can happen when the receiver simply does not understand what the sender is saying. The words used may not be clear to the sender. Such misunderstandings cause daily problems ranging from minor events to serious, costly errors. Sending barriers may include:

- using poor grammar or spelling
- overlooking typographical and formatting errors
- presenting visually unattractive text or inappropriate graphics
- assuming too much or too little about what the receiver already knows
- using inappropriate language (slang, jargon, or too formal or informal phrasing)

Face-to-face nonverbal communication that causes barriers includes:

- distracting mannerisms
- facial expressions that conflict with the words being said
- inappropriate dress or demeanor
- sarcastic or angry tone of voice
- speaking too softly or too loudly

In these situations, the sender's written or verbal message may be lost or undermined by competing nonverbal messages. The sender who does not have a good grasp of the purpose for communicating is likely to relay a confused and ineffective message.

How can the sender overcome barriers? The sender has a responsibility to the receiver to make sure the message is clear and understood. Select the appropriate format for your message, such as an e-mail or a phone call, based on the situation. Do not assume too much or too little about what the receiver already knows. Ask for feedback from the receiver to see if your message came across clearly.

For written documents, follow the rules of writing, grammar, and formatting documents. A well-written and properly formatted document will send a positive message. For face-to-face communication, maintain positive body language and behavior. Keep in mind that speaking loudly does not overcome communication barriers.

Receiving Barriers

A **receiving barrier** can occur when the receiver says or does something that causes the sender's message not to be received. These barriers can be just as harmful to the communication process as sending barriers. The receiver has a responsibility to give attention and respect to the sender. Most receiving barriers can be overcome with a little self-awareness.

Give feedback to let the sender know you received the message. This can be done by asking questions or giving information if needed. Take responsibility for getting clarification if you do not understand the message. For written documents, make sure you read all of what has been written.

The sender has a responsibility to make sure the message was received as intended.

Elena Elisseeva/Shutterstock.com

While *hearing* is physical ability, *listening* is a conscious action. Although senders are responsible for sending clear messages, listeners should be ready to recognize unclear messages. A listener who is willing to accept responsibility for getting clarification will be a more effective communicator.

Section 1.2   Review

 ### Check Your Understanding

1. List the types of professional communication.
2. Describe the importance of planning before communicating verbally.
3. Explain why body language is important in professional communication.
4. How do sending and receiving barriers occur?
5. What is the difference between hearing and listening?

 ### Build Your Vocabulary

As you progress through this course, develop a personal glossary of key terms. This will help you build your vocabulary and prepare you for a career. Write a definition for each of the following terms and add it to your personal glossary.

written communication	body language
Standard English	personal space
visual communication	paralanguage
verbal communication	barrier
nonverbal communication	sending barrier
context	receiving barrier

1 Review and Assessment

Chapter Summary

Section 1.1 Introduction to Professional Communication

- Communication is sending and receiving messages that convey information, ideas, feelings, and beliefs. Professional communication incorporates written, verbal, visual, and digital communication to provide information that is usable in the workplace. It focuses on using technology to create and distribute information. Rhetoric is an important part of professional communication. People communicate for specific reasons, such as to inform, persuade, direct others, make a request, or respond to a request.

- The communication process is a series of actions on the part of the sender and the receiver of a message and the path the message follows. The six elements of the process are the sender, message, channel, receiver, translation, and feedback.

- Business communication may be informal or formal. Informal business communication is casual sharing of information with no customs or rules of etiquette. Formal business communication is information shared with regard to accepted protocol.

Section 1.2 Communicating Effectively

- Communication can be written, verbal, or nonverbal. Written communication is recording words through writing or keying. Verbal communication is speaking. Nonverbal communication uses body language, behavior, and attitude to communicate.

- Barriers to effective communication can be sending or receiving barriers. Sending barriers are the result of something the sender does to prevent communication. Receiving barriers occur when the receiver does something to prevent communication.

Online Activities

Complete the following activities which will help you learn, practice, and expand your knowledge and skills.

Posttest. Now that you have finished the chapter, see what you learned by taking the chapter posttest.

Vocabulary. Practice vocabulary for this chapter using the e-flash cards, matching activity, and vocabulary game until you are able to recognize their meanings.

English/Language Arts. Visit www.g-wlearning.com to download each data file for this chapter. Follow the instructions to complete an English/language arts activity to practice what you have learned in this chapter.

Activity File 1-1: Improving Your Listening Skills

Activity File 1-2: Using Mnemonics

Review Your Knowledge

1. Explain the role of rhetoric in professional communication.

2. List and explain the function of each element in the communication process.

3. What is the role of feedback in the communication process?

4. Describe the direction in which formal communication typically flows.

5. Describe the difference between written and verbal communication.

6. Why is nonverbal communication important?

7. Explain the importance of context in nonverbal communication.

8. Describe appropriate eye contact when communicating with others.

9. Explain why paralanguage is considered a form of nonverbal communication even though it involves use of the voice.

10. Give an example of a sending barrier that can occur with face-to-face communication.

Apply Your Knowledge

1. Each form of professional communication has its own purpose or intent. Language must always be adapted for the needs of the audience. Create a table with three columns. In the first column, list the four purposes for communicating: inform, persuade, request, and direct. In the second column, give a brief description of each. In the last column, give an example of each purpose. Use this table as a reference as you communicate for professional purposes.

2. Initiate an informal conversation with a classmate or an instructor. When the communication process is complete, note each step. Who are the sender and the receiver? What is the message? What channel was used? Was the message translated and how do you know? Receiving feedback signifies whether the communication process was successful. Analyze each step of the communication process to evaluate whether the communication was clear and appropriate.

3. An important part of the communication process is applying communication management skills to recognize the appropriate channel of communication in your organization. Following protocol will help you identify standards for making appropriate communication choices. Identify which channel of communication (letter, memo, formal e-mail, phone call) should be used for the following situations and why.

   A. Asking a colleague where to find information about a company policy.
   B. Confirming a meeting time.
   C. Writing a summary of minutes from a meeting.
   D. Forwarding information to a client.

4. Channels of communication in the workplace are typically formal or informal. Make a list of three ways you, as an employee, would communicate with someone in the workplace who was higher in rank than you. For each channel, write the type of communication and why you chose it. Next, make a list of three ways you would communicate in the workplace with someone who was lower in rank with you. For each channel, write the type of communication and why you chose it.

5. Informal communication generally takes place between friends or peers in a work environment. It does not require following protocol the way formal communication with managers requires. Analyze the standards of informal communication and professional etiquette as they should be applied in the workplace. Make a list of the protocol you would suggest for talking with peers.

6. Nonverbal communication is important in the workplace. Strategies such as eye contact, handshake, and respect of personal space is important when conducting business. Make a list of reasons why you think each of these behaviors is important. What effect does each of these nonverbal communications send?

7. Make a list of five careers in the Arts, A/V Technology & Communications cluster. Next to each career, indicate which channel of communication is used primarily by each career. For example, an actor might use face-to-face conversation to convey his or her message to the audience.

Communication Skills

College and Career Readiness

Reading. Read a magazine, newspaper, or online article about the importance of effective communication for teens. Determine the central ideas of the article and review the conclusions made by the author. Take notes to identify its purpose and intended audience. Demonstrate your understanding of the information by summarizing what you read.

Writing. Rhetoric is the study of writing or speaking as a way of communicating information or persuading someone. Describe a rhetorical technique that a writer can use to provide information or persuade someone. Write an example of the technique you chose.

Speaking. Create a one-act play for two persons that depicts both a positive and a negative interaction between two coworkers. Include notes to the actors about body language and facial expressions. What is the essential difference between the two interactions? How does body language influence whether the message will be received negatively or positively? Write several paragraphs describing your opinion about the impact of body language in the workplace.

Internet Research

Nonverbal Communication. Research the topic of body language and culture in the United States using various Internet resources. Create a table correlating the behavior or body language to what it means. For example, crossed arms usually mean you are being defensive.

Teamwork

Working in a group, describe a time when you either observed or created a sending barrier and a receiving barrier. Solicit feedback from your teammates on what caused the barrier and what you could have done differently to avoid it.

Portfolio Development

College and Career Readiness

Portfolio Overview. When you apply for a job, community service, or college, you will need to tell others why you are qualified for the position. To support your qualifications, you will need to create a portfolio. A *portfolio* is a selection of related materials that you collect and organize to show your qualifications, skills, and talents to support a career or personal goal. For example, a certificate that shows you have completed lifeguard and first-aid training could help you get a job at a local pool as a lifeguard. An essay you wrote about protecting native plants could show that you are serious about eco-friendly efforts and help you get a volunteer position at a park. A transcript of your school grades could help show that you are qualified for college. A portfolio is a *living document*, which means it should be reviewed and updated on a regular basis.

Artists and other communication professionals have historically presented portfolios of their creative work when seeking jobs or admission to educational institutions. However, portfolios are now used in many professions.

Two types of portfolios commonly used are print portfolios and digital portfolios. A digital portfolio may also be called an *e-portfolio*.

1. Use the Internet to search for *print portfolio* and *digital portfolio*. Read articles about each type.

2. In your own words, compare and contrast a print portfolio with a digital one.

CTSOs

Student Organizations. Career and technical student organizations (CTSOs) are a valuable asset to any educational program. These organizations support student learning and the application of the skills learned in real-world situations. Competitive events may be written, oral, or a combination of both. There is a variety of organizations from which to select, depending on the goals of your educational program.

To prepare for any competitive event, complete the following activities.

1. Go to the website of your organization to find specific information for the events. Visit the site often as information changes quickly. If the organization has an app, download it to your digital device.

2. Read all the organization's guidelines closely. These rules and regulations must be strictly followed, or disqualification can occur.

3. Communication plays a role in all the competitive events, so read which communication skills are covered in the event you select. Research and preparation are important keys to a successful competition.

4. Select one or two events that are of interest to you. Print the information for the events and discuss your interest with your instructor.

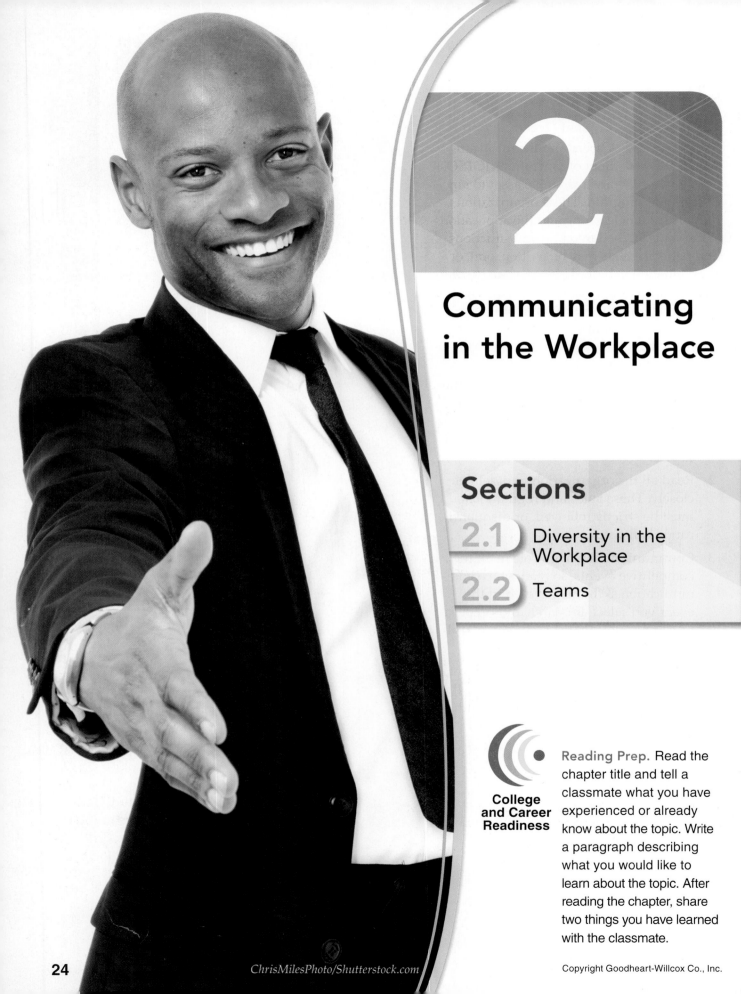

2

Communicating in the Workplace

Sections

2.1 Diversity in the Workplace

2.2 Teams

College and Career Readiness

Reading Prep. Read the chapter title and tell a classmate what you have experienced or already know about the topic. Write a paragraph describing what you would like to learn about the topic. After reading the chapter, share two things you have learned with the classmate.

ChrisMilesPhoto/Shutterstock.com

Check Your Communication IQ ↱

Before you begin the chapter, see what you already know about communication by taking the chapter pretest. The pretest is available at www.g-wlearning.com.

Case Study

Communicating Information

Leah Sanchez, the manager of a small business, needs to inform employees of several changes in the company's emergency procedures. To relay the information, Leah reviewed the new procedures at an employee meeting. She also wrote the following e-mail to the employees and posted the complete document on the company intranet.

NOTICE: NEW EMERGENCY PROCEDURES

In emergency situations, it is the goal of our company to provide immediate action to protect the lives and well-being of all employees. Effective immediately, new emergency response and evacuation procedures will be in effect. Complete evacuation procedures are being distributed to you today. In addition, they are posted on the company intranet. If you have questions, please contact me.

wavebreakmedia/Shutterstock.com

Critical Thinking

1. Is this an effective method of communicating information for the workplace? Why or why not?

2. What other information should have been included when Leah introduced new emergency procedures?

Diversity in the Workplace

Objectives

After completing this section, you will be able to:

- **Explain** the importance of diversity in the workplace.
- **Describe** how to communicate in a diverse workplace.

Key Terms

diversity

culture

intercultural communication

communicative

stereotype

English as a second language (ESL)

Essential Question

Why is diversity important to society?

Diversity

Diversity is having people from different backgrounds, cultures, or demographics come together in a group. Diversity includes age, race, nationality, gender, mental ability, physical ability, and other qualities that make an individual unique.

You interact with a diverse group of people in your school, community, and workplace. For example, a classmate may be from another country. Or, you may work with someone who is disabled. When you begin a career, there is a chance that someone with whom you work will live in another part of the world. You may work for a company in the United States that has employees in another country.

A diverse workforce has many advantages. Diversity can help organizations be more creative, be receptive to customer needs, and find new ways of completing tasks. Diverse employees can help a company create products and services that may be new in the marketplace. New ways of thinking and looking at business are benefits of hiring people with varied backgrounds and experiences. Diversity also increases the pool of potential qualified candidates, which can result in a more effective workforce.

Diversity, however, does not come without its challenges. Special training may be required for employees to learn how to communicate in a diverse workplace. Employees may have to adjust their way of thinking and daily habits to work with a diverse population. Potential employees in the native country of a business may lose job opportunities to diverse candidates.

In order to understand and embrace diversity, culture must be understood. **Culture** is the shared beliefs, customs, practices, and social behavior of a particular group or nation. Culture influences how people respond to the communication and behavior of individuals and organizations. It affects how people think, work, and interact with others.

Diversity is important in schools as well as in businesses.

Konstantin Chagin/Shutterstock.com

Intercultural communication is the process of sending and receiving messages between people of various cultures. It is important to understand the culture of the person with whom you are communicating. Not understanding another person's culture may result in the misinterpretation of verbal and nonverbal communication. For example, in the United States a topic is "tabled" if it is put off for another time. In contrast, the same phrase in Great Britain means to "bring it to the table" for discussion. Additionally, the concept of time may be interpreted differently in some cultures. The workday may not be the 8-hour workday common in the United States.

Communicating in a Diverse Workplace

Working with diverse people requires that individuals learn how to communicate clearly and concisely. This is being communicative. **Communicative** means being willing to talk to people or share information. This sometimes means taking extra time and patience to establish and maintain working relationships. It can also mean taking time to study another person's culture or language so that a spirit of understanding is developed. Diversity should never be a communication barrier or create situations of stereotyping. A **stereotype** is a belief or generalization about a group of people with a given set of characteristics. Stereotyping is not acceptable in any situation.

Remember that diversity is not limited to people from other countries or cultures. Diversity also includes age, gender, abilities, and ethnicity. Be aware of others with whom you interact and show respect. Learning how to listen, speak, write, and communicate clearly with others builds productivity.

Listen Carefully

It is courteous to listen to each person with whom you come in contact. Listening is one of the most important skills you will use in your career. When listening to diverse individuals, extra attention needs to be given. English may not be a person's first language. **English as a second language (ESL)** is the use of English by those with a different native language. Imagine yourself in another country trying to speak a foreign language. It could be frustrating trying to express a thought or idea if you are not fluent in the language. Show the same courtesy to others that you would want if you were in a similar situation.

Just as when listening to a friend or family member, apply these basic courtesies when listening to coworkers.

- Do not interrupt.

- Ask for clarification for any point you do not understand.

- Watch for nonverbal cues.

- Concentrate on what he or she is saying.

- Provide appropriate feedback.

Speak Clearly

Professional communication requires that individuals speak clearly. Using simple language and short sentences can help avoid misunderstandings. Speak slowly and pronounce words clearly. Remember that talking loudly will not necessarily make the person understand what you are saying.

Avoid humor and be aware of topics that are not appropriate in the other person's culture. Do not use technical terms, words, or expressions that someone from another country would not understand. Slang words and jargon are examples of words to avoid. Alternatively, do not speak in a condescending tone.

Be polite and use common courtesies. If the person does not seem to understand what you have said, try to rephrase. There are situations that may require an interpreter. An *interpreter* is a person who translates conversations between individuals who do not speak the same

Maksim Shmeljov/Shutterstock.com

Many international companies and organizations employ interpreters.

language. Many companies doing business internationally have a person on staff to serve as an interpreter.

Write Clearly

If the situation requires written communication, apply the same rules as when speaking. Use short sentences, be brief, and avoid any words that may be misunderstood. Confirm the appropriate method of written communication, such as a letter or e-mail. The rules of good grammar and writing should always be applied.

Be Aware of Body Language

Being aware of body language can help eliminate communication barriers. People from all cultures have specific meanings for nonverbal behavior. Often, two cultures do not always give the same meaning to an action. For example, direct eye contact is not acceptable in some cultures while it is favorable in others. Different cultures have varying standards of how much personal space should be given to other people. Shaking hands may be inappropriate when meeting someone from one culture, while it is common in others. Whenever possible, conduct research to understand what body language cues will be expected by your coworkers. Social etiquette can be very different from what you are used to. Try to understand these differences before communication begins.

Section 2.1 Review

 ### Check Your Understanding

1. What kinds of challenges can diversity present in the workplace?
2. What are some ways to apply basic courtesies when listening to others?
3. Explain how to write in a clear manner so that the message is understood by a diverse audience.
4. What service does an interpreter provide?
5. How can body language affect communication in a diverse workplace?

 ### Build Your Vocabulary

As you progress through this course, develop a personal glossary of key terms. This will help you build your vocabulary and prepare you for a career. Write a definition for each of the following terms and add it to your personal glossary.

diversity

culture

intercultural
  communication

communicative

stereotype

English as a second
  language (ESL)

Teams

Objectives

After completing this section, you will be able to:

- **Describe** teams common in the workplace.
- **Discuss** leadership styles.
- **Identify** the characteristics of effective team members.
- **Explain** the impact of group dynamics on teams.
- **Discuss** the importance of workplace safety.

Essential Question

How are teamwork and leadership related?

Key Terms

team
leadership
leader
interpersonal skills
critical-thinking skills
listening skills
collaboration skills
compromise

time management
personal information management (PIM)
group dynamics
conflict management
conflict-resolution skills
negotiation
mediation

Teams in the Workplace

A **team** is a group of two or more people who work together to achieve a common goal. The terms *team* and *group* are used interchangeably. Teams can be located under one roof, or they can have members located around the world.

The global economy and new technology have influenced how companies conduct business. No longer are workers confined to face-to-face meetings with peers or customers. Many businesses have learned that some of the most qualified people may not be in the city in which the company is physically located. Technology enables team members to communicate virtually by telephone, Internet, and teleconference. This saves companies time and money, and gives them the ability to hire the most qualified employees.

Team Structure

The structure of a team can be formal or informal. A *formal team* is one that comes together for a specific purpose and has an appointed leader. An example is a marketing team created for the specific purpose of promoting the business' products. An *informal team* is one that is usually made up of volunteers and may be considered a social group. A volleyball team that plays on the

weekend is an example. The leader
of an informal group may be elected
by its members or may be a person
who volunteers for the position.

Types of Teams

There are many types of teams
in the workplace. Each organization
has its own types of teams and the
names that they are given. However,
two common types of teams are
functional and cross-functional.

A *functional team* is brought
together for a specific purpose.
Members share the same skill set
and expertise. They may not be
able to perform each job, but they
understand the responsibilities

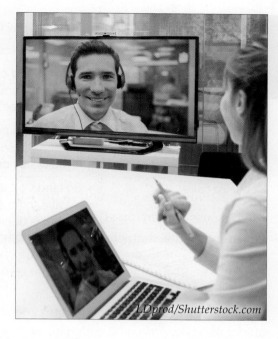

Technology enables
people to work together
without being in the
same location.

LDprod/Shutterstock.com

of each team member. The group comes together as a unit to meet specific
goals. This is common in organizations that have teams such as marketing,
sales, or production. Each team has specific goals and responsibilities it must
meet.

A *cross-functional team* is brought together to solve a specific problem
or task. These teams are sometimes called a *task force*. Representatives from
various functional teams come together for a very specific reason. Task
forces are beneficial for solving issues that affect the entire organization.
Having representation from each group helps establish ownership and
interest in solving an issue for the common good.

Leadership

Leadership is the process of influencing others or making things better.
Certain traits such as honesty, competence, self-confidence, communication
skills, problem-solving skills, and dependability are examples of leadership
characteristics. The ability to set goals, follow through on tasks, and be
forward-thinking are also important leadership abilities.

Teams usually have a leader that is either appointed or elected.
Leaders are those who guide others to a goal. They help bring organization
and focus to a team. A leader has to be able to take responsibility, make
decisions, and inspire members to accomplish tasks.

Being in a leadership position is not always an easy job. Some team
members can be easy to work with, but others can be difficult. Leaders have
to be able to work with different personalities and motivate the group to
accomplish its goals. Each leader has his or her style or may develop a style
based on the personalities of the team.

Three common leadership styles are democratic, autocratic, and laissez-faire,
as shown in Figure 2-1. *Democratic* leadership style is one in which the leader
shares decision making with the group. Democratic leaders encourage other

Common Leadership Styles	
Leadership Style	**Characteristics**
Democratic	• Open and collegial • Invited participation from team • Shares decision making with team members
Autocratic	• Maintains power within the group • Keeps close control over the members of the team • Makes all decisions for the group
Laissez-faire	• Hands-off approach • Little to no direction is provided • Makes decisions only if requested by the team

Goodheart-Willcox Publisher

Figure 2-1   Every leader has his or her own leadership style.

team members to participate in the leadership process. Other leaders use the autocratic style. *Autocratic* leadership style is when a leader maintains all the power within a team. The last common type of leadership is laissez-faire. *Laissez-faire* leadership style is a hands-off approach to leadership. This style leaves the decision-making to the group to decide and manage.

Characteristics of Effective Team Members

Effective teams are those that accomplish the defined goals. This can only happen when the members are cooperative and focused on the assigned tasks. Effective team members are individuals who contribute ideas and personal effort. They are cooperative and work well with others on their team and outside of the team. Successful team members are productive and work to see the team achieve its goals. Individuals who are positive contributors demonstrate leadership qualities even if they are not in a leadership role.

Interpersonal Skills

Individuals with well-rounded skills are an asset to a team. A skill is something a person does well. **Interpersonal skills** are skills that help people communicate and work well with each other. There are many interpersonal skills that individual team members possess that can help the group be effective.

Some examples of important interpersonal skills for an effective team are as follows:

- **Critical-thinking skills** are the ability to interpret and make reasonable judgments and decisions by analyzing a situation. Then, a solution or process can be applied so that a productive action can be taken. Applying critical-thinking skills in a team situation can help the group problem-solve in a more efficient manner.

- You will recall that *verbal skills* are the ability to communicate effectively using spoken or written words. Possessing good verbal skills helps identify an appropriate strategy when writing or speaking to a team member.

- *Nonverbal skills* are the ability to communicate effectively using body language, eye contact, touch, personal space, behavior, and attitude. As you learned in Chapter 1, nonverbal skills can send loud messages in spite of what you might say.

- **Listening skills** are the ability of an individual to hear what a person says as well as understand what is being said. Listening is required for all positive communication.

- **Collaboration skills** are being able to work with others to achieve a common goal. This includes sharing ideas and compromising when the greater good of the team is at stake. To **compromise** is to give up an individual idea so that the group can come to a solution. Collaboration and compromise are two important skills to learn in the workplace.

Teams are effective when the individual members are communicative. Members must interact with each other in a positive manner for the team to be successful. Individuals should apply appropriate verbal, nonverbal, and listening skills. Applying the communication process is necessary for team members to work together effectively.

Exploring Communication Careers

Arts, A/V Technology & Communications

Reporter

The information you read about current events and breaking news in newspapers, magazines, and online is gathered and written by reporters. Reporters research and write articles on news and events happening internationally, nationally, and locally. Research is often done by conducting interviews with people along with searching documentation. Reporters are often assigned to investigate and write news articles on a specific topic, such as area schools, police, or local government. Typical job titles for this position also include *journalist, staff writer, news reporter*, and *correspondent*.

Some examples of tasks that reporters perform include:

- Investigate topics for news stories.

- Interview people about events and their experiences for news stories.

- Write news articles of varying lengths.

- Cultivate relationships with people relevant to their assigned subject area.

Reporters are required to have a bachelor degree in journalism or communication. Some employers hire applicants with a degree in a related subject, such as English or political science. Knowledge of grammar rules and other writing skills are also required.

What Is Business Protocol?

Protocol is customs or rules of etiquette. Business protocol refers to the customs and etiquette rules found in the professional world. As a new employee, it can be challenging to learn business protocol on the job. When you are in a new situation that calls for etiquette with which you are unfamiliar, always check with a supervisor or trusted coworker.

Time-Management Skills

Effective teams make great accomplishments. In order to be productive and accomplish the goals that are set, time management skills are needed.

Time management is the practice of organizing time and work assignments to increase personal efficiency. Team members often work on several tasks at the same time. Tasks must be prioritized by determining which ones should be completed before others. The difference between average and excellent workers is often not how hard they work, but how well they prioritize assignments.

Personal information management (PIM) is a system that individuals use to acquire, organize, maintain, retrieve, and use information. An example of a PIM system is Microsoft Outlook in which an individual can keep a schedule, record contact information, and complete other activities that help organize personal information.

If the goal of PIM is to manage a project, project management applications can be used to develop and maintain a schedule. Such programs include Microsoft Project or Gantt Project. A schedule should identify all required tasks for building, testing, and producing the project. *Milestones* are important dates that need to be met to keep the project moving forward. For each milestone, dates are set so that progress can be checked.

Productivity tools are important in one's personal and professional life. A PIM system can help you have the right information at the right time.

Group Dynamics

Group dynamics are the interacting forces within a group. These forces include the attitudes, behaviors, and personalities of all team members. The dynamics of a team are made up of the attitudes of the members and how they interact with each other. Group dynamics can positively or negatively influence how a team reaches its goals.

Member selection is an important contributor to the way a group interacts. Individuals should complement each other's skills and talents. Team size should also be taken into consideration. Depending on the focus, seven to nine members on a team is generally an effective size. Having an odd number of members avoids a tie when voting is used to make decisions.

Group effectiveness should be analyzed and evaluated periodically to determine if the team is meeting its goals. This can be done informally by asking each member to summarize his or her viewpoint on how the team is doing. In a team meeting, each member has an opportunity to give an opinion. Are the goals being met? Is progress being made? Since this is an informal exercise, other team members should feel free to ask questions or make comments.

An informal evaluation can also be done by asking team members to write a summary of the group's progress. These summaries can be anonymous. However, it is more helpful if each person writes his or her name and discusses his or her contribution to the team.

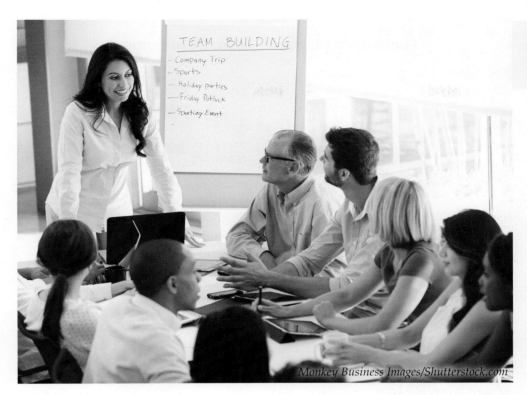

Monkey Business Images/Shutterstock.com

The attitudes of group members affect the group's dynamics.

For a more formal evaluation, a survey can be created and distributed to the team. Specific questions can be asked that will address important goals or topics. The human resources department is a good resource for assistance in creating an effective survey.

Group Process

Group process is how a team comes together to get things done. When teams are organized, they do not necessarily become productive overnight. Psychologist Bruce Tuckman created a group decision-making process that should happen in four stages, as shown in Figure 2-2.

- *Forming.* The group comes together and starts to get to know each other.

- *Storming.* Members express their individual needs and opinions. Conflict can develop at this stage.

- *Norming.* Collaboration and cooperation develop, and the team begins functioning as a cohesive group. Brainstorming is used to work through issues.

- *Performing.* The team is productive and meeting its goals. Members have learned to collaborate and work together.

At some point in the team process, individual members will probably leave the group. When that happens, the team must come together and decide how to work without that team member. This is sometimes called *adjourning.* The process of forming, storming, norming, and performing may start again.

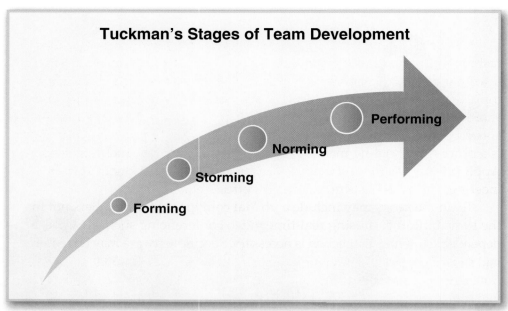

Goodheart-Willcox Publisher

Figure 2-2   Each team goes through this process.

Member Roles

The dynamics of a group are formed by the individual members and their roles within a team. Some members are self-oriented and only concerned about what he or she gets out of the experience. Others are the encouragers who focus on team harmony and are always asking others for opinions. Still other team members are task oriented. These members identify defined tasks and help see that they are accomplished. It is important that each team member assume the role to which he or she is best suited. For example, the person who always takes good notes can be effective as the recorder in the group. Examples of member roles are shown in Figure 2-3.

The *Belbin Team Inventory* is a personality test devised by Meredith Belbin to help individuals to define their roles within a team. It is focused on how individuals behave in a team environment. Nine team roles are part of the test. For teams that want to formally assess roles, this test can help accomplish that task.

Group Member Roles

Compromiser	Initiator	Recorder
Encourager	Innovator	Spokesperson
Explorer	Leader	Summarizer
Information Seeker	Prioritizer	Timekeeper

Goodheart-Willcox Publisher

Figure 2-3   Group members can take on one or more unique roles.

Team Meetings

Meetings are the primary way teams come together in an organized fashion for discussion of topics and issues. Some meetings may be informal in which members meet for a short time to casually discuss a topic. However, there are times when formal meetings are necessary and should be run in an organized manner. Formal meetings usually require an agenda and someone to officially lead the meeting. *Parliamentary procedure* is a process for holding meetings so that they are orderly and democratic. Applying *Robert's Rules of Order* is an effective way to conduct a formal meeting. Figure 2-4 lists guidelines for effective meetings.

Team meetings may include a virtual component for members not in the same building. If using real-time video conferencing such as Skype, a dependable Internet connection is necessary. Specific software may be required and should be installed before the meeting begins. It is important that the camera is positioned so that the people who are speaking can be clearly seen. A high-quality microphone is required so that conversations are clear.

If a meeting is conducted using a web seminar website such as GoToMeeting, similar guidelines apply. There is no camera, but the Internet connection is important as well as the quality of the microphone. Software will be required, so it should be downloaded before the conference begins.

Group Conflict

Every group faces conflict at some point in the group process. Conflict is not always negative. Sometimes creative solutions come from people who disagree on a subject. Conflict is negative when it becomes destructive, and the team can no longer reach its goals.

When conflict arises, some team members show passive behavior. *Passive behavior* is accepting the things that happen without trying to change them. Other members show aggressive behavior. *Aggressive behavior* is expressing individual needs with little interest in or respect for others' needs. Still other team members are assertive. *Assertive behavior* is expressing personal opinions while showing respect for others.

Guidelines for Effective Meetings		
Before the Meeting	**During the Meeting**	**After the Meeting**
• Identify purpose • Select participants • Reserve room and time • Send meeting invitation • Prepare agenda	• Follow the agenda • Adhere to parliamentary procedures • Lead conversation • Respect others' time	• Review notes • Complete tasks

Goodheart-Willcox Publisher

Figure 2-4   Completing these tasks before, during, and after a meeting can help make it more effective.

The team leader and members are responsible for monitoring conflicts that could affect the success of the team. Negative conflicts can throw a group off course. **Conflict management** is the process of recognizing and resolving team disputes in a balanced and effective way. When it is clear that a dispute is escalating, members should work to resolve the negative conflict.

Conflict-resolution skills are the skills required to resolve a situation in which a disagreement could lead to hostile behavior, such as shouting or fighting. A conflict-solving model can help a team develop conflict-resolution skills. See Figure 2-5 for an example of a conflict-resolving model.

1. Acknowledge conflict and define the problem. If the conflict is not recognized, resolution will not happen. Team members should apply positive verbal and nonverbal skills during this stage.

2. Analyze and discuss the issue. List the facts and get opinions on the issue. The issue should be analyzed, including the facts and the opinions.

3. Break into groups or brainstorm as a group for potential solutions. Critical-thinking skills are required. *Brainstorming* is group discussion in which individuals generate as many ideas as possible within a set amount of time. When brainstorming, there are no bad ideas; all are listed for consideration.

4. Solve the problem and come up with solution. After all alternatives have been discussed, the team should be able to recommend one or more solutions. Collaboration is needed from individual team members.

5. Evaluate alternatives and reach *consensus*. Individual team members agree on the decision that the team makes.

6. Implement the solution and then follow up. The solution or process is applied and the outcome is reviewed.

 Green Team

There are many ways to go green in the workplace. Assembling an employee green team is a good place to start. Most green teams start out by addressing employee habits in the workplace, such as implementing a recycling program and eliminating the use of plastic water bottles. Some green teams evolve their mission to help employees make environmentally-friendly decisions in their personal lives as well. A green team can prepare a presentation about hybrid vehicles or about the importance of eating locally grown produce.

Green teams may also look for ways to make the operations of the business more environmentally friendly. Companies can improve shipping routes to consume less fuel, implement online systems that replace paperwork, and keep electronic records. Another way for a green team to expand its mission is to involve consumers and customers. Companies that work toward sustainability are socially responsible and create goodwill.

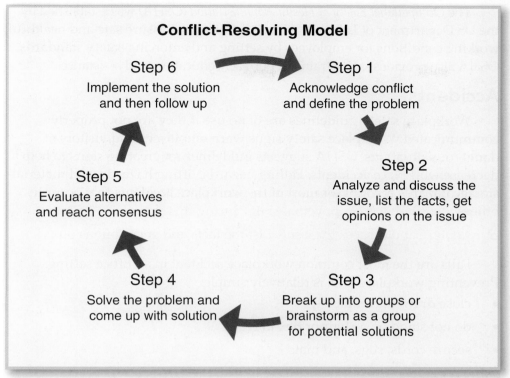

Conflict-Resolving Model

Step 6
Implement the solution
and then follow up

Step 1
Acknowledge conflict
and define the problem

Step 2
Analyze and discuss the
issue, list the facts, get
opinions on the issue

Step 5
Evaluate alternatives
and reach consensus

Step 4
Solve the problem and
come up with solution

Step 3
Break up into groups or
brainstorm as a group
for potential solutions

Goodheart-Willcox Publisher

Figure 2-5   Follow these steps to aid in conflict resolution.

Formal methods such as negotiation or mediation are required to settle some group conflicts. **Negotiation** is when individuals involved in a conflict come together to discuss a compromise. During negotiation, both parties are willing to give up something to meet the other party in the middle. For extreme conflicts, mediation may be needed. **Mediation** is the inclusion of a neutral person, called a *mediator*, to help the conflicting parties resolve their dispute and reach an agreement.

If handled well, conflicts can strengthen the bonds between group members. Learning from those disputes can help the group to avoid them as they move forward toward their goals. However, if the conflict is not fully resolved, it can result in a reoccurring problem in the group.

Workplace Safety

Individuals should be aware of workplace safety for themselves as well as for those with whom they work. Employers, schools, and other organizations and facilities are responsible for providing an environment that is safe for everyone on the premises.

Maintaining a safe workplace is the joint responsibility of the employer and employee. The employer makes sure the facility and working conditions are such that accidents are unlikely to occur. The employee uses common sense and care while at the office. Always read and understand equipment safety manuals, follow safety instructions, and abide by safety requirements.

The *Occupational Safety & Health Administration (OSHA)* was established by the US Department of Labor in 1970. Its mission is to assure safe and healthful working conditions for employees by setting and enforcing safety standards. OSHA also provides safety training, outreach, education, and assistance.

Accidents

Workplace safety guidelines are of no use if they are not properly communicated. Workplace safety signs warn employees and visitors of dangerous situations. OSHA suggests guidelines for creating signs to help decrease workplace accidents. Falling hazards, lifting hazards, and material-storage hazards account for most of the workplace accidents that occur in offices.

Falling Hazards

Falls are the most common workplace accident in an office setting. Preventing workplace falls is relatively simple:

- close drawers completely
- do not stand on a chair or box to reach
- secure cords, rugs, and mats
- obey safety signs

Lifting Hazards

Lifting hazards are sources of potential injury from improperly lifting or carrying items. Most back injuries are caused by improper lifting. To avoid injuries from lifting:

- make several small trips with items rather than one trip with an overly heavy load
- use dollies or handcarts whenever possible
- lift with the legs, not with the back
- never carry an item that blocks vision
- obey safety signs

Material-Storage Hazards

Material-storage hazards are sources of potential injury from the improper storage of office equipment or other items. A cluttered workplace is an unsafe workplace. Material stacked too high can fall on employees. Paper and files that are stored on the floor or in a hall are a fire risk. To prevent material-storage injuries:

- do not stack boxes or papers on top of tall cabinets
- store heavier objects on lower shelves
- keep aisles and hallways clear
- obey safety signs

Emergencies

There are many types of emergencies that can happen at school, at work, or in a social environment. Individuals are responsible for understanding how to react in an emergency at work, school, or another facility.

Emergency procedures are a series of actions taken to minimize risks in the event of an emergency. The first line of defense in all emergencies is to stay calm. This makes it easier to follow the emergency procedures established by the organization. The seriousness of the emergency should be evaluated in order to determine what type of help is required. Be aware of facility exits and how to evacuate the premises if necessary. If there is a medical emergency, follow established procedures to give appropriate assistance, and call for help if needed.

Some emergency situations for which you should be prepared are:

- fire
- natural disasters such as a tornado, earthquake, or hurricane
- medical emergencies such as heart attack, stroke, fainting, burns, or cuts
- bomb threats

If emergency guidelines have not been given to you at school or work, request that they be reviewed.

Section 2.2 Review

 Check Your Understanding

1. Identify types of teams in the workplace.
2. List three common leadership styles.
3. List some examples of interpersonal skills needed for teams to be effective.
4. Explain the importance of group dynamics on a team.
5. Who is responsible for workplace safety?

 Build Your Vocabulary

As you progress through this course, develop a personal glossary of key terms. This will help you build your vocabulary and prepare you for a career. Write a definition for each of the following terms and add it to your personal glossary.

team
leadership
leader
interpersonal skills
critical-thinking skills
listening skills
collaboration skills
compromise

time management
personal information
    management (PIM)
group dynamics
conflict management
conflict-resolution skills
negotiation
mediation

2 Review and Assessment

Chapter Summary

Section 2.1 Diversity in the Workplace

- A diverse workplace includes people from different backgrounds, cultures, and demographics. Diversity includes age, race, nationality, gender, mental ability, physical ability, and other unique qualities. A diverse workplace has many advantages, along with some challenges. Intercultural communication is important to the success of a diverse workplace.

- When working with people from different cultures, individuals must be communicative. Diversity should never be a communication barrier or create situations of stereotyping. Ways to communicate in a diverse workplace include listening carefully, speaking clearly, writing clearly, and being aware of body language.

Section 2.2 Teams

- A team is a group of two or more people who work together to achieve a common goal. There are many different teams found in a workplace, but two common team structures are formal and informal. Each organization has its own types of teams; however, two common types are functional and cross-functional.

- Being a leader is not always an easy job, but most teams have one. Team leaders are either appointed or elected. Three common leadership styles are democratic, autocratic, and laissez-faire.

- Effective teams are those that accomplish defined goals. This can only happen when members have interpersonal skills that enable people to work well together. Effective teams also have time-management skills to be productive and accomplish the goals that are set.

- Group dynamics are the attitudes, behaviors, and personalities of all team members. They influence how a group will work together to meet its goals. Group process is the way in which a team comes together to accomplish goals. The primary way teams come together for discussion of topics and issues is by holding meetings. During the group process, every group will face conflict at one point.

- It is important for employers and employees to be aware of workplace safety measures. Common accidents that occur in the workplace include falling accidents, lifting accidents, and material storage accidents. Additionally, emergencies can occur in the workplace. Everyone must follow the established emergency procedures in the event of an emergency.

Online Activities

Complete the following activities which will help you learn, practice, and expand your knowledge and skills.

Posttest. Now that you have finished the chapter, see what you learned by taking the chapter posttest.

Vocabulary. Practice vocabulary for this chapter using the e-flash cards, matching activity, and vocabulary game until you are able to recognize their meanings.

English/Language Arts. Visit www.g-wlearning.com to download each data file for this chapter. Follow the instructions to complete an English/language arts activity to practice what you have learned in this chapter.

Activity File 2-1: Using Idioms

Activity File 2-2: Improving Your Reading Skills

Review Your Knowledge

1. How can diversity influence the workforce in a positive manner?

2. Explain why intercultural communication is important in a diverse workplace.

3. Summarize ways to be an effective communicator when listening to and speaking with diverse individuals.

4. Explain the purpose of a formal team.

5. What is an informal team?

6. List the roles that individuals typically play in a group. Write your own definition of each.

7. Describe the purpose of a functional team and a cross-functional team.

8. Describe three common leadership styles. Analyze each style.

9. Analyze the Tuckman theory of group process.

10. Explain the purpose of emergency procedures and how they should be followed in all situations.

Apply Your Knowledge

1. Analyze the communicative effects of the Arts, A/V Technology & Communications career field. How has it influenced society?

2. When communicating with your team, common courtesies must be applied. Create an outline for communication with others in the workplace. Your outline should include these categories: listening skills, verbal skills, and nonverbal skills. Under each category, write appropriate suggestions that explain how each should be applied.

3. It is important to apply critical thinking skills when working with your team to solve problems. Identify a group conflict of which you were a part. Using the conflict-resolving model in Figure 2-5, make a list of actions that could have helped the team solve the conflict.

4. Acquiring interpersonal skills will help you be a successful team member. This chapter introduced critical thinking, listening, and collaboration as interpersonal skills. For each skill, evaluate your own interpersonal skills. How could you apply these skills in a group setting to solve problems?

5. Each group has its own dynamics, depending on the team members and the purpose for forming the group. Create a questionnaire for analyzing and evaluating group dynamics and effectiveness. Survey questions should include factors such as communication, teamwork, commitment, and effectiveness. Questions may be directed to the group for evaluation, to individual contributors, or to both. Create a rating scale that is easy to use and understandable for the person who is completing it.

6. Analyze yourself as a group member. What role do you typically play in a group? Why do you think this role describes you? What skills can you demonstrate to show that you are a productive member of the team?

7. Of the communication skills discussed in this chapter, which skills are most effective for building a consensus among group members? Explain your choice.

8. The conflict-resolving model is a helpful guideline when confronting a conflict within a team. Using the conflict-solving model in Figure 2-5, write a script that could be used to bring consensus on a team challenge of selecting a new meeting time.

Communication Skills

College and Career Readiness

Listening. Hearing is a physical process. Listening combines hearing with evaluation. Effective leaders learn how to listen to their team members. Select a video from the Internet on effective communication strategies for leaders. Analyze the effectiveness of the presentation. Listen carefully and take notes about the main points. Then organize the key information that you heard.

Reading. Ask your teacher for a copy of the emergency procedures and safety rules for your school. Apply appropriate reading techniques to identify the main ideas and purpose of the information that is presented. Ask questions about any procedure that you do not understand.

Speaking. Career-ready individuals understand that demonstrating leadership qualities is a way to make a positive contribution to the team. Identify leadership characteristics that you believe all team members should possess. List your ideas in a chart and share with the class.

Internet Research

Personal Information Management (PIM). Using the Internet, research personal information management (PIM) systems. Identify a system that would work for you. Explain how you can apply a PIM system to your daily schedule to help you complete projects and other tasks.

English as a Second Language. Research the topic of English as a second language (ESL) using various Internet resources. Write several paragraphs explaining the importance of clear communication with those for whom English is not their first language.

Teamwork

Working with your team, create the following lists: standards for safety in your classroom, personal safety standards for individual well being, and emergency guidelines for your classroom. Next, compare the guidelines your team created with those provided by the school. How did your lists compare with those provided by the school? Discuss how to implement personal safety rules, classroom safety rules, and emergency procedures with the class.

Portfolio Development

College and Career Readiness

Objective. Before you begin collecting information for your portfolio, write an objective for the finished product. An *objective* is a complete sentence or two that states what you want to accomplish.

The language in your objective should be clear and specific. Include enough details so you can easily judge when you have accomplished it. Consider this objective: "I will try to get into college." Such an objective is too general. A better, more detailed objective might read: "I will get accepted into the communications program at one of my top three colleges of choice." Creating a clear objective is a good starting point for beginning to work on your portfolio.

1. Decide the purpose of the portfolio you are creating, such as short-term employment, career, community service, or college application.

2. Set a timeline to finish the final product.

3. Write an objective for your portfolio.

CTSOs

 **Parliamentary Procedure.** The Parliamentary Procedure competitive event is an event in which the participants must demonstrate understanding of parliamentary procedures such as *Roberts Rules of Order*. This is a team event in which the group will demonstrate how to conduct an effective meeting. An objective test may be administered to each person on the team that will be evaluated and included in the overall team score. To prepare for the parliamentary procedure, complete the following activities.

1. Read the guidelines provided by your organization.

2. Study parliamentary procedure principles by reviewing Roberts Rules of Order.

3. Practice proper procedures for conducting a meeting. Assign each team member a role for the presentation.

4. Visit the organization's website and look for the evaluation criteria or rubric for the event. This will help you determine what the judges will be looking for in your presentation.

3

Digital Citizenship

Sections

3.1	Communicating in a Digital Society
3.2	Workplace Ethics
3.3	History of Communication

College and Career Readiness

Reading Prep. Arrange a study session to read the chapter aloud with a classmate. Take turns reading each section. Stop at the end of each section to discuss what you think its main points are. Take notes of your study session to share with the class.

Check Your Communication IQ ↪

Before you begin the chapter, see what you already know about communication by taking the chapter pretest. The pretest is available at www.g-wlearning.com.

Case Study

Cyberbullying

Jim Hill is the writer of a popular blog devoted to professional hockey. Last month, he was invited to serve as the luncheon speaker at the annual meeting of the local Sports Writers Association. The association announced on its website that Jim would be the guest speaker.

Shortly after the announcement, Jim began seeing negative comments on his blog from people he did not know. The posts implied that he is a terrible presenter and that he regularly plagiarizes the work of others. Jim was shocked and humiliated at these false statements.

Critical Thinking

1. Explain whether you think Jim is a victim of cyberbullying in the workplace.

2. What actions can Jim take to stop these false statements?

Tyler Olson/Shutterstock.com

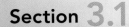

Communicating in a Digital Society

Objectives

After completing this section, you will be able to:

- **Describe** the elements of digital communication.
- **Explain** intellectual property and what it includes.
- **Discuss** the importance of the Electronic User's Bill of Rights.

Key Terms

digital communication	libel
digital citizen	digital footprint
digital literacy	intellectual property
digital citizenship	plagiarism
ethics	piracy
cyberbullying	infringement
netiquette	public domain
slander	open source

?Essential Question

How does digital citizenship have implications for society as a whole?

Digital Communication

Digital communication is the exchange of information through electronic means. Using technology to communicate in the workplace and in one's personal life requires users to be responsible. A **digital citizen** is someone who regularly and skillfully engages in the use of technology such as the Internet, computers, and other digital devices. This requires the knowledge and skills to successfully navigate the Internet to interact with individuals and organizations. Digital communication is comprised of digital literacy and digital citizenship.

Digital Literacy

Digital communication requires digital literacy skills. **Digital literacy** is the ability to use technology to create, locate, evaluate, and communicate information. According to the US federal government, digital literacy skills include the following:

- using a computer or mobile device, including the mouse and keyboard, as well as icons and folders
- using software and applications to complete tasks, such as word processing and creating spreadsheets, tables, and databases

- using the Internet to conduct searches, use e-mail, and register on a website
- communicating online, including sharing photos and videos, using social media, and learning to be an informed digital citizen
- helping children learn to be responsible and make informed decisions online

To learn more about digital literacy skills, visit the US government's digital literacy website.

Digital Citizenship

Digital citizenship is the standard of appropriate behavior when using technology to communicate. Good digital citizenship focuses on using technology in a positive way rather than using it for negative or illegal purposes. People who participate in the digital society have a legal responsibility for their online actions, whether those actions are ethical or unethical. **Ethics** are the principles of what is right and wrong that help people make decisions. Ethical actions are those actions in which the user applies ethics and moral behavior. Unethical actions are those that involve crime or theft while online. These actions can be punishable by law.

It is important to understand the difference between ethical and unethical electronic activities. For example, it is sometimes difficult to know where joking stops and bullying starts. **Cyberbullying** is using the Internet to harass or threaten an individual. It includes using social media, text messages, or e-mails to harass or scare a person with hurtful words or pictures. A victim of cyberbullying cannot be physically seen or touched by the bully. However, this does not mean the person cannot be harmed by his or her actions. Cyberbullying is unethical and can be prosecuted.

StockLite/Shutterstock.com

Digital literacy skills are valuable in professional communication.

Reusing material without permission, such as photocopying pages out of a textbook, is unethical.

l i g h t p o e t/Shutterstock.com

Another unacceptable behavior is flaming. *Flaming* is purposefully insulting someone and inciting an argument on social media. Spamming is equally unethical. *Spamming* is intentionally sending unwanted e-mails or flooding an individual's social media site with unwanted messages.

Netiquette, also known as *digital etiquette*, is etiquette used when communicating electronically. Netiquette includes accepted social and professional guidelines for Internet communication. Netiquette applies to e-mails, social networking, or other contact with customers or peers via the Internet during work hours. For example, using all capital letters in a message has the effect of yelling and is not acceptable. Always use correct capitalization, spelling, and grammar.

Having poor netiquette can also have legal ramifications. **Slander** is speaking a false statement about someone that causes others to have a bad opinion of him or her. **Libel** is publishing a false statement about someone that causes others to have a bad opinion of him or her. Slander and libel can be considered crimes of defamation. It is important to choose words carefully when making comments about others, whether online or face-to-face.

What you post on the Internet never really goes away. A **digital footprint** is a data record of all of an individual's online activities. Even if you delete something you have posted on the Internet, it stays in your digital footprint. Always think before posting to social media sites or sending an e-mail. What you post online today could risk your future college and job opportunities.

Intellectual Property

The Internet provides countless sources for obtaining text, images, video, audio, and software. Even though this material is readily available, this does not make it free to use however you choose. Laws exist to govern the use of media and creative works. The creators or owners of this material have certain legal rights. **Intellectual property** is something that comes from a person's mind, such as an idea, invention, or process. Intellectual property laws protect a person's or a company's inventions, artistic works, and other intellectual property.

Plagiarism is claiming another person's material as your own, which is both unethical and illegal. If you must refer to someone else's work, follow intellectual property laws to ethically acquire the information. Use standard methods of citing sources. Citation guidelines in *The Chicago Manual of Style* or the Modern Language Association's *MLA Handbook* can be helpful.

Piracy is the unethical and illegal copying or downloading of software, files, or other protected material. Examples of protected material include images, movies, and music. Piracy carries a heavy penalty, including fines and incarceration.

Copyright

A *copyright* acknowledges ownership of a work and specifies that only the owner has the right to sell the work, use it, or give permission for someone else to sell or use it. Any use of copyrighted material without permission is called **infringement**. The laws cover all original work, whether it is in print, on the Internet, or in any other form. Scanning or photocopying a document does not make the content yours.

Copyrighted material is indicated by the © symbol or the statement "copyright by." However, lack of the symbol or statement does not mean the material is not copyrighted. All original material is automatically copyrighted as soon as it is in tangible form. An idea cannot be copyrighted. A copyright can be registered with the US Copyright Office, which is part of the Library of Congress. Original material is still legally protected whether or not the copyright is registered.

Fair use doctrine allows individuals to use copyrighted works without permission in limited situations under very strict guidelines. Fair use doctrine allows copyrighted material to be used for the purpose of describing or reviewing the work. For example, a student writing about the material in an original report is an example of fair use. Another is a product-review website providing editorial comment. Fair use doctrine does not change the copyright or ownership of the material used under the doctrine.

In some cases, individuals or organizations may wish to allow others to use their intellectual property without needing permission. Sometimes this type of use assignment is called *copyleft*, which is a play on the word *copyright*.

One popular method of allowing use of intellectual property is a Creative Commons license. A *Creative Commons (CC) license* is a specialized copyright license that allows free distribution of copyrighted work. If the creator of the work wants to give the public the ability to use, share, or advance his or her original work, a Creative Commons license provides that flexibility. The creator maintains the copyright and can specify how the copyrighted work can be used. For example, one type of Creative Commons license prohibits commercial use.

Public domain refers to material that is not owned by anybody and can be used without permission. Material can enter the public domain when a copyright expires and is not renewed. Much of the material created by federal, state, or local governments is often in the public domain. This is because taxpayer money was used to create it. Additionally, the owner of material may choose to give up ownership and place the material in the public domain.

Most information on the Internet is copyrighted, whether it is text, graphics, illustrations, or digital media. This means you cannot reuse it without first obtaining permission from the owner. Sometimes, the owner of the material has placed the material on the Internet for others to reuse. However, if this is not explicitly stated, assume the material is copyrighted and cannot be freely used.

Many websites list rules called the *terms of use* that must be followed for downloaded files. The agreement may come up automatically, for example, if you are downloading a file or software application. If you want to use an image or text from a website, look for the terms of use. Unless the terms of use specifically state that you are free to copy and use the material provided on a website, it must be assumed the material is copyrighted. You cannot reuse the material without permission.

Patent

A *patent* gives a person or company the right to be the sole producer of a product for a defined period of time. Patents protect an invention that is functional or mechanical. The invention must be considered useful and non-obvious, and it must be operational. This means that an idea may not be patented. A process can be patented under certain conditions. The process must be related to a particular machine or transform a substance or item into a different state or thing.

Twin Design/Shutterstock.com

Most brand logos, such as those seen on social media websites, are trademarks.

Trademark

A *trademark* protects taglines, slogans, names, symbols, or any unique method to identify a product or company. A *service mark* is similar to a trademark, but it identifies a service rather than a product. Trademarks and service marks do not protect a work or product. They only protect the way in which the product is described. The term "trademark" is often used to refer to both trademarks and service marks. Trademarks never expire.

The symbols used to indicate a trademark or service mark are called *graphic marks*. Some graphic marks can be used without being formally registered, as shown in Figure 3-1.

Correct Usage of Graphic Marks

TM	Trademark, not registered
SM	Service mark, not registered
®	Registered trademark

Goodheart-Willcox Publisher

Figure 3-1 Graphic marks are symbols that indicate legal protection of intellectual property.

License Agreement

A *licensing agreement* is a contract that gives one party permission to market, produce, or use the product or service owned by another party. The agreement grants a license in return for a fee or royalty payment. When buying software, the purchaser is agreeing to follow the terms of a license. A *license* is the legal permission to use a software program. All software has terms of use that explain how and when the software may be used. Figure 3-2 explains the characteristics of different software licensing.

Alternative usage rights for software programs are typically covered by the *GNU General Public License (GNU GPL)*. The GNU GPL guarantees all

Exploring Communication Careers

Telecommunications Technician

rts, A/V Technology & Communications

The workplace requires workers to have access to the Internet, telephone equipment, and in some situations, cable television. In order for businesses to function effectively, they rely on proper installation and consistent operation of telecommunications equipment. Telecommunications technicians install, maintain, repair, and remove equipment as needed by businesses and organizations. Typical job titles for this telecommunications position include *service technician*, *field technician*, and *communications technician*.

Some examples of tasks that telecommunications technicians perform include:

- Identify and install needed equipment
- Check newly installed devices to ensure they are functioning properly
- Perform maintenance checks on equipment
- Test circuits, wiring, and parts of malfunctioning equipment
- Repair or replace faulty telecommunications equipment
- Show customers how to use equipment

Most of these positions require a certificate or an associate degree. On-the-job training or apprenticeships are often required. Telecommunications technicians must be knowledgeable about equipment as well as possess customer service in order to train customers to use the digital devices. The ability to analyze and troubleshoot technical problems is needed as well.

Characteristics of Software Types			
Characteristics	**Software Type**		
	For-Purchase	**Freeware**	**Shareware**
Cost	• Must be purchased to use • Demo may be available	• Never have to pay for it	• Free to try • Pay to upgrade to full functionality
Features	• Full functionality	• Full functionality	• Limited functionality without upgrade

Goodheart-Willcox Publisher

Figure 3-2 Each type of software has specific licensing permissions.

users the freedom to use, study, share, and modify the software. The term **open source** applies to software that has had its source code made available to the public at no charge. Open-source software can be downloaded and used for free and can also be modified and distributed by anyone. However, part or all of the code of open-source software may be owned by an individual or organization.

Electronic User's Bill of Rights

The *Electronic User's Bill of Rights* details the rights and responsibilities of both individuals and institutions regarding the treatment of digital information. It was originally proposed in 1993 by Frank W. Connolly of American University. It is modeled after the original United States Bill of Rights, although it contains only four articles. The articles are not legally binding, but contain guidelines for appropriate use of digital information. The articles in the Electronic User's Bill of Rights include the following.

- *Article I: Individual Rights* focuses on the rights and freedoms of the users of computers and the Internet. It states "citizens of the electronic community of learners" have the right to access computers and informational resources. They should be informed when their personal information is being collected. They have the right to review and correct the information that has been collected. Users should have freedom of speech and have rights of ownership for their intellectual property.

- *Article II: Individual Responsibilities* focuses on the responsibilities that come with those rights outlined in Article I. A citizen of the electronic community is responsible for seeking information and using it effectively. It is also the individual's responsibility to honor the intellectual property of others. This includes verifying the accuracy of information obtained electronically. It also includes respecting the privacy of others, and using electronic resources wisely.

- *Article III: Rights of Educational Institutions* states the right of educational institutions to access computers and informational resources. Like individuals, an educational institution retains ownership of its intellectual property. Each institution has the right to use its resources as it sees fit.

- *Article IV: Institutional Responsibilities* focuses on the responsibilities that come with the rights granted in Article III. Educational institutions are held accountable for the information they use and provide. Institutions are responsible for creating and maintaining "an environment wherein trust and intellectual freedom are the foundation for individual and institutional growth and success."

Section 3.1 Review

Check Your Understanding

1. List the components of digital communication.
2. What actions are considered cyberbullying?
3. Name two unethical uses of another person's intellectual property.
4. What does a licensing agreement allow?
5. What does the Electronic User's Bill of Rights provide?

Build Your Vocabulary

As you progress through this course, develop a personal glossary of key terms. This will help you build your vocabulary and prepare you for a career. Write a definition for each of the following terms and add it to your personal glossary.

digital communication
digital citizen
digital literacy
digital citizenship
ethics
cyberbullying
netiquette
slander
libel

digital footprint
intellectual property
plagiarism
piracy
infringement
public domain
open source

? **E**ssential **Q**uestion

How do ethics impact workplace decisions?

Workplace Ethics

Objectives

After completing this section, you will be able to:

- **Discuss** the importance of ethical communication in the workplace.
- **Explain** how employers ensure appropriate use of the Internet in a professional setting.
- **Describe** the importance of digital security.

Key Terms

proprietary information
false advertising
social responsibility
acceptable use policy
Internet protocol address
hacking
cookies

phishing
malware
spyware
software virus
firewall
identity theft

Ethical Communication

Digital citizenship requires individuals to apply ethics in all communication. *Ethical communication* is applying ethics to messages to make sure all communication is honest in every way. It is every employee's responsibility to maintain ethical behavior in all communication that represents his or her employer.

Many companies have a communication plan in place to identify how ethical communication about the company is provided to the public. A *code of ethics* is a document that dictates how business should be conducted. This communication plan provides an outline of the appropriate channels of communication for the company. It also includes an analysis of how communication for the company should occur. When creating messages that represent your organization, ask the following questions to analyze if the information is ethical.

- Has confidentiality been honored?
- Has the privacy of the company been protected?
- Is the information presented factual and honest?
- Has appropriate credit been given to contributors of the communication?
- Has copyrighted material been used appropriately?

Some companies establish a code of conduct. A *code of conduct* identifies the manner in which employees should behave while at work or when representing the company. To discourage unethical behavior in the workplace, these suggestions may be considered part of a code of conduct.

- Office equipment should not be used for personal business. This includes using the photocopier and office telephone.

- Negative comments should not be made about the company or those with whom you work.

- Internet access provided by the company should be used only for business purposes. Checking personal e-mail or shopping online is not acceptable.

Confidentiality

Confidentiality means that specific information about a company is never shared except with those who have clearance to receive it. **Proprietary information** is any work created by company employees on the job that is owned by that company. Proprietary information may be called trade secrets. *Trade secrets* refers to information a company needs to keep private to protect from theft. Proprietary information can include many things, such as product formulas, customer lists, or manufacturing processes. The code of conduct should explain that company information may only be shared with permission from human resources. Employees who share proprietary information with outsiders are unethical and, possibly, breaking the law.

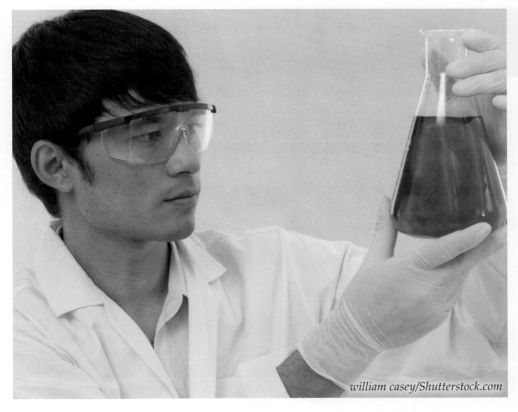

Employees are expected to keep proprietary information a secret.

william casey/Shutterstock.com

Honesty

Careful consideration must be given to the impact company communication has on the public. It may be tempting for those writing messages or representing the business to get caught up in exaggerations or inaccurate claims about the company. The point of view presented should be honest. Marketing messages that persuade the reader to buy or respond in some way must be written according to laws. Laws enforced by the Federal Trade Commission (FTC) dictate that truth in advertising must be followed. **False advertising** is overstating the features and benefits of products or services, making false claims about them. Misrepresenting information, intentionally or unintentionally, can lead to lawsuits, loss of customers, or loss of jobs.

Social Responsibility

Social responsibility is behaving with sensitivity to social, environmental, and economic issues. As a professional communicator, social responsibility may be considered an ethical issue. Communicators must be sensitive to the world around them. Negative communication about society or the environment reflects negatively on the company. Messages should be analyzed to confirm they are not offensive. Questions can be asked to measure whether a message is socially responsible.

- Has confidentiality been honored?

- Has privacy of the company been protected?

- Is the information presented factual and honest?

- Have any negative comments been stated or implied about social issues, such as the environment?

- Have any personal opinions about social responsibility been included?

Professionalism should be the number one priority as you conduct business, whether at home or in the office.

Always use caution when using technology to communicate.

Radu Bercan/Shutterstock.com

Ethical Internet Use

An important aspect of digital citizenship is respecting an employer's property and time. Internet access provided by the company should be used only for business purposes. For example, checking personal e-mail or playing a game online is not acceptable. Most companies have an established acceptable use policy. An **acceptable use policy** is a set of rules that explains what is and is not acceptable use of company-owned and company-operated equipment and networks. Employees are typically made aware of acceptable use policies during training before they are allowed access to the company's computers and network.

Many companies and schools use *filters* that prevent unauthorized Internet surfing or visiting selected websites during working hours. *Censorship* is the practice of examining material, such as online content, and blocking or deleting anything considered inappropriate. Employers are legally allowed to censor information that employees read on the Internet during work hours.

Whether at work or at home, each time you access a search engine or visit a web page, the computer's identity is revealed. The **Internet protocol address**, known as an *IP address*, is a number used to identify an electronic device connected to the Internet. While your personal information cannot be easily discovered, an IP address can reveal your approximate geographic location. Any e-mails you send from your computer or mobile devices have an IP address attached to them. Use caution when doing so.

One way to protect yourself online is to ensure that you are transmitting data over secure web pages. When transmitting private information to a website, check that the site is secure. A secure URL begins with https. The s stands for secure. This is not 100 percent foolproof, but generally is a sign of protection. Secure websites may also display an icon somewhere in the browser to indicate the communication is secure. Be wary of uploading personal information to sites that do not display the protection.

Public Wi-Fi hotspots should be avoided. While convenient, these networks are generally not secure and put your devices at risk by inadvertently exposing data. One definition of **hacking** is illegally accessing or altering digital devices, software, or networks.

Hackers are also able to create illicit hotspots in locations where free or paid public Wi-Fi exists. Users unknowingly connect to the incorrect network, allowing the hacker access to any data being transmitted over that connection. The signal with the best strength may not always be the legitimate hotspot. An easy way to avoid illicit hotspots is to check with an employee of the business providing it. Ask the employee for the name of the network and the access key. If a Wi-Fi authentication screen is asking for credit card information, confirm that the Wi-Fi connection is legitimate.

Cookies

Cookies are bits of data stored on your computer that record information about the websites you have visited. Cookies may also contain the personal information you enter on a website. Most cookies are from

Ethics

Integrity

Integrity is defined as the honesty of a person's actions. Integrity and ethics go hand-in-hand in both personal and professional lives. Employees help establish the reputation of a business in the community. An employee who displays integrity helps create a positive culture for the business, customers, and the community.

legitimate websites and will not harm your computer. Some advertisers place them onto your computer without your knowledge or consent. Marketers use the information for research and selling purposes. If a hacker gains access to your cookies, you are at risk. The cookies can be used to steal personal information you have entered on a website. Cookies also can be used to target you for a scam based on your Internet history.

As a precaution, there are ways to protect your computer from cookies. One way is to prevent them from being accepted by the browser. Most Internet browsers allow you to set a preference to never accept cookies. Check your browser for specific instructions.

Another way to protect your computer is to delete cookies on a regular basis. Still another way to remove cookies is to run a disk cleanup utility.

Phishing

Phishing is the use of fraudulent e-mails and copies of valid websites to trick people into providing private and confidential data. A common form of phishing is sending a fraudulent e-mail that appears to be from a legitimate source, such as a bank. The e-mail asks for certain information, such as a Social Security number or bank account information. Sometimes it provides a link to a web page. The linked web page looks real, but its sole purpose is to collect private information that is used to commit fraud.

Most legitimate organizations do not use e-mail to request this type of information. Never provide confidential information in response to an unsolicited e-mail. Avoid clicking a link to a website in an e-mail. It is better to manually enter the website URL into a web browser. Never open an e-mail attachment that you are not expecting.

Malware

Malware, short for *malicious software*, is a term given to software programs that are intended to damage, destroy, or steal data. Beware of an invitation to click on a website link for more information about an advertisement as the link may trigger malware. One click can activate a code, and the computer could be hacked or infected. Malware comes in many forms including spyware, Trojan horses, worms, and viruses.

- **Spyware** is software that spies on a computer. Spyware can capture information such as e-mail messages, usernames, passwords, bank account information, and credit card information. Often, affected users will not be aware that spyware is on their computer.

- A *Trojan horse* is malware usually disguised to appear as a useful or common application in order to convince people to download and use the program. However, the Trojan horse performs malicious actions on the user's computer, such as destroying data or stealing information. Trojan horses do not self-replicate, nor do they infect other files.

- *Worms* are similar to Trojan horses, except they self-replicate. Worms self-replicate so they can infect other computers or devices. Like Trojan horses, worms do not infect other files.

- A **software virus** is a computer program designed to negatively impact a computer system by infecting other files. A virus may destroy data on the computer, cause programs to malfunction, bring harm to a network, or steal information. Viruses can be introduced to a computer in many ways, such as by downloading infected files from an e-mail or website.

Virus-protection software helps safeguard a computer. It should be used on any device that is connected to the Internet or any type of network. Virus-protection software is also referred to as *antivirus* or *antimalware* software.

Virus-protection software should also have a firewall. A **firewall** is a program that monitors information coming into a computer. It helps ensure that only safe information gets through.

Digital Security

Do not be lulled into a false sense of security when communicating with others online. Be especially careful with those whom you do not know personally. Avoid opening e-mails that look suspicious. Use common sense when deciding what personal details you share, especially your address or Social Security number. Resist the urge to share too much information that could be stolen.

Avoid Identity Theft

Identity theft is an illegal act that involves stealing someone's personal information and using that information to commit theft or fraud. There are many ways that your personal information can be stolen without you knowing it. A lost credit card or driver's license can provide thieves with the

Kues/Shutterstock.com

A security plan includes storing backup of important digital files in a fireproof container.

information they need to steal a person's identity. Criminals will also steal physical mail to commit identity theft. This method is often called *dumpster diving*. However, computer technology has made identity theft through digital means the most prevalent.

Be wary of how much information you share on social networking websites. If you suspect your identity has been stolen, visit the Identify Theft website provided by the Federal Trade Commission for resources and guidance. Time is of the essence, so if this unfortunate situation happens to you, act immediately.

Create a Security Plan

A security plan should be in place for your computer and any databases you maintain, as well as any mobile devices you have. Your employer will assist in creating a plan for your workplace equipment. If you have any suspicions about communicating with someone or giving your information via a website, do not proceed. Investigate the person or the company with whom you are dealing. You may be able to avoid a scam before it is too late.

Consider downloading and running antivirus software for your mobile device. Many people rely on mobile devices. It is important to guard them against viruses that would disrupt a primary means of communication and expose personal data.

You must also plan to protect your mobile devices from theft. If you become careless and leave your smartphone or other device in an unexpected location, your identity can be stolen. You may also be stuck with a large telephone bill. If it is an employer-issued device, you may be responsible for replacing it from your personal funds. To protect your mobile device from use by a thief, create a password to lock it. Have the number of your mobile device in a safe place so that if the unexpected happens, you can contact your service provider.

Secure Passwords

Unfortunately, many people have weak passwords for even their most important accounts, such as banking or credit card accounts. Your employer will have guidelines for creating passwords for work accounts. When creating new passwords, use the tips shown in Figure 3-3.

Security Settings

Become acquainted with the security settings and features of your browser when accessing the Internet from your computer. Change your settings to protect your computer and your information. Enabling a *pop-up blocker* prevents your browser from allowing you to see pop-up ads, which can contain malware.

Back Up Your Computer

An important part of a security plan is backing up the data on your computer. If a virus invades your computer or the hard disk crashes, it may be too late to retrieve your files and computer programs.

Secure Passwords

- Do not be careless or in a hurry.
- Do not use passwords that contain easily guessed information.
- Do not use the same passwords for multiple accounts or profiles.
- Do change your passwords often.
- Do record your passwords on a dedicated and secure hard-copy doccument.

Goodheart-Willcox Publisher

Figure 3-3   Use these tips to create safe, secure passwords.

Your employer will create regular backups of files on your work computer. For your personal computer, put a plan in place to perform regular backups. Decide on a storage device and method for backing up your files. Place the backup in a fireproof container and store it at a location other than your home.

Section 3.2 Review

 Check Your Understanding

1. Describe ethical communication.
2. Explain how following an acceptable use policy is ethical.
3. Discuss the importance of digital security.
4. Explain how to protect a mobile device from theft.
5. Why should a computer be backed up on a regular basis?

 Build Your Vocabulary

As you progress through this course, develop a personal glossary of key terms. This will help you build your vocabulary and prepare you for a career. Write a definition for each of the following terms and add it to your personal glossary.

proprietary information	phishing
false advertising	malware
social responsibility	spyware
acceptable use policy	software virus
Internet protocol address	firewall
hacking	identity theft
cookies	

History of Communication

Objectives

After completing this section, you will be able to:

- **Explain** the evolution of career clusters.
- **Describe** communication during the ancient era.
- **Explain** the evolution of communication in the postclassical era.
- **Describe** communication inventions of the modern era.

Key Terms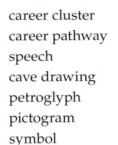

career cluster
career pathway
speech
cave drawing
petroglyph
pictogram
symbol

ideogram
writing
alphabet
telecommunication
movable type
cloud computing

Essential Question

What does the history of communication reveal about its future?

Communication Career Cluster

Communication has evolved through the decades into technology that allows for real-time communication across distances. Modern technology makes it possible for us to connect with others anywhere in the world in real time. Communication has also evolved into an industry that provides employment for countless people. As communication technologies have developed, new careers have emerged.

The Career Clusters Initiative began in 1996 as the Building Linkages Initiative. This was a collaborative effort between the US Department of Education, the Office of Vocational and Adult Education (OVAE), the National School-to-Work Office (NSTWO) and the National Skill Standards Board (NSSB). The goal of the project was to create a reliable set of standards for the integration of academics with workplace skills. Eventually, the organization of the project emerged as career clusters, and the States' Career Clusters Initiative was launched in 2001.

The **career clusters** are 16 groups of occupational and career specialties in the National Career Clusters Framework. In each cluster, three levels of knowledge and skills exist, ranging from broad to specific. The foundation level applies to all levels of the careers. Within the 16 clusters, there are 79 different pathways. A **career pathway** is a subgroup that reflects occupations requiring similar knowledge and skills. The career/occupation level is the highest level of skills and knowledge within a cluster. All levels promote employability, academic, and technical skills.

Originally, communication careers were as part of the Telecommunications, Computers, Arts and Entertainment, and Information sector. Communication careers are now part of the Arts, A/V Technology & Communications career cluster. The career clusters are covered in more detail in Chapter 18.

Prehistory and the Ancient Era: to 500 AD

To appreciate the importance of the communication careers cluster, it is helpful to study the history and evolution of communication. Early communication started as crude speech that evolved over thousands of years. Today, technology allows for real-time communication across distances. Computer programs allow for instant communication with friends and coworkers. News media offer a 24-hour cycle of information to help people stay informed of current events. The evolution of communication will continue for years to come.

Communication has a long history. The first forms of communication began to develop over 100,000 years ago, as shown in Figure 3-4. Each generation has had its own impact on how humans interact with each other to conduct business or meet personal goals.

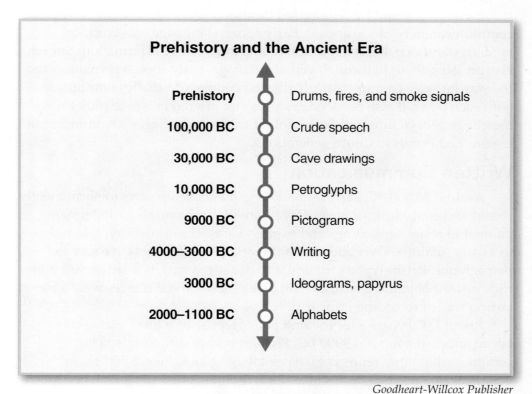

Prehistory and the Ancient Era

Prehistory	Drums, fires, and smoke signals
100,000 BC	Crude speech
30,000 BC	Cave drawings
10,000 BC	Petroglyphs
9000 BC	Pictograms
4000–3000 BC	Writing
3000 BC	Ideograms, papyrus
2000–1100 BC	Alphabets

Goodheart-Willcox Publisher

Figure 3-4   This time line shows communication development from prehistory through the ancient era.

Early humans created images like this one in cave drawings and petroglyphs.

Lukiyanova Natalia / frenta /Shutterstock.com

Verbal Communication

The earliest human communication was nonverbal. Prehistoric humans did not have a spoken or written language. They relied on nonverbal methods such as hand gestures and uttered noises to communicate.

Between one and three hundred thousand years ago, the first verbal communication began to appear. Early spoken language was crude by modern standards, but it allowed humans to exchange information. **Speech** is expressing thought through verbal language. Early speech revolutionized the way humans communicate. It allowed people to verbally communicate with each other. It also replaced gestures and uttered noises to indicate meanings. Storytelling became a tool for tribes and villages to communicate lessons and events to future generations.

Written Communication

Around 30,000 BC, early humans began to develop ways to permanently record and communicate ideas. **Cave drawings** are murals early humans painted to relate happenings and express ideas. These are often referred to as *cave paintings*. Over about 20,000 years, cave paintings gave way to petroglyphs. **Petroglyphs** are similar to cave drawings, but are carved into rock instead of painted or drawn on rock. These carved images were a more lasting way of recording information.

About 1,000 years after the first petroglyphs were used, pictograms began appearing around 9000 BC. **Pictograms** are symbols used for communication that represent what something looks like. **Symbols** are objects or images that represent an idea, thought, or concept. Pictograms represent specific elements that could be put into a certain order to tell a story. An example of a pictogram might be three wavy lines to represent water. Egyptian hieroglyphs are pictograms.

Around 3000 BC, many systems of pictograms evolved into or gave way to ideograms. **Ideograms** are graphic symbols that represent abstract ideas or concepts. To build on the last example, an ideogram of three wavy lines might mean not only "water," but also "wet," "river," "ocean," or "drink." Modern-day examples of ideograms can be seen in the icons used in computer programs. One example is the floppy disk icon that means "save." Floppy disks are no longer used, but the abstract concept of saving your work is still communicated by the ideogram.

Writing is a system of visual communication using symbols, letters, or words. Pictograms and ideograms are considered types of *protowriting*, or very primitive writing. One of the first forms of writing was called *cuneiform writing* after the wedge-shaped tool that was used to mark the writing surface. It was developed between 3500 BC and 3000 BC in Mesopotamia. Cuneiform started as a pictogram system and is considered a type of protowriting.

While ideograms were an advance over pictograms, those systems were not alphabets. An **alphabet** consists of symbols representing basic sounds of a language. These symbols can be put together to form words and sentences. The first true alphabet was developed in the eastern Mediterranean region by the Phoenicians in about 1100 BC. Different cultures developed unique alphabets that still differ today.

Early forms of writing, including cuneiform, were recorded on clay or stone tablets. Eventually, societies developed media to hold written symbols that were more portable. In Ancient Egypt, papyrus was created around 3000 BC. Paper was invented in China around 100 AD. It took about a hundred years for widespread use of paper as a medium for writing. At first, writing on paper was done on scrolls. Scrolls eventually gave way to the codex sometime during the second or third century AD. A *codex* appears like a modern printed book with folded pages bound on one side.

An early form of printing or duplicating writing was developed in China about 220 AD. This was called *block printing*. A large wooden block was carved with the writing in reverse. Then the block was inked. A piece of paper or cloth was placed on the block, transferring the ink to the medium. Printing allowed for multiple copies of a message to be more quickly written for easier distribution.

Telecommunication

Telecommunication is communication over a distance. Early human cultures used drums, smoke signals, and fires to indicate warnings or other messages over long distances. Cultures in western Africa developed a talking drum that could mimic speech. Smoke signals were used by early North American and Chinese cultures.

As cultures advanced, so did the means of telecommunication. Between about 550 BC and 520 BC, Persians developed a system of mail in which messages were delivered on horseback. Other mail systems would develop around the world over the next four or five hundred years.

Ancient Persians are also credited with developing a system of messenger pigeons between 500 BC and 400 BC. This form of telecommunication spread to Greece, Rome, India, and other cultures.

Postclassical Era: 500 AD to 1500 AD

During the postclassical era, cultures and societies advanced and evolved into what would become modern societies. Communication began to spread between cultures at an increasing rate, as shown in Figure 3-5. Trade between cultures required communication and translation between different languages. Changes in religious beliefs and behaviors also had a great impact on how communication evolved, as did conflicts between cultures.

Written Communication

Movable type is a system of printing involving individual letters or symbols that can be assembled to create words, sentences, and passages. The first known movable type system was created in China in 1040 AD. This system used porcelain type. Around 1230 AD, a system of movable type that used metal type was developed in Korea. Movable type quickly spread throughout Asia and Europe.

Johannes Gutenberg of Germany is credited with inventing an improved system of metal movable type and printing press around 1450 AD. Gutenberg's printing press and a version of movable type made it easy to print multiple copies of a document in large quantities. This led to wider distribution and communication of ideas. The Gutenberg system revolutionized the way in which written language is communicated. Within a decade, the Gutenberg system had spread from Germany throughout Europe.

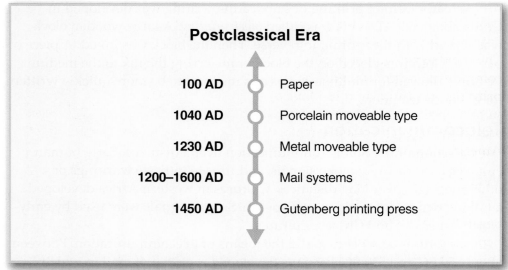

Postclassical Era

100 AD	Paper
1040 AD	Porcelain moveable type
1230 AD	Metal moveable type
1200–1600 AD	Mail systems
1450 AD	Gutenberg printing press

Goodheart-Willcox Publisher

Figure 3-5   This time line shows communication advances during the postclassical era.

Telecommunication

Between 1200 AD and 1600 AD, nations all over the world developed or adopted messenger services and postal systems. These systems allowed printed or written communication to be transmitted over distances. The time needed for the message to be delivered depended on many factors. The distance between sender and receiver and the reliability of the service affected delivery time.

Additionally, as ocean-based trade increased, the need to communicate between ships arose. Maritime flags developed as a means to communicate a ship's country of origin and other information at a distance. This is an example of real-time communication as the receiver could view the message as soon as the sender transmitted it. However, the sender and receiver had to be visible to each other, which is why this is called *line-of-sight communication*.

Modern Era: 1500 AD to present

Societies and technology continued to advance in the modern era, as shown in Figure 3-6. European voyagers sailed to the Americas. The Renaissance and the Age of Discovery began. Global trade and communication networks were established. The rapid expansion of printed communication continued. The printing press appeared in Mexico in 1539, in the Philippines in 1593, and in the English colonies in North America in 1638.

Written Communication

Personal writing instruments began to evolve from the quill pens used in the postclassical era. Pencil lead was first used in the 1790s in both France and Austria. In the 1800s, metal nib pens were developed, which directly replaced

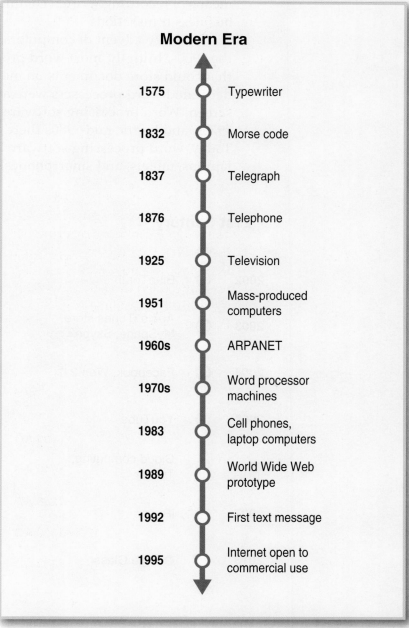

Goodheart-Willcox Publisher

Figure 3-6   There were many exciting new inventions during the modern era that shaped communication as we know it today.

quill pens. In 1884, the first fountain pen was invented. By the 1940s, the ballpoint pen was in use. Each of these devices made it easier for humans to communicate their ideas by recording them on paper.

What is known today as the typewriter began with an invention in Italy in 1575. The device was designed to press type into paper. Over the next three hundred years, various inventors developed new versions of the typewriter or improved on existing versions. The first commercially successful typewriter was invented in 1868 in Milwaukee, Wisconsin. This machine was the first to be called a "typewriter" and to have the now-familiar QWERTY layout of keys. The typewriter became a primary means of recording written communication, especially business transactions.

With the advent of computers, word processing was invented in the 1960s. Initially, most word processors were advanced typewriters that could store documents on magnetic tape or cards. By the late 1970s, dedicated word processors were available, which included a display screen. Word processing software was first introduced in the mid-1970s, and by the mid-1980s there were dozens of programs available. Today, word processing software is found on personal computers, laptops, tablets, and smartphones. It has almost entirely replaced word processor typewriters as the way in which humans record written communication.

Telecommunication

During the modern era, telecommunication expanded substantially. Many significant inventions that changed how humans communicate were perfected in the modern era. These included the telegraph, telephone, radio, television, and Internet. Figure 3-7 shows selected communication inventions in the 21st century.

Telegraph

Several inventors developed various forms of the electric *telegraph* during the early 1800s. The first commercial electric telegraphs were independently developed and patented in England and in the United States in 1837. Samuel Morse

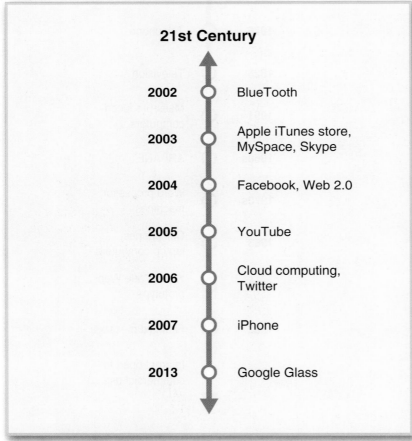

Goodheart-Willcox Publisher

Figure 3-7 Communication developments in the 21st century have largely been related to technology advancements.

was the American inventor, and he developed a code, or language, for use in transmitting messages with a telegraph. For the first time, humans could send and receive complex written messages in real time over long distances. The first transoceanic telegraph line was laid in 1858 between North America and Europe.

Telephone

The invention of the *telephone* allowed humans to verbally communicate over distances without the sender and receiver being in visual contact. Several inventors developed versions of the telephone in the late 1800s. The first patent for the telephone was granted to Alexander Graham Bell in the United States in 1876. By the turn of the 20th century, there were millions of phones installed in the United States.

Early telephones were connected by networks of wires. Later on, wire-based networks were connected by radio and then satellite. The first transoceanic telephone cable was not laid until the mid-1950s. Today, cellular technology allows for completely wire-free telephone service all across the globe.

Radio

The first telephones were limited by the fact that they were wire-based networks. A wireless telegraph, on the other hand, would not have the restriction of a wire-based network. Experiments in wireless telegraphy, which were eventually called *radio*, were conducted as early as the first half of the 19th century.

Inventors made several discoveries during the 1800s that advanced wireless telegraphy. In 1894 Italian Guglielmo Marconi built the first commercially successful wireless telegraphy system. In 1901, he conducted the first successful transoceanic transmission, with the first regular service

Modern advances in written communication and telecommunication sped up the pace of business.

BrAt82 /Shutterstock.com

established in 1907. The first wireless broadcast to include the human voice occurred on December 24, 1906. Verbal communication could be conducted without wires.

Television

Television was the first technology to allow the transmission of both verbal and visual communication between the sender and the receiver. The first television technology was patented in 1884 by German Paul Gottlieb Nipkow. However, Nipkow never actually built it. The first demonstration of television based on Nipkow's system was conducted in Paris in 1909. This system was electromechanical. Experiments on the first electronic television system were conducted later in 1926 in England.

However, several inventors were investigating television, including American Philo Farnsworth. In September of 1927, Farnsworth transmitted the first images with his system, and one year later gave his first public demonstration. Color television was introduced in the United States in 1953, but it took several years for color broadcasts and for the public to purchase color television sets.

Early television signals were transmitted through the air, but in 1948 cable television was introduced. Satellites were used to broadcast television between continents starting in 1962. Home-based satellite television receivers were introduced in the United States in the mid-1970s. Today, television broadcasts can be received via air, cable, satellite, cellular technology, and the Internet.

 Green   Unplug Electronics

If electronics and appliances are turned off at night, will the electric bill be less? The answer is a potential "no." Electronics that are plugged into an outlet use standby power, which is the minimum power usage when the item is plugged in. That means that even if it is turned off, it is still drawing power and costing money to run, just because it is plugged into an outlet. To make sure that computers, monitors, printers, photocopiers, and other electronics will not waste power, unplug them entirely.

It is a common practice in Europe to unplug equipment that is not in use, including lights and computers. Up to 25 percent can be saved on energy costs by just turning off and unplugging equipment at the end of the day. Less energy usage also reduces negative effects on the environment.

Internet

The *Internet* is a global computer network. Its origins date to the 1960s when the US Defense Department developed ARPANET. This was the first computer network to use the Internet protocol. Beginning in 1981, ARPANET was expanded to include academic institutions. Over the next decade, the Internet developed as global computer networks were created. Its use was restricted to government and academic institutions until 1995.

Like the Internet, cloud computing has its roots in the 1960s. **Cloud computing** is using remote servers to store and access data over the Internet rather than on a personal computer or local server. There is no exact date for its invention, but what is thought of today as cloud computing emerged in the mid-1990s. It became popular in 2006 with the introduction of the Amazon Elastic Compute Cloud by Amazon.com. This allows users to access personal content, such as saved files, from anywhere with a Wi-Fi connection. Cloud computing makes even private digital information accessible from any device.

Section 3.3   Review

 Check Your Understanding

1. Summarize the development of writing in the prehistoric era.
2. Explain the importance of the invention of the printing press.
3. What is meant by *line-of-sight communication*?
4. What important telecommunication advances were made during the modern era?
5. How did the Internet develop?

 Build Your Vocabulary

As you progress through this course, develop a personal glossary of key terms. This will help you build your vocabulary and prepare you for a career. Write a definition for each of the following terms and add it to your personal glossary.

career cluster   ideogram
career pathway   writing
speech   alphabet
cave drawing   telecommunication
petroglyph   movable type
pictogram   cloud computing
symbol

Chapter Summary

Section 3.1 Communicating in a Digital Society

- Digital communication is the exchange of information through electronic means. It requires digital literacy skills and appropriate digital citizenship behavior.

- Intellectual property is something that comes from a person's mind, such as an idea, invention, or process. Copyrights, patents, and trademarks can protect intellectual property rights. Material that is in the public domain refers to material that is not owned by anyone and can be used without permission. Products or services can be protected by issuing a licensing agreement which is a contract that gives one party permission to use a product or service owned by someone else.

- The Electronic User's Bill of Rights details the rights and responsibilities of both individuals and institutions regarding the treatment of digital information.

Section 3.2 Workplace Ethics

- Ethical communication is applying ethics to messages and other documents to make sure all communication is honest in every way. The workplace requires that employees be ethical in all communication that represents the organization. Confidentiality and social responsibility are important topics to all organizations and businesses.

- Internet access provided by a company should be used only for business purposes. Most companies have an acceptable use policy that explains what is and is not acceptable use of company-owned and company-operated equipment.

- Identity theft is an illegal act that involves stealing someone's personal information and using that information to commit theft or fraud. It is important to protect equipment, data, and your digital footprint against theft by putting a security plan in place.

Section 3.3 History of Communication

- Communication has evolved into an industry that employs countless people. The National Skill Standards Board Act developed a system to categorize careers based on common knowledge and skills. These categories were revised in 1999 to the career cluster model.

- The first forms of communication evolved over 100,000 years ago when nonverbal exchange was used. Early verbal exchanges led to cave drawings and other images used to convey ideas and record information. Writing eventually developed and the invention of paper enabled better communication. As cultures evolved, the need for connecting with people over a distance became important. Smoke signals were some of the first forms of telecommunication used in North America and China.

- In the postclassical era, communication advanced and modern societies developed. Johannes Gutenberg invented the first printing press which changed the way written language was communicated. Telecommunication also evolved and messenger systems and postal systems began to develop.

- The modern era brought with it the Renaissance and the Age of Discovery. Communication evolved rapidly. Pens, typewriters, and eventually computers changed the way humans communicated with each other. The telegraph, telephone, radio, television, and Internet led the way to an ever-changing timeline in the evolution of communication.

Online Activities

Complete the following activities which will help you learn, practice, and expand your knowledge and skills.

Posttest. Now that you have finished the chapter, see what you learned by taking the chapter posttest.

Vocabulary. Practice vocabulary for this chapter using the e-flash cards, matching activity, and vocabulary game until you are able to recognize their meanings.

English/Language Arts. Visit www.g-wlearning.com to download each data file for this chapter. Follow the instructions to complete an English/language arts activity to practice what you have learned in this chapter.

Activity File 3-1: Improving Your Reading Skills

Activity File 3-2: Improving Your Editing Skills

Review Your Knowledge

1. Explain the importance of digital citizenship.
2. Explain what intellectual property is and what it includes.
3. What is fair use doctrine?
4. How does open-source software differ from other forms of software?
5. Describe measures companies put in place to ensure their employees use the Internet appropriately while at work.
6. Differentiate between a code of ethics and a code of conduct.
7. List examples of ways that a company can monitor use of the Internet by employees.

8. Describe the most common form of phishing.
9. How does virus protection software help safeguard a computer?
10. Explain the history and evolution of career clusters.

Apply Your Knowledge

1. Create a list of acceptable behaviors that are considered good examples of netiquette. Next to each, explain why these behaviors are necessary in a digital society.
2. Select a topic related to digital citizenship, such as social media use or identity theft. Prepare a presentation to illustrate the implications of your topic on individuals, society, and businesses. Give your presentation to the class.
3. Analyze the legal and ethical responsibilities required as a professional in the arts, audio/visual technology, and communications workplace.
4. Photocopying copyrighted material is illegal and unethical. What is your opinion of a friend photocopying a textbook chapter instead of buying the textbook? Do you think that duplicating copyrighted materials is illegal, unethical, or both? Do you think the fair use doctrine would apply in this situation?
5. Professional marketing communication regularly involves persuasive messages. Advertisements that claim weight loss overnight or white teeth in four hours attempt to persuade the audience to purchase a product. How do these communication messages impact society? Does the advertiser's point of view sway the audience? What social responsibilities does marketing have to society? Write several paragraphs discussing your opinion.

6. Identify a list of social responsibilities a business has to society, such as protecting the environment or supporting the community. Once the list is complete, analyze each social responsibility and why you think it is important for businesses and professional communicators.

7. Summarize the evolution of communication. Which part of the evolution of communication do you think is more important and reflective of our communication today? Write several paragraphs to describe your opinion.

8. The time line for the 21st century in Figure 3-7 shows selected communication inventions. Create your own detailed time line of communication inventions between 2000 and present day.

Communication Skills

College and Career Readiness

Reading. Imagery is descriptive language that indicates how something looks, feels, smells, sounds, or tastes. After you have read this chapter, find an example of how the author used imagery to appeal to the five senses. Analyze the presentation of the material. Why did you think this appealed to the senses? How did this explanation create imagery? Did it influence the mood of the reader?

Writing. Generate your own ideas relevant to using digital technology in the appropriate manner. Use multiple authoritative print and digital sources and document each. Write several paragraphs about your findings to demonstrate your understanding of digital citizenship.

Speaking. Most people in the United States act as responsible and contributing citizens. How can a person demonstrate social and ethical responsibility in a digital society? Can you think of ways that are not discussed in this chapter? Present to your class.

Internet Research

Copyright. Copyright laws protect intellectual property. Conduct an Internet search for *copyright law violation example*. Select an example and discuss the law and how it was violated. What copyright issues were at stake? Write your findings and cite your sources using the *Chicago Manual of Style* or your choice of reference guide.

Teamwork

Working with your team, identify and analyze examples of ethical responsibilities that a professional communicator, such as a person in marketing, has to society. How can a professional exhibit ethical conduct?

Portfolio Development

College and Career Readiness

Checklist. Once you have written your portfolio objective, consider how you will achieve it. It is helpful to have a checklist of components that will be included in your portfolio. The checklist will be used to record ideas for documents and other items that you might include. Starting with a checklist will help you brainstorm ideas that you want to pursue.

The elements that you select to include in your portfolio will reflect your portfolio's purpose. For example, if you are seeking acceptance into art school, create a portfolio that includes your best artwork.

1. Ask your instructor for a checklist. If one is not provided, use the Internet and research Student Portfolio checklists. Find an example that works for your purpose.

2. Create a checklist. This will be your roadmap for your portfolio.

CTSOs

 **Objective Test.** Some competitive events for CTSOs require that entrants complete an objective component of the event. This event will typically be an objective test that includes terminology and concepts related to a selected subject area. Participants are usually allowed one hour to complete the objective test component of the event.

To prepare for an objective test, complete the following activities.

1. Read the guidelines provided by your organization.

2. Visit the organization's website and look for objective tests that were used in previous years. Many organizations post these tests for students to use as practice for future competitions.

3. Look for the evaluation criteria or rubric for the event. This will help you determine what the judge will be looking for in your presentation.

4. Create flash cards for each vocabulary term with its definition on the other side. Ask a friend to use these cards to review with you.

5. Ask your instructor to give you practice tests for each chapter of this book. It is important that you are familiar with answering multiple choice and true/false questions. Have someone time you as you take a practice test.

Unit

2

Writing Basics

Professional Communication

Why It Matters

Communication is based on language. This is true for letters, e-mails, reports, verbal conversations, and any type of message. To be an effective and professional communicator, you must understand the rules of the English language. If you use language that is not correct English, your message may be misunderstood. Even worse, you may be viewed as lacking professionalism.

Proper writing is required in the workplace. Messages that are well written project a professional image and command attention from the reader. Good writers learn the rules of grammar and punctuation and follow the steps in the writing process. By doing so, you can create documents that reflect qualities of clarity, conciseness, courtesy, and correctness.

Chapters

Chapter **4** Grammar Skills

Chapter **5** Grammar Mechanics

Chapter **6** Writing Process

Chapter **7** Writing Style

While studying, look for the activity icon  **for:**

- Pretests and posttests
- Vocabulary terms with e-flash cards and matching activities
- Videos
- Self-assessment

G-WLEARNING.com

Video

Before you begin this unit, scan the QR code to view a video about professional communication. If you do not have a smartphone, visit www.g-wlearning.com.

Diego Cerva/Shutterstock.com

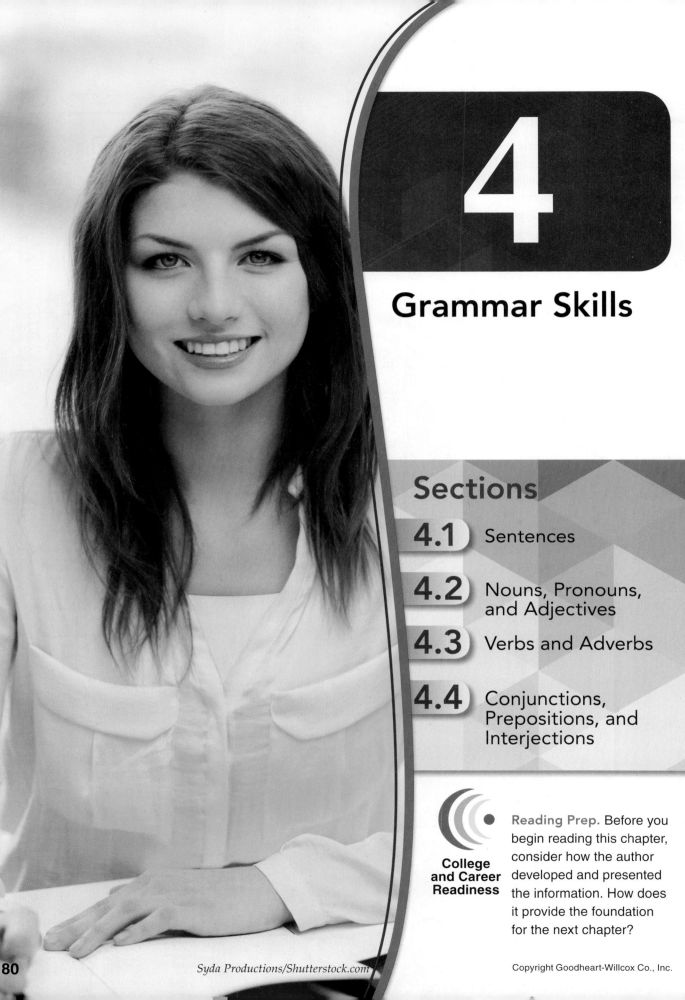

4

Grammar Skills

Sections

4.1 Sentences

4.2 Nouns, Pronouns, and Adjectives

4.3 Verbs and Adverbs

4.4 Conjunctions, Prepositions, and Interjections

College and Career Readiness

Reading Prep. Before you begin reading this chapter, consider how the author developed and presented the information. How does it provide the foundation for the next chapter?

Syda Productions/Shutterstock.com

Check Your Communication IQ ↗

Before you begin the chapter, see what you already know about communication by taking the chapter pretest. The pretest is available at www.g-wlearning.com.

Case Study

Correct Grammar

Jason Wells works in human resources at a small company. He has reviewed cover messages and résumés from applicants for a customer service position. Jason wants to interview four people. After reading several applications, he has selected three candidates to interview.

Jason is debating between two people to select as the fourth candidate. Emily Bahri has the appropriate education. She has worked in customer service for several years. However, Jason noted several grammatical errors in Emily's cover message and résumé. Connie Wong has the appropriate education, but her experience is limited compared with Emily. Connie's letter and résumé are clear, courteous, and concise, with no grammatical errors.

EDHAR/Shutterstock.com

Critical Thinking

1. Which candidate do you think Jason will invite for an interview? Explain.

2. What is being communicated nonverbally when a cover message and résumé have spelling or grammar mistakes?

Sentences

Objectives

After completing this section, you will be able to:

- **Describe** how sentences are structured.
- **Summarize** types of sentence structure.

Key Terms

ssential
uestion

What can you learn about the English language by studying sentences?

grammar
sentence
subject
predicate
direct object
indirect object
phrase

clause
independent clause
dependent clause
subordinating clause
restrictive clause
nonrestrictive clause

Sentence Parts

Words in the English language are classified as one of eight different *parts of speech*: noun, pronoun, verb, adjective, adverb, conjunction, preposition, and interjection. **Grammar** is the study of how words and their components come together to form sentences. It is a set of rules for using language properly. The rules of English grammar relate to how the parts of speech are used to form the sentences with which people communicate. The brief definitions of the parts of speech in Figure 4-1 will help you understand the following discussion of sentence parts. You will learn more about each part of speech later in this chapter.

A **sentence** is a group of words that expresses a complete thought. Consider the two examples that follow. Are these sentences?

> Under the desk.
>
> The book is under the desk.

The first example does not give a complete thought. More information is needed to understand how *under the desk* relates to an action, person, or thing. The second example is a sentence because it provides enough information for a complete thought.

Eight Parts of Speech

Part	Definition	Examples
Noun	A word naming a person, place, or thing.	girl school book
Pronoun	A word taking the place of a noun.	she it they
Verb	A word showing action or state of being.	run sing is
Adjective	A word describing a noun or pronoun.	tall young round
Adverb	A word describing a verb, adjective, or another adverb.	quickly very nearby
Conjunction	A word connecting words, phrases, or sentences.	and but or
Preposition	A word relating nouns or pronouns to other words in a sentence.	under to for
Interjection	A word expressing strong emotion.	wow oh hey

Goodheart-Willcox Publisher

Figure 4-1   The eight parts of speech are noun, pronoun, verb, adjective, adverb, conjunction, preposition, and interjection.

Subjects and Predicates

A sentence has two main parts: a subject and a predicate. The **subject** is the person speaking or the person, place, or thing the sentence describes. The **predicate** describes an action or a state of being for the subject.

Subjects

Nouns and pronouns are discussed in detail later in this chapter. Both nouns and pronouns can serve as the subject of a sentence. Consider this sentence.

| Anne will sing.

Business Protocol

Workspace

Employees are expected to keep company workspaces clean and in order. When using a shared copier, do not leave paperclips or other supplies behind. If you take breaks or eat lunch in the common eating area, clean up dishes, utensils, and food packaging. Keep your personal space clean and free from clutter.

What person, place, or thing does the sentence describe? The sentence gives information about Anne, who is the subject of the sentence. In the examples that follow, the subjects are shown in italics.

> *Elena* writes beautiful poems.
>
> *They* left the party before midnight.
>
> The *school* has nine classrooms.
>
> The *dog* has a white house in the backyard.

When a sentence discusses more than one noun or pronoun, it has a compound subject. In the examples that follow, the compound subjects are shown in italics.

> *Mario and Chin* play video games after school.
>
> The *cars and trucks* were parked behind the building.

In some sentences, the subject is not stated, but it is understood. This form is often used when speaking directly to a person. In the examples that follow, *you* is the understood subject of each sentence.

> Run home and tell your mother about the accident.
>
> Read all of the instructions before answering the questions on the test.

Each subject in the earlier examples is called a simple subject. A simple subject is just the nouns or pronouns about which the sentence gives information. A complete subject is the simple subject and the words that describe it. In the examples that follow, the complete subjects are shown in italics.

> *The fresh, hot bread* has a wonderful smell.
>
> *The payment for admission* includes snacks.

Predicates

The simple predicate of a sentence includes only the verb or verbs that show action or state of being. In the examples that follow, the simple predicates are shown in italics.

> My brother *cleaned* his room.
>
> Julia and I *will attend* a concert at the park.
>
> Ms. Chung *is* the principal.

A compound predicate contains two or more verbs joined by *and* or another conjunction. Both verbs describe action or state of being for the subject. In the examples that follow, the compound predicates are shown in italics.

> Mr. Romero *rose* to his feet *and addressed* the audience.
>
> The shipping clerk *wrapped* the package *and mailed* it.

The complete predicate of a sentence includes the verb and other information that tells what the subject is or does. In the examples that follow, the complete predicates are shown in italics.

> Ms. Chung *is the principal.*
>
> My brother *cleaned his room.*
>
> Julia and I *attended a concert at the park.*

Objects and Complements

Sentence predicates often contain objects. A **direct object** is someone or something that receives the action of the verb. In the first example that follows, *Mr. Rosenbaum* is the person who performs the action. *Reads* is the action performed (the verb). *Story* is the direct object—the thing that receives the action of the verb. In the following examples, the objects are shown in italics.

> Mr. Rosenbaum reads a *story* to his class every Monday.
>
> The little boy threw the *ball*.
>
> The cows ate the *hay*.

A predicate that contains a direct object can also contain an indirect object. An **indirect object** names something or someone for whom the action of the verb is performed. It often comes before the direct object in the sentence. In the first example that follows, *gave* is the action (the verb). *Present* is the direct object. *Me* is the indirect object. In the following examples, the indirect objects are shown in italics.

> Grandmother gave *me* a birthday present.
>
> The teacher gave the *students* instructions for the test.
>
> The boy gave the *dog* a biscuit.

A predicate with a verb that shows a state of being may contain a subject complement. A subject complement is an adjective that describes the subject or a noun that renames or tells what the subject is. In the first example that follows, *beautiful* (an adjective) is a subject complement that describes *dress* (the subject of the sentence). In the second example, *captain* is a subject complement that renames *Jamal*.

> Your new dress is *beautiful*.
>
> Jamal is *captain* of the team.

Phrases and Clauses

Sentences can be very short, such as *He is*. Longer sentences can contain phrases and clauses that add more information to the sentences. Correctly structuring phrases and clauses will convey the meaning you intend listeners and readers to receive.

Phrases

A **phrase** is a group of words that act together to convey meaning in a sentence. Both complete subjects and complete predicates can contain phrases. Phrases can be short or long; however, a phrase does not contain both a subject and a predicate. Some examples of phrases are shown in Figure 4-2.

Phrases	
Type of Phrase	**Example**
Noun	*Watching movies* is my favorite hobby.
Verb	The sale *has been running* all week.
Adjective	The rookie is a *quick, strong* player.
Adverb	He climbed the ladder *very quickly*.
Preposition	She made uniforms *for the team*.

Goodheart-Willcox Publisher

Figure 4-2   The words in a phrase act together to convey meaning.

Clauses

A **clause** is a group of words within a sentence that has a subject and a predicate. When a clause gives a complete thought and could stand alone as a separate sentence, it is called an **independent clause**. In the following examples, the independent clauses are shown in italics. Note that the third example has two independent clauses.

> *Jane will head the team* because she has the most experience.
>
> Since we arrived late, *we missed the opening speech*.
>
> *I read a novel*, and *she watched a movie*.

A clause that requires the rest of the sentence to provide a complete thought is called a **dependent clause**. A dependent clause used alone is a writing error and is often called a *sentence fragment*. Subordinating clauses, restrictive clauses, and nonrestrictive clauses are types of dependent clauses.

A **subordinating clause** is joined to the rest of the sentence with a subordinating conjunction, such as *since, because, when, if,* or *though*. In the following examples, the subordinating clauses are shown in italics.

> I cannot attend the meeting, *though I am interested in the topic.*
>
> *When we land*, everyone will leave the plane.
>
> *Because the rain was very heavy*, a flash flood warning was issued.

A **restrictive clause** is a type of dependent clause that is essential to the meaning of the sentence. The clause identifies a particular person or thing. In the following examples, the restrictive clauses are shown in italics. In the first example, the clause identifies one particular boy on the team. In the second example, the clause identifies a particular group of students. In the third example, the clause identifies a particular vase.

> The little boy on the team *who has a broken arm* will not play.
>
> Students *who do not follow the rules* will be banned from participation.
>
> The vase *that you dropped* was very valuable.

Can you identify the types of clauses in this sentence? "When playing team sports, everyone should play by the rules."

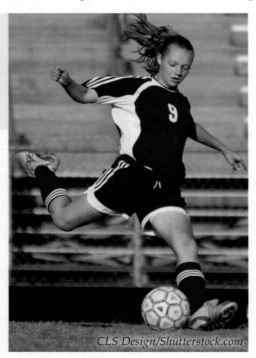

CLS Design/Shutterstock.com

A **nonrestrictive clause** provides information that is not essential to the meaning of the sentence. The clause provides information that may be helpful. However, the receiver can understand the message without that information. In the following examples, the nonrestrictive clauses are shown in italics.

> Mark West, *who loves to swim,* is the only boy on the team.
>
> The bicycle, *which is dirty and rusty*, is an antique.

Sentence Structure

Sentences are structured as simple sentences, compound sentences, or complex sentences. A simple sentence has one independent clause and no dependent clauses. It often contains one or more phrases. The subject or predicate of a simple sentence can be compound. The first example has a compound subject. The second example has a compound predicate.

> Paula and Jan ate lunch in the cafeteria.
>
> Alberto will ride his bike this afternoon and swim tomorrow.
>
> The cart rolled down the narrow, winding road.
>
> Julie is an administrative assistant.

A compound sentence has two independent clauses joined by a conjunction, such as *and* or *but*. Examples of compound sentences are as follows.

> Paula ate lunch in the cafeteria, and Kim ate lunch in the park.
>
> Aman invited me to study with him, but I had other plans.
>
> A heavy rain fell, and the game was delayed.

Complex sentences have an independent clause and one or more dependent clauses. Examples of complex sentences are as follows. The first example has one independent clause (shown in italics) and one dependent clause. The second example has one independent clause (shown in italics) and two dependent clauses.

> When you write a business letter, *you should use clear and concise language.*
>
> *Mrs. Parsons*, who lives on Maple Street, *complained about the noise*, which was keeping her awake at night.

A sentence that has two independent clauses and one or more dependent clauses is called a compound-complex sentence (or a complex-compound sentence). Examples of compound-complex sentences are as follows.

> Mrs. Parsons complained about the noise, which was keeping her awake at night, but the police officer did not file a report.
>
> Whenever she dines at a restaurant, she orders a salad, and this helps her stay healthy.

When writing business documents, varying the type and length of the sentences you use can make the message more interesting. Your goal is to make the message flow smoothly from one thought to the next and be easy to understand. Using too many short sentences can make the message seem choppy with disconnected thoughts. Using too many long, complex sentences can make the message difficult to understand.

Reading level is a measure of the difficulty of a written message. It is often correlated to a grade or age range. *Readability* is a measure of whether the document is easy to read. You can use the spelling- and grammar-checking features of a word processing program, such as Microsoft Word, to see the readability statistics of a passage, as shown in Figure 4-3. In this example, one paragraph contains four sentences.

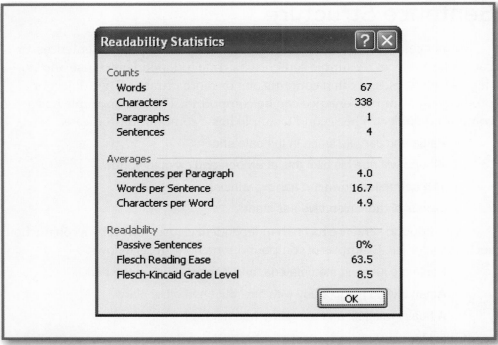

Goodheart-Willcox Publisher

Figure 4-3   Use a built-in feature of Microsoft Word to show readability statistics for a selected passage or the entire document.

Section 4.1   Review

 Check Your Understanding

1. What are the two main parts of a sentence?
2. Describe the difference between a direct and an indirect object.
3. What are the five types of clauses?
4. List the four types of sentences.
5. Define *reading level*.

 Build Your Vocabulary

As you progress through this course, develop a personal glossary of key terms. This will help you build your vocabulary and prepare you for a career. Write a definition for each of the following terms and add it to your personal glossary.

grammar	clause
sentence	independent clause
subject	dependent clause
predicate	subordinating clause
direct object	restrictive clause
indirect object	nonrestrictive clause
phrase	

Nouns, Pronouns, and Adjectives

Objectives

After completing this section, you will be able to:

- **Explain** the use of nouns and pronouns.
- **Summarize** the correct use of adjectives.

Key Terms

noun	adjective
collective noun	article
possessive noun	definite article
pronoun	indefinite article
antecedent	demonstrative adjective

Essential Question

Why do we need pronouns?

Nouns and Pronouns

As you learned earlier, nouns and pronouns are used as the simple subject in sentences. They can also serve as a direct object, an indirect object, and the object in a prepositional phrase. Pronouns can be used to take the place of a noun. They should properly relate to the nouns they replace.

Nouns

A **noun** is a word that names a person, place, or thing. Nouns help you point out your best friend, tell someone about your hometown, or ask your brother to pass the potatoes. Without nouns, communicating would be very difficult. *Maria, Chesterfield Park,* and *potatoes* are examples of nouns.

A proper noun names a particular person, place, or thing. *Mr. Thomas, Atlanta,* and *Empire State Building* are examples of proper nouns. A common noun describes a person, place, or thing in general terms. *Teacher, city,* and *building* are examples of common nouns. In the following examples, the nouns are shown in italics.

> The *boy* and his *bike* were wet from the *rain*.
>
> *Central Park* has a soccer *field*.
>
> *Carrots* are my favorite *vegetable*.

Singular and Plural Nouns

Nouns can be singular or plural. A singular noun names one person, place, or thing. *Girl*, *carrot*, and *bus* are examples of singular nouns. A plural noun indicates more than one person, place, or thing. *Girls*, *carrots*, and *buses* are examples of plural nouns. The plural form of a noun is created in one of several ways, as shown in Figure 4-4.

Irregular nouns are those that do not follow the guidelines described in Figure 4-4 for making plurals. Rather than adding *s* or *es* to the singular form, the plural form often has a different spelling from the singular form. In other cases, the singular and plural forms are spelled the same. Examples of irregular nouns are as follows.

Singular	Plural
child	children
man	men
woman	women
goose	geese
person	people
deer	deer
barracks	barracks

Guidelines for Making Nouns Plural

Guidelines	Singular	Plural
For most nouns, add *s* to the singular form to create the plural form.	cat rock football	cats rocks footballs
For nouns that end in *sh*, *ch*, *s*, *x*, *z*, or similar sounds, add *es* to the singular form.	bush box class blitz	bushes boxes classes blitzes
For nouns that end in a consonant and a *y*, change the *y* to *i* and add *es*.	city baby	cities babies
For nouns that end in *o* preceded by a vowel, add *s* to the singular form. For most nouns that end in *o* preceded by a consonant, add *s* to form the plural. For some exceptions, add *es*.	stereo radio memo piano potato	stereos radios memos pianos potatoes
For many nouns that end in *f* or *fe*, change the *f* sound to a *v* and add *s* or *es* to the singular form. For others, keep the *f* and add an *s*.	life knife roof	lives knives roofs

Goodheart-Willcox Publisher

Figure 4-4   These guidelines outline how to make singular nouns plural.

A **collective noun** refers to a group or unit that contains more than one person, place, or thing. *Army, class, committee,* and *team* are examples of collective nouns. Although a collective noun refers to a group of people or things, these nouns can also be plural or singular. In the following examples, the collective nouns are shown in italics.

> The British *army* crossed the river; the French and Italian *armies* went by another route.
>
> The Mendoza *family* left the park, but the Chung and Olson *families* remained.
>
> During our safari, we saw one *herd* of elephants and two *herds* of zebras.

Because the way to form the plural of nouns varies, you probably will not remember the proper form for every word you want to use. When you are unsure about the plural form of a noun, check a dictionary. Dictionaries typically do not show the plural form of nouns that are formed simply by adding *s* or *es* to the singular form. However, the plural form is typically shown when the noun is irregular (tooth and teeth), ends in *o*, or ends in a consonant and a *y*. Figure 4-5 shows a sample dictionary entry that indicates the plural form of a noun.

Possessive Nouns

A **possessive noun** indicates ownership by the noun or an attribute of the noun. For most singular nouns, the possessive form is created by adding an apostrophe and an *s* to the noun. The possessive noun can come before or after the item owned. In the first example that follows, *girl's* is a

---

Exploring Communication Careers

Archivist

An *archive* is a collection of valuable records or historically significant documents. An archivist creates and manages archives. They are specially trained in preserving original material, such as computer files, photographs, music, film, and paper documents. Helping people find and secure original material is also part of the job responsibilities. Typical job titles for this visual arts position include *collections manager, museum archivist,* and *records manager.*

Some examples of tasks that archivists perform include:

- Obtain historically valuable items.

- Appraise permanent records and historically valuable documents.

- Preserve records, documents, and objects.

- Copy records to an appropriate format, such as digital or film.

- Create and maintain an organizational system for an archive.

- Direct the safekeeping of items in an archive.

Archivists are expected to have a bachelor degree, but most positions require a master degree. Several years of experience in similar fields are also expected.

city ('si-tē)

n. pl cities

1. A population center larger than a town.
2. A municipality incorporated in the United States.
3. The inhabitants of a city as a group.

Figure 4-5   This is an example of an online dictionary entry. Notice the icon that can be clicked to hear the pronunciation of the word.

possessive noun signifying ownership of books by one girl. In the second example, *manager's* is a possessive noun showing ownership of the attribute of friendliness. In the third example, *Gloria's* is a possessive noun indicating ownership of a bracelet. The apostrophe and *s* are added to the final word in compounds words, as shown in the last example.

The *girl's* books were placed in her locker.

My new *manager's* friendliness was reassuring.

The lost bracelet was *Gloria's*.

My *sister-in-law's* garden contained many types of flowers.

Possessive nouns indicate ownership. "Alex used the library's books to write his report."

For most plural nouns, an apostrophe is added to form the possessive noun. In the first example that follows, *girls'* is a plural possessive noun indicating the ownership of jackets by two or more girls. When a noun has an irregular plural that does not end in *s*, an apostrophe and an *s* are added to form the possessive, as in the second and third examples.

The *girls'* jackets were neatly stacked on the bleachers.

The *women's* dinner was held in James Hall.

The *children's* games taught them math skills.

In some cases, adding an *s* to a word that already ends in *s* or an *s* sound results in an awkward pronunciation for the word. In those cases, the possessive is still formed using an apostrophe and an *s*. However, the extra *s* or *es* sound is not pronounced. Such words are often proper names.

> *Mrs. Phillips's* home is located by the river.
>
> The *Foxes's* relatives are coming to dinner.
>
> The *Ganges's* banks were lined with trees.

Pronouns

A **pronoun** is a word that replaces a noun in a sentence. They can refer to people or things. Pronouns allow messages to flow smoothly without repeating nouns or noun phrases over and over. For example, you could begin a paragraph with a sentence that refers to Mr. Joseph Patel and then use the pronoun *he* to refer to Mr. Patel in later sentences. Pronouns should properly relate to the words they replace. When pronouns are not used correctly, the meaning of the sentence will be unclear.

Antecedents

The word that gets replaced with a pronoun is its **antecedent**. Most pronouns have antecedents, but some typically do not. The pronoun *I*, which refers to the speaker, and the pronoun *you*, which refers to the person being addressed, usually do not have antecedents. In the following examples, the pronouns are shown in italics. In the second example, *girls* is the antecedent of *they*. In the third example, *ball* is the antecedent of *it*.

> *I* am sure that *you* will win.
>
> The girls lost the game, and *they* were very upset.
>
> Shelia hit the ball before *it* touched the ground.

Personal Pronouns

Personal pronouns refer to specific persons or things. To correctly use pronouns, you need to consider their properties: number, gender, person, and case. The number of a pronoun indicates whether it is singular (referring to one person or thing) or plural (referring to more than one person or thing). Gender indicates whether the pronoun refers to a male, a female, or an object without gender. Always use pronouns that agree with their antecedents in number and gender. Examples are shown in Figure 4-6.

Pronouns			
Pronouns	**Number**	**Gender**	**Example**
she, her	Singular	Feminine	Monica left *her* coat by the door.
he, him	Singular	Masculine	James arrived late, and *he* missed the kickoff.
it	Singular	Neutral	The ball was hit hard, and *it* went out of the park.
they, we	Plural	Neutral	The children played hard, and *they* grew tired.

Goodheart-Willcox Publisher

Figure 4-6   Pronouns indicate number and gender.

Personal pronouns can be in one of three persons. A pronoun in *first person* refers to someone who is speaking or writing. A pronoun in *second person* refers to someone who is being addressed. A pronoun in *third person* refers to someone being discussed. Examples of pronouns in first, second, and third person are as follows.

First person

I am happy to be home.

Give the information to *us*.

Second person

Alicia, will *you* return on Monday or Tuesday?

Chet, *your* project is finished.

Third person

Pablo was tired, so *he* went home.

The children ate lunch and then *they* played in the park.

The case of a pronoun indicates the way it is used in a sentence. *Nominative case* pronouns are used as the subject in a sentence or as subject complements. *Objective case* pronouns are used as direct objects, indirect objects, or objects of prepositions. *Possessive case* pronouns show ownership. Examples are shown in Figure 4-7. Note that some pronouns, such as *you* and *it*, can be either nominative or objective, depending on how they are used in a sentence.

Other Pronouns

Other types of pronouns include interrogative pronouns, relative pronouns, demonstrative pronouns, indefinite pronouns, and adjective pronouns. These pronouns do not indicate gender, but they can indicate number. Some pronouns fall into more than one category, depending on their use in the sentence.

Interrogative pronouns, which are used to ask a question, include *what*, *which*, *who*, *whom*, and *whose*. Typically, these pronouns do not have a known

Pronoun Case		
Case	**Pronouns**	**Examples**
Nominative	I, you, he, she, it, we, they, who	*I* am happy to be home. *You* should be careful. *Who* made this cake?
Objective	me, you, him, her, it, us, them, whom	*Whom* does Charles trust? Give *me* a ream of paper. Pass the bucket to *him*.
Possessive	my, mine, your, yours, his, her, hers, it, its, our, ours, their, theirs, whose	*My* notes were unclear. Bring *your* homework to school. *Whose* phone is ringing?

Goodheart-Willcox Publisher

Figure 4-7   Pronouns can be nominative, objective, or possessive case.

antecedent. The pronoun represents something or someone unknown. The suffix *ever* is sometimes used with interrogative pronouns to form words such as *whoever* or *whatever*. In the example that follows, *who* is used as an interrogative pronoun.

| *Who* answered the telephone?

Relative pronouns are used to begin dependent clauses in complex sentences. Relative pronouns include *who, whom, whose, which, what,* and *that.* The pronouns *who, whom,* and *whose* are used to refer to a person. *Which, what,* and *that* are used to refer to an animal or object. In the example that follows, *who* is used as a relative pronoun.

| The woman *who* came to the door asked for directions.

Demonstrative pronouns identify or direct attention to a noun or pronoun. *This, that, these,* and *those* are demonstrative pronouns. *This* and *that* refer to singular nouns or pronouns. *These* and *those* refer to plural nouns or pronouns. *This* and *these* are generally used to refer to something nearby. *That* and *those* are generally used to refer to something at a distance.

Nearby

This was damaged during shipment.

At a distance

Those will be shipped from another city.

Indefinite pronouns generally refer to an object or person that has been identified earlier or does not need specific identification. Examples of indefinite pronouns include *some, none, one, every, neither, other, both, each, any, such,* and *another.* Compound examples include *everyone, somebody, anyone, anything,* and *someone.* In the example that follows, *some* is used as an indefinite pronoun.

| *Some* will be thrown in the trash.

Some pronouns can also be used as adjectives or in adjective clauses. Examples include *some, none, all,* and *who.* In the example that follows, *some* is used as an adjective pronoun.

| Would you like *some* fruit?

Adjectives

An **adjective** is a word that modifies a noun or pronoun. Adjectives may provide details about the noun or pronoun that give you a better understanding of the person, place, or thing. In the first example that follows, *brilliant* and *bold* are adjectives that expand the meaning of *colors.* Adjectives can also define limits. In the second example that follows, *two* is an adjective that limits the meaning of *students,* the word it modifies or describes. Some adjectives are made from proper names and always begin with a capital letter, as shown in the third example.

| *Brilliant, bold* colors were used in the painting.

| *Two* students passed the exam.

| *African* lions live in family groups called "prides."

Adjectives often come before the words they modify, as shown in the previous examples. In some cases, adjectives follow the nouns or pronouns they modify, as shown in the first example that follows. Adjectives that are subject complements follow a linking verb and rename or describe the subject. The second example contains an adjective used as a subject complement.

> This will not lead to anything *good*.
>
> Wilma is *tired*.

Two or more related adjectives that appear before a noun or pronoun and equally modify it are called coordinate adjectives. These adjectives should be separated by the word *and* or by commas. However, not all adjectives that appear in a sequence are coordinate adjectives. In the first example that follows, *old* and *rusty* are coordinate adjectives describing the shovel. In the second example, *new* and *soccer* describe a ball, but are not coordinate adjectives.

> The *old*, *rusty* shovel had a broken handle.
>
> The *new soccer* ball has a blue cover.

When the order of the adjectives before a noun can be arranged without changing the meaning of the sentence, the adjectives are typically coordinate adjectives. For example, you might say the *old, rusty shovel* or the *rusty, old shovel*. You would not, however, say *soccer new ball* instead of *new soccer ball*.

Forms of Adjectives

Most adjectives have three forms: positive, comparative, and superlative. Positive adjectives describe, but do not compare, people or things. Comparative adjectives compare two people or things. Superlative adjectives compare three or more people or things. Examples of adjectives are shown in Figure 4-8.

> **Positive**
>
> The *small* book was on top of the stack.
>
> **Comparative**
>
> The red book was *smaller* than the blue book.
>
> **Superlative**
>
> The red book was the *smallest* of the books.

Forms of Adjectives		
Positive	**Comparative**	**Superlative**
large	larger	largest
happy	happier	happiest
low	lower	lowest
beautiful	more beautiful	most beautiful
eager	more eager	most eager
good	better	best
less	lesser	least

Goodheart-Willcox Publisher

Figure 4-8   Adjectives can be positive, comparative, or superlative forms.

Articles

An **article** is an adjective that limits the noun or pronoun it modifies. The adjectives *the, a,* and *an* are articles. Articles come before a noun, pronoun, or noun phrase and can be definite or indefinite. The **definite article** *the* refers to a specific noun. The **indefinite articles** *a* and *an* typically refer to a noun in a general way. Use *a* before words that begin with a consonant sound and *an* before words that begin with a vowel sound. Articles need not be repeated before each noun in a series of nouns. In the following examples, the articles are shown in italics.

> *The* cat chased *the* mouse.
>
> *A* cat will sometimes come when called.
>
> *The* counselor has *an* open, caring attitude.
>
> *The* letter, envelope, and stamp were placed on *the* desk.

Demonstrative Adjectives

This, that, these, and *those* are demonstrative adjectives. A **demonstrative adjective** is used before a noun to indicate number and location. *This* and *that* are used with singular words. *These* and *those* are used with plural words. *This* and *these* indicate a location that is near the speaker. *That* and *those* indicate a location that is not near the speaker. Refer to the examples that follow.

> *This* food is delicious.
>
> *That* boat is moored at another pier.
>
> *These* children sing well.

These same words are demonstrative pronouns when they take the place of a noun. Review the section on pronouns earlier in this chapter for examples of demonstrative pronouns.

Section 4.2 Review

Check Your Understanding

1. Explain the difference between a proper noun and a common noun. Give examples of each.
2. What is the advantage of using pronouns?
3. Explain what someone should do when he or she cannot remember the plural form of an irregular noun.
4. Describe the purpose of adjectives.
5. What is a coordinate adjective?

Build Your Vocabulary

As you progress through this course, develop a personal glossary of key terms. This will help you build your vocabulary and prepare you for a career. Write a definition for each of the following terms and add it to your personal glossary.

noun
collective noun
possessive noun
pronoun
antecedent
adjective

article
definite article
indefinite article
demonstrative adjective

Verbs and Adverbs

Objectives

After completing this section, you will be able to:

- **Explain** the use of verbs.
- **Describe** the appropriate use of adverbs.

Key Terms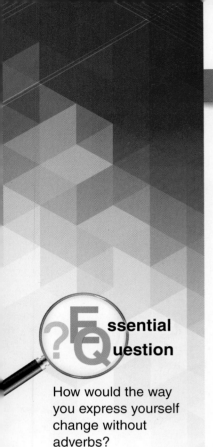

verb	third person
active voice	present participle
passive voice	past participle
present tense	dangling participle
past tense	gerund
future tense	infinitive
first person	adverb
second person	

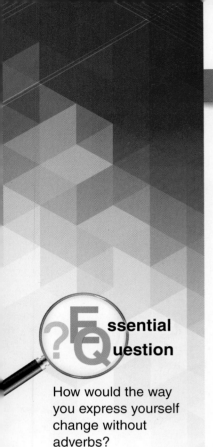

Essential Question

How would the way you express yourself change without adverbs?

Verbs

A **verb** is a word that shows action or state of being. Using verbs, you can recount the action in a basketball game or explain that a salad tastes delicious. Verbs may be the most important of the parts of speech. Only a verb can express a complete thought by itself, having *you* as the understood subject.

Types of Verbs

A verb can be one of two basic types: those that show action or those that show a state of being. Examples of action verbs include *read, sing, run, count, laugh, go,* and *eat*. Examples of verbs that show a state of being are *be, is, are, was, were,* and *am*. In the examples that follow, the verbs are shown in italics.

> I *count* the money when the store closes.
>
> Sue, *eat* your vegetables.
>
> I *am* hungry.
>
> Go! (*you* is the understood subject)

Linking Verbs

Verbs that show a state of being are also called linking verbs when they relate a subject to a subject complement. In the first example that follows, the verb *is* links the subject (Ralph) to the subject complement (a tall boy).

> Ralph *is* a tall boy.
>
> Kendra *was* the president of the club.

Daniel Korzeniewski/Shutterstock.com

The sentence, "Andrew is winning the race" uses a helping verb. Which word is it?

Helping Verbs

Verbs that work with a main verb to show action are called helping verbs (or auxiliary verbs). These verbs express little meaning on their own. However, they help make the meaning of the main verb clear. Examples of helping verbs include *be, been, am, is, are, was, were, has, had, have, do, does, did, can, could, may, might, will, would, should, shall,* and *must.* In the following examples, the helping verbs are shown in italics.

> He *is* calling your name.
>
> Movies *are* shown in a dark room.
>
> She *has* walked around the track.
>
> I *should* press the fabric after sewing each seam.

Compound Verbs

A compound verb consists of two or more verbs in the same sentence. The verbs can be main verbs and helping verbs, as shown in the first example that follows. A compound verb can include two or more main verbs and no helping verbs, as shown in the second example.

> Jim *will climb* to the top of the hill.
>
> Pedro *ran* to the fence and *jumped* over the gate.

Properties of Verbs

Verbs can have one or more of five different properties: voice, mood, tense, person, and number. Understanding the properties of verbs can help you create messages that are free of verb errors.

Voice

An action verb can be in either active voice or passive voice. In **active voice**, the subject of the sentence performs the action. In the first example that follows, the subject (Alfred) performs the action (rowing). In **passive voice**, the subject of the sentence is acted upon, as in the second example.

> Alfred *rowed* the boat.
>
> The boat *was rowed* by Alfred.

Sentences written in active voice are considered to be more direct and easier to understand than those written in passive voice. Sentences in passive voice can seem wordy or awkward. However, using passive voice is appropriate in some cases. When you do not know who performed the action, use passive voice, as in the following example. Passive voice is often used in writing scientific papers to make actions or conclusions sound more objective.

> The car *was stolen*.

Mood

The mood of a verb relates to the way in which the speaker or writer wants the sentence to be understood. The indicative mood is most commonly used. It expresses a straightforward statement of fact or opinion or asks a question. The imperative mood states a command or a direct request. The subjunctive mood expresses an idea, suggestion, or hypothetical situation. Examples of sentences in each mood are as follows.

The subjunctive mood is used to give a suggestion. "You should practice your music more often."

Jacob Gregory/Shutterstock.com

Indicative

The snowstorm raged for two days.

When will the new printer be delivered?

Imperative

Leave the building.

Please pass your papers to the front.

Subjunctive

I recommend that you hire three assistants.

If I were you, I would read this book.

Tense

The *tense* of a verb indicates when the action or state of being takes place. The **present tense** of a verb indicates that the action or state of being takes place now. The **past tense** indicates that the action or state of being has already occurred. For many verbs, the past tense is formed by adding *ed* to the present tense. Examples include *walk/walked*, *hunt/hunted*, and *look/looked*. For irregular verbs, the spelling of the past tense varies. Examples include *run/ran*, *drink/drank*, and *pay/paid*. The **future tense** indicates that the action or state of being will occur at a later time. The future tense is formed by adding *will* before the present tense of the verb. Examples of verb tense are as follows.

Present tense

The horse runs around the paddock.

Past tense

The horse ran around the paddock.

Future tense

The horse will run around the paddock.

Verb tenses can be further divided into simple and perfect tenses. The simple tenses are the present, past, and future tenses discussed above. The perfect tenses are used to express that something happens over or during a certain time. The *present perfect tense* is formed by adding *have* or *has* to the past tense. The *past perfect tense* is formed by adding *had* to the past tense. The *future perfect tense* is formed by adding *will have* to the past tense. Examples of the perfect tenses are as follows.

Present perfect tense

The horse has run around the paddock. (just now)

Past perfect tense

The horse had run around the paddock. (last week, perhaps)

Future perfect tense

The horse will have run around the paddock. (next week, perhaps)

Person

Verbs can be in one of three persons. A verb in **first person** refers to an action of someone who is speaking or writing. A verb in **second person** refers to an action of someone who is being addressed (you). A verb in **third person** refers to an action of someone being discussed. Examples are as follows.

First person

I am getting ready to go.

Second person

You are not alone.

Third person

They are waiting.

Number

A verb should agree in number with related nouns or pronouns. Verbs that relate to *I* should always be singular. Verbs that relate to *you* should always be plural, even when one person is being addressed. Verbs that relate to nouns or pronouns used in the third person (someone spoken about) should agree in number with the nouns or pronouns.

> **First person, singular verb**
>
> I am thirsty.
>
> **Second person, plural verb**
>
> You are late for the meeting.
>
> **Third person, singular verb**
>
> The girl runs every day.
>
> **Third person, plural verb**
>
> The girls and boys run every day.

When a sentence has two or more simple subjects connected by *and*, the verb should be plural. When a sentence has two or more singular subjects connected by *or* or *nor*, the verb should be singular.

> **Third person, plural verb**
>
> Tom, Roger, and Aydin *sing* every day.
>
> **Third person, singular verb**
>
> Tom or Roger *sings* tenor.

Verb Forms

Understanding verb forms, such as participles, gerunds, and infinitives, can help you write clear and creative messages. These verb forms are also called *verbals*.

Participles

A **present participle** is a verb form that indicates action is in progress or ongoing. It can also be used as an adjective. To create a present participle,

Green   Lunch

Lunchtime is an opportunity to go green. The most environmentally friendly lunch option is to bring lunch in a reusable container. Any packaging waste generated from a packed lunch should be recycled. Most employers now have the option to recycle paper, plastic, and aluminum.

Getting delivery or takeout inevitably ends with a large amount of packaging waste, not to mention the fuel cost involved. If it is necessary to have lunch delivered or to get takeout, join coworkers in placing a large order. This is more efficient than many small, separate orders. If you go out for lunch, try biking or walking instead of driving.

Use reusable plates, utensils, and napkins whenever possible. Disposable versions of these items usually cannot be recycled after they are soiled and will end up in landfills.

add *ing* to the present tense. Examples include *eating*, *drawing*, and *working*. A **past participle** indicates that action has been completed. A past participle is the same as the past-tense form discussed earlier.

> **Present participle**
>
> Angie is *painting* a picture.
>
> The *running* water makes a soothing sound.
>
> **Past participle**
>
> Angie *painted* a picture last week.

A **dangling participle** is a writing error in which a participle phrase modifies nothing or the wrong person or object. In the following incorrect example, the phrase implies that the birds were paddling down the stream. This is not likely the writer's intent.

> **Incorrect**
>
> Paddling down the stream, the birds were startled.
>
> **Correct**
>
> As we were paddling down the stream, the birds were startled.

Gerunds

A **gerund** is a verb form used as a noun. Gerunds are formed by adding *ing* to the present tense of a verb. Examples of gerunds include *eating*, *shopping*, *talking*, *playing*, and *counting*. Gerunds can serve as the subject of a sentence, a subject complement, or the object of a verb or preposition.

> *Shopping* is my favorite hobby.
>
> I love *jogging*.
>
> She does not appreciate my *snoring*.
>
> He was arrested for *speeding*.

Infinitives

An **infinitive** is the word *to* and a verb in its simple present form. Examples include *to eat, to read, to see, to touch*, and *to find*. An infinitive or infinitive phrase can serve as a noun, adjective, or adverb. The examples that follow show infinitive phrases and their uses in the sentences.

> *To cry* over spilled milk seemed a waste of time. (noun, subject)
>
> Her dream is *to win*. (noun, subject complement)
>
> She intended *to buy a new car*. (noun, direct object)
>
> He found a way *to earn more money*. (adjective)
>
> He yelled *to get her attention*. (adverb)

A split infinitive occurs when an adverb is placed between the word *to* and the verb. Examples of split infinitives include *to barely see, to slowly read*, and *to quickly jump*. A split infinitive can be useful for emphasizing the adverb. The phrase *to boldly go* may sound more forceful or dramatic than *to go boldly*. This is largely a matter of the writer's opinion. In the past, some grammar rules deemed a split infinitive to be a writing error. However, this structure is now widely accepted.

The sentence, "Tropical fish are colorful" uses a positive adverb.

Adverbs

An **adverb** is a word that describes a verb, adjective, clause, or another adverb. Adverbs tell how, when, or where something is done. They can also limit or qualify a description. In the first example that follows, *beautifully* tells how Jose sang and *yesterday* tells when he sang. Both adverbs modify the verb *sang*. In the second example, *fast* tells how the girl ran. *Very* qualifies the adverb *fast*. In the third example, *perhaps* qualifies the first clause of the sentence. In the last example, *finally* modifies the rest of the sentence (an independent clause).

> Jose sang *beautifully yesterday*.
>
> The girl ran *very fast*.
>
> *Perhaps* this answer is correct, but I am not sure.
>
> *Finally*, she will finish her work.

Forms of Adverbs

Adverbs have three forms: positive, comparative, and superlative. Positive adverbs describe, but do not compare, actions or qualities. Comparative adverbs compare two actions, conditions, or qualities. Add *er* or *more* to create the comparative form of most adverbs. Superlative adverbs compare three or more actions, conditions, or qualities. Add *est* or *most* to create the superlative form of most adverbs.

> **Positive**
>
> Aysha drives *fast*.
>
> The painting is *beautiful*.
>
> **Comparative**
>
> Aysha drives *faster* than Janet.
>
> Jia Li's painting is *more beautiful* than Jeanette's painting.
>
> **Superlative**
>
> Aysha drives *fastest* of all contestants.
>
> Jia Li's painting is the *most beautiful* of all the paintings.

Some adverbs do not have comparative or superlative forms. Examples of these adverbs include *almost, before, here, there, now, then, too, very,* and *never*. These adverbs express qualities or conditions that are not suitable for comparison. Some adverbs, such as *little, much, bad,* and *well,* have irregular comparative and superlative forms. Consult a dictionary when you are unsure about how to form the comparative or superlative form of an adverb.

Conjunctive Adverbs

Conjunctive adverbs, such as *however*, *therefore*, and *also*, connect or introduce clauses or phrases in a sentence. They help clarify the ideas in the sentence. In the first example that follows, *therefore* connects two independent clauses in the sentence. In the second example, *then* introduces the main clause of the sentence. In the third example, the adverb comes at the end of the sentence. Examples of conjunctive adverbs are shown in Figure 4-9.

> The snow fell heavily; *therefore*, the roads were slippery.
>
> *Then*, rearrange the numbers, beginning with the smallest one.
>
> He went to the grocery store; he did not buy anything, *however*.

Conjunctive Adverbs				
accordingly	finally	likewise	otherwise	still
again	however	meanwhile	rather	then
besides	indeed	next	similarly	therefore
certainly	instead	now	so	yet

Goodheart-Willcox Publisher

Figure 4-9   Conjunctive adverbs help clarify the ideas in a sentence.

Section 4.3   Review

 Check Your Understanding

1. What are the two basic types of verbs? Give examples of each.
2. List the five properties of verbs.
3. How is a gerund formed?
4. Describe the three forms of adverbs.
5. Explain the role of conjunctive adverbs.

Build Your Vocabulary

As you progress through this course, develop a personal glossary of key terms. This will help you build your vocabulary and prepare you for a career. Write a definition for each of the following terms and add it to your personal glossary.

verb
active voice
passive voice
present tense
past tense
future tense
first person
second person

third person
present participle
past participle
dangling participle
gerund
infinitive
adverb

Conjunctions, Prepositions, and Interjections

Objectives

After completing this section, you will be able to:

- **Demonstrate** the use of conjunctions and prepositions.
- **Explain** the purpose of interjections.

Key Terms

conjunction
coordinating conjunction
subordinating conjunction

correlative conjunction
preposition
interjection

Essential Question

How do prepositional phrases make communication easier?

Conjunctions and Prepositions

Conjunctions and prepositions are important parts of speech because they connect words, phrases, or clauses to other elements in the sentence. Expressing a thought with clarity without using these words would often be difficult.

Conjunctions

A **conjunction** is a word that connects other words, phrases, or sentences. There are three types of conjunctions: coordinating, subordinating, and correlative. Each type has a particular use in connecting elements in sentences.

Coordinating Conjunctions

Coordinating conjunctions join two or more sentence elements that are of equal importance. The elements may be words or clauses. Examples of coordinating conjunctions include *and, or, nor, but, yet, so,* and *for.* In the first example that follows, *and* joins the three words *coats, gloves,* and *hats.* In the second example, *but* joins two independent clauses.

> The coats, gloves, *and* hats are in the closet.
>
> He invited me to a play, *but* I did not go.

Subordinating Conjunctions

Subordinating conjunctions connect dependent clauses to independent clauses. Examples include *although, because, since,* and *unless.* Since the subordinating conjunction introduces the dependent clause, it comes at the

AnetaPics/Shutterstock.com

An example of a sentence using a correlative conjunction is, "The puppy could neither sit nor stay."

beginning of the clause. However, the dependent clause can come before the independent clause, as in the first example that follows, or after it, as in the second example.

> *Because* the day was warm, I did not wear a jacket.
>
> I did not wear a jacket *because* the day was warm.

Correlative Conjunctions

Correlative conjunctions are pairs of words or phrases that work together to connect elements in a sentence. Examples include *both/and, either/ or, not only/but also, rather/than,* and *neither/nor.* The elements connected can be words, phrases, or clauses. Refer to these examples.

> *Both* students *and* teachers attended the assembly.
>
> The triathlon includes *not only* running, *but also* swimming and cycling.
>
> *Either* eat your broccoli *or* leave the table.
>
> I would *rather* run in the park *than* wash the dishes.
>
> He *neither* read the book *nor* studied for the exam.

Prepositions

A **preposition** is a word that connects or relates its object to the rest of the sentence. The English language has dozens of prepositions. Examples of prepositions include *to, at, by, under, of, beside, over,* and *during.* More examples are shown in Figure 4-10. The object of a preposition can be a noun, phrase, or objective case pronoun. A prepositional phrase consists of the preposition, its object, and any related adjectives and adverbs. In the following examples, the prepositional phrases are shown in italics.

Prepositions				
about	behind	from	onto	underneath
above	below	in	outside	until
across	beneath	inside	over	up
after	beside	into	past	upon
along	by	like	since	versus
among	down	near	through	with
around	during	of	to	within
at	except	off	toward	without
before	for	on	under	

Figure 4-10   There are dozens of prepositions in the English language.

> The cards are *on the table*.
>
> The hat is *beside the very pretty dress*.
>
> She mailed the package *to him*.

Prepositional phrases often show location in space or time for the object of the phrase. In the first two examples below, the prepositional phrases show location in space. In the third example, the phrase shows location in time.

> The book is *on the floor*.
>
> The paper is *underneath the stapler*.
>
> The leaves change color *in the fall*.

Prepositional phrases can serve as adverbs in a sentence. In the example that follows, *without pain* tells how the man ran the race.

> The man ran the race *without pain*.

Interjections

Interjections are probably the least used of the parts of speech. However, they play an important role in expressing strong emotions. An **interjection** is a word that expresses strong emotion, such as surprise, fear, anger, excitement, or shock. An interjection can also express a command. Examples of interjections include *wow, oh, hey, ouch, well,* and *hurray*. An interjection can appear at the beginning of a sentence that expresses strong emotion. The sentence can end with a period or an exclamation point, depending on how forceful the writer wants the sentence to be. In the following examples, the interjections are shown in italics.

> *No*, don't touch that!
>
> *Oh*, you surprised me.
>
> *Well*, I am insulted by that remark!

Interjections can also appear alone with an exclamation mark, with the following sentence providing more information. This makes the interjection seem more forceful. When an interjection expresses surprise, it can be followed by a question mark rather than an exclamation mark.

> *Ouch!* That hurts.
>
> *Hurray!* We won the game.
>
> *What?* You can't be serious.

Interjections should be used sparingly in formal business communication, such as letters and reports. For example, an interjection might be used when quoting someone's spoken words. Interjections can be effective in advertising materials or sales promotions. These messages are more informal and are designed to grab the reader's attention. However, interjections should still be used sparingly.

Section 4.4   Review

 Check Your Understanding

1. What is the function of conjunctions and prepositions in English?
2. Name the three types of conjunctions.
3. How is a preposition different from a conjunction?
4. Describe what is included in a prepositional phrase.
5. Explain the role of interjections in business communication.

 Build Your Vocabulary

As you progress through this course, develop a personal glossary of key terms. This will help you build your vocabulary and prepare you for a career. Write a definition for each of the following terms and add it to your personal glossary.

conjunction   preposition
coordinating conjunction   interjection
subordinating conjunction
correlative conjunction

4 Review and Assessment

Chapter Summary

Section 4.1 Sentences

- A sentence is a group of words that expresses a complete thought. The two parts of a sentence are the subject and the predicate. Sentence predicates often contain objects, which can be either direct or indirect, and complements. Longer sentences can contain phrases and clauses that add more information to the sentences.

- Sentences are structured as simple sentences, compound sentences, or complex sentences. A simple sentence has one independent clause and no dependent clauses. A compound sentence has two independent clauses joined by a conjunction. Complex sentences have an independent clause and one or more dependent clauses.

Section 4.2 Nouns, Pronouns, and Adjectives

- Nouns and pronouns are used as the simple subjects in sentences. A noun is a person, place, or thing. Nouns can be common or proper; singular or plural; collective; and possessive. A pronoun replaces a noun in a sentence.

- An adjective is a word that modifies a noun or pronoun. Adjectives can be positive, comparative, or superlative. Adjectives include definite and indefinite articles.

Section 4.3 Verbs and Adverbs

- A verb is a word that shows action or state of being. Verbs can have one or more of five properties which are voice, mood, tense, person, and number. Verb forms help the writer create clear messages. Verb forms include participles, gerunds, and infinitives.

- An adverb is a word that describes a verb, adjective, clause, or another adverb. Just like adjectives, adverbs can also be positive, comparative, or superlative. Adverbs can also be conjunctive.

Section 4.4 Conjunctions, Prepositions, and Interjections

- Conjunctions and prepositions connect words, phrases, or clauses to other elements in the sentence. Conjunctions can be coordinating, subordinating, or correlative. A preposition connects or relates objects to the rest of the sentence. All the words related to a preposition make up the prepositional phrase.

- An interjection is a word that expresses strong emotion or command. Interjections can introduce a sentence or appear alone with an exclamation mark or question mark.

Online Activities

Complete the following activities which will help you learn, practice, and expand your knowledge and skills.

- **Posttest.** Now that you have finished the chapter, see what you learned by taking the chapter posttest.

- **Vocabulary.** Practice vocabulary for this chapter using the e-flash cards, matching activity, and vocabulary game until you are able to recognize their meanings.

- **English/Language Arts.** Visit www.g-wlearning.com to download each data file for this chapter. Follow the instructions to complete an English/language arts activity to practice what you have learned in this chapter.

Activity File 4-1: Improving Your Editing Skills

Activity File 4-2: Using Word Division

Review Your Knowledge

1. List the eight parts of speech.

2. Describe the difference between a phrase and a clause.

3. Summarize how the following are typically constructed: simple sentence, compound sentence, and complex sentence.

4. Differentiate between a noun and pronoun.

5. Describe what it means for a pronoun to be in first, second, and third person.

6. What is the role of articles in English?

7. Explain the difference between passive voice and active voice, and the advantages of using each.

8. Name and describe the three forms of adverbs.

9. What is a prepositional phrase?

10. How can an interjection be written to seem more forceful?

Apply Your Knowledge

1. What is the origin of the word *grammar*? Interpret your findings and write several paragraphs about what you learned.

2. In each sentence that follows, identify and label the simple subject, complete subject, simple predicate, complete predicate, direct object, indirect object, subject complement, and prepositional phrase. Note that some sentences will not have all of these parts.
   A. The large box contains office supplies.
   B. Return the book to the library.
   C. This man is the committee chairperson.
   D. The large flower arrangement of roses and lilies was beautiful.

3. Identify the nouns and pronouns in the sentences that follow.
   A. She is keying quickly and accurately.
   B. Certainly, I will complete the finance report.
   C. What do you recommend?
   D. Some items will be returned to the store.

4. Write several paragraphs that describe an activity, sport, or hobby that interests you. Use each of the eight parts of speech at least once. Use at least one simple sentence, one compound sentence, and one complex sentence. Pay particular attention to the correct usage of verbs. When you are finished, edit the document to check for correct grammar.

5. Identify the conjunctions, prepositions, and interjections in the sentences that follow.
   A. The cat is hiding beneath the chair.
   B. Well, that book was a disappointment.
   C. Not only will I run the race, but also I will win it.
   D. The dog is running toward the ball.

Communication Skills

College and Career Readiness

Speaking. Select three of your classmates to participate in a discussion panel. Acting as the team leader, name each person to a specific task such as time-keeper, recorder, etc. Discuss the topic of using Standard English versus using texting language in the workplace. Keep the panel on task and promote democratic discussion.

Listening. Active listeners know when to comment and when to remain silent. Practice your listening skills while your instructor presents this chapter. Participate when appropriate and build on his or her ideas.

Writing. It is important for an employee to apply both technical and academic skills in the workplace. Writing is an academic skill that is applied each day in personal and work life. Write a paragraph describing why writing is considered an academic skill. How do you think good writing skills will help you in your professional career?

Internet Research

International Grammar. Research how grammar functions in another language, such as Spanish, German, or Japanese, using various Internet resources. Compare the parts of speech and grammar rules to those of Standard English. Prepare a brief handout for your class that explains the major differences.

Teamwork

Texting language is not Standard English and is always inappropriate in professional communication. With your team, discuss whether you agree or disagree with this statement. Then, create a list of words and phrases commonly used in text messages that are inappropriate to use in the workplace.

Portfolio Development

College and Career Readiness

Hard Copy Organization. As you collect material for your portfolio, you will need an effective strategy to keep the items clean, safe, and organized for assembly at the appropriate time. Structure and organization are important when working on an ongoing project that includes multiple pieces. A large manila envelope works well to keep hard copies of documents, photos, awards, and other items. A three-ring binder with sleeves is another good way to store your materials.

Plan to keep similar items together and label the categories. For example, store sample documents that illustrate your writing or technology skills together. Use notes clipped to the documents to identify each item and state why it is included in the portfolio. For example, a note might say, "Newsletter that illustrates desktop publishing skills."

1. Select a method for storing hard copy items you will be collecting.

2. Create a master spreadsheet to use as a tracking tool for the components of your portfolio. You may list each document alphabetically, by category, date, or other convention that helps you keep track of each document that you are including.

3. Record the name of each item and the date that you stored it.

CTSOs

Teamwork. Some competitive events for CTSOs have a teamwork component. If it is a team event, it is important that the competing team prepare to operate as a cohesive unit.

To prepare for teamwork events, complete the following activities.

1. Review the rules to confirm whether questions will be asked or if the team will need to defend a case or situation.

2. Practice performing as a team by completing the team activities at the end of each chapter in this text. This will help members learn how to interact with each other and participate effectively.

3. Locate a rubric or scoring sheet for the event on your organization's website to see how the team will be judged.

4. Confirm whether visual aids may be used in the presentation and the amount of setup time permitted.

5. Make notes on index cards about important points to remember. Team members should exchange note cards so that each evaluates the other person's notes. Use these notes to study. You may also be able to use these notes during the event.

6. Assign each team member a role for the presentation. Practice performing as a team. Each team member should introduce him- or herself, review the case, make suggestions for the case, and conclude with a summary.

7. Ask your instructor to play the role of competition judge as your team reviews the case. After the presentation is complete, ask for feedback from your instructor. You may also consider having a student audience to listen and give feedback.

5

Grammar Mechanics

Sections

5.1 Punctuation

5.2 Capitalization and Numbers

5.3 Structure and Word Choice

College and Career Readiness

Reading Prep. As you read the chapter, record any questions that come to mind. Indicate where the answer to each question can be found: within the text, by asking your teacher, in another book, on the Internet, or by reflecting on your own knowledge and experiences. Pursue the answers to your questions.

Check Your Communication IQ ➦

Before you begin the chapter, see what you already know about communication by taking the chapter pretest. The pretest is available at www.g-wlearning.com.

Case Study

Accuracy

Chloe Williams works at a real estate company. Her supervisor asked her to order T-shirts printed with the company name. Employees will wear the T-shirts at the company picnic. Chloe prepared a letter requesting one dozen T-shirts. When editing the letter, Chloe thought, "Maybe I should be perfectly clear and request 12 T-shirts." A paragraph from Chloe's letter appears below.

> Please send me 12 dozen T-shirts, style 345, all in size large for $10.95 each. Print this name on all the T-shirts: Jackson's Realty.

Chloe was shocked when 144 T-shirts arrived at the office two weeks later. Since the T-shirts have custom printing, they cannot be returned.

michaeljung/Shutterstock.com

Critical Thinking

1. What mistake did Chloe make that caused this problem?

2. What additional information could she have included in the order that would have not caused confusion?

Punctuation

Objectives

After completing this section, you will be able to:

- **Describe** how to use terminal punctuation correctly.
- **Explain** the use of internal punctuation.

Key Terms 📲

punctuation	parentheses
period	semicolon
abbreviation	colon
question mark	apostrophe
exclamation point	contraction
internal punctuation	hyphen
comma	permanent compound
dash	quotation marks

?EQ essential Question

How would communication change without punctuation?

Terminal Punctuation

In writing, **punctuation** consists of marks used to show the structure of sentences. These marks guide readers and help them understand the meaning of sentences and passages. They indicate separations of words into sentences, clauses, and phrases.

Punctuation marks used at the end of a sentence are called *terminal punctuation*. Terminal punctuation marks include periods, question marks, and exclamation points.

Periods

A **period** is a punctuation mark used at the end of a declarative sentence. A *declarative sentence* is one that makes a statement. As you learned in Chapter 4, a sentence has a subject and a predicate and expresses a complete thought. A period signals to the reader that the expressed thought has ended. Periods provide structure to paragraphs, which can contain several sentences. The sentences in the following examples end with periods.

> The final exam will be on May 26.
>
> Alma traveled to Lexington to visit her friend.
>
> Andrew rented a car for his vacation trip.

Periods are also used to divide parts of an abbreviation or signal the end of an abbreviation. An **abbreviation** is a shortened form of a word or letters used to stand for a word or term. An initial is an abbreviation for a person's name using only the first letter of the name or names. An initial that stands for a given name is typically followed by a period. Do not use a period in US state abbreviations or in those for academic degrees, such as master of arts (MA). When an abbreviation ending in a period comes at the end of a declarative sentence, the period also serves to end the sentence. Examples of words and their abbreviations are shown in Figure 5-1.

Periods are used after numbers and letters in some types of lists, such as outlines or numbered lists. In the partial outline example, periods follow the numbers and letters.

Punctuation
I. Terminal punctuation

   A. Periods

      1. Sentences

      2. Abbreviations

   B. Question marks

   C. Exclamation points

II. Internal punctuation

   A. Commas

   B. Colons

Common Abbreviations

Word	Abbreviation	Sentence
association	assoc.	The Park Assoc. will host a picnic.
captain	Capt.	Capt. Hook was a pirate.
company	co.	Send the check to Johnson Co.
doctor	Dr.	Dr. Chung is a surgeon.
Earl Dale, John Fitzgerald Kennedy	E. D. JFK	E. D. Ross quoted a speech by JFK.
Kentucky	KY	The last line of the address is: Monticello, KY 42633.
master of arts	MA	Shelia Reins, MA, teaches this class.
mister	Mr.	Mr. Diaz voted for the motion.
superintendent	supt.	The supt. of the building unlocked the door.

Goodheart-Willcox Publisher

Figure 5-1   These are common abbreviations along with examples of how they appear in sentences.

In a vertical numbered list, each number is followed by a period. The text of each item in the list ends with a period only if it is a complete sentence. If the item is not a complete sentence, do not use a period.

> Follow these steps.
>
> 1. Carefully read the contracts.
> 2. Check the accuracy of all numbers.
> 3. Sign your name on each copy of the contract.
> 4. Return the contracts by overnight mail.

Question Marks

A **question mark** is punctuation used at the end of an interrogative sentence. An *interrogative sentence* is one that asks a question. As with a period, the question mark signals the reader that the expressed thought has ended. Along with periods, they provide structure to paragraphs. A question mark can be used after a word or sentence that expresses strong emotion, such as shock or doubt.

> Will the plane arrive on time?
>
> Did she travel to Lexington to visit her friend?
>
> Has he rented a car for his vacation trip?
>
> What? Are you serious?

A question mark can be part of a sentence that contains a quote. Place the question mark inside the quotation marks when the quote asks a question. Place the question mark outside the quotation marks if the entire sentence asks a question.

> Teresa asked, "Will the work be finished soon?"
>
> Did he say, "The sale will end on Friday"?

Exclamation Points

An **exclamation point** is a punctuation mark used to express strong emotion. Exclamation points are used at the end of a sentence or after an interjection that stands alone. An exclamation point can be used at the end of a question rather than a question mark, if the writer wishes to show strong emotion.

> Stop hurting me!
>
> Hurrah! This is great.
>
> Will you ever grow up!

As with question marks, an exclamation point can be part of a sentence that contains a quote. Place the exclamation point inside the quotation marks when the quote expresses the strong emotion. Place the exclamation point outside the quotation marks if the entire sentence expresses the strong emotion.

> All of the students shouted, "Hooray!"
>
> She said, "you are disqualified"!

An exclamation point is used to express strong emotion. "We won the game!"

Monkey Business Images/Shutterstock.com

Internal Punctuation

Punctuation marks used within a sentence are called **internal punctuation**. These marks include commas, dashes, parentheses, semicolons, colons, hyphens, apostrophes, and quotation marks.

Commas

A **comma** is a punctuation mark used to separate elements in a sentence. The elements can be items in a series, clauses, phrases, words of direct address, parts of dates, parts of addresses, or missing (understood) words. Commas provide breaks or pauses in a sentence. These breaks help readers more easily understand sentences.

Commas are used to separate items in a series. The items can be words, phrases, or independent clauses joined by a conjunction such as *and, or, but, so,* or *yet.* Place a comma after each item in the series that comes before the conjunction. Some style guides recommend omitting the last comma.

A comma is also used before a coordinating conjunction that joins two independent clauses. If the clauses are very short, the comma can be omitted.

> Apples, pears, or grapes will be on the menu.
>
> She won the game by hitting the ball, running the bases, and sliding home.
>
> Maria sang a ballad, Chin-Sun read a poem, and Henry played the piano.
>
> The sun rose, and the birds began to sing.
>
> Stand up and smile.

A dependent clause that comes at the beginning of a sentence should be followed by a comma. When a dependent clause comes at the end of a sentence, a comma is not needed.

> If you want to arrive on time, you must leave now.
>
> You must leave now if you want to arrive on time.

Commas are used to separate some words or phrases from the rest of the sentence. Place a comma after an introductory word or phrase, including a phrase that introduces a quote. Place a comma before and after an adverb, such as *however* or *indeed*, when it comes in the middle of a sentence.

> Yes, I will attend the meeting.
>
> After reading the story, the students wrote answers to the questions.
>
> He answered, "I am not hungry."
>
> To Carla, Shane seemed depressed.
>
> Preparing a delicious meal, however, requires using fresh ingredients.

Some explanatory phrases are restrictive, providing information that is essential to the meaning of the sentence. Restrictive clauses are not separated by commas, as shown in the examples that follow. Commas are used to separate a nonrestrictive explanatory word or phrase from the rest of the sentence.

> **Restrictive**
>
> The game that was cancelled has been rescheduled.
>
> The famous poet Carl Sandburg gave a presentation.
>
> **Nonrestrictive**
>
> The game, which we lost, was exciting.
>
> Gloria's husband, Jorge, drove the car.

When an adjective phrase contains coordinate adjectives, use commas to separate the coordinate adjectives. As discussed in Chapter 4, coordinate adjectives equally modify a noun or pronoun. Remember, not all adjectives that appear in a sequence are coordinate adjectives.

> **Coordinate adjectives**
>
> The *long*, *hot* summer was finally over.
>
> **Not coordinate adjectives**
>
> The *tall brick* building has a black roof.

Commas are used to separate words used in direct address. The words can be proper nouns (as in the first example), the pronoun *you*, or common nouns (as in the second example). When the nouns of direct address come within the sentence (rather than at the beginning), a comma is placed before and after the nouns of direct address. See the third example that follows.

> Quon, please answer the next question.
>
> Everyone, please sit down.
>
> After lunch, boys and girls, I will read a story.

Commas are used to separate elements in dates and addresses. When a date is expressed in the month-day-year format, commas are used to separate the year. When only the month and year or a holiday and year are used, a comma is not needed.

> On December 7, 1941, Japan attacked Pearl Harbor.
>
> In January 2010 she retired from her job.
>
> The race took place on Labor Day 2011.

A comma is used after the street address and after the city when an address or location appears in general text.

> Mail the item to 123 Maple Drive, Columbus, OH 43085.
>
> He arrived in Boise, Idaho, yesterday.

A comma is used to indicate missing words that can be understood without being repeated. In the example that follows, *I have relatives* is understood rather than stated each time.

> In Oregon I have six relatives; in Kansas, eight; in Maine, two.

Dashes and Parentheses

A **dash** is a punctuation mark that separates elements in a sentence or signals an abrupt change in thought. The dash is more properly called an *em dash*. This name comes from its width, which is the same as the uppercase letter M.

A dash provides a stronger break than a comma. To give a break mild emphasis, use a comma. To give a break strong emphasis, use a dash.

> My history teacher, an avid reader, visits the library every week.
>
> My history teacher—an avid reader—visits the library every week.

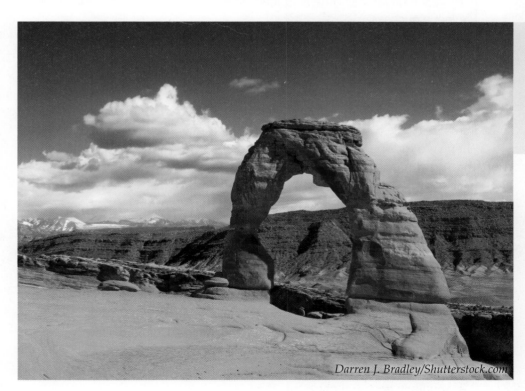

Darren J. Bradley/Shutterstock.com

A comma is used after the city when a location appears in general text. For example, "Arches National Park is located 5 miles north of Moab, Utah."

Use a dash to signal an abrupt change in thought in a sentence. If the words come in the middle of a sentence, use a dash before and after them.

> I thought you would—oh, never mind.

> I need my car keys—I've lost them again—so I can drive to work.

Parentheses are punctuation marks used to enclose words or phrases that clarify meaning or give added information. They always appear as a pair. Place a period that comes at the end of a sentence inside the parentheses only when the entire sentence is enclosed in parentheses.

> Deliver the materials to the meeting site (the Polluck Building).

> Please review the table. (The table is in Appendix A.)

Use parentheses to enclose numbers or letters in a list that is part of a sentence. When the words that introduce a list could be a complete sentence, use a colon before the list, as shown in the second example that follows.

> Revise the sentences to correct errors in (1) spelling, (2) punctuation, and (3) capitalization.

> Bring your sewing machine and basic sewing supplies: (a) cutting mat, (b) rotary cutter, and (c) thread.

A nonrestrictive explanatory word or phrase can be separated from the rest of the sentence by commas, dashes, or parentheses. Both dashes and parentheses provide a stronger break than commas. Note the use of these marks in the examples.

> The contributions of three students, Mark, Elena, and Hoshi, made the event a success.

> The contributions of three students—Mark, Elena, and Hoshi—made the event a success.

> The contributions of three students (Mark, Elena, and Hoshi) made the event a success.

Semicolons

A **semicolon** is an internal punctuation mark used to separate clauses or some items in a series. A semicolon provides a stronger break than a comma.

When two independent clauses in a sentence are not joined by a coordinating conjunction, use a semicolon to separate the clauses.

> Twelve students took the test; two students passed.

> The bike ran over a nail; the tire went flat.

> I left; however, she stayed.

Items in a series are typically separated by commas. However, when at least one item in the series already contains commas, semicolons are used to separate the items. Using semicolons makes identifying the separate elements easier.

> We visited Newark, New Jersey; Portland, Maine; Concord, New Hampshire; and New York, New York.

> The group included Mr. Roberts, an auditor; Ms. Keys, a forensic accountant; and Mr. Lopez, the company president.

Ethics

Bias-Free Language

As you go to work or school each day, you may encounter others who categorize people using biased words and comments. Using age, gender, race, disability, or ethnicity as a way to describe others is unethical and sometimes illegal. Use bias-free language in all of your communication, whether verbal or printed, to show respect for those with whom you come in contact.

Colons

A **colon** is an internal punctuation mark that introduces an element in a sentence or paragraph. The elements can be words, phrases, clauses, or sentences. The colon also provides a stronger break than a comma.

> The bag contains three items: a book, a pencil, and an apple.
>
> You need to practice these activities: keying numbers quickly and proofreading carefully.
>
> She failed the test for one reason: she did not study.
>
> He considered several alternatives: He could keep working in a difficult situation and say nothing. He could report his boss for harassment. He could find a new job.

A colon is also used after a phrase, clause, or sentence that introduces a vertical list. See the following example.

> Follow these steps:
>
> 1. Identify the problem.
> 2. Talk to the people involved.
> 3. Consider possible solutions.
> 4. Select the best alternative.
> 5. Implement the solution.

Colons are used in other situations that do not relate to the structure of a sentence. Some of these uses are shown in Figure 5-2.

Apostrophes

An **apostrophe** is a punctuation mark used to form possessive words and contractions. Possessive words show ownership. An apostrophe or an apostrophe and an *s* are added to many nouns to create the possessive form. Note that possessive pronouns, such as *her, our, mine,* and *their,* do not use an apostrophe. To review more information about possessive words, see

Using Colons	
Use	**Example**
Business letter salutation	Dear Mrs. Martinez:
Introduction of a definition	note: a brief written record
Hours and minutes	Meet me at 5:45 p.m.
Title and subtitle	*Star Wars: The Force Unleashed*
Reference note between city and publisher	*Webster's New World College Dictionary.* Cleveland: Wiley Publishing Inc., 2014.

Goodheart-Willcox Publisher

Figure 5-2 Shown here are examples of where colons may be used.

Chapter 4. Examples of possessive nouns with apostrophes are shown in the sentences that follow.

> Akeno's dress was red.
>
> The boys' bikes were parked by the building.
>
> This year's crop was poor.

A **contraction** is a shortened form of a word or term. It is formed by omitting letters from one or more words and replacing them with an apostrophe to create one word—the contraction. Examples of contractions and the words they represent are shown in Figure 5-3.

Apostrophes can be used to indicate that letters are omitted from words for brevity or writing style. For example, in a poem the final *g* might be omitted from words ending in *ing*. Note that these uses are not preferred for business writing.

> Leisure suits were in style in the '60s. (1960s)
>
> The candidates will meet to discuss activities of the gov't. (government)
>
> Rock 'n' roll will never die. (and)
>
> The bells were ringin', and the choir was singin'. (ringing, singing)

Apostrophes are used in forming the plural of single lowercase letters. The apostrophe helps the reader avoid misunderstanding the sentence. For example, without the apostrophe, *a's* would be read *as*. Apostrophes are not used to form the plural of capital letters unless the meaning would be unclear without an apostrophe.

> The word *Mississippi* has four s's and two p's.
>
> She got all Bs on her progress report.

\multicolumn{3}{c}{**Contractions**}		
Words	**Contraction**	**Sentence**
do not	don't	Don't leave until after dinner.
does not	doesn't	He doesn't want to go to the movies.
you are	you're	While you're reading, I will listen to music.
I am	I'm	I'm sorry I'm late.
is not	isn't	She isn't ready to go.
he has	he's	He's playing golf today.
I have	I've	I've read three books this week.
I will	I'll	I'll let you know later.
will not	won't	She won't finish the work on time.
I would	I'd	I'd be happy to oblige.

Goodheart-Willcox Publisher

Figure 5-3   These are common contractions along with examples of how they appear in sentences.

Kobby Dagan/Shutterstock.com

"The self-confident dancers displayed their talent at the festival." Is the hyphen in this sentence used correctly?

Hyphens

A **hyphen** is a punctuation mark used to separate parts of compound words, numbers, or ranges. Compound words that always have a hyphen are called **permanent compounds**. Temporary compounds are created as needed by the writer. Hyphens are also used in word division.

Many compound words have a hyphen between elements. Examples include *close-up, mother-in-law,* and *voice-over*. These nouns always have hyphens. Some adverbs, such as *out-of-doors*, always have hyphens. A dictionary can be used to find permanent compound words.

> The close-up was blurry.
>
> My mother-in-law made dinner.
>
> The wedding was held out-of-doors.

In many cases, the writer must decide whether to use hyphens in compound words based on how they are used in a sentence. Compound adjectives typically have hyphens when they come before the words they modify, but not when they come after them.

> The well-done pot roast was delicious.
>
> The delicious pot roast was well done.
>
> These out-of-date books should be thrown away.
>
> Throw away the books that are out of date.

In some words that have prefixes, a hyphen is used between the prefix and the rest of the word. Examples of prefixes include *all, ex, pre,* and *self.* Words with these prefixes are used in the following examples.

> The all-inclusive report was presented at the meeting.
>
> My ex-wife has custody of our children.
>
> These quilt patterns are from the pre-Civil War era.
>
> My self-imposed discipline helped me reach my goals.

Hyphens are also used in numbers that are expressed as words. Figure 5-4 describes some of these uses and gives examples.

When a word is divided at the end of a line of text, a hyphen is used between parts of the word. See Figure 5-5 for guidelines for dividing words.

Using Hyphens

Use	Example
Fractions expressed in words	one-half, two-thirds
Numbers less than 100 that have two words	twenty-one, forty-three
Social Security numbers, telephone numbers, or serial numbers	987-65-4325, 1-800-555-0124
Between letters of a word that is spelled out, as when writing dialogue	That's spelled T-w-y-f-o-r-d-s.

Goodheart-Willcox Publisher

Figure 5-4   Hyphens may be used in numbers and ranges.

Word Division Guidelines

- Do not divide a word that has one syllable or is a contraction.
- Divide words only between syllables.
- When a word already contains a hyphen, divide it only at the existing hyphen.
    - Example:
    - self-
    - assured
- Divide solid compound words between the two base words.
    - Example:
    - down-
    - town
- Do not place a single letter of a word at the end of a line.
    - Incorrect:
    - a-
    - gain
- Do not place only one or two letters of a word at the beginning of a new line.
    - Incorrect:
    - quick-
    - ly
- Divide between two single-letter syllables that come together in a word.
    - Example:
    - situ-
    - ation
- Avoid dividing proper names.

Goodheart-Willcox Publisher

Figure 5-5   Use these guidelines for dividing words.

Quotation Marks

Quotation marks are used to enclose short, direct quotes and titles of some artistic or written works. (Long quotes are set apart from the paragraph and are not enclosed in quotation marks.) Quotation marks can also be used to show irony or nonstandard use of words. A direct quote is a restatement of someone's exact words, as shown in the first example. A general statement that relays a similar thought does not use quotation marks, as shown in the second example.

> "Which color do you want," he asked.

> He asked which color you want.

A sentence with a direct quote often has an explanatory phrase, such as *he said* or *she replied*, that refers to the person speaking. The phrase is followed by a comma (or a colon in more formal situations) when it comes before the quote. A comma comes before the phrase when the phrase follows the quote. The quoted words can also be split, with the phrase coming between them. The words quoted are enclosed in double quotation marks, as shown in the examples.

> Martin replied, "Sales have increased by 50 percent during the last quarter."

> "It's time to go home, children," said the teacher.

> "Now that everyone is here," Susan said, "we can begin."

A quote need not be a complete sentence; it can be a word or a phrase as spoken or written by someone. See the examples that follow.

> When the mayor refers to "charitable giving," does that include gifts to all nonprofit organizations?

> The announcer mentioned that the news about the economy "has been positive for two months."

When a quote contains another quote, the quote within a quote is enclosed in single quotation marks. See the first example. Notice the placement of the period in the first example. Periods and commas always go inside closing quotation marks. The placement of a question mark in relation to quotation marks varies. When the entire sentence is a question, place the question mark outside a closing quotation mark. When only the quote is a question, place the question mark inside a closing quotation mark. The same logic applies to the use of an exclamation point with quotation marks.

> He answered, "Niran said, 'Order shirts for everyone on the team.'"

> Did he say, "The project will be delayed"?

> He asked, "Who will work on Saturday?"

> The cheerleaders shouted, "Go team!"

When writing a dialogue, the words of each speaker are enclosed in quotation marks. The speakers are often identified at the beginning of the dialogue, but not with each statement that follows. Begin a new paragraph each time the speaker changes. When the words of one speaker require two or more paragraphs (with no interruptions), place an opening quotation mark at the beginning of each paragraph. Place a closing quotation mark at the end of the last paragraph.

> Anna arrived at the office and greeted her coworker, Joan. "Good morning. You're getting an early start today."
>
> "Yes, I have some reports I need to finish this morning."
>
> "I will be in a meeting until around one o'clock. Would you like to go to Strong's Deli for a late lunch?"
>
> "That sounds great. See you later."

Titles of complete books, movies, and other artistic works are typically shown in italics. Titles of shorter works, which may also be part of a larger work, are shown in quotation marks. Examples include articles in magazines, chapters in a book, short poems, episodes of a television or radio show, sections or special features of a website, and titles of songs.

> "Books and Journals" is the first chapter in *The Chicago Manual of Style*.
>
> "When and Where" is a favorite episode of *Warehouse 13* fans.

Quotation marks are used to enclose words that are meant to show irony. In the first example that follows, the writer is implying that Connie was not really busy. Quotations marks are also used to enclose words used in a nonstandard way. In the second example, the term *sinking ship* is used to describe a failing business—not a real ship.

> Although Connie had the afternoon off, she was too "busy" to help me.
>
> In a survey of small businesses, one in five managers said their companies are "sinking ships."

Use the grammar checker in your word processing software to help you locate possible errors in punctuation, as well as capitalization and word usage in your documents. Figure 5-6 shows the spelling and grammar checker in Microsoft Word.

Be aware, however, that a grammar checker is not perfect. Some things the grammar checker raises as possible errors may not be errors. Proofread and evaluate suggestions given by the grammar checker before accepting the changes. In Figure 5-6, the program has identified an error. The comma and quotations marks are missing before the quote. However, the suggested solution is not appropriate.

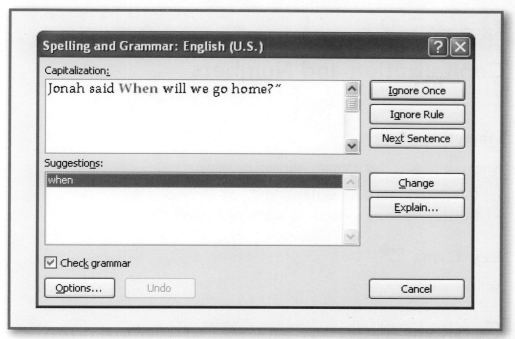

Goodheart-Willcox Publisher

Figure 5-6   Microsoft Word includes an option for checking grammar with spelling. However, it is still up to the user to decide whether the suggestions are appropriate.

Section 5.1   Review

 Check Your Understanding

1. How do readers benefit from punctuation?
2. Give examples of terminal punctuation.
3. List seven types of internal punctuation.
4. When is an interrogative sentence used?
5. Explain how commas are used in a series.

 Build Your Vocabulary

As you progress through this course, develop a personal glossary of key terms. This will help you build your vocabulary and prepare you for a career. Write a definition for each of the following terms and add it to your personal glossary.

punctuation	parentheses
period	semicolon
abbreviation	colon
question mark	apostrophe
exclamation point	contraction
internal punctuation	hyphen
comma	permanent compound
dash	quotation marks

Capitalization and Numbers

Objectives

After completing this section, you will be able to:

- **Use** capitalization correctly.
- **Express** numbers correctly in words or figures.

Key Terms

capitalization

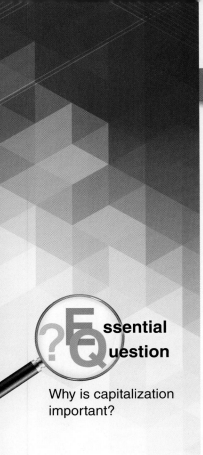

?Essential Question

Why is capitalization important?

Capitalization

Capitalization is writing a letter in uppercase (B) rather than lowercase (b). Capital letters signal the beginning of a new sentence and identify important words in titles and headings. This helps readers see the structure of paragraphs, reports, articles, and other messages. Capital letters are also used for proper nouns, for some abbreviations, in personal and professional titles, and for parts of business letters.

Sentences

A sentence begins with a capital letter. Numbers that begin a sentence should be spelled as words, and the first word should be capitalized. If the number is very long, consider revising the sentence so the number is not at the beginning. The first word in a quote within a sentence should be capitalized if the quote is a complete sentence.

> He was elected mayor.
>
> Thirty-three students took part in the graduation ceremony.
>
> He said, "Wait for me by the door."
>
> "What," she asked, "do you want me to do?"

Headings, Titles, and Documents

Capital letters are used in headings for reports, articles, newsletters, and other documents. They are also used for titles of books, magazines, movies, and other works. Use the guidelines that follow for headline-style capitalization.

- Capitalize the first word and the last word in a heading or title.

> *Gone with the Wind*

- Capitalize all other important words in a heading or title.

  The Adventure of the Hansom Cabs

  Softly He Goes into the Night

- For numbers with hyphens in a heading or title, capitalize both words.

  Twenty-One Candles

- Do not capitalize articles or prepositions within a heading or title. When a title and subtitle are written together, the first word of the subtitle is capitalized regardless of the part of speech. Note that the title and subtitle are often separated by a colon.

  The Finest Story in the World

  Tales of Troy: Ulysses the Sacker of Cities

- Do not capitalize coordinating conjunctions (*yet, and, but, for, or,* and *nor*) in a heading or title.

  Pride and Prejudice

  Never Marry but for Love

- Do not capitalize parts of names that normally appear in lowercase (Hans von Luck).

  Panzer Commander: The Memoirs of Colonel Hans von Luck

Business documents, such as letters and memos, use capital letters to begin certain document parts. Capitalize the first word in the salutation and the complimentary close for a letter. Capitalize the heading words (To, From, Date, and Subject) in a memo. Some style guides recommend using all capitals for these words.

  Dear Mrs. Stockton:

  Sincerely yours,

Proper Nouns

Proper nouns begin with a capital letter. Recall that a proper noun is a word that identifies a specific person, place, or thing. Examples include names

Green   Reusable Bags

Bring reusable bags to the store instead of accepting disposable plastic ones. Over one trillion plastic bags are used every year around the world. This poses a problem because a single plastic bag can take up to 1,000 years to break down in a landfill. Simply throwing these bags in the trash can be harmful to wildlife and contaminate soil and water.

In the United States, only 1 percent of plastic bags are recycled.

Alternatively, reusable bags save thousands of pounds of landfill waste every year. Many stores are now offering incentives to customers who take their purchases home in reusable bags.

of people, pets, nationalities, schools, cities, regions, and buildings. Directional words (north, south, west, and east) are capitalized when they refer to a region. Proper nouns are capitalized in the examples that follow.

> Joe Wong is the principal of George Rogers Clark High School.
>
> My dog, Susie, is three years old.
>
> We live in Tampa, Florida.
>
> The family drove west as they traveled through the South during their vacation.
>
> This is my favorite Chinese restaurant.
>
> The meeting will be held in the Fountain Square Room.

Abbreviations and Titles

Some abbreviations use capital letters. Titles that come before a name and some that come after a name use capital letters. Use the guidelines that follow for capital letters with abbreviations and titles.

- Capitalize initials used in place of names.

> E. J. Roberts is on the committee.
>
> UCLA won the football game.

- Capitalize abbreviations that are made up of the first letters of words.

> HTML stands for hypertext markup language.
>
> FAA stands for Federal Aviation Administration.

- Capitalize the name of months and days and their abbreviations.

> Mon. is the abbreviation for Monday.
>
> Jan., Feb., and Mar. are in the first quarter of the year.

- Capitalize abbreviations for names of states and countries.

> NY is a state in the United States.
>
> The price is given in US dollars.

- Capitalize abbreviations for directional terms and location terms in street addresses.

> She lives at 123 NW Cedar Ave.

- Capitalize call letters of a broadcasting company.

> My favorite television show is on CBS.
>
> Radio station WFLW plays easy-listening music.

- Capitalize abbreviations that note an era in time.

> The article included a map of Europe for the year 1200 BC.

- Capitalize titles that come before personal names.

> Sen. Carl Rogers called Mr. Juarez and Dr. Wang.
>
> Sister Catherine sings in the choir.

- Capitalize seniority titles (Jr., Sr.) after names.

  | Mr. Thomas O'Malley, Jr., spoke at the ceremony.

- Capitalize abbreviations for academic degrees and other professional designations that follow names.

  | Carlos Herrera, MD, testified in the court case.

  | Jane Patel, LPN, was on duty at the hospital.

Number Expression

Numbers can be expressed as figures or as words. In some cases, as in legal documents and on bank checks, numbers are written in both figures and words. When the two expressions of a number do not agree, readers are alerted to ask for clarification.

Number expression guidelines are not as widely agreed upon as rules for punctuation and capitalization. Follow the guidelines in this section for general writing. If you are writing a research report or an article for a particular group or publication, ask whether there are number expression guidelines you should follow for that item.

Numbers Expressed as Words

Refer to the guidelines that follow for expressing numbers as words.

- In general writing, use words for numbers one through nine. (See other style guides for exceptions to this guideline.)

  | One dog and three cats sat on the porch.

Maridav/Shutterstock.com

Numbers used in measurements are expressed as figures. "We picked 6 pounds of apples."

- Use words for numbers that are indefinite or approximate amounts.

  | About fifty people signed the petition.

- Use words for numbers one through nine followed by *million, billion,* and so forth. For numbers 10 or greater followed by *million, billion,* and so forth, use a figure and the word.

  | Two million people live in this region.

  | The relief organization serves 12 million people.

- Use words for a number that begins a sentence. If the number is long when written as words, consider revising the sentence so it does not begin with a number.

  | Twenty copies of the report were prepared.

- When two numbers come together in a sentence, use words for one of the numbers.

  | On the bus, there were 15 ten-year-olds.

- Use words for fractions. Note that a hyphen is placed between the words.

  | Place one-half of the mixture in the pan.

- Use words for numbers with *o'clock* to express time.

  | Come to my house for lunch at eleven o'clock.

Numbers Expressed as Figures

Numbers in table format are typically expressed as figures. The following guidelines should be used for expressing numbers as figures in general writing.

- Use figures for numbers 10 and greater. (See other style guides for exceptions to this guideline.)

  | She placed an order for 125 blue ink pens.

- When some numbers in a sentence are 9 or less and some are 10 or greater, write all the numbers as figures.

  | The box contains 5 books, 10 folders, and 15 pads of paper.

- Use figures with a dollar sign to express amounts of money. Do not use a decimal and two zeros when all dollar amounts in a sentence are even amounts.

  | The total amount is $18,395.40.

  | The charges were $5, $312, and $89.

- For an isolated amount less than $1, use figures and the word *cents.* When an amount less than $1 appears with other amounts greater than $1, use figures and dollar signs for all of the numbers.

  | Buy a cup of lemonade for 75 cents.

  | The prices were $12.50, $0.89, and $12.45.

- For a large, even dollar amount, use the dollar sign, a figure, and a word, such as *million* or *billion*.

  | The profits for last year were $5 million.

- Use figures for days and years in dates.

  | On February 19, 2015, the court was not in session.

- Use figures for mixed numbers (a whole number and a fraction) and for decimals.

  I bought 3 1/2 yards of red fabric.

  The measurements are 1.358 and 0.878.

- Use figures with *a.m.* and *p.m.* to express time. However, use *noon* and *midnight* to express these two times.

  The assembly will begin at 9:30 a.m.

  The baby was born at noon on June 15.

  The restaurant closes at midnight.

- Use figures in measurements, such as distance, weight, and percentages.

  We drove 258 miles today.

  The winning pumpkin weighs 50 pounds.

  Sales have increased 20 percent in the last year.

- Use figures to refer to pages, chapters, figures, or parts in a book.

  Open your book to Chapter 3, page 125.

  Refer to Figure 6 on page 72 for an example.

Section 5.2 Review

Check Your Understanding

1. What does it mean to capitalize a letter?
2. Which words should not be capitalized in a heading or title?
3. How should the numbers one through nine be written?
4. Words are used for fractions. What else is needed?
5. When some numbers in a sentence are 9 or less and some are 10 or greater, how should all the numbers be written?

Build Your Vocabulary

As you progress through this course, develop a personal glossary of key terms. This will help you build your vocabulary and prepare you for a career. Write a definition for the following term and add it to your personal glossary.

capitalization

Structure and Word Choice

Objectives

After completing this section, you will be able to:

- **Explain** the use of parallel structure in sentences.
- **Select** the proper use of commonly misused words and terms.

Key Terms

parallel structure

Essential Question

How is parallel structure important to proper grammar?

Parallel Structure

Parallel structure is a method of writing in which similar elements are expressed in a consistent way or presented in the same pattern. The elements can be words, phrases, or clauses. Using parallel structure in sentences, paragraphs, and lists makes messages easier for readers to understand.

Words and Phrases

To create parallel structure, use the same word or phrase form for all items in a series of words or phrases. The first example that follows, in which the structure is not parallel, is awkward. Gerunds and infinitives are mixed in the series. The second example uses infinitives to create a parallel structure. Note that *to* can be used before each word in the infinitive series or just before the first word. In the last example, gerunds are used to form the series.

> **Not parallel**
> She likes swimming, to read, and painting.
>
> **Parallel**
> She likes to swim, to read, and to paint.
>
> He wants to hike, swim, and ride his bicycle.
>
> She likes swimming, reading, and painting.

Verb forms and tenses should be constructed in a parallel pattern. Compare the two examples that follow. The first sentence uses verbs in the present and past tense, creating a structure that is not parallel.

> **Not parallel**
> She *waits* until the last day to begin her work, *caused* problems in the lab, and her commitment to the project *was lacking*.
>
> **Parallel**
> She *waits* until the last day to begin her work, *causes* problems in the lab, and *lacks* commitment to the project.

In the first example that follows, adverbs and verbs are mixed, creating a structure that is not parallel. In the second example, only adverbs are used to express the message. The structure is parallel.

> **Not parallel**
> He was asked to do his work very fast, keep it quiet, and be accurate.
>
> **Parallel**
> He was asked to do his work quickly, quietly, and accurately.

In a series of prepositional phrases, it is acceptable to include the preposition only before the first object if all items in the series use the same preposition. If not, include the preposition before each object.

> **Incorrect**
> She placed air fresheners *in* the living room, the bedroom, the bathroom, and *under* the sink.
>
> **Correct**
> She placed air fresheners *in* the living room, *in* the bedroom, *in* the bathroom, and *under* the sink.

Clauses

Clauses in a series should be written in a parallel pattern. Do not change the form of one clause in the series or change the voice of the verb. In the first example that follows, the series has two clauses and an infinitive phrase. The second example has three parallel clauses.

> **Not parallel**
> The teacher told the students that they should read the chapter, they should answer the review questions, and to do some practice drills.
>
> **Parallel**
> The teacher told the students that they should read the chapter, answer the review questions, and do some practice drills.

Exploring
Communication Careers

Arts, A/V Technology & Communications

Music Composer

Music composers write original music that individual musicians and musical groups perform. Often people think of only popular music or orchestras needing the services of a music composer. However, the makers of films, television shows, and video games also require composers. Another typical job title for this position is *music arranger*.

Some examples of tasks that composers perform include:

- Write music and lyrics for orchestras, musicians, movies, television, or video games.
- Write jingles for marketing and advertising agencies.
- Arrange existing music into new configurations.
- Study and listen to music of various styles for inspiration.
- Play one or more instruments to help compose music.
- Help musicians in the recording of their music.

Classic composition jobs, such as those with an orchestra, require a bachelor degree in music composition, music theory, or a related field. Knowledge of an instrument can be helpful as well as familiarity with computer programs used for recording and editing music.

In the first example that follows, two items in the series use active voice and one uses passive voice. The second example has three parallel clauses each using active voice.

> **Not parallel**
> We will review the report, read the recommendation, and a decision will be made.
>
> **Parallel**
> We will review the report, read the recommendation, and make a decision.

In a vertical list of numbered or bulleted items, use the same pattern for all items. For example, use all complete sentences or all single words or phrases.

> **Not parallel**
> For the camping trip, you will need several items:
>
> - towels
> - swimsuits
> - Bring hiking shoes.
> - Sunscreen and insect-repellant spray are a must.
> - birder's handbook
> - A compass would be helpful.
>
> **Parallel**
> For the camping trip, you will need several items:
>
> - towels
> - swimsuits
> - hiking shoes
> - sunscreen
> - insect-repellant spray
> - birder's handbook
> - compass

Word Choice

Selecting the correct words helps writers and speakers convey messages that will be understood in the way they intend. Many words in the English language are often confused with other words or simply misused. A *homonym* is a word that sounds the same as another word, but has a different meaning and spelling. For example, the words *ensure* and *insure* have different meanings. However, they can be easily confused for one another.

Many other words are also misused or confused. Consult a dictionary whenever you are not sure about the meaning or proper use of a word. Several examples of frequently misused words and their meanings are shown in Figure 5-7.

Commonly Misused Words

Words	Meaning	Example
advice	Guidance or suggestion given	My advice is to leave it here.
advise	To give guidance or warn	I advise you to wait until tomorrow.
affect	To influence	Will this error affect my grade?
effect	A result or outcome	His speeches have a positive effect on the voters.
	To cause	Can the group effect a change in policy?
all together	Everyone or everything in one place	The students are all together at the school.
altogether	Completely, wholly	He was altogether convinced of her innocence.
concurrent	Happening at the same time	The concurrent meetings begin at noon.
consecutive	Following one after the other	The consecutive meetings will take all afternoon.
continual	Repeated quickly	The continual interruptions were annoying.
continuous	Without pause or interruption	The continuous noise of the engine kept me awake.
farther	At a more distant place	We will walk one mile farther today.
further	To a greater extent, more	He will evaluate the possible solution further.
less	Not as great (for something that cannot be counted)	He is less enthusiastic than she is.
fewer	Not as great (for things that can be counted)	She has fewer books than he does.
imply	To suggest indirectly	He implied that I was ignorant.
infer	To conclude or reason	I inferred from his tone that he was angry.
lie	To recline or rest	I will lie down for a nap after lunch.
lay	To put or place	Lay the watch on your dresser.
precede	To come before	The teacher will precede the students into the room.
proceed	To move forward, take action	I will proceed with the operation.
raise	To lift, grow, build, or increase	Please raise my salary.
rise	To get up	I will rise from my chair and take a walk.
set	To place or put	Set the groceries on the table.
sit	To be seated	Please sit in the front row.

Goodheart-Willcox Publisher

Figure 5-7   These are frequently misused words along with examples of how they correctly appear in sentences.

Section 5.3   Review

 Check Your Understanding

1. What is parallel structure?
2. How can you create a parallel structure of words or phrases?
3. How can you create a parallel structure of clauses?
4. Give examples of two words that are commonly misused in the English language.
5. What should you do if you are uncertain of the meaning or correct usage of a word?

 Build Your Vocabulary

As you progress through this course, develop a personal glossary of key terms. This will help you build your vocabulary and prepare you for a career. Write a definition for the following term and add it to your personal glossary.

parallel structure

Chapter Summary

Section 5.1 Punctuation

- Terminal punctuation signals the end of a sentence. Periods, question marks, and exclamation points are considered terminal punctuation.

- Internal punctuation separates a sentence into phrases and clauses. These marks include commas, dashes, parentheses, semicolons, colons, apostrophes, hyphens, and quotation marks.

Section 5.2 Capitalization and Numbers

- Capitalization means writing a letter in uppercase instead of lowercase. Sentences begin with a capital letter, even if a number begins the sentence. The important words in a heading or title are usually capitalized. Proper nouns are capitalized as are some abbreviations.

- Numbers may be expressed as figures or words. In general, spell out numbers one through nine, but use figures for numbers 10 and greater.

Section 5.3 Structure and Word Choice

- To create parallel structure, express similar elements in similar ways. Using the same word or phrase form in a series creates parallel structure. Likewise, using one form of a clause or voice of a verb in a series forms parallel structure.

- Many words are often confused or misused. Consult a dictionary if you are unsure of the meaning or correct usage of a word.

Online Activities

Complete the following activities which will help you learn, practice, and expand your knowledge and skills.

Posttest. Now that you have finished the chapter, see what you learned by taking the chapter posttest.

Vocabulary. Practice vocabulary for this chapter using the e-flash cards, matching activity, and vocabulary game until you are able to recognize their meanings.

English/Language Arts. Visit www.g-wlearning.com to download each data file for this chapter. Follow the instructions to complete an English/language arts activity to practice what you have learned in this chapter.

Activity File 5-1: Improving Your Editing Skills

Activity File 5-2: Identifying Misused Words

Review Your Knowledge

1. How is terminal punctuation different from internal punctuation?
2. When is a dash used in a sentence?
3. What is the rule for using a semicolon?
4. Give two uses of an apostrophe and explain how each is used.
5. When is a hyphen used in a sentence?
6. What is a permanent compound? Give an example.
7. What is a proper noun?
8. What is the general rule for using numbers expressed as words and expressed as figures?
9. Explain the meaning of parallel structure and why it is important.
10. Why is word choice important in professional communication?

142 **5 Review and Assessment**

Apply Your Knowledge

1. Edit the following sentences, revising each to correct errors in punctuation.
   - A. How many records are in the filing cabinet.
   - B. When the project is finished; send an invoice to our office.
   - C. This answer is not oh, I understand now.
   - D. His self assured smile was charming.

2. Edit the following sentences, revising each to correct errors in capitalization.
   - A. The store clerk said, "this sweater is on sale."
   - B. eight cars were involved in an accident near chicago, il.
   - C. I met mr. chen at the philadelphia museum of art to view paintings by italian artists.
   - D. eduardo works at the homeless shelter with sister elizabeth.

3. Edit the following sentences, revising each to correct errors in number expression.
   - A. Please purchase six soccer balls, 12 softballs, and five basketballs for use on the playground.
   - B. For mowing this small lawn, I will pay you twenty-five dollars.
   - C. The bell rings to signal lunchtime at 12 p.m.
   - D. 25 paintings are on display at the small gallery.

4. Edit the following sentences, revising each to make the items in a series have parallel structure.
   - A. To prepare for a presentation, you should study the material you will discuss, writing an outline, and practicing the delivery.
   - B. The park provides a perfect place for hiking, to ride a bike, to play tennis, and having a picnic.
   - C. He placed signs announcing the garage sale at the corner, the end of the street, the end of the driveway, and near the house.
   - D. The students will gather in the gym, the teacher will announce the contest winners, and prizes will be awarded by the principal.

5. Edit the following sentences, selecting the word that correctly completes each sentence.
   - A. Can you (advise, advice) me on how to handle this issue?
   - B. The girls' basketball team has five (less, fewer) players than the boys' basketball team.
   - C. How do you wish to (precede, proceed)?
   - D. The grocer will (ensure, insure) that the produce is fresh.

Communication Skills

College and Career Readiness

Reading. Affix means to add a prefix or suffix to a root word. Read about prefixes and suffixes. Explain what each one means. Give examples of words with prefixes and suffixes.

Writing. Standard English means that word choice, sentence structure, paragraphs, and the format of communication follow standard conventions used by those who speak English. Research the topic of college access. Write an informative report consisting of several paragraphs to describe your findings. Edit the writing for proper syntax, tense, and voice.

Speaking. What do you think the old adage "necessity is the mother of invention" means? Find examples of how the need for various punctuation marks has sparked their invention. Identify a need for a new punctuation mark, and invent one to meet the need. Present to your class.

Internet Research

History of Punctuation. Research the history of punctuation using various Internet resources. Why was punctuation first developed? When did punctuation become standardized? Write several paragraphs describing what you learned. Use correct punctuation as you write and edit your document.

Teamwork

Working with your team, identify five pairs of words or terms that are often confused or misused (other than ones listed in this chapter). Write the definition of each word. Then, work with the other teams in your class to compile a list that includes the words and their definitions.

Portfolio Development

College and Career Readiness

Digital Presentation Options. Before you begin collecting items for a digital portfolio, you will need to decide how you are going to present the final product. For example, you could create an electronic presentation with slides for each section. The slides could have links to documents, videos, graphics, or sound files. This will dictate file naming conventions and file structure.

Websites are another option for presenting a digital portfolio. You could create a personal website to host the files and have a main page with links to various sections. Each section page could have links to pages containing your documents, videos, graphics, or sound files. (Be sure you read and understand the user agreement for any site on which you place your materials.)

Another option is to place the files on a CD. The method you choose should allow the viewer to easily navigate and find items. There are many creative ways to present a digital portfolio.

Establish the types of technology that are available for you to create a digital portfolio. Will you have access to cameras or studios? Do you have the level of skill needed to create videos?

Decide the type of presentation you will use. Research what will be needed to create the final portfolio product.

CTSOs

Writing. Many competitive events for CTSOs require students to write a research paper. The paper must be submitted either before the competition or when the student arrives at the event. Written events can be lengthy and require a lot of preparation, so it is important to start early.

To prepare for a written event, complete the following activities.

1. Read the guidelines provided by the organization. The topic to be researched will be specified in detail. Also, all final format guidelines will be given, including how to organize and submit the paper. Make certain you ask questions about any points you do not understand.

2. Research the topic. Begin your research early. Research may take days or weeks, and you do not want to rush the process.

3. Set a deadline for yourself so that you can write at a comfortable pace.

4. After you write the first draft, ask an instructor to review it and give feedback.

5. Once you have the final version, go through the checklist for the event to make sure you have covered all of the details. Your score will be penalized if you do not follow instructions.

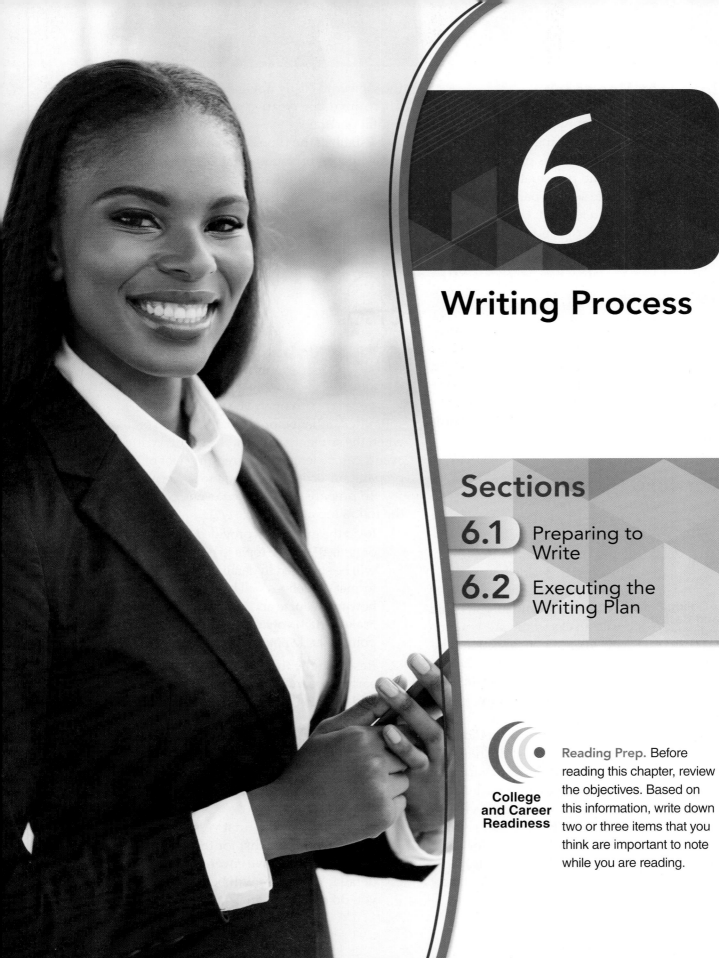

6

Writing Process

Sections

6.1 Preparing to Write

6.2 Executing the Writing Plan

College and Career Readiness

Reading Prep. Before reading this chapter, review the objectives. Based on this information, write down two or three items that you think are important to note while you are reading.

Check Your Communication IQ

Before you begin the chapter, see what you already know about communication by taking the chapter pretest. The pretest is available at www.g-wlearning.com.

Case Study

Persuasion

Christopher Cohen wants to persuade the executive board of a marketing firm to expand its staff for a cost of $125,000. The board chairperson has agreed to review his written proposal. Christopher knows the chairperson and the board do not want to spend more money. His proposal needs to be convincing.

While preparing the proposal, Christopher found statistics and background data that support his position. Once he identified the information to include, Christopher began his document:

> This proposal will convince you we need to hire three additional telemarketing employees as soon as possible. The cost to our organization will be about $125,000 annually. However, once you consider our needs and weigh the benefits, there will be no doubt this action is desirable.

Goodluz/Shutterstock.com

Critical Thinking

1. Which approach did Christopher choose to take for his proposal?

2. Do you think it is likely to work? Why or why not?

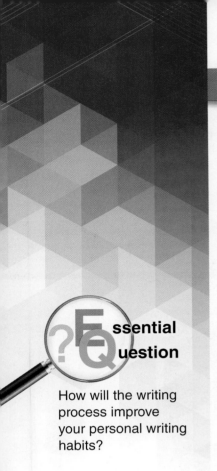

Section 6.1

Preparing to Write

Objectives

After completing this section, you will be able to:

- **Explain** each step in the writing process.
- **Describe** the steps in the prewriting stage.

Essential Question

How will the writing process improve your personal writing habits?

Key Terms 🔗

writing process

four Cs of communication

medium

writer's block

audience

primary audience

secondary audience

demographics

public relations

scope

direct approach

indirect approach

outline

Writing Process

The **writing process** is a set of sequential steps for each writing task that includes prewriting, writing, postwriting, and publishing. These steps are shown in Figure 6-1.

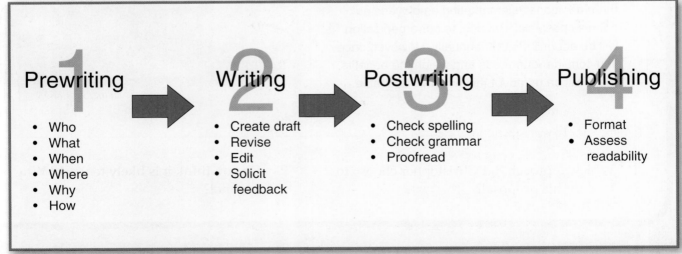

1 Prewriting

- Who
- What
- When
- Where
- Why
- How

2 Writing

- Create draft
- Revise
- Edit
- Solicit feedback

3 Postwriting

- Check spelling
- Check grammar
- Proofread

4 Publishing

- Format
- Assess readability

Goodheart-Willcox Publisher

Figure 6-1 There are four stages in the writing process.

146

By following the four-step writing process, you will learn to critique and revise your own writing to achieve the four Cs of communication. The **four Cs of communication** are the qualities of clarity, conciseness, courtesy, and correctness. These standards apply to all types of written communication. Communication that contains errors or poor language usage reflects negatively on both you and the business for which you work. Using abbreviations and spelling common to text messaging is *not* acceptable in most business organizations.

You probably already use the writing process even if you do not consciously think about it. Take the time to break down the steps of the process, and analyze how to approach each one. This will help you become a better and more efficient writer. The writing process relieves the stress of writing, because it turns each task into a manageable activity. Writing begins with the knowledge that you will be your own first critic. It is polished until you are ready to publish or share the work with a reviewer. Putting this process into action helps to create a satisfactory finished product.

Prewriting

The first step in the writing process is *prewriting*, which is the planning stage. Prewriting tasks are shown in Figure 6-2. During prewriting, you will define the purpose and topic of your writing as well as analyze the audience. Once these steps have been completed, you will gather the information, research ideas, organize your thoughts, and choose a medium. The **medium** is the form of communication that you will use. It may be written, visual, oral, or digital.

The prewriting tasks should be done in the order that works best for the writing assignment. For example, if you need to write a formal report, you can read and research similar reports before planning your own. On the other hand, simpler writing tasks such as a letter or e-mail might require you to find detailed information after most of the content is planned.

Prewriting Checklist

- ❏ *Who* is the audience?
- ❏ *What* do you want to communicate?
- ❏ *When* must the document be complete?
- ❏ *Where* is the information?
- ❏ *Why* are you writing?
- ❏ *How* should the information be organized?

Goodheart-Willcox Publisher

Figure 6-2   Use this checklist in the prewriting stage.

Business Protocol

Punctuality

Employees are expected to be on time to begin work each day. You should be at your workspace ready to work when you are to begin your day. It is not acceptable to arrive at your starting time, hang up your coat, talk to your coworkers, and then go to your workstation. If your starting time is 8:00 a.m., you should begin working at 8:00 a.m. rather than 8:15 a.m. It is equally important to be on time to meetings scheduled throughout the day.

A good way to begin the prewriting stage is to use the journalistic approach. The *journalistic approach* is asking *who, what, when, where, why,* and *how* questions. Answering these basic questions will help gather information. Journalists use the approach as a formula for getting a complete story. However, the order of the questions may vary depending on the situation. Ask the most important question first when you begin the process.

Spending time to completely explore a topic at the beginning makes you less likely to need to backtrack. Approaching a writing task without a plan can be very intimidating and often causes writer's block. **Writer's block** is a psychological condition that prevents a writer from proceeding with the writing process. The writer feels unable to begin the writing task. It is easier to write when you are adequately prepared.

Who Is the Audience?

The **audience** is the person or group to whom the message is directed. They are the receivers of the message. The audience should be analyzed to evaluate their interest in what you have to say. You can then adapt the language and determine the best way to gain their attention.

Communication can have a primary audience and a secondary audience. The **primary audience** is made up of those directly involved in the purpose for the communication. These are the people who will act on the content of the message. After reading, the primary audience should feel that their points of view were considered and their concerns were addressed. The **secondary audience** is made up of those who need to know the communication took place. These individuals may or may not be interested in all the details. They receive copies of the communication and, typically, only have to read it.

Using demographics can help analyze an audience. **Demographics** are information about a group of people. Characteristics such as gender, age, and level of education of the audience may influence the topic and how the information is conveyed. The more you know about the individuals, the better you will be able to deliver the message on a level to which they can relate.

If the audience is a group with which you have had previous contact, you will probably know the best way to communicate with them. Their reactions can be anticipated because you know their background or some other information about them. If you do not personally know the audience, you may still have some general knowledge about them. For example, if you are a teacher presenting to other teachers, most people in the audience will have a similar background. You will probably know ways to interact with them to capture their attention.

Another important factor in analyzing the audience is to determine whether the individuals are internal or external to the organization. An *internal audience* has a specific background and experience. It can be assumed they have a basis for and can relate to at least some of the information that is being conveyed.

An *external audience* will probably need more background information about your topic. When dealing with an audience external to the organization, it is important to exhibit positive public relations skills and promote goodwill for the organization. For example, vocabulary or important data may have to be introduced. **Public relations** is applying communication skills that promote goodwill between a business and the public. Other businesses, customers, and the general public may judge the communication from a different perspective than the writer.

What Do You Want to Communicate?

Knowing what ideas you want to communicate helps focus on the purpose of the message. Your message will begin by selecting a subject area. The subject area will then be narrowed down to a specific topic.

After the topic is selected, it is necessary to consider the proper scope of the content for the message. The **scope** is the guideline of how much information will be included. Keeping ideas focused on the main purpose is an important aspect of the prewriting stage.

When you want the reader to do something in response to the message, be specific about the expectations. Clearly state what actions are being requested using a polite, firm tone. In some cases, the message itself clarifies the reasons for the requested action. In others, you might need to explain the benefits of an action or the reasons for a request.

For example, suppose you are writing to inform fellow employees of a company blood donation drive. One purpose of the communication is to tell them where and when the event will take place. Another purpose is to persuade them to volunteer. In this case, mentioning the benefits of participating is as important as requesting the specific action.

When Must the Document Be Complete?

In business, deadlines are an important consideration. An announcement that is poorly timed may not accomplish what you thought it would. A late proposal, no matter how brilliant, is essentially worthless. Establishing priorities and managing your time will help accommodate all steps of the writing process.

If a specific deadline has not been given, set one for yourself. Deadlines will help determine what you can accomplish given the specific circumstances. When a message needs an immediate response, there may not be enough time to complete extensive research. On the other hand, if there is a month to assemble a report, thoroughly study the topic.

Where Is the Information?

The topic dictates where to look for source material. For example, if writing about a competitive product, you may need to obtain brochures and other literature from the manufacturer. Other sources of information may include colleagues, existing correspondence and reports, databases, searches on the Internet, and print or online newspapers and trade journals. Be prepared to track down what is needed in a timely manner so that you can write a message with substance while meeting the deadline.

Researching requires the application of media literacy skills. *Media literacy skills* include accessing, analyzing, evaluating, and communicating information in various formats that include print and online. When reviewing print or digital materials, it is necessary to access, analyze, and evaluate what is being read. Each source should be reviewed for bias and credibility. Keep in mind that what appears in the media may not always be truthful or accurate. It is the responsibility of the writer to decide which sources are accurate and which ones have been driven by profit or politics. When writing a message, your credibility is at stake. It is important to thoroughly research sources that are used.

As you gather information, always check the facts to be sure the data is accurate. Are names, dates, prices, and statements accurate? If there is a question about any information, be sure to verify the facts. Review the findings to distinguish fact from opinion. Determine if your idea agrees with company policies and procedures. Locate any explanatory material that should be attached.

Always properly credit any information used from any source. As soon as information is in tangible form, it is protected by copyright laws. Using someone else's information as though it is your own is *plagiarism*. It is both illegal and unethical. If you have any questions on the proper procedure for referencing a source, consult an appropriate style guide, such as *The Chicago Manual of Style*, Modern Language Association's *MLA Handbook*, American Psychological Association (APA) publication manual, or other accepted style manual.

Gathering information takes time and patience. Sometimes, long hours are needed to meet a deadline.

pio3/Shutterstock.com

Why Are You Writing?

When you write, there is a reason for doing so. Recall that the purpose for communicating will usually fall into one of these broad categories:

- inform

- instruct

- respond to a request

- make a request

- persuade

It is important to identify the primary purpose, or *intent*, of the message before you begin writing. By doing so, you will be able to make decisions about the communication process. A clear and concise message will help the receiver understand what is expected as a response or feedback.

How Should the Information Be Organized?

Once you have the needed information, determine the approach of the document. Decide on the order in which the information will be presented, and create an outline. Both are important to produce a polished, final document.

Determine Approach

The *approach* of the document is how the information is presented. Most houses have a front door and a back door. This provides a good analogy for the two ways in which a topic can be approached. A person can come in through the front door by using a direct approach. A person can also use the back door by using an indirect approach.

With the **direct approach**, the topic is introduced first and then followed by descriptive details. The direct approach is desirable for most written communication, particularly when the reader is expecting a straightforward message. To use a direct approach, organize and present the information in the clearest and most logical way. Begin with a statement of the main idea and move on to support it with details.

 Green   Reusable Water Bottles

Drinking water is good for a person's health. However, drinking water out of a disposable water bottle is bad for the environment and can be bad for a person's health. According to National Geographic, over 80 percent of water bottles end up in landfills. Just like plastic bags, plastic water bottles do not biodegrade. Instead, they break down into smaller and smaller pieces over time, polluting soil and water with harmful chemicals.

Additionally, the plastic in which the water is bottled can be harmful to a person's health. The type of plastic used to bottle water is typically safe when used one time. When the bottle gets reused, which it often does, it will leach harmful chemicals and bacteria with each sip. A more healthful choice is to use a reusable water bottle made from a safe, durable plastic that is washed frequently.

Note in the following two examples how the individuals use the direct approach to organize information. In each of the examples, the main idea is presented first. Then, the supporting information is presented.

- Ikumi Wantanabe wrote a proposal of her one-year plan for increasing sales. She decided to organize her materials chronologically. This shows how the plan will unfold month by month.

- Alexandra Ford prepared a report summarizing staff changes and key events in her company's branch offices. She organized the information alphabetically by city: first Albuquerque, then Atlanta, followed by Birmingham, and so on.

With the **indirect approach**, details are given first and are then followed by the main idea. Begin with information that prepares the reader to respond how you want him or her to respond. Use the indirect approach when you need to persuade the reader with a request.

The next two situations call for an indirect approach. Note how information is presented. The details are given first, while the main message is presented later.

- Cameron Smith has to tell her production team that they must work overtime for the next two months. She began the message by emphasizing the benefits of overtime: bonus pay and higher profit sharing. Then she went on to detail the long hours it will take to meet a difficult production deadline.

- Chris DeLorenzo must announce the new employee safety program in the company newsletter. He began his article by citing the current accident rate. Then he explained how the new program has been developed to reduce accidents and to conform to regulations. At the end, Chris listed each new safety procedure.

Develop an Outline

An **outline** is a guideline that helps identify the information to be presented and its proper sequence. An outline helps to ensure related ideas are covered in the same section. Not every writing task requires a formal outline. However, most writing tasks can be improved by first jotting down the points you want to make.

For complex communication, a formal outline helps organize and clarify the relationship between ideas and sections of content. Start by selecting the key points. *Key points,* or main ideas, are the topics that help achieve the purpose for writing. Under each item, list its supporting points and any necessary details under those. Then, consider the approach you determined earlier and the order in which you want to present the information.

One way to write an outline is to make a numbered list of the key points. Record the items in the order in which you think of them. Then, reorder the items until they reflect the order in which the information will be presented. **Figure 6-3** shows an outline. The outline is a tool that helps you to organize the document, find the direction, and start writing.

Status of Search for New Production Assistant

I.   Position is still open
    A.   No new hire to date
    B.   Five candidates interviewed, but none met criteria
    C.   No further response from advertisement

II.   HR manager has stayed on top of the situation
    A.   Contacting search firms for referrals
    B.   Evaluating wage/compensation package
    C.   Contracting with a temporary agency

III.   HR manager has a plan for filling the position
    A.   Continue an aggressive search
    B.   Evaluate job description

Goodheart-Willcox Publisher

Figure 6-3   A formal outline is an organizational tool to use during the prewriting stage.

Section 6.1   Review

 Check Your Understanding

1. What are the four steps of the writing process?
2. Explain how the journalistic approach can be useful during the prewriting stage.
3. Describe the two types of audiences.
4. List the two types of approaches that can be used for writing.
5. Describe the purpose of an outline.

Build Your Vocabulary

As you progress through this course, develop a personal glossary of key terms. This will help you build your vocabulary and prepare you for a career. Write a definition for each of the following terms and add it to your personal glossary.

writing process	demographics
four Cs of communication	public relations
medium	scope
writer's block	direct approach
audience	indirect approach
primary audience	outline
secondary audience	

Executing the Writing Plan

Objectives

After completing this section, you will be able to:

- **Identify** each step of the writing stage.
- **Describe** the importance of the postwriting stage.
- **Explain** the publishing process.

Key Terms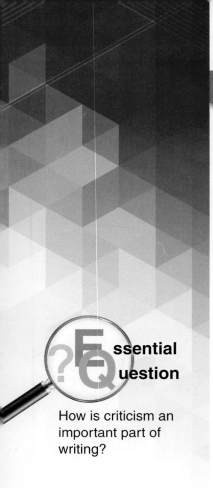

revising	proofreading
editing	publishing
objectivity	formatting
criticism	layout
constructive criticism	readability
destructive criticism	

Essential Question

How is criticism an important part of writing?

Writing

Once the prewriting tasks are completed, you are ready to begin the writing stage. This is step two in the writing process. The *writing* stage includes creating rough drafts and getting ideas "on paper." The goal of the writing stage is simple: get your ideas on paper in sentence form. Following the writing checklist in Figure 6-4 will help guide you through the process.

After a first draft is completed, you will revise the content. Edit the sentences and language as many times as necessary until you are satisfied.

Creating the First Draft

To begin the writing stage, start by creating a first draft. Since the reader will not see the first draft, it does not matter where you begin. You can begin

---

Writing Checklist

- ❏ Create the first draft of the document.
- ❏ Revise the first draft to improve the message.
- ❏ Edit the draft for correct grammar, mechanics, spelling, and word usage.
- ❏ Solicit feedback from others to help perfect the final document.

Goodheart-Willcox Publisher

Figure 6-4 Use this checklist in the writing stage.

at the top of the outline and work to the bottom. Or, you may decide to start somewhere in between. Often, opening and closing paragraphs are easier to write once the rest of the content is drafted.

Resist the urge to revise as you write. Plan to revise after the whole draft is completed. Knowing that you will revise as many times as needed allows you to move quickly.

As you write, do not worry about the organization of the material. Move things around if the flow is out of order, but organizational problems can often be more clearly seen when you read the whole document. Include more information, rather than less. It is usually easier to delete content later than to backtrack to determine how to add missing content.

While writing the first draft, do not worry about precision. For example, the placement of headings and spacing can be left for the revision stage. Also, how sentences sound is not important in the first draft. Do not stop to wonder about sentence structure, word choice, or grammar. There will be time to evaluate and polish in the revision stage. Instead, maintain your train of thought and get all the information "on paper." The more you get sidetracked making revisions, the longer it will take to get the information down. It will be harder to continue writing after each pause.

By writing without stopping to make decisions, you can quickly complete a first draft of a short document. A first draft based on the outline in Figure 6-3 is shown in Figure 6-5. This first draft needs revising and proofreading, but the writer has successfully put all of the ideas of the outline in sentence form.

Exploring Communication Careers

Broadcast Technician

To *broadcast* means to transmit by radio or television. The primary job of a broadcast technician is to facilitate broadcasting. Setting up and installing equipment used during radio or television programs are the responsibilities of this telecommunications position. Broadcast technicians also monitor sound and video quality and adjust equipment as needed to maintain high quality standards. Typical job titles for this position include *broadcast engineer*, *production assistant*, *broadcast operations engineer*, and *audio engineer*.

Some examples of tasks that broadcast technicians perform include:

- Set up, install, and operate broadcast equipment.

- Monitor and adjust equipment to ensure high-quality sound or video.

- Copy or edit sound or graphics onto videotape.

- Maintain and coordinate repairs on equipment.

- Maintain programming logs as required by the Federal Communications Commission.

Broadcast technicians need a minimum of a high school diploma for most positions. Certain jobs require some college or an associate degree. Many companies provide on-the-job training for their broadcast equipment, but others look for candidates who have received training at a vocational school.

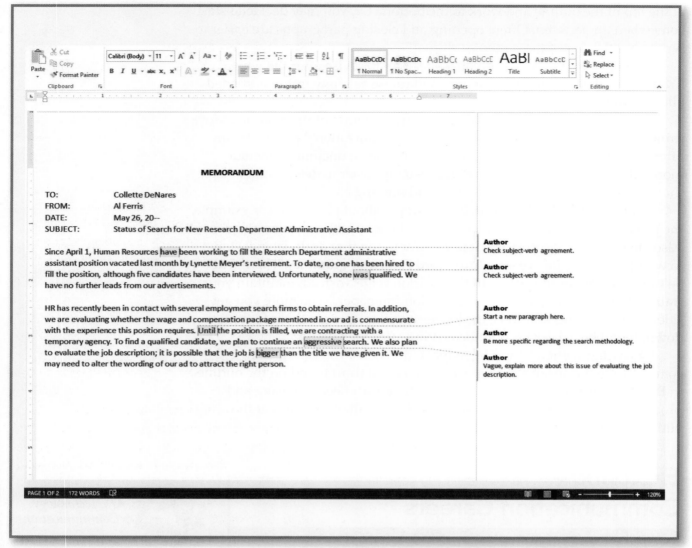

Figure 6-5   A revised document is shown in Microsoft Word. Word's track changes feature has been used to keep track of changes.

Revising

Once you have your draft complete, improve the quality of the message by revising it. **Revising** is the process of rewriting paragraphs and sentences to improve organization and content. It also involves checking the structure of the document as a whole.

Start revising by reviewing aspects that affect the whole message such as content and organization. Once those aspects are sound, work from the next-largest units to the smallest units. After all, there is no need to struggle with a sentence if you might remove the entire paragraph.

Learn to ask questions about the first draft. Honestly answer those questions from a reader's point of view. One way to read your writing from a reader's point of view is to distance yourself from it. After the first draft and revision are finished, take a break from writing. Go to lunch, go to a meeting, or do some other work and let the draft sit overnight. Better still, let it sit over the weekend. The longer the break, the newer the draft will seem when you finally look at it again. Taking a break from the writing allows you to review it with more objectivity. To have **objectivity** is to be free of personal feelings, prejudices, or interpretations.

Make changes whenever needed. Figure 6-6 shows how each line of questioning can help refine your writing. Many writers need

---

How to Refine Your Writing

Once you have a first draft of the document, ask these questions.

- Did you use the correct approach: direct for good or neutral news; indirect for bad news?
- Is the message effective? Is the reader likely to respond in the desired manner?
- Has all necessary information been included?
- Is the document oriented to the reader?
- Does your document as a whole:
    - fully and clearly present the information and ideas?
    - address the specific audience being addressed?
    - use the style and tone most suitable for the situation?
    - use the format most suitable for the situation?

Once you have considered your document as a whole, consider each of the paragraphs.

- Do paragraphs flow logically?
- Does each paragraph have a clearly identified topic sentence?
- Does the first paragraph:
    - tell your reader what the main points are going to be?
    - focus on the reader's point of view?
- Does the concluding paragraph:
    - briefly reinforce the main point?
    - leave the reader with a clear view of how to react or respond?
- Does each of the middle paragraphs:
    - have a clear organizational structure so the reader can easily follow the ideas?
    - include only information that supports the main points?
    - include only information that causes the reader to respond in the desired way?
    - consider and respond to possible objections the reader might make to the main points?
    - clearly relate to the paragraphs before and after it?

Once you are satisfied with each paragraph, consider each sentence.

- Do sentences flow logically?
- Have you eliminated needless repetitions?
- Does each sentence:
    - clearly and completely state its point?
    - support the main idea?
    - work with the sentence before and after it to form a smooth, easy-to-read paragraph?
    - contain strong nouns and verbs when possible instead of too many modifiers?
    - contain modifiers placed next to the words they modify?
    - express agreement between sentence parts, such as subjects and verbs?
    - express ideas in parallel construction?
    - avoid unnecessary words and phrases?
    - have a style and tone consistent with the rest of the document?

Once you are satisfied with each sentence, consider the words.

- Is each word the best choice, considering the:
    - reader's knowledge of the topic?
    - situation's level of formality?
    - level of specificity you are trying to achieve?
    - tone you are trying to achieve?
    - emotional impact you are trying to make or trying to avoid?

Goodheart-Willcox Publisher

Figure 6-6   These questions can help refine the document.

to go through several revisions of the first draft before achieving an acceptable final draft.

Editing

Editing is a more-refined form of revising. It is focused on sentence construction, wording, and clarity of ideas. Where revising focuses on constructing the content, editing is polishing the document until it is in finished form.

For example, verify that each heading in a document reflects the content within the section. Headings should be checked for consistency and adherence to style. Sentences must be edited and checked for correct grammar, mechanics, spelling, and word usage.

Grammar is the study of how words and their components come together to form sentences. Grammar is also a set of rules for using language correctly. Using correct grammar to write documents is necessary to convey a clear and concise message.

Editing for correct grammar and usage demands a good command of the English language. If your skills are lacking in this area, take time to review the rules of grammar. Consult a reference manual to ensure that grammar and usage are correct. For word usage, variety, and clarity, keep a dictionary and thesaurus on hand. Printed or online versions can be used, depending on personal preference.

Soliciting Feedback

During the writing stage, you might have someone review the document and offer feedback. As you will recall, feedback is the receiver's response to a message. It is always helpful to have a reviewer who understands the reader's point of view. In business, it is common for important documents to be reviewed by several people before distribution. This suggests that professional people know the importance of good writing.

When individuals are willing to review your writing, help them provide the feedback you need. Make sure they understand the situation for which the document is written. Do not hesitate to direct the review by asking questions. For example, ask, "Are you able to follow my directions in the third paragraph?"

Finally, be a good listener and demonstrate professional etiquette. When a reviewer suggests a change, many writers feel offended and immediately leap to defend what was written. Feedback is sometimes translated as criticism. **Criticism** is a comment that expresses unfavorable judgment or disapproval of a person or action.

If a reviewer suggests a change or has difficulty with something, try to understand why. This person is trying to help you rather than criticize. **Constructive criticism** is giving well-reasoned opinions about the work of others. Keep an open mind when listening to others' opinions about your work. Ask questions to help solve the problem. In short, recognize that the reviewer is providing a critique of the writing, not criticizing the writer. Being defensive will make it difficult to convince people to review your work.

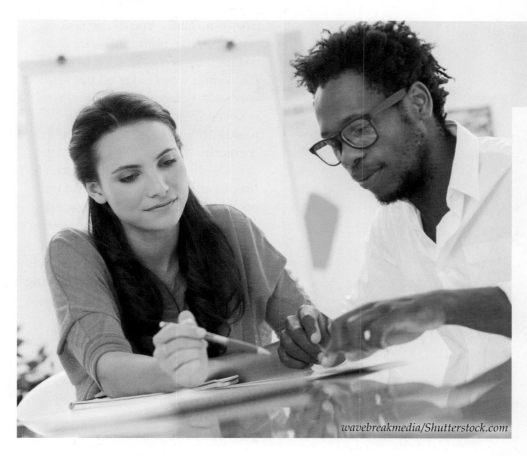

Constructive criticism can provide valuable feedback for improving the document.

wavebreakmedia/Shutterstock.com

There will be occasions in the workplace when it will be necessary for you to give constructive criticism. Keep the following behaviors in mind.

- Control your body language and tone of voice.

- Begin and end with a positive remark or compliment.

- Comment on the qualities of the work, not on the individual person.

- Offer specific suggestions, not vague comments.

- Give the other person the chance to respond.

Avoid giving destructive criticism. **Destructive criticism** is a judgment given with the intention of harming or offending someone. This behavior is unproductive for the workplace.

Postwriting

Step three in the writing process is the postwriting stage. In the *postwriting* stage, a final edit of the work is completed. Your written work will often be judged by its correctness and appearance. Errors distract from the message and suggest you were careless in preparing the communication. For this reason, proofreading is an important part of the postwriting stage.

Proofreading is checking the final copy for correct spelling, punctuation, and for typographical errors. The first step in proofreading is to use the software's grammar and spelling checker. However, this

Mills Studio/Shutterstock.com

Proofreading helps the writer make sure that written communication is free of errors.

does not relieve you of the task of proofreading. Some software may not pick up errors that occur when the wrong word is keyed but spelled correctly. For example, when "you" is keyed instead of "your", the words are incorrect but are spelled correctly.

Use the following guidelines for proofreading. Not every point will need to be used on every writing task. Your judgment will indicate how much attention is needed.

- Proofread for content by slowly reading the copy, concentrating on the accuracy of the message.

- First use the spelling and grammar checker, then proofread on the computer screen.

- Print a copy and proofread it again; mark errors on the printout.

- Read the copy aloud.

- Enlist a coworker to be a proofreading partner. Read aloud from the printed copy while your partner checks against the final document on screen. It is easier to catch subtle mistakes with another set of eyes.

Try to put some time between the tasks of revising, proofreading, and making final changes. Again, you will be more objective if some time has elapsed between readings of the document. As you proofread, be on the lookout for these types of mistakes:

- incorrect word usage that changes the meaning of the sentence

  | The courts have ruled that this type of business activity is <u>now legal</u>.

  The intended meaning: The activity is not legal. Change *now* to *not*, or *legal* to *illegal*.

- errors in names, titles, addresses, dates, numbers, amounts of money, time

  | The project is expected to be complete by <u>May 32</u>.

- errors of transposition

  | The meeting <u>be will</u> held next Friday.

- errors in fact or logic

  | The company's fiscal year runs from <u>December through January</u>.

- errors or problems in formatting

Figure 6-7 shows standard *proofreaders' marks* universally used by writers and editors to note errors and changes. It is a good idea to learn this standardized system and use it when proofreading printed material. The marks can be understood by anyone in the event someone else is reviewing or keying the changes. When marking the printout, use a red pen so the notations are easy to spot. If another reviewer has used red, select a different color.

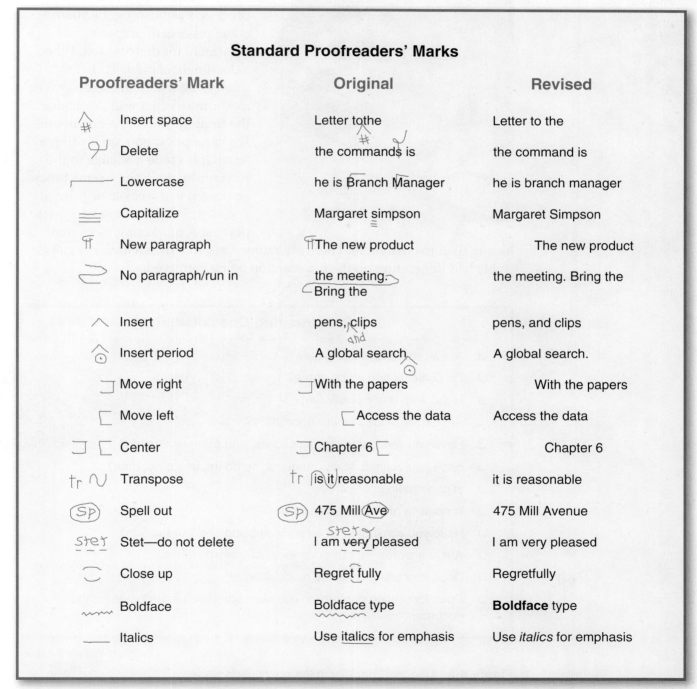

Standard Proofreaders' Marks

Proofreaders' Mark	Original	Revised
Insert space	Letter tothe	Letter to the
Delete	the commands is	the command is
Lowercase	he is Branch Manager	he is branch manager
Capitalize	Margaret simpson	Margaret Simpson
New paragraph	The new product	The new product
No paragraph/run in	the meeting. Bring the	the meeting. Bring the
Insert	pens, clips	pens, and clips
Insert period	A global search	A global search.
Move right	With the papers	With the papers
Move left	Access the data	Access the data
Center	Chapter 6	Chapter 6
Transpose	is it reasonable	it is reasonable
Spell out	475 Mill Ave	475 Mill Avenue
Stet—do not delete	I am very pleased	I am very pleased
Close up	Regret fully	Regretfully
Boldface	Boldface type	**Boldface** type
Italics	Use italics for emphasis	Use *italics* for emphasis

Goodheart-Willcox Publisher

Figure 6-7   Standard proofreaders' marks should be used when editing a document in printed form.

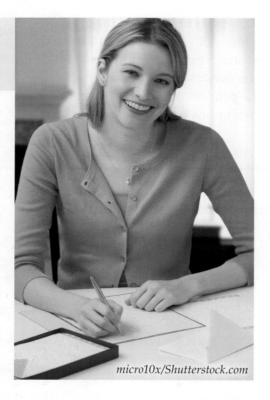

A letter might be published by being mailed to the receiver.

micro10x/Shutterstock.com

The checklist in Figure 6-8 summarizes the proofreading tasks. Use this checklist as a guide each time you evaluate your work.

Publishing

The final step in the writing process is publishing. **Publishing** is the process of preparing a document for distribution. When a document is published, it is made available to the receiver. The medium selected will determine the final format of the document. For example, if you are writing a letter, it is made available to the receiver by mailing. A report may be posted to a website or printed and distributed to the appropriate parties. A marketing piece may be e-mailed to customers. There are many ways in which a message can be published depending on the information being conveyed.

Proofreading Checklist

❑ Are all sentences complete?

❑ Do subjects and verbs agree?

❑ Is the verb tense consistent?

❑ Are terms defined where necessary?

❑ Have you eliminated jargon, clichés, and pompous words?

❑ Have you verified dates, amounts, numbers, and other data?

❑ Is punctuation correct?

❑ Is spelling of proper nouns correct?

❑ Have you eliminated all errors in spelling and word usage?

❑ Are any words left out or unnecessary words left in?

❑ Does formatting enhance readability?

❑ Does formatting conform to business standards appropriate for the document?

Goodheart-Willcox Publisher

Figure 6-8   Use this checklist in the postwriting stage.

Part of the publishing stage is formatting the document. **Formatting** is the placement and style of type in a document. Formatting is important because it affects how the message is presented to the reader. Considerations in formatting include the font, font size, and layout. **Layout** is the relationship of the text to white space. A good layout is essential to readability. **Readability** is a measure of whether the document is easy to read.

Typical business documents that require formatting include letters, memos, reports, and proposals. E-mail may also need formatting. For example, you may decide that a numbered or bulleted list, boldface, or underlining is needed to show emphasis.

When preparing formal business documents, it is important to follow standard formatting guidelines. These guidelines are covered in detail in Chapter 9.

Section 6.2 Review

 Check Your Understanding

1. Summarize how to write a first draft of a document.
2. Describe the difference between revising and editing.
3. How can a person make sure he or she gets quality feedback?
4. Explain the importance of the postwriting stage.
5. What does it mean to publish a document?

 Build Your Vocabulary

As you progress through this course, develop a personal glossary of key terms. This will help you build your vocabulary and prepare you for a career. Write a definition for each of the following terms and add it to your personal glossary.

revising   proofreading
editing   publishing
objectivity   formatting
criticism   layout
constructive criticism   readability
destructive criticism

Chapter Summary

Section 6.1 Preparing to Write

- Quality writing is achieved by following the four stages of the writing process: prewriting, writing, postwriting, and publishing. The goal of the writing process is to produce a well-written document that effectively achieves your purpose. Following the four Cs of communication helps achieve this goal.

- The prewriting stage involves thinking about, planning, and researching your goals in an orderly fashion. During prewriting, you will define the purpose and topic of your writing as well as analyze the audience. Once these steps have been completed, you will gather the information, research ideas, organize your thoughts, and choose a medium.

Section 6.2 Executing the Writing Plan

- The initial task in the writing stage is to create a first draft. During the writing stage, you will revise and edit drafts of the document. The final draft of the document can be reviewed by peers or coworkers who will provide feedback to help you perfect your work.

- The postwriting stage is when the document is proofread. Proofreading involves checking for grammar and spelling errors, as well as checking other mechanics of writing.

- The publishing stage is when the completed document is sent or made available to the reader. Before sending the document to the reader, it should be properly formatted.

Online Activities

Complete the following activities which will help you learn, practice, and expand your knowledge and skills.

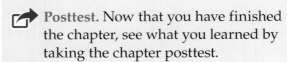 **Posttest.** Now that you have finished the chapter, see what you learned by taking the chapter posttest.

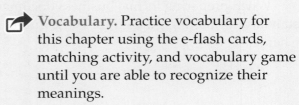 **Vocabulary.** Practice vocabulary for this chapter using the e-flash cards, matching activity, and vocabulary game until you are able to recognize their meanings.

English/Language Arts. Visit www.g-wlearning.com to download each data file for this chapter. Follow the instructions to complete an English/language arts activity to practice what you have learned in this chapter.

Activity File 6-1: Using Antonyms

Activity File 6-2: Improving Your Editing Skills

Review Your Knowledge

1. What are the four Cs of communication?
2. How can writer's block be avoided?
3. Explain how demographics can help analyze an audience.
4. When is the direct approach desirable?
5. Explain when the indirect approach is appropriate.
6. Summarize the writing stage.
7. How should the process of revising be approached?
8. What does it mean to be objective?
9. List examples of guidelines for proofreading.
10. Explain why feedback is sometimes perceived as criticism. How can professionalism be demonstrated when receiving feedback?

Apply Your Knowledge

1. Create a flowchart that shows the four steps of the writing process. Add any notes that will help you as you complete writing assignments. Use this as a reference as you write professional documents.

2. Read an opinion piece in a newspaper or magazine. Compose a letter to the editor supporting or disputing the editorial position. Using the writing process described in this chapter, create the document.

3. You can learn about a situation using the journalistic approach of asking *who, what, where, when, why,* and *how.* Select a message you recently received, such as an e-mail from a friend or an article in a magazine. Analyze the situation by identifying the *who, what, when, where, why,* and *how* of the message.

4. Interpret and communicate the following information. Phillip Jenkins, public relations director for a public utility, must write a press release regarding an accident at one of the utility's plants. Three employees received minor injuries, were treated at the local hospital, and are in good condition. They will return to work in two days. The utility company for which Phillip works has been criticized in the past for allowing unsafe working conditions. However, these are the first injuries reported in many years. Consider what information Phillip needs to include in the press release in an effort to address the feelings of other plant workers and their families, company executives, the community, and the press. Which approach will you use: direct or indirect? Create an outline for Phillip's announcement applying the steps of prewriting.

5. Using the outline created in the last activity, write a draft of the press release applying the steps of the writing process.

6. Using the draft of the outline created in the last activity, compose the press release. Use appropriate proofreading and editing techniques to finalize the document.

7. Which publishing option would you select for the press release that you just created? What alternatives are available?

8. You have just written and published a press release. Part of your responsibility is to create a message for the employees at the company where the accident occurred. How will you adapt the message to this audience? Will the audience be primary or secondary readers? Explain your approach.

Communication Skills

College and Career Readiness

Speaking. Communication careers require that individuals be able to participate and contribute to one-on-one discussions. Developing intrapersonal communication skills is one way to achieve career opportunities. As your instructor lectures on this chapter, contribute thoughtful comments when participation is invited.

Listening. Engage in a conversation with someone you have not spoken with before. Ask the person how he or she manages time. Actively listen to what that person is sharing. Next, summarize and retell what the person conveyed in conversation to you. Did you really hear what was being said?

Writing. To become career ready, it is important to learn how to communicate clearly and effectively by using reason. Create a flowchart that includes the steps in the journalistic approach for writing (*who, what, when, where, why, how*). How can the steps of this flowchart be applied in critical thinking situations as well as in the writing process?

Internet Research

Communication Careers. Using various Internet resources, research the current job opportunities and general qualifications for a communication career that interests you. Use the Arts, A/V Technology & Communications Career Cluster as a starting point. Describe the lifestyle implications and physical demands of the position. Write a one-page report about job prospects that evaluates your findings. Use correct grammar, punctuation, and terminology to write and edit the document.

Teamwork

Knowing how to give and accept constructive criticism is a requirement in the workplace. Working with your team, create a list of rules that should be followed when giving criticism to a peer. Next, create a list of rules that should be followed when receiving criticism.

Portfolio Development

College and Career Readiness

Digital File Formats. A portfolio will contain documents you created electronically as well as documents that you have in hard copy format that will be scanned. It will be necessary to decide file formats to use for both types of documents. Before you begin, consider the technology that you might use for creating and scanning documents. You will need access to desktop publishing software, scanners, cameras, and other digital equipment or software.

For documents that you create, consider using the default format to save the files. For example, you could save letters and essays created in Microsoft Word in DOCX format. You could save worksheets created in Microsoft Excel in XLSX format. If your presentation will include graphics or video,

confirm the file formats that are necessary for each item. Use the appropriate formats as you create the documents.

Hard copy items will need to be converted to digital format. Portable document format, or PDF, is a good choice for scanned items, such as awards and certificates.

Another option is to save all documents as PDF files. Keep in mind that the person reviewing your digital portfolio will need programs that open these formats to view your files. Having all of the files in the same format can make viewing them easier for others who need to review your portfolio.

CTSOs

Performance. Some competitive events for CTSOs have a performance component. The activity could potentially be a decision-making scenario for which your team will provide a solution and present to the judges.

To prepare for the performance component of a presentation, complete the following activities.

1. On your CTSO's website, locate a rubric or scoring sheet for the event.

2. Confirm whether visual aids may be used in the presentation and the amount of setup time permitted.

3. Review the rules to confirm whether questions will be asked or if the team will need to defend a case or situation.

4. Make notes on index cards about important points to remember. Use these notes to study. You may also be able to use these notes during the event.

5. Practice the performance. You should introduce yourself, review the topic that is being presented, defend the topic being presented, and conclude with a summary.

6. After the performance is complete, ask for feedback from your instructor. You may also consider having a student audience listen and give feedback.

7

Writing Style

Sections

7.1 Style and Tone

7.2 Sentence Style

College and Career Readiness

Reading Prep. Before reading this chapter, flip through the pages and make notes of the major headings. Analyze the structure of the relationships of the headings with the concepts in the chapter.

Minerva Studio/Shutterstock.com

Check Your Communication IQ ➦

Before you begin the chapter, see what you already know about communication by taking the chapter pretest. The pretest is available at www.g-wlearning.com.

Case Study

Complete Information

Danielle Greco is a self-published author whose book *Modern Home Renovation* is for sale on her website. She received an e-mail from William Salinas, a customer who purchased the book online. William was charged $28.45 and questioned the price of the book in his e-mail. He said he expected to be charged $24.95, the price advertised on the website. Danielle realized the price is higher because she forgot to list the shipping cost. This is the copy on the website:

> Every homeowner should have *Modern Home Renovation* on the shelf. This book will help you learn how to remodel your home and make it a showplace. Your friends and neighbors will wonder how you learned to be so creative without a contractor. For a limited time, you can buy this book for only $24.95. Don't waste time—order today!

vgstudio/Shutterstock.com

Critical Thinking

1. Did Danielle use the four Cs of communication in her copy? Explain.

2. Rewrite the copy to make it more clear and concise. Be sure to include the shipping cost.

Style and Tone

Objectives

After completing this section, you will be able to:

- **Explain** how to create an appropriate style and tone when writing.
- **Describe** how to select words that convey meaning and adjust to the needs of the audience.

Key Terms

writing style	euphemism
tone	condescending
formal language	bias-free words
informal language	situation
slang	jargon
connotation	cliché

?Essential Question

How can writing style and tone impact the success of a message?

Creating Writing Style and Tone

Writing style refers to the way in which a writer uses language to convey an idea. It reflects the numerous decisions the writer must make regarding word choice and construction of sentences and paragraphs.

The style you use creates a tone. **Tone** is an impression of the overall content of the message. Is it friendly or hostile, demanding or courteous, sensitive or insensitive? Ask yourself or a reviewer if your writing has a tone that is both professional and friendly.

Judge your writing based on the four Cs of communication. When developing a writing style, look for opportunities to make the writing clear, concise, courteous, and correct. Doing so will help your writing show respect and sensitivity, leaving the reader with a positive impression.

Use Formal Language

Formal language is language that is used in a workplace environment. Standard English is the norm. Standard English language usage follows accepted rules for spelling, grammar, and punctuation. It should be used for all documents, such as reports, presentations, letters, and e-mail. Professional writing must use formal language.

Informal language is language used in a casual situation without applying the rules of grammar. Most people use informal language with friends and family. An example of informal language is the language you probably use when texting with your friends. Texting language, such as using the letter *u* instead of the word *you*, is not acceptable in business writing. **Slang** is words and phrases that are not considered part of Standard English. For example, you may say you are "hanging out with a friend." "Hanging out" is slang that may mean *visiting a friend*.

Consider Meaning

Good writers look for fresh, clear words to describe and express ideas. They are also always aware that words should be handled with care. Words have an exact meaning according to the dictionary, but sometimes words convey other meanings outside of their definition. A word's meaning can vary according to the context in which it is used. Recall that *context* is the environment or setting in which something occurs or is communicated. The context of a word is the words or paragraphs surrounding it that can help explain its meaning.

In some cases, however, context is not enough. The real meaning of words resides in the mind of the reader or the listener. The **connotation** of a word is its meaning apart from what it explicitly names or describes. This is where the shades of meaning become a concern for the writer.

An example of connotation is the word *foreign*. In spite of its definition of referring to something outside one's own country, the word may also have a negative connotation. The word *foreign* can be associated with the idea of *other*, meaning *not one of us* or *not like us*. In the business world, the word *international* is most often used in place of the word *foreign*.

When revising your writing, review both the context and connotation of your words. This will help you avoid the common problems of misunderstanding or misinterpretation. For example, if you describe an office facility as *adequate*, one reader may interpret *adequate* as *sufficient*. Another reader may interpret *adequate* to mean *close to the lower limit of quality or acceptability*. Each of these readers has a different impression of the facility.

Review the context and connotation of the writing style to avoid misunderstandings.

BlueSkyImage/Shutterstock.com

Ethics

Code of Ethics

Most companies establish a set of ethics that employees must follow. The code of ethics outlines acceptable behavior when interacting with coworkers, suppliers, and customers. Some businesses even post their code of ethics on their websites. As an employee, it is important to know the code of ethics so you can make correct decisions on behalf of the company.

Consider the words *defective* and *broken*. Both are used to describe something that does not work properly. A customer may claim a product is defective while the manufacturer claims it is broken. The shades of meaning clash because *defective* implies manufacturer responsibility while *broken* implies user responsibility.

Some words may sound acceptable in conversation but may come across as harsh in writing. For those words, you may need to find a euphemism. A **euphemism** is a word that expresses unpleasant ideas in more pleasant terms. For example, instead of saying, "this phone system is *cheaper*," the preferred euphemism is *less expensive*. In another example, the *customer service department* used to be commonly called the *customer complaint office*. The new term reflects a desire by the business to service a customer's needs. Some businesses even use the term *customer care* to communicate greater sensitivity to the customer's needs. Use euphemisms when needed, but use them wisely.

Avoid language that is condescending. To be **condescending** means to assume an attitude of superiority. Use words the reader will understand but not interpret to mean the writer feels superior to the reader. For example, an explanation that is too basic to make sure the reader understands may be condescending. Estimate what level of knowledge the reader should have on the topic to avoid insulting the reader's intelligence.

Choose Positive or Neutral Language

It is easier to get results by expressing a positive tone rather than a negative one. For example, it is always better to emphasize what you *can* do rather than what you *cannot* do. Notice how these two sentences create different feelings when you read them.

Negative

We cannot mail your package by overnight express mail.

Positive

You can choose to have the package sent by two-day air or three-day ground service.

Many words tend to automatically cause negative reactions. Similarly, there are words that generally have a positive effect on readers. The words italicized in the following sentences tend to create good feelings.

We hope you will be able to take *advantage* of this one-time offer.

Loyal customers like you *deserve* the very best.

It is our *pleasure* to offer you a free trial of this new product with no strings attached.

Of course, no writer can make all messages sound positive. To maintain integrity, it is often impossible to avoid information that a reader will not like to receive. Nevertheless, try to avoid negative language. When a message is likely to make the reader unhappy, search for neutral words to soften the reaction.

Review the words in the list that follows. Think about how a message using the words on the left will be received. The words on the right mean the same thing but are neutral and better accepted by a reader. Use a thesaurus or dictionary when you need a neutral word or phrase to communicate a negative message.

Negative	Neutral/Positive
cannot	unable to
cheap	affordable/less expensive
defective	malfunctioning
fault	responsibility
misinformed	unaware
neglect	forget
regret	apologize
wrong	incorrect

Apply Sensitive Language

When writing for professional purposes, it is important to use language free of bias. A *bias* is a tendency to believe that some ideas or people are better than others, which often results in acting unfairly. **Bias-free words** are neutral words imparting neither a positive nor negative message. For example, gender, ethnicity, and age cannot be inferred from bias-free words. Using gender neutral words, such as *server* rather than *waiter* or *waitress*, focuses the reader on the job or the individual's qualifications instead of the gender of the individual. Rather than saying, "we hired a *young man* for the manager job," state, "we hired a *new manager*." When a disability must be referenced, use a specific term such as *hearing impaired* or *physically disabled*. Do not use outdated terms that are now considered offensive.

Choosing Words

It is important to carefully think about the words you use. Consider the intended meaning and the connotation the words might have in the mind of the receiver. There are word choices you can make that will increase the likelihood readers will respond as desired. Focus on using words that are precise and familiar.

Be Precise

Some words are more precise than others. When precise language is used, the readers will be better able to understand the message. This will help them to respond in the desired way. For example, this phrase is vague:

"I would like to receive your feedback on this proposal *as soon as possible*."

On the other hand, giving a specific date is clear and precise:

"I would like to receive your feedback on this proposal *no later than Friday, March 25*."

This makes it more likely the information will be delivered when it is needed. Precise words also make writing more interesting to read, as shown in Figure 7-1. Notice how much easier it is to create a mental picture when precise words are used.

Figure 7-1   The more specific the word, the easier it is to create a mental image.

Always keep in mind, however, that writing style is not about formulas. Sometimes it makes more sense to write in general terms before getting specific. For example, it might be best to first describe a new spa service in general terms as *a new personal service* before specifically stating it is a *Dead Sea salt scrub*.

Simple, everyday words will help attract and hold the reader's attention. Long words look difficult to the reader and may actually be difficult to read. In contrast, short, familiar words have more force and clarity. They also contribute to easier readability of sentences.

Select Familiar Words

As you edit your writing, make an effort to eliminate less familiar words. Read the sentences aloud to check whether the words will quickly and clearly convey the message. This is especially important if the message will be delivered to the public. In general, always aim to create a document that is easy to read and understand.

Unfamiliar	Familiar
utilize	use
terminate	end
endeavor	try
demonstrate	show
ascertain	find out
query	ask
initiate	begin
procure	get
peruse	review/read
converse	talk

Use Jargon Sparingly

Language should be adapted to fit the situation. The **situation** is all of the facts, conditions, and events that affect your message. Some situations call for documents to be written using industry language, or jargon. **Jargon** is language specific to a line of work or area of expertise. It is the technical terminology or vocabulary that is used in a field or subject area. Various professions and industries have specific words and phrases that are familiar to those who work in that field. These words may not be understood by those outside of the field. For example, stockbrokers talk about *bull* and *bear* markets. Retailers talk about *retail*, *wholesale*, and *markdown prices*. These are examples of industry language. Jargon may also be considered slang or *technical language* in the specific industry.

Jargon speeds up the communication process only if the reader shares your area of expertise. However, if readers are unfamiliar with the technical terms used, they may not understand the message. Even if your readers know the words, avoid trying too hard to impress them with insider vocabulary.

Avoid Buzzwords and Clichés

Using buzzwords can also make it look as though you are trying too hard to impress the reader. Be aware of whether popular words are still current and if they are appropriate for the audience. Using an outdated word makes writing sound out of touch or not current. There also is a chance that a reader will not be familiar with a trendy word or phrase. This can result in a communication breakdown.

Exploring
Communication Careers

Choreographer

Most times when you see a dance performance on television, in a movie, in a play, or at a concert, a choreographer has been involved. Choreographers create dance routines. It is the primary responsibility of this position to decide what steps the dancers will take. They will often teach the steps and routines to the dancers. Directing rehearsals of the routine is also part of the job responsibilities. Typical job titles for this performing arts position include *creative director*, *artistic director*, and *dance director*.

Some examples of tasks that choreographers perform include:

- Create dance routines.
- Select music, sound effects, or spoken narratives to accompany the dance.
- Audition people for parts in a dance routine.
- Direct rehearsals of dance routines.
- Advise dancers how to move to create the desired effect.

Choreographers are required to have a high school diploma for most positions. The ability to be creative is essential. Being knowledgeable about dance movements and how to safely execute them is also required. Choreographers need to have people skills in order to teach steps to dancers and direct rehearsals.

To make your writing concise, do not use clichés. **Clichés** are overused, commonplace, or trite language. Often, clichés are not well received by the reader because it seems the writer is not being original. Knowing the audience can help determine whether using a cliché is acceptable. Some examples of clichés from everyday speech are:

- easy as pie
- like finding a needle in a haystack
- it's not rocket science

There are also clichés that show up almost exclusively in business writing:

- Dear Valued Customer:
- Enclosed, please find…
- Per your request…
- We are hereby requesting…

Because clichés are, by definition, commonplace, they will not necessarily compel the reader to act. Readers may not even understand a message with clichés since they are likely to skip over them as they read. With a little imagination, it is possible to find new ways to express old ideas. Instead of the cliché, "We appreciate your business," you might end a letter with a more personal remark. "As one of our best customers, you have helped Jetson Markets reach our sales goal for the year. Thank you!"

Adjust to the Needs of the Audience

The tone of a professional message may be formal or informal. A formal tone may be appropriate for a message that is being conveyed to management or clients. An informal tone might be better suited for communication with coworkers or for a marketing piece.

Choose words that are appropriate for the audience.

Andrey_Popov /Shutterstock.com

If you know your audience well, it is acceptable to use personal pronouns in your message. *I, me, my, you, your, he, she, it, we,* and *they* are examples of personal pronouns. If you use *I,* be careful not to overuse the word and sound like you are bragging.

Marketers often use the personal pronoun *you* in marketing pieces. This is known as using the "you" attitude. Statements such as "we look forward to hearing from you" influence the reader to connect to the sender. The message sounds more personal, helpful, and friendly.

Notice how the personal pronouns make the following message sound friendly and sincere:

> Dear Mr. Stephenson:
>
> I have enclosed the agreement we discussed last week for your services on the sales conference video. If the terms meet with your approval, please sign both copies of the agreement and return them to me for my signature. I will promptly return your copy so that we can begin our collaboration on the video.
>
> All of us on the conference-planning committee look forward to working with you.
>
> Sincerely,

In professional communication, personal pronouns may be inappropriate if the message is representing a business or organization. Make certain you know the purpose of the message and the makeup of the audience.

Section 7.1 Review

 Check Your Understanding

1. Why is it important to judge your writing on the four Cs of communication?
2. Give an example of connotation.
3. Explain why bias-free language should be used in the workplace.
4. What is the advantage of using simple, precise words in your messages?
5. Explain when it is appropriate to use a formal tone and when it is appropriate to use an informal tone.

 Build Your Vocabulary

As you progress through this course, develop a personal glossary of key terms. This will help you build your vocabulary and prepare you for a career. Write a definition for each of the following terms and add it to your personal glossary.

writing style

tone

formal language

informal language

slang

connotation

euphemism

condescending

bias-free words

situation

jargon

cliché

Sentence Style

Objectives

After completing this section, you will be able to:

- **Describe** ways to structure sentences that are clear and concise.
- **Explain** how to compose effective paragraphs.

Key Terms

redundancy   transition

Essential Question

How does sentence style contribute to effective paragraphs?

Structuring Clear and Concise Sentences

As a writer, you must arrange words so sentences convey a meaningful unit of thought. Being aware of techniques for writing sentences helps improve your writing style. You can make your writing not only clearer, but also more interesting to read.

Balance Sentence Length

Short, simple sentences are more understandable than long, complex ones. However, too many short, simple sentences can be boring. In some cases, they make the entire text hard to read. To judge the best length of a sentence, identify if the reader can immediately recognize the main idea.

Aim to make sentences short enough to be clear, but avoid writing a series of choppy sentences. Joining clauses and adding phrases will make sentences flow smoothly and add variety to your writing. These are the keys to achieving balance and keeping the reader's interest. Notice the difference in the following examples.

Draft

The company hopes the plant will open next spring. The plant will cover 200 acres. It will house 700 people. These employees are currently spread around the city in four different offices.

Revision

With much anticipation, the company plans to open the new plant next spring. The 200-acre campus will house 700 employees who are currently spread around the city in four different offices.

While revising and editing, read sentences aloud to gain a different perspective on the sentence structure. When you find several short sentences, consider combining some into longer sentences to help the flow and clarity. When you lengthen sentences, always reread to make sure the writing is still crisp and clean. Learning to critically read your own writing takes practice. At first, it will take longer to reread and hear or see the flaws. However, as you continue to practice revising and editing, this discipline will help improve your writing.

Choose Active or Passive Voice

Verbs show the action in a sentence. They can also either directly or indirectly tell the reader what the subject is doing or has done. You could say that verbs are the heart of the sentence. Recall that when a verb is in the *active voice*, the subject is performing the action. In the *passive voice*, the subject receives the action.

> **Active voice**
>
> He explained the policy.
>
> The company approved the plan.
>
> **Passive voice**
>
> The policy was explained.
>
> The plan was approved.

The following sentences are written in active voice. The simple subject is shown in bold and the verb is underlined.

> The **company** <u>hired</u> her in 2014.
>
> **First Mutual, Inc**. <u>offers</u> financial planning services.
>
> The **union members** <u>rejected</u> the proposal for nonunion hiring.

All of these sentences are clear and concise. Each one precisely tells what action the subject took. Notice the lessening of the verb's impact when it is written in the passive voice.

> She <u>was hired</u> by the **company** in 2014.
>
> Financial planning services <u>are offered</u> by **First Mutual, Inc**.
>
> The proposal for nonunion hiring <u>was rejected</u> by the **union members**.

 **Green**   Electronic Waste

It is important to recycle so that landfills do not become overloaded. Just as paper, plastic, and aluminum are often recycled, electronics should also be properly disposed of, not just placed in the trash.

Electronic waste includes computers, cell phones, and batteries of all kinds. All electronic waste can and should be recycled. The batteries in electronic devices contain hazardous chemicals and will harm the environment if discarded in a landfill. Many electronics retailers and community groups provide electronics recycling services. Before discarding electronic waste, research how the item should be properly disposed of.

Out-of-use electronic equipment can also be donated. Often, charities and community groups that are in need of equipment can refurbish and use older equipment. However, if the equipment is beyond repair, make sure the equipment is properly recycled.

When you use the active voice in writing, the message comes across in a stronger tone. Active voice is best when you need to be direct and have no reason to soften the message.

Passive voice is perfectly acceptable in writing. However, it should be used with thought given to the purpose it serves. Therefore, in the earlier example, the passive-voice version of the sentence would be the correct one to use. Here are some appropriate uses of the passive voice:

When the doer is unknown

The building was constructed in 1984.

(Who constructed the building is unknown.)

When the doer is unimportant

Your order was shipped on Thursday.

(The shipper is unimportant.)

When the doer of the action should not be mentioned out of tact or diplomacy

An error was made in the computation of your taxes.

(The person who made the error is not identified.)

When the action is more important than the doer, as in formal reports

Forty charge-account customers were surveyed regarding their spending habits.

(The customers are more important than who conducted the survey.)

In these situations, passive voice is effective. In other situations, you may need to choose active voice. Keep in mind, active voice emphasizes immediacy and adds vitality to your writing.

When using passive voice, give thought to the purpose it serves.

StockLite/Shutterstock.com

Write Concise Sentences

Effective business writing does not have *any* frills. When you write for business, it is your job to get the point across as concisely as possible. Every sentence and every word within the sentence should contribute to the overall message in a meaningful way. Businesspeople have a lot to do and want anything they read to quickly get to the point. The reader does not want to stop and think about what you are trying to communicate. Instead, the reader wants to immediately identify the issue so that a productive decision can be made.

Read the following examples. Notice how the lack of conciseness in the first example detracts from the message. On the other hand, the second example is stated in a more concise manner.

> **Draft**
>
> While I was away from my desk for a few short moments today, your package arrived from a delivery service. It was shortly before lunch. Imagine my surprise when I opened it to find the CD of photographs for the meeting I attended at 9:00 a.m.! Now it is too late to include your photos for consideration in the brochure.
>
> **Revision**
>
> The CD you sent by overnight mail arrived today at 11:30 a.m. Unfortunately, the meeting to discuss photography for the brochure was at 9:00 a.m., so I was not able to present your photos for consideration in the brochure.

When your writing is concise, you do not waste time explaining every detail of the situation. Subsequently, the reader does not waste time either.

Writing Effective Paragraphs

Effective paragraphs are a series of well-written, coherent sentences arranged in a meaningful order. Think of a paragraph as having three main parts: topic sentence, developmental sentences, and closing or summarizing sentence.

The topic sentence introduces and summarizes the main ideas that are being presented. This can be accomplished in one or two well-written sentences. The topic sentence is followed by the developmental sentences. These sentences include important information about the main idea of the message. After the idea has been well explained, the closing follows. Every well-written paragraph closes with a summary of the main idea of the message.

Apply Logic

Writing is logical when you have presented and connected ideas so that they make sense to the reader. Logic is tied to the order in which your thoughts are arranged in the writing, whether on paper or in digital form. Ask yourself these questions.

- Does the first paragraph introduce the topic?
- Are the points made in a logical sequence?
- Does each paragraph build on the previous one?

michaeljung./Shutterstock.com

Check for organization and logic when revising a written message.

Following the writing process of prewriting, writing, and postwriting will help establish a logical flow in each paragraph.

Remember that when you write the first draft, your goal is to get all your thoughts down without stopping. The revision stage is the time to check the organization of your work. Does the order make sense to the reader? Is a technical term used in paragraph two, but not defined until paragraph four? Does the piece jump from point A to point C without covering point B? It is common to find that paragraphs need to be moved around to tighten the logical flow. Taking the time to do this will ensure that the work makes sense to the reader.

Control Paragraph Length

There is no standard for how many sentences a paragraph should contain. Paragraph length will vary according to subject matter and sentence construction. Sometimes, a paragraph may consist of only one sentence, although these are generally avoided. The one-sentence paragraph is often used effectively as the opening or closing of a message.

Always keep the audience in mind as you write. Generally, as with sentences, readers want paragraphs to be short and clear. Shorter paragraphs help readers to skim and scan. These techniques for reading and absorbing information are discussed in Chapter 17. When you revise a draft, notice if there are long paragraphs. If so, look for places where it makes sense to begin a new paragraph. Do not force a break if it would not be logical. In most cases, however, you will find that long paragraphs have points where a break can be made.

Avoid Redundancies

A **redundancy** is repeating a message or saying the same thing more than once. Two or more words may have the same meaning or two or more sentences may say essentially the same thing. This can confuse or irritate the reader. In the following example, a manager is asking a staff member to follow up on an issue after a meeting. After reading the draft, try to identify the redundancy. Then, look at the revision to see how the repetition has been eliminated. Also notice the changes add clarity, conciseness, and precision to the writing.

> **Draft**
>
> At Monday's status meeting, you mentioned there is a potential for cost overruns on the Jamison Park project. If you feel there could be cost overruns, I need an itemized list of what specific items are likely to incur additional costs so that we can discuss these with the team.
>
> Would you please send me a summary listing areas of potential overruns and the reason that is causing each item to run over budget? I would like to have this before next Monday's status meeting so we can discuss the details with the team.
>
> **Revision**
>
> At Monday's status meeting, you mentioned potential cost overruns on the Jamison Park project. Please send me a summary listing the items that may run over budget and the cause of each overrun. I would like to have this by Friday so we can discuss the details with the team at next Monday's meeting.

Use Transitions

The key to connecting thoughts between sentences and paragraphs is the use of transitions. **Transitions** are words, phrases, and sentences that connect ideas and clarify the relationship between sentences and paragraphs. Review the following examples. The transitions are shown in bold.

> The promotion will begin on September 15. **Consequently**, sales should be brisk during October.
>
> Your account is seriously past due. **As a result**, your charge privileges are temporarily suspended.
>
> Let's examine the reasons for the new procedure. **First**, we need a process that is more efficient.

Transitions prepare the reader for what is coming and move the reader from one idea to another. They aid the reader's understanding of the message. Transitional words and phrases also add balance to sentence length when used to connect two short sentences.

Notice how paragraph two reads more smoothly than paragraph one, while paragraph three overuses transitions. The transition words are shown in bold.

> **Paragraph 1**
>
> We are increasing the price of the new merchandise. Regular customers will still get a discount on large-volume purchases. They will be able to take advantage of this discount only if they place orders every 60 days or less.
>
> **Paragraph 2**
>
> We are increasing the price of the new merchandise, **but** regular customers will still get a discount on large-volume purchases. **However**, they will be able to take advantage of this discount only if they place orders every 60 days or less.
>
> **Paragraph 3**
>
> We are increasing the price of the new merchandise, **but**, **on the other hand**, we will still give a discount to our regular large-volume purchasers. **Accordingly**, these purchasers will be able to take advantage of this discount only if they place orders every 60 days or less.

Without transitions, writing will sound choppy, the relationship among ideas will be unclear, and readers may be confused. But, when these connectors are overused, your writing will sound overly wordy as in paragraph three. Choosing the right mix of transitions will help you achieve a smooth and readable writing style.

The English language has many useful transitional words and phrases that serve various purposes. To use them appropriately, be aware of how they add meaning and make the writing more effective. Figure 7-2 lists commonly used transitions and their purpose.

Choose Direct or Indirect Approach

Paragraphs may be constructed using a direct or indirect approach. As you will recall, with the *direct approach*, the main idea is followed by descriptive details. The direct approach is a very readable format and is

Using Transitions		
Purpose	**Transition**	
Introduce a topic	first in addition	besides
Review a point	in other words that is	in conclusion to summarize
Compare items	likewise in the same way	similarly in contrast
Introduce examples	for example for instance	namely including
Provide contrast	however on the other hand but	yet in contrast on the contrary
Show cause	consequently because therefore	accordingly as a result
Concede a point	granted of course	to be sure certainly
Guide a reader through time	after again eventually earlier	later next now ultimately
Guide a reader through space	above below	nearby
Conclude	overall finally	in conclusion to summarize

Goodheart-Willcox Publisher

Figure 7-2   Useful transitions help lead the reader through the message.

most often used in business writing. With the *indirect approach,* details precede the main idea of the paragraph. Review the following examples.

Direct

We are pleased to inform you that your application for membership in the Writer's Association of America (WAA) has been accepted. As a member, you will have access to all of the benefits described in the attached brochure. To begin taking advantage of your WAA membership, please click on the link below to complete the online member registration form.

Indirect

Thank you for your application for membership in the Writer's Association of America (WAA). Each year we receive applications from several thousand published writers such as yourself who have excellent credentials and writing samples. Regrettably, we are able to admit only a few new members each year and must decline your application. We hope you will continue to enjoy the nonmember benefits we offer.

By using the indirect approach, the reader is prepared for the bad news. The writer is able to state the bad news in words that do not offend.

Section 7.2 Review

 Check Your Understanding

1. How can a writer balance sentence length?
2. How does using active voice affect a message?
3. Why is it important to be concise when writing for business?
4. Explain why paragraph length is important to the reader.
5. How do transitions in a sentence influence a reader?

 Build Your Vocabulary

As you progress through this course, develop a personal glossary of key terms. This will help you build your vocabulary and prepare you for a career. Write a definition for each of the following terms and add it to your personal glossary.

redundancy   transition

Chapter Summary

Section 7.1 Style and Tone

- Writing style refers to the way in which a writer uses language to convey an idea. Tone is an overall impression of the writing. Standard English is the norm in business writing and helps create an acceptable style and tone. When writing, consider the meaning of words, choose positive or neutral language, and apply sensitive language.

- When choosing words, use precise language, select familiar words, use jargon sparingly, and avoid buzzwords and clichés. This will help you meet the needs of the audience and set a professional tone.

Section 7.2 Sentence Style

- Short, simple sentences are more understandable than long, complex ones. Use active voice when you need to be direct. Use a passive voice to downplay a situation and soften the tone.

- Paragraphs have an introduction, developmental sentences, and a closing sentence. Use logic when writing and control the length of a paragraph. Avoid redundancies, use transitions, and decide whether to use a direct or indirect approach.

Online Activities

Complete the following activities which will help you learn, practice, and expand your knowledge and skills.

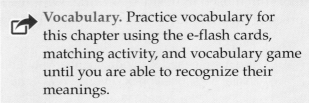 **Posttest.** Now that you have finished the chapter, see what you learned by taking the chapter posttest.

Vocabulary. Practice vocabulary for this chapter using the e-flash cards, matching activity, and vocabulary game until you are able to recognize their meanings.

English/Language Arts. Visit www.g-wlearning.com to download each data file for this chapter. Follow the instructions to complete an English/language arts activity to practice what you have learned in this chapter.

Activity File 7-1: Improving Your Editing Skills

Activity File 7-2: Using Synonyms

Review Your Knowledge

1. Explain what is meant by the *context* of a word.
2. Give an example of a euphemism.
3. Why is it important to use jargon sparingly?
4. Why avoid buzzwords in business writing?
5. Give an example of a cliché used in business writing.
6. When is it acceptable to use personal pronouns in business writing?
7. Why is it important to structure clear and concise sentences?
8. Describe the elements of an effective paragraph.
9. When is writing considered logical?
10. Explain when to use a direct approach in a message and when to use an indirect approach in a message.

Apply Your Knowledge

1. A euphemism is a word that expresses unpleasant ideas in more pleasant terms. Create a list of euphemisms with which you are familiar. What do they really mean?

2. Create a spreadsheet entitled *Workplace-Suitable Language*. In column one of a spreadsheet, list buzzwords, clichés, or slang you frequently encounter. In column two, identify whether the word or phrase is appropriate to use in business writing. If it is not, find a workplace-suitable substitute. For example, "I'm with it" is *not* appropriate in business and can be translated to "I agree."

3. Select a career that interests you. Make a list of five industry words, or jargon, that are used in that career. Next to each, write the definition. Did you know the definition of each term or did you have to research to find the meaning? Write a one- to two-page paper about the career you selected. Be sure your paper includes each of the jargon words you defined.

4. Rewrite the following draft of an e-mail to improve word choice and sentence and paragraph construction. Use an appropriate style and tone.
We received an order of 50 luminescent bulbs yesterday from your outfit. Needless to say, we cannot ship it until we receive a cashier's check because of your questionable credit rating. We want your business. We're sure you have a good excuse for your credit history, but a bird in the hand is worth two in the bush. In other words, we need the greenbacks before we release the goods. No hard feelings, just send the check. Have a grand day!
Sincerely,

5. Read the negative messages that follow. Rewrite each message with a positive tone.
   A. I was not able to give my presentation because the equipment was broken.
   B. My coworker neglected to schedule the meeting.
   C. The regional manager gave us wrong directions to the conference venue.
   D. We need to find cheaper airfare for the clients.

6. Bias-free words should be used when writing for business purposes. Locate a message in a newspaper or magazine or on a website that you believe has biased language in it that refers to gender, ethnicity, or age. Identify instances where the language can be modified to be unbiased. What strategies should have been used? Rewrite the message using appropriate bias-free words.

7. Print an article from an online newspaper or magazine. Analyze the style and tone of the article. Identify the situation and the intended audience. Critique the message regarding word usage, word choice, and sentence and paragraph construction. Did the writer adapt the language to fit the situation and the audience? Why or why not?

8. Identify which of the following sentences are written in passive voice. Rewrite those sentences that would be better in the active voice. Also, rewrite any sentences that you feel could be clearer. Explain how your changes are more effective for each communication.
   A. The site for the new company headquarters was selected by the committee.
   B. Our chemist tested the perfume samples.
   C. The quota was not met by the sales team last month.
   D. The amendment was approved by a majority of the board members.
   E. For some reason, the manager believed that we had left our job early.
   F. Several steps are being taken by our staff to improve customer service.
   G. Smoking is prohibited in the entire building.
   H. This shipment should be examined for damage.

Communication Skills

College and Career Readiness

Reading. After you have read this chapter, identify the explicit details, as well as the author's main idea for the chapter. Draw conclusions about the author's purpose. Share your findings with the class.

Writing. Writing style is the way in which a writer uses language to convey an idea. Select a page or pages of notes you have taken during a class. Evaluate your writing style and the relevance, quality, and depth of the information. Once you have done so, write a one-page paper that synthesizes your notes into complete sentences and thoughts. Organize your material so that it is logical to the reader. Describe what you have learned to the class.

Critical Thinking. To become career ready, it is necessary to utilize critical-thinking skills in order to solve problems. Give an example of a problem you needed to solve that was important to your success at work or school. How did you apply critical-thinking skills to arrive at a solution?

Internet Research

Formal and Informal Language. Research the terms *formal language* and *informal language*. Analyze what is meant by each. Next, create a list of standards that characterize formal language and a separate list of standards that characterize informal language. Create a list of rules that instruct a writer when to apply formal or informal language to a document.

Teamwork

With your team, create a list of long or complicated words or phrases that might be used in business writing. Examples include *commensurate with*, *disseminate*, *predisposed*, and *subsequent to*. List each of the words and phrases on a dry-erase board or flip chart. As a team, work together to think of simpler words or phrases to replace each list item. Use a thesaurus if one is available.

Portfolio Development

College and Career Readiness

File Structure. After you have chosen a file format for your documents, determine a strategy for storing and organizing the materials. The file structure for storing digital documents is similar to storing hard copy documents.

First, you need a place to store each item. Ask your instructor where to save your documents. This could be on the school's network or a flash drive of your own. Next, decide how to organize related files into categories. For example, certificates might be the name of a folder with a subfolder Community Service Certificates and a subfolder that says School Certificates. Appropriate certificates would be saved in each subfolder. The names for folders and files should be descriptive but not too long.

1. Decide on the file structure for your documents.

2. Create folders and subfolders on the school's network drive or flash drive on which you will save your files.

CTSOs

Communication Skills. Some competitive events judge communications skills. Students must be able to exchange information with the judges in a clear, concise manner. This requirement is in keeping with the mission of CTSOs: to prepare students for professional careers. Both written and oral communication skills will be judged. The evaluation will include all aspects of effective writing, speaking, and listening skills.

To prepare for the communication skills component of an event, complete the following activities.

1. Visit the organization's website and look for specific communication skills that will be judged as a part of a competitive event.

2. Spend time to review the essential principles of communication, such as grammar, spelling, proofreading, capitalization, and punctuation.

3. If you are making a written presentation, ask an instructor to evaluate your writing. Review and apply the feedback so that your writing sample appears professional and correct.

4. If you are making an oral presentation, ask an instructor to observe and listen for errors in grammar or sentence structure. After you have received comments, adjust and practice the presentation several times until you are comfortable with it.

5. Review the college and career readiness activities that appear at the end of each chapter of this text specific to reading, writing, listening, and speaking skills.

Unit

3

Writing Professional Communication

Professional Communication

Why It Matters

Understanding the writing process is necessary when creating professional documents such as correspondence, reports, technical documentation, and social media. There are standard writing techniques that should be followed in order to produce the desired result. By following these techniques, high-quality content can be created.

Readers of professional documents also expect to see information formatted and designed in an appropriate style that lends to readability and clarity of content. Documents that are poorly designed can send a message to the reader that the document was not given the attention that was required. It can also project an unprofessional image that can cause a writer to be dismissed from a job.

Chapters

While studying, look for the activity icon **for:**

- Pretests and posttests
- Vocabulary terms with e-flash cards and matching activities
- Videos
- Self-assessment

Video

Before you begin this unit, scan the QR code to view a video about professional communication. If you do not have a smartphone, visit www.g-wlearning.com.

Arek_malang/Shutterstock.com

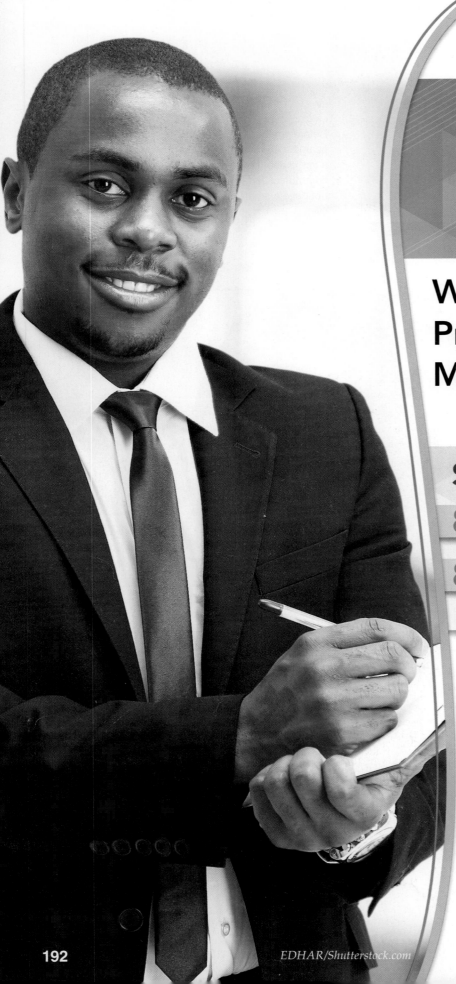

8

Writing Professional Messages

Sections

8.1 Messages That Inform or Instruct

8.2 Messages That Request or Persuade

College and Career Readiness

Reading Prep. As you read this chapter, stop at the Section Reviews and take time to answer the questions. Were you able to answer these questions without referring to the chapter content?

EDHAR/Shutterstock.com

Check Your Communication IQ ↪

Before you begin the chapter, see what you already know about communication by taking the chapter pretest. The pretest is available at www.g-wlearning.com.

Case Study

Courteous Request

Abby Cornish is in charge of the student activity program at a small college. This summer she will be hosting a group of international students who are studying English.

Abby wants to provide the students with cultural activities during their stay. She e-mails the local theater to request a group rate for 20 students, one in a wheelchair. She hopes to get tickets for a matinee on one of two Saturdays in August. To make this a fun learning experience, she inquires about a backstage tour as well. Abby drafted the following message to the theater manager.

I would like to arrange for a group of international students to attend a performance of *The Lion King*. Do you have a large block of seats available either Saturday, August 5 or 12? Also, do you offer a student or group discount? Do you offer backstage tours? We would like to stay after the performance and get a short informational tour if possible.

I need this information from you by June 15. Thank you very much.

Minerva Studio/Shutterstock.com

Critical Thinking

1. Identify the information missing from Abby's request.
2. Rewrite her message to improve the writing style and format.

Messages That Inform or Instruct

Objectives

After completing this section, you will be able to:

- **Explain** how to write an effective message that informs.
- **Summarize** the writing process for a message that instructs.

Key Terms

confirmation message
transmittal message

instructions
directions

Essential Question

How is the success of an informational message measured?

Messages That Inform

A common reason for writing messages is to provide information to customers, colleagues, or supervisors. Professional communication always informs the audience. Putting information in writing avoids miscommunication. It makes it more likely that you will get the result you want. Also, written documents provide a record that can be used later.

The direct approach works well when sending a positive message.

There are two general approaches to writing a message that informs: direct and indirect. Selecting which approach to use should be the first decision you make. This decision is based on whether the information will be received by the reader as positive, neutral, or negative.

Karramba Production/Shutterstock.com

Positive or Neutral Messages

When you write messages that contain positive or neutral information, a direct approach is usually the best choice. Use the following steps for a positive or neutral message.

1. **State your reason for writing.** Since the reader wants the information or will welcome positive news, a simple statement that introduces the topic is enough. If the subject line in an e-mail message can achieve this, you can go directly to the next step.

2. **Provide the information**. Using active voice, write simple, clear sentences that convey the information. Use formatting to clarify the content. You can divide the topic into paragraphs, use numbered or bulleted lists, or use headings.

3. **Close courteously**. The final paragraph of your message should be courteous and professional. If you want the reader to do something, make the request in direct, clear language.

Figure 8-1 shows how a direct, positive message flows smoothly and logically.

Negative Messages

An indirect approach uses the reverse of the positive-message organizational plan. Giving the explanation first buffers the negative part of the message. An indirect message can be organized using the following steps.

1. **Begin with an explanation**. Show that you understand the reader's point of view. Make statements that show empathy, and anticipate the reader's response by addressing possible objections or concerns up front.

2. **State the negative information in positive language**. Be honest, but choose words that are tactful and respectful. For example, instead of saying, "the museum does not offer a group discount to nonmembers," say, "our group discount policy applies only to members of the museum."

3. **Close courteously**. Be as positive as possible, but only offer hope for a different response in the future if it is realistic. Otherwise, be firm but not harsh. In the museum example, the closing might invite the reader to become a member and supply information on how to do so.

In Figure 8-2, the sender explains to the receiver that he is not the chosen speaker for a sales conference. This message uses the indirect approach because

As we discussed, I have reserved 12 more rooms for the sales meeting at the Marion Hotel in downtown Chicago. The reservation is for four nights, arriving September 9. All the accommodations will be on the fifth floor.

Please confirm the number of rooms with the hotel, and make any cancellations no later than August 31. I am forwarding the confirmation e-mail from the hotel with all the details.

Let me know if there is anything more I can do to help you. Have a great meeting.

Goodheart-Willcox Publisher

Figure 8-1   This is a positive informational message.

All the managers have expressed their interest in speaking at the opening ceremony of the annual sales meeting next month. It is nice to know everyone is willing to step forward, but unfortunately, the time is very limited.

I have weighed the pros and cons of having a speaker with your experience and ability to motivate, versus letting the reps hear from one of the newer managers on our team. Considering that you will be available to interact with the team all week, I have decided to put Tabitha on the program to represent the managers. Having recently worked for our biggest competitor, I believe the staff will benefit from what she can tell us about leveraging her past experience to achieve huge success on our team.

Mike, I am confident that your leadership will shine throughout the week at the breakout sessions. I know the reps are looking forward to working closely with you.

Goodheart-Willcox Publisher

Figure 8-2   This message between colleagues uses the indirect approach.

the sender knows the receiver will be disappointed with the news. She uses reasoning to bolster her decision. Sincere, courteous compliments are included to buffer the receiver's disappointment. However, to be too complimentary could be seen as patronizing. Also note the sender's tone is firm. Nothing she said would open the door to negotiations about the decision.

Routine Informational Messages

Writers frequently send informational messages that are routine in nature. As with other types of written communication, the formality of a routine message depends on the audience. However, a casual, friendly tone is usually appropriate. Common routine informational messages include confirmation messages and transmittal messages.

Confirmation Message

A **confirmation message** is a message written to confirm a verbal agreement made with a customer, client, or colleague. A manager writing to coworkers to confirm a meeting would write a short, informal e-mail message. In contrast, a message written to a customer to confirm a service agreement would be written more formally.

Confirmation messages are a guard against miscommunication. This is especially important when dealing with customers, because miscommunication can lead to anger and frustration. Confirming correct dates, times, and locations of events prevents mistakes that can hurt customer and coworker relationships. Following up on oral agreements or information given verbally provides a record for future reference and shows professionalism. Confirmation messages are also useful when you want to verify something you indirectly learned. Checking with a colleague or customer before acting on secondhand information shows common sense and respect.

The message in Figure 8-3 confirms a verbal agreement. The message is both detailed and congenial and follows the guidelines given in Figure 8-4.

As agreed in our telephone conversation yesterday, I have reserved exhibit space K for you at the national convention of the Association of Rare Book Dealers, which will be held in Austin, Texas, on the days of December 2–4.

The enclosed diagram shows the exhibit area layout. Your space is highlighted so you will know precisely where you are located in relation to the other exhibits. This is an excellent location—in the mainstream of convention traffic—and I am sure you will be happy with it.

Details concerning electrical outlets and other facilities in the exhibit area are described on the back of the exhibit-area layout. If you have any additional needs or questions, please do not hesitate to contact me. We will do everything possible to accommodate your needs.

The cost for the three days is $2,400. We will need payment for half that amount ($1,200) by November 15 to hold your space. The remainder is to be paid when you arrive at the convention.

I extend you a warm welcome to Austin and hope the convention will be a very successful occasion for you and your company.

Goodheart-Willcox Publisher

Figure 8-3   This is a formal confirmation message from a business to a client.

Guidelines for Writing a Confirmation Message

❑ Clearly and specifically state the circumstances to which you are referring.

❑ Provide complete and accurate information that reflects your best notes or memory.

❑ If any part of the agreement is unclear, ask questions rather than make assumptions.

❑ Ask the reader to confirm that the information is correct. If necessary, invite additional feedback to ensure that you and the reader have a mutual understanding and agreement.

Goodheart-Willcox Publisher

Figure 8-4   Follow these guidelines when writing a confirmation message.

Transmittal Messages

A **transmittal message** is routine communication accompanying documents or other materials attached to e-mails or sent by a delivery service. One of the main purposes of the message is to serve as a record of when something was sent. The message may also include information you would tell the reader if you were to deliver the materials by hand.

The level of formality of a transmittal message depends on the reader and the situation. Letters to customers or e-mails to colleagues are often informal messages adding little important information. On the other hand, a writer might include a formal transmittal message to introduce the report. Transmittals that accompany official business documents such as proposals, bids, contracts, or formal reports may have legal implications and, therefore, must be carefully worded.

The informally written transmittal message in Figure 8-5 identifies the transmitted documents and explains relevant information. This message is both brief and congenial, provides the needed information, and follows the guidelines in Figure 8-6.

Messages That Instruct

A message that instructs provides information to use an item or perform a task in an effective manner. This is accomplished by providing specific how-to instructions or directions for the reader. **Instructions** are steps that must be followed in sequence in order to accomplish a task. If the sequence is not followed, the reader may not be able to successfully complete the goal. Instructions should be presented in a numeric list format. **Directions** are steps to get from point A to point B. They are generally used to navigate to a geographical location. Directions may be presented in a bulleted list.

Attached are the photos I selected for our exciting fall brochure. It should be a winner!

You will find two photos labeled for page 7 of the brochure. Photo 7a is my preference; however, my concern is that the colors will appear too dark in the finished brochure. If this might be a problem, photo 7b would work well. It portrays a similar fashion, but in lighter colors.

Please let me know what you think. With your input and approval, we will begin layout and copy work on Monday, right on schedule.

Goodheart-Willcox Publisher

Figure 8-5   This is a transmittal message written from one colleague to another.

Guidelines for Writing a Transmittal Message

❑   Identify or describe what is being sent. Make the message brief unless you need to provide full details about what you are sending.

❑   State why the item is being sent if you think the recipient will be puzzled.

❑   Explain anything about the contents of the transmitted item that you think is important for the recipient to know.

Goodheart-Willcox Publisher

Figure 8-6   Follow these guidelines when writing a transmittal message.

When writing messages that instruct, use precise terms. Revise and edit to eliminate unnecessary words. Unclear instructions and directions cause frustration at the very least. In the worst case, they can cause things to go terribly wrong.

Compare these instructions for using a recording device.

Directions guide a person from point A to point B.

Unclear

The amber-colored button on the back panel activates the recording option when moved from left to right.

Clear

Slide the orange switch on the back from left to right to begin recording.

aslysun/Shutterstock.com

Notice that the second version starts with a verb. This construction is better because the sentence identifies the action for the reader. The revised instruction also uses clearer language. *Orange* is used instead of *amber*, *begin* instead of *activate*, and *back* instead of *back panel*. Take the time to revise and edit written instructions until sentences are short and clear.

Sometimes, it may seem easier to give verbal instructions rather than writing long explanations. However, conversations are not easy to remember. Often, notes jotted down in a hurry are unreadable or inaccurate. How many times have you heard someone say, "I cannot read my own writing"? With written instructions, the coworker can focus on each task as the need arises. The writer has taken responsibility for ensuring the reader is able to carry out the instructions with ease. The message shown in Figure 8-7 provides an example of clear directions written in a logical sequence.

 Green Lighting

Every building must be well-lit in order for people to live and work safely. Simple behavioral changes can make a big impact in the cost of lighting. Take advantage of the natural daylight that comes in through windows and skylights. Turn off lights when they will not be in use, such as when leaving a room. Dim lights when strong lighting is not needed, such as around computer monitors.

Lighting can also be modified to be more environmentally friendly. Remove or disconnect unnecessary light fixtures, as they draw power whether they are on or off. Replace or retrofit light fixtures that are not energy efficient. Install automatic sensors to turn lights on and off when people enter and exit rooms. Outdoor lighting can be fitted with timers or photocells to turn them on when it gets dark outside.

I appreciate you volunteering to help with Vicki's surprise party! Here's how I'd like you to pitch in:

1. Call Lindy's Deli (555-9284) this week and place the attached order; tell them I want to pick it up at 10 a.m. on June 5.
2. Check with Dave Lundeen in Promotions (ext. 284) to see if we can use the helium tanks to blow up about 50 balloons. Please let me know by Friday if he gives the okay; otherwise, I'll need to make different arrangements.
3. Make sure Vicki is kept busy in the back office on the morning of June 5. We'll be preparing the conference room for the party at that time, so we want to keep her busy!
4. Bring Vicki to the conference room at 11:45 under the guise of a staff meeting. The door will be shut and the lights will be off, but we'll be ready for you.

Thanks so much for the help—and by all means, keep your lips sealed.

Goodheart-Willcox Publisher

Figure 8-7   This message is an example of detailed instructions.

Section 8.1) Review

Check Your Understanding

1. What is the most common reason for writing a business message?
2. What tone should be used for routine informational messages?
3. Describe a confirmation message and its purpose.
4. What is the purpose of a transmittal message?
5. What goal does an instructional message aim to reach?

Build Your Vocabulary

As you progress through this course, develop a personal glossary of key terms. This will help you build your vocabulary and prepare you for a career. Write a definition for each of the following terms and add it to your personal glossary.

confirmation message   instructions
transmittal message   directions

Messages That Request or Persuade

Objectives

After completing this section, you will be able to:

- **Explain** the steps for writing a message that makes a request.
- **Discuss** the approach that should be used when responding to a request.
- **Describe** the steps for writing a message that attempts to persuade the reader.

Key Terms

request
routine request
special request
diplomacy
frequently asked question (FAQ)
courtesy response
persuade

persuasive message
AIDA
marketing
sales message
propaganda
press release
advertisement

Essential Question

Why is persuasion ethical?

Making Requests

A **request** asks the reader for some type of action or response. In the workplace, people regularly send and receive routine requests. **Routine requests** are expected by the receiver. Examples of routine requests include requests for materials, information, and services.

Other requests are not routine in nature. They are more complex and require explanation. These are considered special requests. **Special requests** require planning and an approach that will create a positive response.

For example, consider a request that requires extra work or to change the way something is normally done. This type of request will inconvenience the reader. You need to convince the reader to accept the special request. Choose the indirect approach, and start with an explanation of the reasons for making the special request. The words you use should show courtesy and diplomacy. **Diplomacy** is the tactful handling of a situation to avoid offending the reader or arousing hostility. Diplomacy goes beyond saying *please* and *thank you*.

Read the message in Figure 8-8. Notice how the writer is careful to explain the situation. He expresses willingness to pay for the services provided, if necessary. The writer also offers to share information with the reader as a courtesy.

I am the Office Manager for our company and have been given the task to research ways in which we can expand and modernize our laboratory. Our lab was organized many years ago when we were a very small company. Over the years, we have been fortunate to expand our business and greatly increase the number of staff we employ. Our engineers, chemists, scientists, and executives need a modern space with brand new technology at their fingertips.

I am inquiring to see if you have sample model layouts and recommendations for equipment and materials to create a new lab. We are very interested in reviewing any resources that you may have to share with us.

Also, I visited your website and noticed that you also have a virtual tour of labs you have helped create for other customers. If you could give me a password to log into the demo site, I would appreciate it.

If your department is not the correct contact for new lab purchases, I would appreciate it if you could direct me to the appropriate division of your company.

Thank you very much, Mr. Lipscomb. If we are successful in our lab redesign, we would be happy to serve as a reviewer of your services.

Goodheart-Willcox Publisher

Figure 8-8   This message is requesting a special favor.

Exploring Communication Careers

Commercial Designer

How a product looks is the result of the work of the commercial designer. Commercial designers develop the design for manufactured products such as toys, electronics, and cars. They use their artistic ability coupled with knowledge of how a product will be used by the consumer. The goal is to create the most appealing and functional product possible. Typical job titles for this visual arts position include *industrial designer, product designer,* and *product design engineer.*

Some examples of tasks that commercial designers perform include:

- Analyze research on product use, marketing, and materials to drive designs.

- Sketch designs for products.

- Work with engineering, marketing, production, and sales departments in developing products.

- Present designs to company executives.

- Modify designs based on market research.

Commercial designers need a minimum of a high school diploma and some college coursework. However, many jobs require a bachelor degree in commercial design or a related field. People skills are also required to successfully work with others to develop products and make product demonstrations.

Balance is the key to writing effective requests. Avoid including too much or too little information. Think about what the recipient needs to know and write accordingly. See the examples in Figure 8-9. The messages progress from too little information, to just the right amount of information, to too much information.

Be Clear, Specific, and Accurate

When you make a request, the most important thing is to put yourself in the reader's place. Analyze what you write to make sure the reader will not have to struggle to determine the request. Plainly state what you want and be as specific as possible. If there is more than one item or question, use bullets to list them.

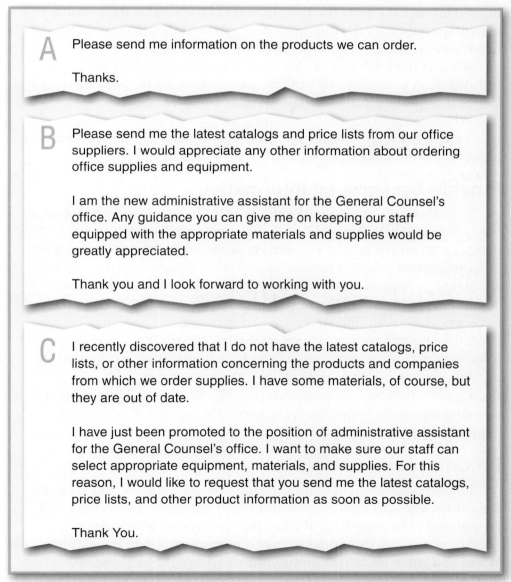

A   Please send me information on the products we can order.

Thanks.

B   Please send me the latest catalogs and price lists from our office suppliers. I would appreciate any other information about ordering office supplies and equipment.

I am the new administrative assistant for the General Counsel's office. Any guidance you can give me on keeping our staff equipped with the appropriate materials and supplies would be greatly appreciated.

Thank you and I look forward to working with you.

C   I recently discovered that I do not have the latest catalogs, price lists, or other information concerning the products and companies from which we order supplies. I have some materials, of course, but they are out of date.

I have just been promoted to the position of administrative assistant for the General Counsel's office. I want to make sure our staff can select appropriate equipment, materials, and supplies. For this reason, I would like to request that you send me the latest catalogs, price lists, and other product information as soon as possible.

Thank You.

Goodheart-Willcox Publisher

Figure 8-9   Message A contains too little information. Message B contains just the right amount of information. Message C contains too much information.

Business Protocol

Polite Language

When speaking to others at work, use respectful and polite language at all times. Use polite phrases such as "please," "thank you," and "you are welcome" whenever possible. Choose words that show respect to others. Never use profane words or phrases. To do so is inappropriate and unacceptable workplace behavior.

If you are requesting information, consider if the reader might be confused by your request. Is there a title, number, or other feature that will the reader help identify the information you need? Make sure to include all of the necessary information, and double-check to make sure it is accurate.

Provide Adequate Information for a Response

When making requests, think about what the reader will have to consider. Are there any decisions to be made? If so, include information to ensure you get what you want as opposed to what the reader gives you. For example, if someone is making dinner reservations for you, state your preferences, such as the restaurant and preferred time. Include the number of people in your party and consider other questions that might arise. Does the restaurant have more than one location in the area? Is the restaurant more important than the dining time? If you fail to think through the details in advance, you might not be happy with the results.

Also, let the reader know exactly when you need to have the request fulfilled. Plan your schedule to allow enough time for the reader to respond. If time is important, call or e-mail before sending the request.

When a request requires something be sent to you, include all information needed by the reader. Include your name, address, phone number, and e-mail address on any correspondence.

Provide Background Information

Sometimes background information must be provided for the reader. When you supply background information, the reader can be more helpful with regard to your request. He or she might be able to anticipate other needs that you may not realize you have. Always explain why you are making a request unless you are sure the reader knows the reason. You might receive a negative response or no response if the reader is not comfortable fulfilling your request. For example, a human resources department may have restrictions on sharing certain types of employee information. Explaining why you need such information is critical to the decision about whether or not to release the information.

Figure 8-10 shows a request that provides background information, allowing the reader to quickly and completely respond. Readers will appreciate this approach.

Be Courteous

Be courteous when making a request. The words *please* and *thank you* are always appropriate. It is more effective to ask rather than to demand. People tend to be more helpful when they are treated with respect.

Your courtesy should be sincere, but avoid going to the extreme. When you come on too strongly, your words might be perceived by the reader as insincere. "Words cannot express how grateful the entire department is for your contribution to this project" may sound insincere. It is better to say, "the entire department is grateful for your contribution to this project."

> Last March, we ordered several cases of 100 percent cotton rag stock from your paper division. We were very pleased with the quality of this paper and would like to place another order. Unfortunately, we have disposed of the boxes and cannot locate the exact stock number of the paper. Your catalog describes over ten varieties of cotton rag stock, and we are not certain which one we ordered.
>
> Can you help me by checking your records to find the exact product ordered by Print Co. in March of this year? We ordered the stock in both white and cream. I would appreciate a confirmation of the product numbers, paper weight, and price so that we might place a new order as soon as possible.
>
> Thank you for your help.

Goodheart-Willcox Publisher

Figure 8-10   This brief message is a request for information.

When you feel a simple thank-you will not suffice, it may be appropriate to offer to return a courtesy or favor. For example, if you are conducting a survey, offer to share the results. If you are assembling a proposal, let readers know their contributions will be acknowledged.

Be Reasonable

Make sure that your request is reasonable. It is improper to ask someone to do something that is unethical. It is also unfair to ask someone to do something outside of normal job functions or that requires an extreme sacrifice. You are more likely to get cooperation when the reader does not feel pressured or exploited.

When requesting something that creates work for the reader, find a way to make the task easier. Perhaps you need a speaker on short notice. Maybe you want the reader to complete a lengthy questionnaire. In these situations, you can use an indirect approach. Explain why you are making the request and acknowledge that it might be inconvenient. Balancing your request with courtesy and background information will help you get the response you need.

Responding to Requests

Like requests, responses to customers, colleagues, and supervisors deal with both routine and special matters. Some requests might require you to confer with others, such as when an exception to a policy is involved. Other requests might require you to retrieve information from sources inside or outside of the company. In some cases, you might need to organize information in a certain way to benefit the reader.

Goodwill is the advantage an individual or an organization has due to its good reputation; it cannot be bought. Every employee needs to build goodwill with colleagues, customers, and clients. Companies build goodwill through providing consistent, quality service. To build goodwill, consider how you would respond to a request from a supervisor or top executive. Apply the same amount of attention to all other requests. Every request is a prospect for a new or continued relationship. Ultimately, these relationships have an impact on your future success within an organization. Your attitude toward others and responding to their needs is an important aspect of building a successful career.

Form Response

Businesses that sell a product or service receive routine requests for information from customers. Company websites and social media pages anticipate these requests by providing extensive information. A company website may also have a **frequently asked questions (FAQ)** page that provides answers to common customer questions.

However, there are situations that require that a customer be contacted individually. Companies balance the need to provide quick, accessible answers to customers with the need to build goodwill with individual attention.

If a phone call to a customer is needed, a script can provide information for customer service to place the call. If a written request is needed, a form-type response can be used. Form-type responses have standard language to ensure consistency and help avoid problems or confusion about a product or service. The message can be customized when a special situation demands a specific response.

Some form-type responses are sent by e-mail. Others are printed on company stationery or postcards. Technology allows for customization of responses that go out to large numbers of customers. For example, instead of *Dear Customer*, each greeting or salutation addresses the customer by name. A good form letter or e-mail:

- uses language that expresses warmth and friendliness whether the message is positive or negative

- is addressed to each individual recipient by name

- communicates that the request is important and welcome

- tells the reader how to get additional information or assistance

The form response in Figure 8-11 was prepared as an automatic response to customers who write to a company about its environmental policies.

Companies also prepare marketing pieces that accompany answers to reoccurring questions. These pieces of communication may be sent to a customer with or without a transmittal message.

Thank you for writing to us about changes in our packaging to make it more environmentally friendly. We are always pleased to hear from customers concerning our contribution to a greener planet.

To show our appreciation for your feedback, we are sending you a brochure about our new line of organic bath products with samples for you to try. Look for these items in the mail within the next few days. Please be sure to let us know how you like them.

Again, thank you for your interest in our products. Please do not hesitate to write or call our 800 number below if we can assist you in any way with the use of our products.

Goodheart-Willcox Publisher

Figure 8-11   This is an example of a form response that a business might send to a customer.

Courtesy Response

The **courtesy response** is a message written to confirm that a message was received and action was taken. A common courtesy response is to thank a colleague for information or for fulfilling a request. Another is to tell someone you received a request and will need additional time to respond.

Courtesy responses to customers provide businesses with opportunities to build trust and are a gesture of goodwill. For example, businesses often send e-mails to customers who order online to confirm that the order was received. The message shown in Figure 8-12 is an example of this type of response.

This e-mail is to inform you that your BuyBooks account has been successfully created. Your account is immediately active and you may now submit online orders. Should you have any questions, do not hesitate to e-mail us at BuyBooks@e-mail.com. We also appreciate any feedback you have for us, so please feel free to send us comments to the same address.

Please take a moment to review our privacy policy at http://buybooks.e-mail.com.

We look forward to serving you!

Goodheart-Willcox Publisher

Figure 8-12   This is a courtesy response to inform a customer that an account has been activated.

Nonroutine Response

Many business situations require responses that do not fit a set pattern. These are classified as nonroutine responses. When responding to a nonroutine response:

- begin with a friendly or courteous statement
- open with a positive comment
- use the indirect approach if you cannot respond positively
- be complete and specific
- consider readability

Use language that is clear, concise, and specific. Completely answer each question or comment, even when responding to several. If possible, provide answers in the same order that the writer used.

Avoid long paragraphs and too many details. If the response is lengthy, look for ways to break up the text with lists or headings.

Build goodwill. When responding to a negative message, if possible, offer to do something extra as a gesture of friendliness.

Read the nonroutine response in Figure 8-13. Notice how the response meets the guidelines presented here.

Writing Messages to Persuade

Suppose you want to sell your manager on a great idea that will boost sales. Maybe you need to write a letter to a customer to persuade them to pay an overdue account. To **persuade** someone is to convince that person to take the course of action you propose. A **persuasive message** is a message to convince the reader to take a certain course of action. Each persuasive message has a specific purpose and desired outcome. Your purpose for writing is to convince readers of the value of your product, service, idea,

---

Thank you for your letter on May 23 requesting information on our shrink-wrap and multiple-packaging equipment.

The enclosed fact sheets list the technical data and the price information you requested. In addition to packaging equipment, our company also manufactures other products that would be beneficial to your operations, particularly your canned foods division. Fact sheets for those products are also enclosed.

I would be pleased to visit your location and make a formal presentation of our product line at a time that works for you. Please let me know when you wish to schedule a meeting.

Thank you for the opportunity to introduce our line of products to you. You may call me at 617-555-4400 if you have further questions or if you wish for additional information.

Goodheart-Willcox Publisher

Figure 8-13   This is a formal message to a customer in response to a request for information.

or suggestion. The goal, or outcome, is to convince the reader to do or take action on what you are requesting. You must demonstrate that you have a solution to a problem of which the reader may or may not be aware.

Persuasive messages generally follow a communication model called AIDA. **AIDA** is an acronym that stands for attention, interest, desire, and action. Figure 8-14 illustrates the AIDA model. When beginning to organize the content of your communication, these elements are essential to building a persuasive message.

- **Attract the reader's attention**. A persuasive message needs to catch the reader's interest in the opening paragraph. It is important to know your target audience and what will grab attention. Start the message with a strong introduction, and keep the information brief and to the point. The goal is to capture the reader's interest so that the message is read in its entirety.

- **Build the reader's interest**. Once you have the reader's attention, hold it with a writing style and tone that will build interest. Use language and a style that is easy to read and understand. The message will hold the reader's interest if you can give evidence that your suggestions will help the reader to achieve, have, or do something. Think about all of the possible objections and questions the reader might have.

- **Create desire for the product or service**. There are two basic appeals to build desire: appeal to emotions or appeal to reason. Appealing to emotions may be appropriate for requests such as donating to charity or volunteering for after-work events. An appeal to reason may be used to show the company leaders how going green will reduce expenses. The target audience will dictate which approach you use based on your prior experiences with the reader.

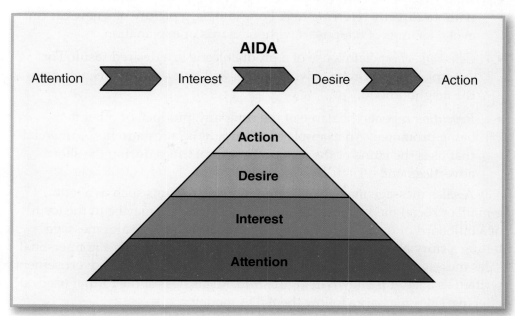

Goodheart-Willcox Publisher

Figure 8-14   Persuasive messages generally follow the AIDA model.

210   Chapter 8   Writing Professional Messages

- **Encourage the reader to take action.** If you want the reader to respond, you must ask them to do something. To encourage action, emphasize the positive points of your ideas, service, product, or company. If you do not ask the reader to take action, do not expect any action to be taken.

In the workplace, persuasive messages are used in marketing. **Marketing** consists of persuasive activities that identify, anticipate, and satisfy customer needs. Nearly every persuasive message sells something, even if it is only a point of view, idea, or goodwill. Our society sometimes looks at marketing as intrusive and deceptive. However, ethical companies that demonstrate social responsibility use marketing in a positive manner. By communicating about products and services that help individuals, information is shared that can improve the standard of living.

A **sales message** is used to persuade the reader to spend money for a product or service, either immediately or later. An effective sales message attracts attention while selling the features and benefits of the product or service. These messages are also known as **propaganda** as their purpose is to influence the audience with biased information. Propaganda typically uses emotion rather than logic to persuade the audience to take action. It has its own point of view and makes assumptions about the audience. Examples of *propaganda techniques* are as follows.

- *Bandwagon* encourages the audience to become part of a group or act because other people are acting in the same way, such as by supporting a cause or by buying a certain product. For example, "Every kid in America loves Crazy Shoes!"

- *Testimonial* is when a famous person or public figure recommends or promotes a product. One famous example is the basketball player Michael Jordan promoting Nike products.

- *Transfer* uses the emotion evoked by a symbol to encourage action without directly referring to it. For example, a picture of a new car can evoke feelings of happiness without words or explanation.

- *Cause and effect* claims use of a product leads to a desired result. For example, "SuperGreen Lawn Services will give you the greenest grass in the neighborhood."

- *Repetition* repeats the name of the company, product, or other item being promoted. An example of this might be a restaurant commercial that uses the name of the restaurant several times during the short advertisement.

A sales message may be delivered in many formats such as a letter, e-mail, or social media message. Some sales messages may be in the form of a billboard or on a hot air balloon. A **press release** is a sales message telling a story about and by a company. An **advertisement** is a nonpersonal sales message that is paid for by a sponsor. An example of an advertisement written as a letter is shown in Figure 8-15. Regardless of the format used, all effective sales messages follow the AIDA model.

Copyright Goodheart-Willcox Co., Inc.

**435 South Ironwood Drive
South Bend, Indiana 46675
219-555-5667 Fax 219-555-1234**

«Date»

«Name»
«Street»
«City, State, ZIP»

Dear «Name»:

Pancho Gonzales...Rod Laver...Fred Perry...Margaret Court...Billie Jean King...John Newcombe...Arthur Ashe...John McEnroe...Chris Evert...Pete Sampras...Venus Williams...

Attract attention. Those who receive Tennis Monthly will be familiar with these names, so reader attention is captured.

Build interest. The writer explains the reason for name dropping and gradually builds sufficient interest for the reader to want to learn more.

Pardon me for name dropping, but I have exciting news about these and other all-time tennis greats that I want to share with *Tennis Monthly* readers. You know, of course, that each of these players blazed the pro circuit in one era or another, leaving an indelible imprint on tennis history. But did you know that they were also prolific writers on the subject?

Tennis Monthly has arranged to issue a series of books of major writings of twenty of the greatest names in tennis. The first is Rod Laver on *Tennis*, followed by similar books by those whose names are instantly recognized by every tennis enthusiast.

I think you will find every volume in this series immensely exciting. Each will be profusely illustrated by America's leading tennis artist, Eklund Nillsen, and will be handsomely bound in a rich-looking leather-like cover. The price of each book will be only $29.95, including postage.

Use the enclosed card to order your copy of Rod Laver on *Tennis*. I will accept your personal check or credit card now or I can bill you later. As each volume is released, I will send you advance notice. I don't think you will want to miss a single one.

SPECIAL BONUS! If your order reaches me before May 15, I will include—absolutely free—a beautifully illustrated, 24-page booklet, *Back to Fundamentals*. It could make a big difference in your game!

Sincerely,

Chris Hemby
Editor

Enclosure

Encourage action. Sufficient desire has been created for the reader to ask, "How do I get this series?" This question is answered and a bonus is offered as an incentive to take action.

Create desire. The reader has to become interested enough to want to own the product.

Goodheart-Willcox Publisher

Figure 8-15 The four steps of AIDA are illustrated in this letter.

Attract the Reader's Attention

Ask a question that makes a strong point about the need for what you are selling, the unique feature of the product, or an opportunity that is too hot to pass up.

> Do you remember last winter when we had twelve inches of snow and the stores ran out of shovels?

Think of something that the reader needs or wants. Then, explain why your product or service will meet those needs or wants. Use a provocative statement to get the reader's attention.

> You, too, can be a millionaire!

Make a special offer or the opportunity to get a free sample.

> Discover a new and better way to stay healthy by having fresh fruit delivered directly to your door each month. Without any cost to you, we will send you a sample of our citrus fruits if you sign up for our newsletter on our website.

Build the Reader's Interest

An effective sales message has a positive reader-oriented tone that captures the attention of the recipient. A positive tone stresses the favorable and plays down the unfavorable.

> **Unfavorable**
>
> It takes up to a month to receive the product from the factory. We appreciate your patience.
>
> **Favorable**
>
> Once you place your order, you will receive the product directly from the factory in about 30 days.

A good sales message only promises what the company can deliver. It does not rely on exaggeration to make a sale. You are more likely to win the respect and allegiance of readers if you make reasonable, sound offers of products or services.

> **Exaggerated**
>
> We will never, ever miss your call because our operators are standing by at all times.
>
> **Balanced**
>
> We do our best to keep our customer service operators available to you 24 hours a day, seven days a week.

Convey that you value your own dignity as well as that of the reader. Talking down, lecturing, or accusing can ruin any attempts at persuasion.

> **Talking down**
>
> Although we are very large and successful, Conover-Crane makes no distinction between small businesses like yours and giant corporations.
>
> **Building up**
>
> Family-run businesses like yours are important to Conover-Crane.

Create Desire for the Product or Service

To create desire, you can appeal to emotions or reason. The approach will depend on the situation, your knowledge of the reader, and your experience regarding what works best.

Appeal to emotions

You will sleep better, feel better, and look better after you spend a night on a Support Rest mattress.

Appeal to reason

Because of its superior construction, the Support Rest mattress conforms to your body so you sleep in optimum physical comfort that promotes energy and vigor throughout the day.

Anticipate Questions and Objections

Anticipate questions and objections the reader may have. Then, provide information to answer those questions or overcome those objections. Readers may have questions regarding prices, or how long a special offer will be valid. Objections may be related to evidence backing up statements and claims, or lack of an included sample.

Encourage the Reader to Take Action

All good sales messages close with a call to action. Remember to do these three things in your messages to increase reader response:

- make a specific request or call for action
- make it easy for the reader to respond

Make it easy for the reader to understand the request.

Lisa F. Young/Shutterstock.com

- motivate the reader to respond promptly by giving some reason or incentive

Make a specific request or call for action

Please call our toll-free number today to receive your free copy of *The Complete Gourmet* cookbook.

Make it easy for the reader to respond

Just complete the attached order form and receive free shipping within the next 14 days. Or, call 1 (877) 555–2442 or visit our website to order.

Provide a reason or incentive to respond

The first 500 callers will receive an original lithograph from the esteemed artist Jorgen Hansford.

Section 8.2   Review

 Check Your Understanding

1. Name five things a person should do when making a request.
2. Name three types of response messages that are used in the workplace.
3. Explain the importance of goodwill.
4. What is the goal of a persuasive message?
5. Describe the AIDA model.

 Build Your Vocabulary

As you progress through this course, develop a personal glossary of key terms. This will help you build your vocabulary and prepare you for a career. Write a definition for each of the following terms and add it to your personal glossary.

request
routine request
special request
diplomacy
frequently asked question (FAQ)
courtesy response
persuade

persuasive message
AIDA
marketing
sales message
propaganda
press release
advertisement

Chapter Summary

Section 8.1 Messages That Inform or Instruct

- The most common reason for writing business messages is to inform. Positive and neutral messages that inform should be straightforward and direct. Negative messages should buffer the news by using the indirect approach. Examples of routine informational messages are confirmation and transmittal messages.

- A message that instructs is one that provides information to use an item or perform a task in an effective manner. Instructions are steps that must be followed in sequence in order to accomplish a task. Directions are steps to get from point A to point B.

Section 8.2 Messages That Request or Persuade

- A request asks the reader for a type of action or response. Requests may be routine which are expected by the reader. Other requests are not routine and require explanation. These are considered special requests.

- Responses to a request may be a form response, a courtesy response, or a nonroutine response. Each requires consideration and care.

- Writing persuasive messages requires convincing the reader to take action such as a sales message for example. Persuasive messages should use the AIDA model that attracts the reader's attention, builds the reader's interest, creates desire for the product or service, and induces the reader to take action.

Online Activities

Complete the following activities which will help you learn, practice, and expand your knowledge and skills.

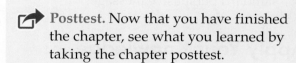 **Posttest.** Now that you have finished the chapter, see what you learned by taking the chapter posttest.

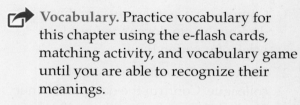 **Vocabulary.** Practice vocabulary for this chapter using the e-flash cards, matching activity, and vocabulary game until you are able to recognize their meanings.

English/Language Arts. Visit www.g-wlearning.com to download each data file for this chapter. Follow the instructions to complete an English/ language arts activity to practice what you have learned in this chapter.

Activity File 8-1: Improving Your Editing Skills

Activity File 8-2: Improving Your Reading Skills

Review Your Knowledge

1. List and describe three steps of an organizational plan for writing negative messages.

2. List and describe three steps of an organizational plan for writing a positive or neutral message.

3. Name two common routine informational messages.

4. Why is sequence important when writing directions?

5. Explain the difference between instructions and directions.

6. How does a routine request differ from a special request?

7. Explain the role of a form-type response.

8. Summarize how to approach the writing of a nonroutine response.

9. How can the reader's interest be built in a persuasive message?

10. How does a sales message differ from a standard persuasive message?

Apply Your Knowledge

1. Compose a negative message that declines an employee's request for a week of vacation time.

2. Write a confirmation message to a colleague. Confirm the dates and venue for the sales conference that will take place next month.

3. Compose a transmittal message that will accompany a product purchased by a customer.

4. Write a message that requests all members of your team to attend a company meeting on Friday. Use a positive or neutral tone.

5. Create a set of instructions for completing a time sheet for employees in your company. After you finish the draft, write an e-mail that includes the information.

6. Write a message requesting customers to volunteer to complete a survey. This information will be placed on the company's Facebook page.

7. Write a sales message promoting a service you could provide for a fee. Consider your hobbies, interests, and talents. For example, if you like to take pictures or give parties, you could sell yourself as a photographer or event planner. Use the AIDA model to write your message. Incorporate the assumptions about the audience, the purpose of your message, and the solution you can provide for the customer. After you write a draft of the message, select the type of sales message you will use. You may choose a letter, advertisement, or another type of propaganda.

8. There are many types of propaganda used in marketing and advertising. Bandwagon and testimonial are examples. Name other propaganda techniques with which you are familiar. What assumptions about the audience do these techniques assume?

9. Advertisements are messages that attempt to persuade. Select an advertisement from a newspaper or magazine. Which propaganda technique was used? Identify the purpose of the message. What assumptions did the writer make about the audience? Were solutions offered to the audience so that the desired outcome was clear?

Communication Skills

College and Career Readiness

Speaking. There will be many instances when you will be required to persuade the listener. When you persuade, you convince a person to take a proposed course of action. Prepare for a conversation with your principal about the importance of having snow days in the winter. Request the principal's assistance in rewriting the snow day policy for your school. Plan and deliver a focused presentation that argues your case and shows solid reasoning.

Listening. Active listening is fully participating as you process what others are saying. Practice active listening skills while listening to a news report on the radio, the television, or a podcast. Select a single story and prepare a report in which you analyze the following aspects of the business story: the speaker's audience, point of view, reasoning, stance, word choice, tone, points of emphasis, and organization.

Writing. You may have been taught to treat others how you would like to be treated. This is often referred to as the "golden rule." Productively working with others who have a background different from yours may require that you learn to treat others as they wish to be treated. Conduct research about cultural differences related to personal space, time, gestures, and body language. List four differences and how you would approach each.

Internet Research

Federal Trade Commission. Advertising is regulated by the Federal Trade Commission (FTC). Research the website of the FTC to find information about advertising laws. Write several paragraphs to describe your findings.

Teamwork

Bring several advertisements or sales brochures to class. Find examples to show how each meets the AIDA model and discuss them with your team. Next, write an advertisement for a product of your choice using the advertisements as an example. Adapt the language you use to the purpose and intent of your advertisement.

Portfolio Development

College and Career Readiness

Certificates. Exhibiting certificates you have received in your portfolio reflects your accomplishments. For example, a certificate might show that you have completed a training class. Another one might show that you can key at a certain speed. Include any certificates that show tasks completed or your skills or talents. Remember that this is an ongoing project.

Plan to update when you have new certificates to add.

1. Scan the certificates that will be in your portfolio.
2. Give each document an appropriate name and save in a folder or subfolder.
3. Place the hard copy certificates in a container for future reference.
4. Record these documents on your master spreadsheet that you started earlier to record hardcopy items. You may list each document alphabetically, by category, date, or other convention that helps you keep track of each document that you are including.

CTSOs

Business Communication. The *Business Communication* competitive event may consist of an objective test that covers multiple topics. Participants are usually allowed one hour to complete the event. One of the topics that will be included in the event is written communication concepts. Effective communicators work to perfect the mechanics of written communication. By participating in the business communication event, you will have an opportunity to showcase your written communication skills.

To prepare for the objective business communication test, complete the following activities.

1. Study the vocabulary words at the beginning of each chapter in this book. Make sure you understand each definition.
2. Study the grammar concepts presented in this text.
3. Review the chapter summary for each chapter in this unit.

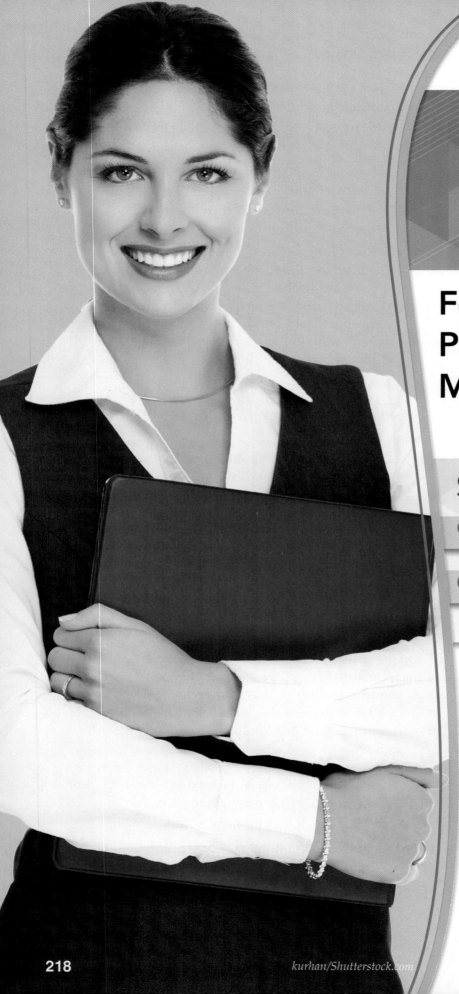

9

Formatting Professional Messages

Sections

9.1 Formatting Letters

9.2 Formatting Memos and E-mails

College and Career Readiness

Reading Prep. Scan this chapter and look for information presented as fact. As you read this chapter, try to determine which topics are fact and which are the author's opinion. After reading the chapter, research the topics and verify which are facts and which are opinions.

kurhan/Shutterstock.com

Check Your Communication IQ 📤

Before you begin the chapter, see what you already know about communication by taking the chapter pretest. The pretest is available at www.g-wlearning.com.

Case Study

Timely Response

Mike Flores is the manager of Greenway West, a resort in Tampa, Florida. He regularly corresponds with clients who plan to visit Greenway West for both business and pleasure.

In September, Cassie Bingham inquired about holding a meeting at the resort in December. Mike received her phone call and mailed an information packet to her the next day. However, by October, Cassie had not responded. As of October 16, the December dates he had discussed with Cassie were still open. Mike decided to write to her to encourage her to make a decision.

Alexander Lukatskiy/Shutterstock.com

When you called in September about accommodations for your December 3–7 meeting, I tentatively reserved a block of meeting and residence rooms for your group. I wanted to make certain I had rooms for you in case you decided to choose Greenway West for your conference. If you are still thinking about hosting your conference here (and I certainly hope you are), I will need to hear from you by October 25. This is the latest date on which I can guarantee accommodations for the dates you requested.

Since we last spoke, the resort has completed work on a solarium with an indoor pool. I've enclosed a colorful brochure to let you see for yourself. I hope yours is one of the first groups to use these new facilities!

Critical Thinking

1. Should Mike send this message as a letter, memo, or e-mail? Why?

2. Format this message to create a final document. Use your choice of letter, e-mail, or memo.

Formatting Letters

Objectives

After completing this section, you will be able to:

- **Discuss** the importance of formatting basics for business letters.
- **Identify** standard formatting elements and styles appropriate for business letters.
- **Explain** how to address an envelope.

Key Terms

format
white space
typeface
font
block-style letter
modified-block-style letter
inside address
salutation

mixed punctuation
open punctuation
complimentary close
signature block
reference initials
enclosure notation
copy notation
postscript

Essential Question

How does the format of a document help you infer its purpose?

Formatting Basics

In business, document types are characterized not only by different purposes, but also by different formats. By using the appropriate format, the reader can immediately tell what type of document is being received.

Readers expect professional documents to appear a certain way. **Format** is how written information is presented on a printed page or screen. Another term for format is *layout*. *Standard formatting* is a generally accepted way to format a document so its appearance follows a convention. Writers use standard formatting so their business documents are consistent in appearance with what the reader expects.

The appearance of a document is the first impression your writing makes on the reader. That first glance at the message should be an open invitation to the receiver. The arrangement of text and graphics in relation to the white space on the page determines the visual appeal to the reader. **White space** includes margins, space between paragraphs, and any other blank space on the page. Without properly formatted elements, the reader can easily become lost or distracted. If the message lacks visual appeal, it may be discarded even before it is read.

Readability is a measure of how easy it is for the reader to understand your writing and locate information within a document. Readability is achieved through a combination of clear writing and effective formatting. Together, these elements help obtain the response you need from the reader.

Writing is most readable when it is presented in small segments with adequate white space. Information presented in long paragraphs is uncomfortable and physically tiring to read, since the reader's eyes are given few breaks. Use the following techniques to enhance readability.

- Introduce the message with a short paragraph.
- Use standard fonts and sizes.
- Use parallel structure.
- Use organizational symbols, such as bulleted and numbered lists.

A well-formatted document appears open and inviting.

Introductory Paragraph

No one likes to sort through a long paragraph right at the beginning of a document. A short paragraph should be written for the message that concisely introduces the main idea. This paragraph should prepare the reader for the information to follow.

Standard Fonts and Sizes

Typeface is the definition of the characteristics that make up a set of letters, numbers, and symbols. The typography helps to create the tone of the document. The **font** is the typeface, size, and style of characters. Standard font types and font sizes vary by organization or business. Often, the default font of the word processing application used by a business determines the standard.

The default font for body text in Microsoft Word 2013 is 11-point Calibri. Many organizations have adopted this as the standard. However, the traditional standard is 12-point Times Roman or Times New Roman. Always follow the standard set by your instructor or organization.

For e-mails, it is often accepted to use the default font in e-mail software. Many e-mail–reader applications strip out all formatting. This leaves the reader with plain text, so any applied formatting is lost.

Parallel Structure

Recall that *parallel structure* is a method of writing in which similar elements are expressed in a consistent way or presented in the same pattern. When formatting a document, parallel structure occurs when similar sections or elements contain similar patterns of words to show they are of equal importance. It is easily created when words or sentences are used in writing in similar ways. Elements that form a pattern should be worded in a consistent manner. For example, you can begin each item in a list with an action verb, or *ing* word.

> During the meeting, three topics will be covered:
> - *redesigning* the company website
> - *distributing* new marketing materials
> - *implementing* sales strategies

Parallel structure can happen at the word, sentence, paragraph, or section level. It will help the reader quickly and easily understand how the document is organized.

Organizational Symbols

Important information or related items should be highlighted by using bulleted lists, numbered lists, asterisks, underlining, or boldface type to help organize a message. Numbered lists should be used only when the order of the items is important, such as directions. If the order of the items is not important, use a bulleted list.

Always treat lists consistently throughout a document. For example, do not use round bullets in one list and square bullets in the next.

Standard Letter Format

Letters are messages printed on stationery and should conform to workplace standards. Stationery used for business purposes is often letterhead stationery. A *letterhead* includes information about an organization, such as its name, address, contact information, and a logo. Letterhead is preprinted on high-quality paper so organizations do not have to key this information on every correspondence.

Businesses generally use one of two standardized letter formats: block or modified block. The **block-style letter**, as shown in Figure 9-1, is formatted so all lines are flush with the left margin. No indentions are used. Appropriate guidelines for spacing between the date, inside address, greeting, letter body, and signature block need to be followed.

The **modified-block-style letter** places the date, complimentary close, and signature to the right of the center point of the letter. All other elements of the letter are flush with the left margin. Figure 9-2 shows a letter formatted in the modified-block style. The decision to indent the paragraphs needs to be considered, depending on the guidelines of the workplace.

 Green   Paper Consumption

Our "paperless society" still creates many reasons to print material rather than to save our information digitally. According to the EPA, the average office worker in the United States will use approximately 10,000 sheets of paper in a year. Consider how much paper, ink, toner, and electricity is needed to print those pages. Businesses can reduce the consumption of paper and other materials by adopting a few simple practices.

Instead of accepting a printed telephone directory, the Internet can be used to locate phone numbers and addresses of people and businesses. Rather than receive paper statements from banks and other financial institutions, request online statements. Most utility and credit card companies have online billing options and may provide special rates for businesses that participate. Many publications also have online subscription services. All of these online resources decrease the amount of paper that is printed and mailed, reducing the consumption of not only paper and ink, but also of fuel needed to physically transport them.

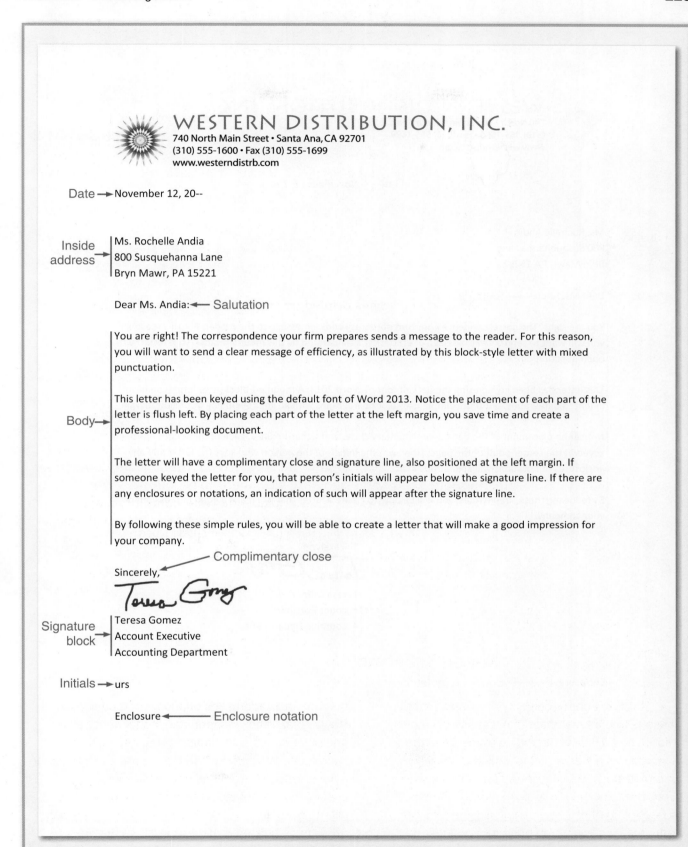

WESTERN DISTRIBUTION, INC.
740 North Main Street • Santa Ana, CA 92701
(310) 555-1600 • Fax (310) 555-1699
www.westerndistrb.com

Date ➞ November 12, 20--

Inside address ➞ Ms. Rochelle Andia
800 Susquehanna Lane
Bryn Mawr, PA 15221

Dear Ms. Andia: ◀— Salutation

You are right! The correspondence your firm prepares sends a message to the reader. For this reason, you will want to send a clear message of efficiency, as illustrated by this block-style letter with mixed punctuation.

This letter has been keyed using the default font of Word 2013. Notice the placement of each part of the letter is flush left. By placing each part of the letter at the left margin, you save time and create a professional-looking document.

Body ➞

The letter will have a complimentary close and signature line, also positioned at the left margin. If someone keyed the letter for you, that person's initials will appear below the signature line. If there are any enclosures or notations, an indication of such will appear after the signature line.

By following these simple rules, you will be able to create a letter that will make a good impression for your company.

Complimentary close

Sincerely,

Teresa Gomez

Signature block ➞ Teresa Gomez
Account Executive
Accounting Department

Initials ➞ urs

Enclosure ◀———— Enclosure notation

Goodheart-Willcox Publisher

Figure 9-1   This letter is formatted in block style with mixed punctuation.

Date ➔ November 12, 20--

Inside
address ➔ Ms. Rochelle Andia
800 Susquehanna Lane
Bryn Mawr, PA 15221

Dear Ms. Andia: ◄— Salutation

You are right! The correspondence your firm prepares sends a message to the reader. For this reason, you will want to send a clear message of efficiency, as illustrated by this modified-block-style letter with open punctuation.

Body ➔ This letter has been keyed using the default font of Word 2013. A modified-block-style letter can have indented paragraphs, but this example uses block paragraphs with all lines beginning at the left margin.

Notice the placement of the date, complimentary close, and signature lines. Each of these lines has been keyed at the center point of the page. However, the initials of the person who keys the letter and any enclosures or notations will appear flush left.

By following these simple rules, you will be able to create a letter that will make a good impression for your company.

Complimentary close
Sincerely, ◄

Teresa Gomez

Signature ➔ Teresa Gomez
block   Account Executive
Accounting Department

Initials ➔ urs

Enclosure ◄—— Enclosure notation

Goodheart-Willcox Publisher

Figure 9-2 This is the same letter shown in Figure 9-1 but formatted in modified-block style. It also uses open punctuation.

Standard Letter Elements

Block-style and modified-block-style letters have the same line spacing and top, bottom, and side margins. Both also contain the same standard letter elements:

- date
- inside address
- salutation
- body
- complimentary close
- signature
- notations

Date

The date consists of the month, day, and year. The month is spelled in full. The day is written in figures and followed by a comma. The year is written in full and consists of numbers. For example:

December 18, 20--

Inside Address

The **inside address** is the name, title, and address of the recipient. The two examples that follow show how to format an inside address.

Mr. Angelo Costanzo, Manager
Griffin Plumbing Supply Co.
1987 Susquehanna Avenue
Wilkes-Barre, PA 18701

Ms. Denise Rodriquez
President & CEO
Urban Development Council
150 Grosvenor Avenue
Washington, DC 30005

For addresses in the United States, the last line must state the city, state, and zip code. Note that the state abbreviation is always two letters and in all capitals.

Salutation

The **salutation** is the greeting in a letter and always begins with *Dear*. This is followed by the recipient's first name or, according to your relationship, title and last name.

There are two types of punctuation used in letters. **Mixed punctuation** is a style in which a colon is placed after the salutation and a comma after the complimentary close. **Open punctuation** is a style in which there is no punctuation after the salutation or complimentary close.

Mixed Punctuation	**Open Punctuation**
Dear Perry:	Dear Perry
Dear Mr. Fisher:	Dear Mr. Fisher
Dear Katherine:	Dear Katherine
Dear Dr. Randall:	Dear Dr. Randall

Always address a letter to a specific person, unless it is being intentionally directed to an organization. It may take a phone call or Internet search to get the correct name, but it is worth the effort to personalize business messages. Also, make sure the receiver's name is correctly spelled and the appropriate title use, such as *Dr.*, *Mr.*, or *Ms.* The title *Mrs.* is rarely used in business writing. Spell out and capitalize titles such as *Professor* and *Reverend.* If you are unsure of a person's gender, use the full name:

> Dear Pat Cashin:
>
> Dear Ryan Gulati:

If you need to write a letter without the name of a specific person, do not use traditional greetings, such as *Dear Sir* or *Gentlemen.* You may use *Ladies and Gentlemen*; however, the best course is to use words that describe the role of the person:

> Dear Customer:
>
> Dear Circulation Manager:
>
> Dear Editor:

Body

The *body* of the letter is the message. Format the body according to the block or modified-block style. Most businesses use the block style. Single-spaced letters are standard; however, some businesses prefer the default setting of the word processing software used. In Microsoft Word 2013, the default line spacing is 1.08.

When addressing a letter, take time to think about the person to whom the letter is going so that you can use his or her proper name and title.

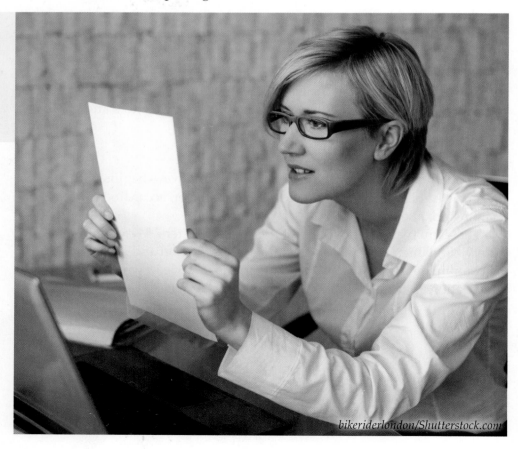

bikeriderlondon/Shutterstock.com

Complimentary Close

The **complimentary close** is the sign-off for the letter. Only the first word is capitalized. Mixed or open punctuation is used in the complimentary close, but be consistent with the style used in the salutation. The complimentary close follows the body of the letter and is appropriately spaced, as shown in Figure 9-1 and Figure 9-2. The most commonly used closings are:

Accountability

Businesses and employees are expected to display accountability, which is the act of being responsible for activities and behavior. An innocent error is not considered unethical behavior; however, not taking responsibility for the error is unethical.

Mixed Punctuation	Open Punctuation
Sincerely,	Sincerely
Sincerely yours,	Sincerely yours
Cordially,	Cordially
Cordially yours,	Cordially yours

Signature Block

The writer's name and title are called the **signature block** or *signature*. The writer's job title and department appear beneath the name, unless a letterhead is used that contains this information. Begin the signature block below the complimentary close. The blank lines of space are used for the handwritten signature.

Sincerely,

Margaret Shaw
Coordinator
Business Development

When the message is from the company rather than an individual, the company name may appear in all-capital letters below the complimentary close. In this situation, there is no signature.

Sincerely,

JIMENEZ-BRADFORD REALTY

Notations

Letters may include reference initials. **Reference initials** indicate the person who keyed the letter. If the writer keyed the letter, initials are not included. Reference initials are lowercase letters.

Cordially yours,

Margaret Shaw
Senior Vice President

smb

An **enclosure notation** alerts the reader to materials that are included in the mailing along with the letter. Spell out and capitalize the word *Enclosure*. If there is more than one enclosure, indicate the number of items included or list them. The word *Attachment* may be used instead of the word *Enclosure*.

Enclosures

Enclosures: 3

Enclosures: Statement
              Check
              Letter

A **copy notation** is needed when others are being sent a copy of the letter. The notation appears below the signature, as shown in Figure 9-1 and Figure 9-2. If there are enclosure notations or reference initials, the copy notation appears below these. Use *c* for copy or *cc* for carbon copy or courtesy copy. The copy notation is followed by a colon and a list of the full names of individuals receiving copies.

cc: Tina Ricco
      Gary Kowalski

Additional Letter Elements

There are three additional letter elements that are sometimes used in business letters: attention line, subject line, and postscript.

Attention Line

There is a wealth of resources available to the writer such as the Internet and company databases that make it largely unnecessary to address correspondence without an individual's name. However, if this circumstance does occur, substituting a position or department title for a specific name is

If an individual's name and title are not readily available when writing a letter, conduct research to find the necessary information.

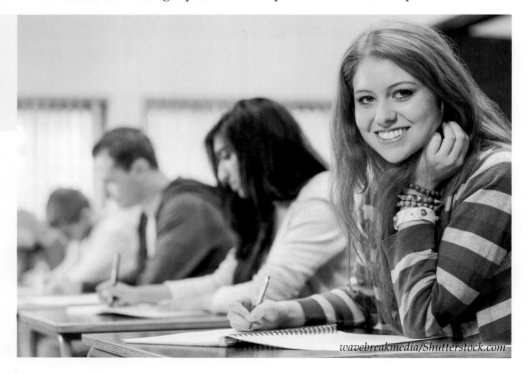

wavebreakmedia/Shutterstock.com

a good solution. For example, you may know the marketing manager is to receive the letter, but cannot find the name of the person. In this situation, it is appropriate to include an attention line that says *Attention Marketing Manager*. This line is positioned as part of the inside address:

> Attention Marketing Manager
>
> Urban Development Council
> 150 Grosvenor Avenue
> Washington, DC 30005

Subject Line

A subject line in a letter is used like a subject line in an e-mail. It helps the reader know the content of the message before reading. The subject line may be in all caps or initial caps and the word *subject* is optional. The subject line appears after the salutation and before the body of the letter.

> Dear Mr. Ramito:
>
> SUBJECT: MINUTES OF SUMMER MEETING
>
> Thank you for attending the summer meeting of the *Green Entrepreneur* that was held last month in Orlando. We appreciate your attendance and your contribution to this meeting…

Postscript

Postscript means *after writing* and is information included after the signature. In business letters, the postscript is no longer used to represent an afterthought. For example, in the past a writer may have included an omission as a postscript, such as:

> P.S. I forgot to tell you we're moving. After June 1, you can reach us at our new address.

With word processing software, the need for postscripts disappeared. If you discover that something important was omitted from the body of a letter, simply edit the letter and include it.

Occasionally, however, a writer uses a postscript to emphasize or personalize a point. Sales letters often use postscripts for special effect.

> P.S. Remember, our sale ends this Thursday. Don't miss the wonderful savings in store for you!

Use postscripts sparingly. Frequent use of postscripts may suggest to the reader that you did not plan your message.

Envelopes

If you are physically mailing a letter, it is necessary to address an envelope. Most businesses generally use a standard size 10 envelope, which is 4 1/8″ by 9 1/2″. The US Postal Service recommends the address be in all capital letters with no punctuation, as shown in Figure 9-3.

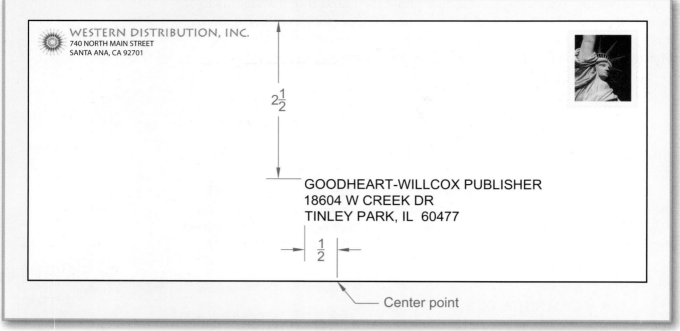

Goodheart-Willcox Publisher

Figure 9-3   This envelope is properly formatted.

To properly fold and insert the letter into the envelope, fold the bottom third up, then the top third down. Place the folded letter in the envelope so the dateline is facing up toward the flap of the envelope. The last fold will be at the bottom of the envelope.

Section 9.1 | Summary

 Check Your Understanding

1. Define *standard formatting* and explain why it is used.
2. What techniques can be used to enhance readability?
3. Explain the difference between block-style and modified block-style.
4. List the seven standard elements of a letter.
5. Explain how to prepare an envelope.

 Build Your Vocabulary

As you progress through this course, develop a personal glossary of key terms. This will help you build your vocabulary and prepare you for a career. Write a definition for each of the following terms and add it to your personal glossary.

format	mixed punctuation
white space	open punctuation
typeface	complimentary close
font	signature block
block-style letter	reference initials
modified-block-style letter	enclosure notation
inside address	copy notation
salutation	postscript

Formatting Memos and E-mails

Objectives

After completing this section, you will be able to:

- **Identify** standard formatting elements and styles appropriate for memos.
- **Identify** standard formatting elements and styles appropriate for business e-mail.
- **Explain** common productivity tools available in most e-mail software.

Key Terms 📩

memo
template
guide word

notation
blind copy

Essential Question

What do the formatting similarities of memos and e-mails tell you about professional communication?

Formatting Memos

Memorandums, more commonly called **memos**, are hardcopies used for intra-office communication. Memos are similar to e-mails in purpose and design, but they are more effective when the writer wants a printed communication or assumes the reader will want a hardcopy for his or her records. Executives and departments that issue policies and other formal messages often use memos attached to e-mails as a means of communicating with employees.

Memo Parts

Memos are usually created and printed on forms with the company name and logo at the top. You may also create memos using **templates**, which are predesigned forms supplied in word processing software.

The word *memorandum* or *memo* appears in large letters at the top, followed by the guide words. The **guide words** are the words *to, from, date*, and *subject* that appear at the top of the memo, as shown in Figure 9-4. These words often appear in all caps.

To Line

The name of the recipient(s) appears in the TO: line. Omit courtesy titles such as Mr. or Ms. Names may be in list format or on a single line separated with commas.

TO:	Tyler A. Dembowsky
	Edward Josi
	Jeannette Loria
TO:	Tyler A. Dembowsky, Edward Josi, Jeannette Loria

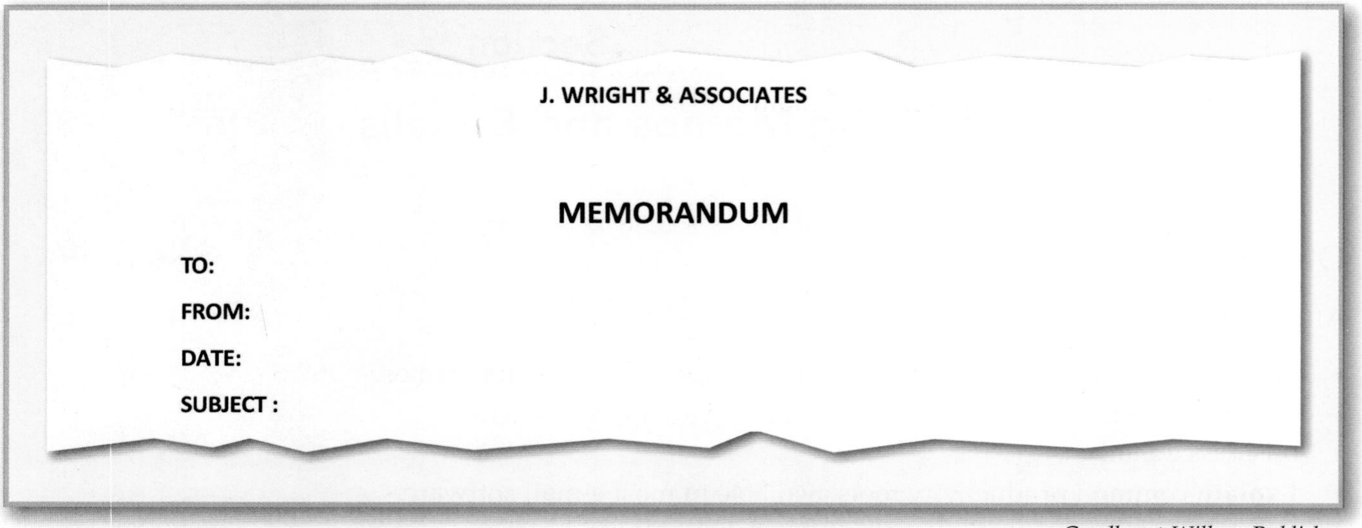

J. WRIGHT & ASSOCIATES

MEMORANDUM

TO:

FROM:

DATE:

SUBJECT :

Goodheart-Willcox Publisher

Figure 9-4   A preprinted memo form may contain this information.

If the list of recipients is very long, you may choose to key the word *Distribution* in the TO: line and list the names at the bottom. The names should be in alphabetical order or in order of position (from highest to lowest) in the company or department.

> Distribution:
>
> Tyler A. Dembowsky
> Edward Josi
> Jeannette Loria
> Ann Peabody
> David Horowitz

If a memo is being sent to a group of employees, use the name of the group instead of listing all the individual names.

> TO: Customer Care Associates

From Line

In the FROM: line, fill in your full name or the name of the person for whom you are keying the memo. It is optional for the sender to initial the typed name before the memo is sent.

> FROM: Jose Ortez

The writer may choose to include his or her job title:

> FROM: Jose Ortez, Marketing Director

Date Line

The DATE: line contains the date that the memo is being sent. Spell out the name of the month. Include the full year in numbers.

> DATE: August 1, 20--

Subject Line

In the SUBJECT: line, indicate the subject in language that clearly states the topic. Be concise. Also, capitalize the main words in the subject line.

| SUBJECT: Merit Increases

Body

When keying a memo, begin the message below the subject line, as shown in Figure 9-5. The paragraphs are positioned flush left. Key the message in a single-spaced format with a double space between paragraphs. As in letters, the business may prefer to use line spacing of 1.08, which is the default of Word 2013.

Special Notations

Notations at the bottom of the memo are used to indicate specific things to the reader. For example, *c* or *cc* indicates copies are being sent. Another notation is *bc* for **blind copy**, which is used when sending a copy of the memo to someone without the recipient's knowledge.

If copies are being sent to others, add the notation *cc* (*copy* or *courtesy copy*) line and the list of names at the bottom of the memo. The blind copy notation appears at the bottom of the file copy and the copy for the recipient who is blind copied, but not on the copy for the primary recipient.

| cc: Tyler A. Dembowsky
| Edward Josi
| Jeannette Loria

Exploring
Communication Careers

Commercial Photographer

There are many types of photographers. Commercial photographers take pictures of individuals, groups of people, or objects. Some photographers photograph people and merchandise to use for product advertisements in print or online. Photojournalists shoot pictures that capture current events or breaking news stories for media outlets. All photographers must be able to use digital cameras to capture their subjects. Typical job titles for this position include *photojournalist*, *photo editor*, and *studio photographer*.

Some examples of tasks that photographers perform include:

- Select and set up appropriate photographic equipment.

- Use measuring devices and formulas to estimate light levels and distances for desired photographs.

- Take photographs of subjects, including people, places, and objects, in a studio or on location.

- Use software applications to produce finished images and prints.

Related experience is required for most photographer positions. Some positions require an associate degree or completion of a photography certificate, while other positions require a bachelor degree.

Other notations include *Confidential*, *Attachments*, and *Enclosures*. It is traditional to also include the preparer's initials in lowercase when someone other than the writer keys the memo. These notations follow the same formatting guidelines as letters and are shown in Figure 9-5.

Formatting E-Mail

Businesses generally have policies for using e-mail as well as disclaimers and other guidelines for sending e-mail correspondence. Figure 9-6 shows an example of an e-mail completed in business style. E-mail is formatted similarly to a printed memo.

Header

In the TO: line, key the names of the recipients from whom you want a response or who have a primary interest in the topic. Use the COPY: line for names of those who are receiving the information as secondary recipients. Normally, a reply is not expected from those who are copied.

You may opt to send blind copies, but use this option sparingly. In most business situations, it is courteous to let the reader know all who are receiving the e-mail. However, for an e-mail sent to a large number of people outside of an organization, it is courteous to use the blind copy function to ensure the e-mail addresses of the recipients remain private. If all recipients are listed in the BLIND COPY: line, the only e-mail address each recipient can see is the sender's address.

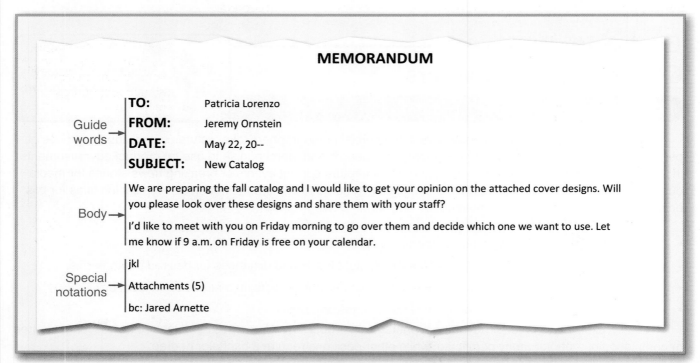

Goodheart-Willcox Publisher

Figure 9-5   This sample memo is properly formatted.

Limit the subject of each e-mail to one topic and clearly and concisely state the subject. For example, a subject of "Hello" is not suitable, but "Business Report 8/14" may be appropriate. By focusing the topic and the content of the e-mail, readers can more easily keep track of subsequent replies.

Salutation

E-mail tends to be more informal than letters. In most businesses and organizations, people address each other by their first names in e-mails. You may use the salutation "Dear" as in a letter, depending on whether you are writing a formal or informal e-mail. Some companies have adopted the style of using very informal salutations, such as addressing customers by first name.

If the company policy is to use informal forms of address, even to outside customers, follow the policy. However, the general rule is to use traditional salutations. Use your judgment based on your relationship with the recipient and the rules of the organization. If you address the recipient by first name in person, it is usually correct to do the same in written communication.

Message

Format the e-mail message the same as a letter or a memo. Use appropriate spacing, as shown in Figure 9-6. Adhere to netiquette when writing both personal and business e-mails. *Netiquette*, or Internet etiquette, is a set of guidelines for appropriate behavior on the Internet, including e-mail, and should always be followed. These rules include the accepted

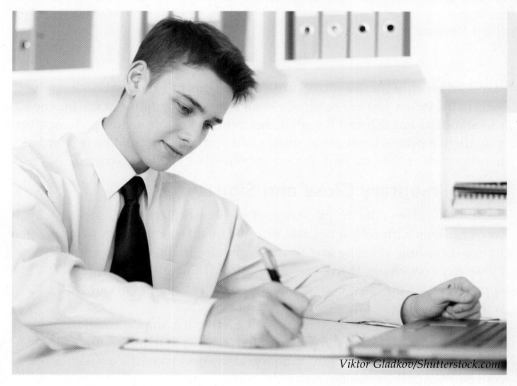

Viktor Gladkov/Shutterstock.com

When writing messages for business, take time to plan the message and use appropriate netiquette.

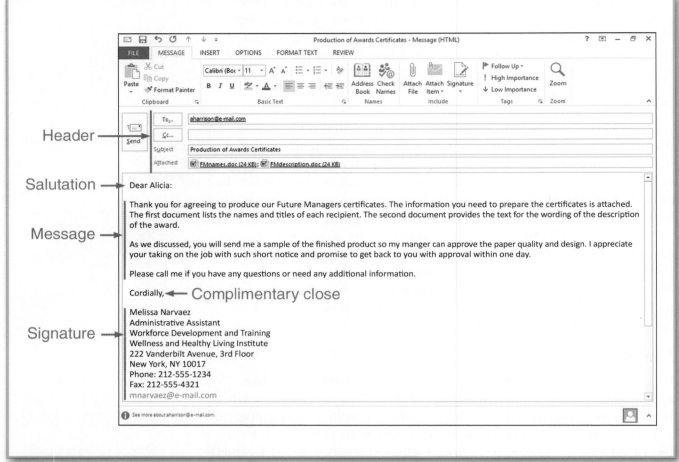

Goodheart-Willcox Publisher

Figure 9-6   This e-mail is properly formatted.

standards within the organization as well as general standards that apply externally. When you are sending e-mail as a representative of the business, use Standard English and the spell check feature before sending. Remember, you are in a professional environment and your e-mail could be forwarded to others who might make judgments about what you have written.

Complimentary Close and Signature

E-mails often take the place of routine phone calls and face-to-face conversations with colleagues and external business associates. Writers often forego including a closing and formal signature in these kinds of messages. However, a courteous thank-you at the end of the message is usually appropriate for business correspondence. This is a judgment call for the writer or a matter of organizational standards.

For e-mails that are used in place of a letter, it is important to include a complimentary close just as in a printed letter. It is standard to include your full name and contact information at the bottom of the e-mail for the convenience of the reader.

E-mail programs allow the user to set up the signature to be automatically inserted. In the signature block, include your name, job title, department, and contact information. It is customary to include the e-mail address in the signature, since many e-mail programs display the sender's full name instead of the e-mail address.

Attachments

Take care when sending attachments to ensure the recipient can handle the size and type of file. Many e-mail servers have limits on the size of files that can be received. Also, because viruses can be spread through attachments, check to make sure the recipient is comfortable receiving attachments or to notify them that an e-mail you will be sending will contain an attachment. It is standard practice in business to delete, without reading, any e-mail that has an attachment unless the attachment is expected.

E-mail Replies

Respond as quickly as possible to e-mails. Stay with the original topic in your reply. If you want to bring up a new topic, send a new e-mail and note the topic in the subject line. Creating a new e-mail with a new subject line makes it easier to keep the information flow understandable. Additionally, it allows both the sender and recipient of the e-mail to electronically file and organize the e-mail.

When you are out of the office, use the automated reply feature to send a message stating when you will return. This is a professional courtesy. It allows the sender to know you are unavailable, rather than being careless about responding.

E-mail Productivity Tools

As you may recall, *personal information management (PIM)* is a system that individuals use to acquire, organize, maintain, retrieve, and use information. Productivity tools common to most e-mail software can be a component of a PIM system.

- *Address book.* The contacts or address book lists the names of all employees on the system and inserts the name when you key a few letters. Many similar names might be in the system, so always check to make sure the correct names have been selected before clicking the Send button. Address books also have search features to help you find names and other information, such as employee job title, location, and phone number.

- *Send options.* Send options let you set criteria before you send an e-mail. Some of the criteria that can be set include the level of urgency, confidentiality, and being notified when the e-mail is opened or deleted.

- *Reply options.* The reply options allow you to determine who receives the reply. You can choose to reply only to the sender or to all recipients of the e-mail. Most e-mail readers also have a setting for including the original message beneath the reply. The e-mail subject line is usually given the prefix RE: to indicate it is a reply.

- *Forward.* The forward option allows you to send a message you have received to a new recipient. The e-mail subject line is usually given the prefix FW: to indicate it is a forwarded message. Once you click the Forward button, you can add multiple e-mail addresses to the TO: line.

- *Folders.* Folders are used to store e-mails you have sent or received. You can also store drafts of e-mails you are planning to send. Folders can be set up by topics, names, or any other filing system you prefer. If your organization has a standard filing system, be sure to use it.

- *Views.* The view feature allows you to sort e-mails in various views. For example, you can choose to sort by names, topics, dates, size, or other criteria. Sorting by name is a quick way to see all e-mails you have received from a particular coworker.

- *Trash.* E-mails that you delete are sent to the trash folder. Depending on how your e-mail software is set up, e-mails in the trash folder may be immediately discarded or kept until you manually empty the trash folder. Be sure to check for the automatic emptying setting, because once an e-mail is deleted from the trash folder, it cannot be retrieved.

- *Calendars and planning tools.* Many e-mail systems include tools that help you plan and organize your work. These tools are like a handheld daily planner. You can schedule meetings, set reminder alarms, and schedule reoccurring tasks.

Section 9.2 Review

 Check Your Understanding

1. When are memos used?
2. List the parts of a memo.
3. How is e-mail formatted?
4. Summarize appropriate behavior when replying to e-mails.
5. How can e-mail software help in personal information management?

Build Your Vocabulary

As you progress through this course, develop a personal glossary of key terms. This will help you build your vocabulary and prepare you for a career. Write a definition for each of the following terms and add it to your personal glossary.

memo   blind copy
template
guide word
notation

Chapter Summary

Section 9.1 Formatting Letters

- Appropriate formatting makes a professional impression with your written correspondence in any business situation. When writing, always use an introductory paragraph, standard fonts, parallel structure, and organizational symbols to format a document for readability.

- Letters may be block style or modified-block style and either open or mixed punctuation can be used. Business letters have standard elements that include date, inside address, salutation, body, complimentary close, and signature. Additional elements in a business letter may include an attention line, subject line, and notations.

- If an envelope is necessary, follow standard formatting guidelines.

Section 9.2 Formatting Memos and E-mails

- Memos are generally used for interoffice communication. Memos have a heading that includes the guide words *to*, *from*, *date*, and *subject*. There is no salutation or closing for a memo, but special notations may be used.

- E-mails are commonly used in business and are formatted similarly to a memo. Business e-mails should have a salutation and closing.

- A personal information management (PIM) system is a system that individuals use to acquire, organize, maintain, retrieve, and use information. Instituting a personal information management system can help you have the right information at the right time and in the correct form.

Online Activities

Complete the following activities which will help you learn, practice, and expand your knowledge and skills.

Posttest. Now that you have finished the chapter, see what you learned by taking the chapter posttest.

Vocabulary. Practice vocabulary for this chapter using the e-flash cards, matching activity, and vocabulary game until you are able to recognize their meanings.

English/Language Arts. Visit www.g-wlearning.com to download each data file for this chapter. Follow the instructions to complete an English/language arts activity to practice what you have learned in this chapter.

Activity File 9-1: Improving Your Editing Skills

Activity File 9-2: Improving Your Formatting Skills

Review Your Knowledge

1. Explain what standard formatting is and why it is used in the workplace.
2. What is readability?
3. Describe how parallel structure is achieved.
4. Explain the difference between mixed punctuation and open punctuation.
5. List and describe three types of notations used in letters.
6. How should a long list of recipients be noted on a memo?
7. What line spacing should be used for a memo?
8. What is the general rule used to determine if you can address somebody by their first name in a business e-mail?

9. Why should you alert a recipient that an e-mail you will be sending will contain an attachment?

10. Explain the importance of using a personal information management (PIM) system.

Apply Your Knowledge

1. Rewrite the following draft of a business letter so that it is properly formatted to increase its readability. Use a block format with open punctuation.

    Ms. Genevieve LeMond 7214 Mulberry Street DeKalb, IL 61616 June 20, 20--

    Dear Genevieve. I am sorry I cannot be at the PER meeting for the final, official goodbye to you as a fellow pollution-control champion. I personally want to communicate how strongly I feel about you as a mentor. No one can prepare better waste-containment strategies, rally support for earth-friendly activities, or use her knowledge more effectively to make changes at the community level! I've also admired your ability to communicate with officials at large corporations and persuade them to support our grassroots efforts. Now, as you enter a new life phase of your career, I hope you find new challenges to attack with your talents. And whatever you choose to pursue next, may it bring you satisfaction. Sincerely. Minerva Harvet Executive Director

2. There are multiple letter templates provided in Microsoft Word. These templates help the writer in formatting professional documents. Select the template for business letterhead. Create your own letterhead to use for letters that you will compose for business purposes.

3. You work at the Woodlake History Center. Each year the center hosts an employee family picnic. This year you are the picnic committee chair. Write an e-mail to your committee members to tell them the date, time, menu, and activities planned for the picnic (supply your own details). Use formatting such as bullets, asterisks, numbers, underlining, and boldface type to emphasize important information.

4. Netiquette is important in the workplace as well as in your personal life. Make a list of the rules of netiquette that you consider to be important.

Communication Skills

College and Career Readiness

Reading. Select several chapters of this textbook. Identify two generic features that are used in each chapter. Compare and contrast how each feature is used. Why do you think the author chose those particular features to apply in multiple chapters?

Writing. You have decided to volunteer for a nonprofit organization. Compose an informative letter or e-mail that you might send to an organization. Convey the information clearly and accurately through the effective organization of the content. Edit and revise your work until the ideas are refined and clear to the reader.

Speaking. Maintaining a healthy lifestyle has an impact on how you function physically and mentally. What unhealthy behaviors could have an effect on how well you do your job? How do you think employers should deal with behaviors that affect the personal health of their employees? Present to your class.

Internet Research

E-mail. Research the advantages and disadvantages of using e-mail for business purposes using various Internet resources. Did your research result in information that was new to you? Share your lists with your classmates.

Teamwork

Working with your team, research e-mail software. Make a chart showing at least five options, the system requirements, and the cost to purchase. One of the software options should be freeware. Write a memo to your supervisor (your teacher) listing the options and recommending an e-mail software program.

Portfolio Development

College and Career Readiness

Community Service. Community service is an important quality to show in a portfolio. Serving the community shows that a candidate is well rounded and socially aware. In this activity, you will create a list of your contributions to nonprofit organizations. Many opportunities are available for young people to serve the community. You might volunteer for a park clean-up project. Perhaps you might enjoy reading to residents in a senior-living facility. Maybe raising money for a pet shelter appeals to you. Whatever your interests, there is sure to be a related service project.

1. Create a Microsoft Word document that lists service projects or volunteer activities in which you have taken part. Use the heading "Community Service" on the document along with your name. List the name of the organization or person you helped, the date(s) of service, and the activities that you performed. If you received an award related to this service, mention it here.

2. Save the document in an appropriate folder.

3. Update your spreadsheet to reflect the inclusion of this Community Service document.

CTSOs

Extemporaneous Speaking. Extemporaneous speaking is a competitive event you might enter with your CTSO. This event allows you to display your communication skills, specifically your ability to organize and deliver an oral presentation. At the competition, you will be given several topics from which to choose. You will also be given a time limit to create and deliver the speech. You will be evaluated on your verbal and nonverbal skills as well as the tone and projection of your voice.

To prepare for an extemporaneous speaking event, complete the following activities.

1. Ask your instructor for several practice topics so you can practice making impromptu speeches.

2. Once you have a practice topic, jot down the ideas and points to cover. An important part of making this type of presentation is that you will have only a few minutes to prepare. Being able to write down your main ideas quickly will enable you to focus on what you will actually say in the presentation.

3. Practice the presentation. You should introduce yourself, review the topic that is being presented, defend the topic being presented, and conclude with a summary.

4. Ask your instructor to play the role of competition judge as you give the presentation. Afterward, ask for feedback from your instructor. You may also consider having a student audience listen and give feedback.

5. For the event, bring paper and pencils to record notes. Supplies may or may not be provided.

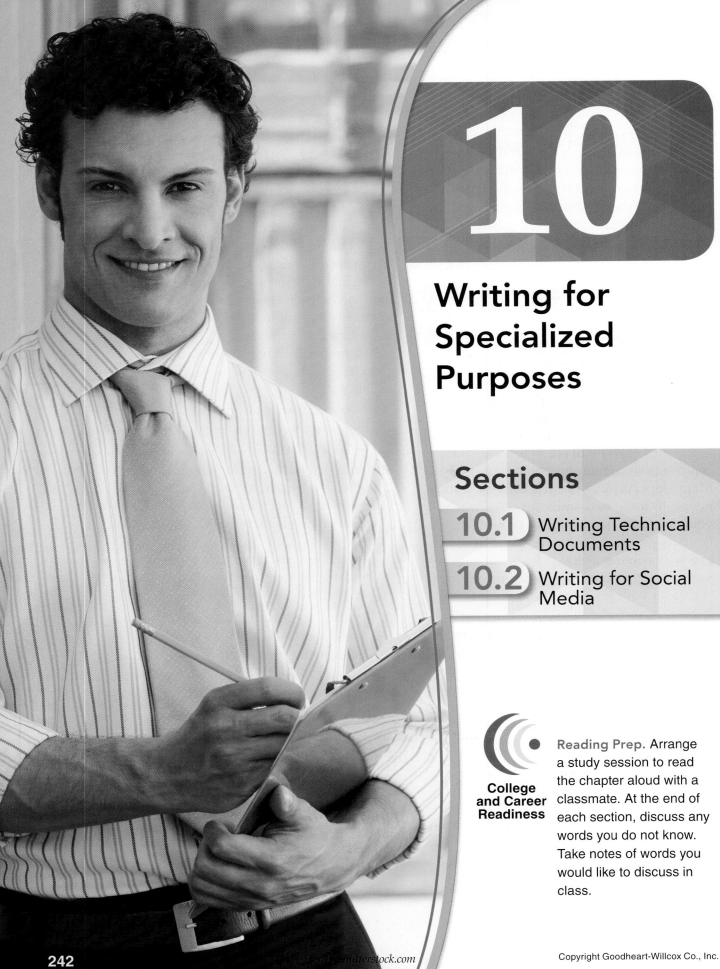

10

Writing for Specialized Purposes

Sections

10.1 Writing Technical Documents

10.2 Writing for Social Media

Reading Prep. Arrange a study session to read the chapter aloud with a classmate. At the end of each section, discuss any words you do not know. Take notes of words you would like to discuss in class.

College and Career Readiness

Shutterstock.com

Check Your Communication IQ

Before you begin the chapter, see what you already know about communication by taking the chapter pretest. The pretest is available at www.g-wlearning.com.

Case Study

Writing for Social Media

Jeanine Enomoto has a new job as a professional writer for an advertising business. As part of the communication plan for interacting with customers, it was decided that social media will play an important role for Trinity Media Tech. The first assignment for Jeanine was to start tweeting for the business.

Jeanine's supervisor, Kyle Oliver, requested to meet with her to discuss the social media writing approach for the company. To prepare, Jeanine created a list of steps she would take to write the copy. Kyle was not familiar with Twitter and was appalled at Jeanine's ideas, including the use of contractions and abbreviations in professional communication.

Jeanine was caught off guard and was not prepared to support her actions. She returned to her office in a state of frustration.

Minerva Studio/Shutterstock.com

Critical Thinking

1. What could Jeanine have done to be better prepared for this meeting?

2. How could Jeanine have communicated the appropriate process for writing for social media so that her supervisor would understand her approach?

Writing Technical Documents

Objectives

After completing this section, you will be able to:

- **Describe** a technical document.
- **Explain** the purpose of instructions.
- **Explain** the purpose of manuals.
- **Discuss** the importance of technical descriptions.

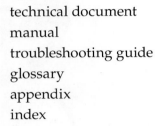

Essential Question

What makes instructions easy to follow?

Key Terms

technical document
manual
troubleshooting guide
glossary
appendix
index

description
object description
object
mechanism
process description
process

Technical Documents

Technical writing makes complex or specialized information more usable and accessible. A **technical document** is one that informs or instructs the reader how to use mechanical, technological, or scientific information. Readers often reference technical documents to learn how to assemble, use, or repair an object, a mechanism, or a process.

Two examples of technical documents are instructions and manuals. As you will recall, instructions are steps that must be followed in sequence to accomplish a task. *Instructions* can also be documents that contain steps to tell a user how to perform a task. A **manual** is a comprehensive, multi-section document covering a technical topic that often includes a combination of instructions and other documentation. With complex

kurhan/Shutterstock.com

Technical documents are used in many industries to teach readers how to accomplish certain tasks.

subjects, a manual is often required. A manual is also known as a *handbook* or *user guide*.

Instructions for products are typically in the form of a document that is inserted in a product package. Some instructions may appear on the packaging of the product. Manufacturers regularly post these on their website in PDF format under a customer service or similar tab. This makes it convenient for users to download the document at their convenience. Most instructions in the United States are in English and another language.

A manual has multiple pages and may be bound and have a cover, similar to a book. If there are only a few pages, they may be stapled. Most manuals are printed in black and white. However, for higher-end products, they may be printed in color. They are also made available on the manufacturer's website. Like instructions, manuals are usually printed in multiple languages.

Instructions

An instructions document lists and describes the steps that must be followed in sequence to complete a task. In some cases, only three or four short sentences will be needed. In other cases, complex subjects can require hundreds of pages to take the reader through the appropriate steps.

The goal of instructions is to guide the reader through completing a task effectively and efficiently. Following the steps in the writing process can help you write effective technical documents. The writing process is shown in Figure 10-1. The prewriting stage will guide you in gathering information.

- *Who is the audience?* Identify your target reader. Do you expect the audience to have special skills or prior knowledge of the content?

- *What do you want to communicate?* What is the intended outcome or goal for the instructions? Will readers be able to successfully assemble an item or understand a process?

- *When must the document be completed?* Identify when you want or need to finish the document. Allow enough time for the writing task without having to rush.

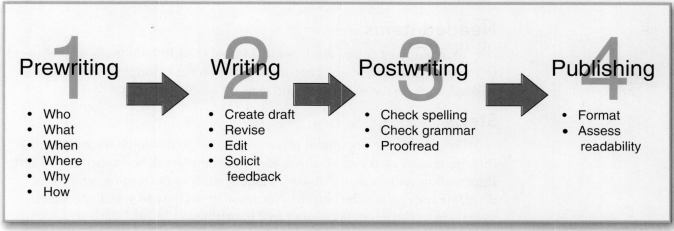

Goodheart-Willcox Publisher

Figure 10-1   There are four stages in the writing process.

- *Where is the information?* Gather the information about the product for which you will be writing instructions. It is necessary to completely understand how to use the product before directing others to use it.

- *Why are you writing?* Identify the purpose of the document. Are you writing instructions to help the reader use an item or perform a task?

- *How should the document be organized?* Instructions should be presented in an orderly manner using the direct approach. Most technical documents have an accepted format that should be used.

Once prewriting is complete, you will begin the writing stage. Writing starts with creating a draft. After the draft is written, revise and edit until you achieve a document that is error-free.

Effective instructions typically include a title, an introduction, a list of needed items, steps, and a conclusion. An instructions document is shown in Figure 10-2.

Title

A useful title clearly communicates what is being presented in the document. For example, the title *Brakes* does not provide enough information for the reader to anticipate what will follow. The title *Installing Drum Brakes* provides the specific information a reader needs to know.

Introduction

The introduction provides an overview. Similar to introductions in other types of documents, it identifies the purpose of the document. It also explains why it is important to read the instructions rather than skip them. An introduction may include:

- definitions of technical terms

- knowledge or skills required of the user

- expected outcomes

- general warnings

- time frame needed to complete the instructions

- advice on how to effectively use the instructions

Needed Items

To avoid frustration, readers must know if additional items are required to complete the instructions before beginning. For example, if a nail is needed, include the exact type and size.

Steps

The core of the document is the steps. The goal is to provide enough information in each step so the reader can complete it. Too much or too little information will cause confusion. Visuals, such as flowcharts, graphs, or illustrations, can also be helpful. Information on how to select and insert visuals in a document is covered in Chapter 12.

Title

Introduction

Steps

Conclusion

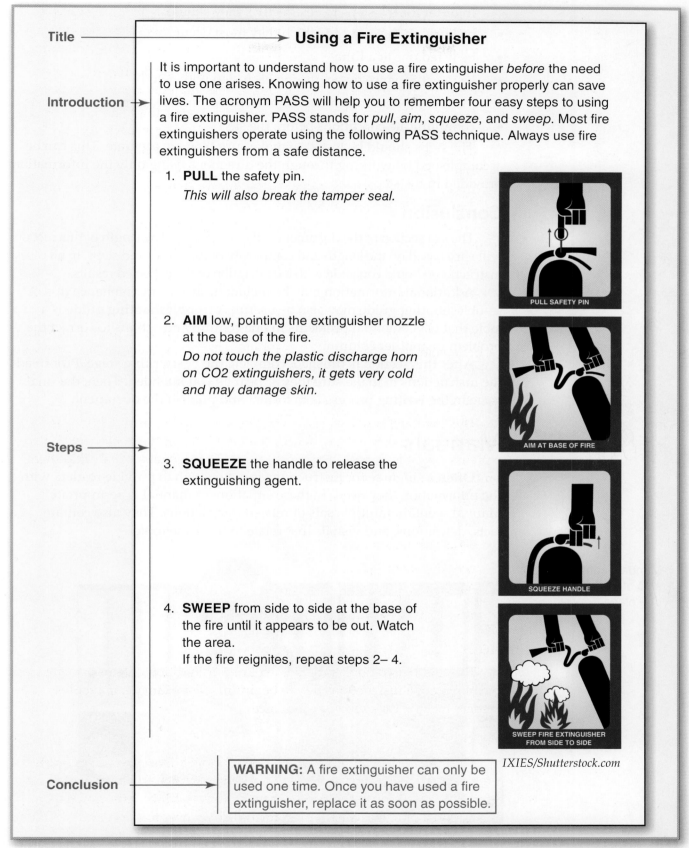

Using a Fire Extinguisher

It is important to understand how to use a fire extinguisher *before* the need to use one arises. Knowing how to use a fire extinguisher properly can save lives. The acronym PASS will help you to remember four easy steps to using a fire extinguisher. PASS stands for *pull*, *aim*, *squeeze*, and *sweep*. Most fire extinguishers operate using the following PASS technique. Always use fire extinguishers from a safe distance.

1. **PULL** the safety pin.
   This will also break the tamper seal.

2. **AIM** low, pointing the extinguisher nozzle at the base of the fire.
   Do not touch the plastic discharge horn on CO2 extinguishers, it gets very cold and may damage skin.

3. **SQUEEZE** the handle to release the extinguishing agent.

4. **SWEEP** from side to side at the base of the fire until it appears to be out. Watch the area.
   If the fire reignites, repeat steps 2–4.

WARNING: A fire extinguisher can only be used one time. Once you have used a fire extinguisher, replace it as soon as possible.

PULL SAFETY PIN

AIM AT BASE OF FIRE

SQUEEZE HANDLE

SWEEP FIRE EXTINGUISHER FROM SIDE TO SIDE

IXIES/Shutterstock.com

Goodheart-Willcox Publisher

Figure 10-2   Instructions provide the reader with information needed to complete a task successfully.

In order for the steps to be effective, they should:

- be listed in the order in which they must occur

- be listed one at a time

- be in active voice by beginning each step with a verb

- include subheadings if the list of steps becomes lengthy

- communicate conditions before the step

The steps should be tested to make sure they are accurate. This can be accomplished by working through the directions using only the information provided in the steps.

Conclusion

The last section of the document is the conclusion. The length of this section will vary based on the length and complexity of the numbered steps. In all cases, instructions should conclude with a description of the expected results.

Additional information may be included, such as maintenance tips. A troubleshooting guide may also be useful. A **troubleshooting guide** is a table that lists potential problems in one column and actions to correct the problem in another column.

After this section is finished, complete the postwriting stage. Proofread the instructions to make sure they appear as you intended. Then, the final stage in the writing process is to format and publish the document.

Manuals

Often a single set of instructions is not enough to provide readers with the information they need. In these situations, a manual is appropriate. Manuals contain multiple sets of related instructions. They also contain facts, definitions, and visuals that relate to the same topic.

Manuals contain many sets of instructions in one place.

Daniel M Ernst/Shutterstock.com

A manual is organized into sections or chapters which are placed in logical order. A section or chapter includes a set of related instructions or visuals. An effective manual may include these parts:

- title
- table of contents
- introduction
- instructions
- glossary
- appendix
- index

Technical descriptions may also be one of the parts of a manual. Technical descriptions will be explained later in the chapter.

Title, Table of Contents, and Introduction

Like other technical documents, the title of a manual should be both descriptive and concise. The title should state the topic of the information contained in the manual.

The *table of contents* is a map to the information contained within the manual. It should include the title of each section, any subtitles or subheadings, and the exact page numbers where each section can be found. In addition to the main table of contents, specialized lists can be included. For example, a separate list can be included that lists each figure and its page number.

The introduction to the manual is similar to the introduction of an instructions document. However, it has the potential to be longer. Its purpose is to the lay the foundation for more information than a single set of instructions.

Instructions

The steps in each set of instructions are the heart of the manual. The information in each section should be presented in a uniform manner. Figures, such as flowcharts, should be numbered consistently throughout the document.

Glossary, Appendix, and Index

For ease of use, a glossary, appendix, and index can be added to a manual. A **glossary** is an alphabetical listing of terms used in the manual and their definitions. The glossary appears at the back of the manual.

An appendix is often placed at the back of a manual. An **appendix** contains additional information that would be helpful to the reader but is not necessary to complete the numbered steps. It is too cumbersome to be included with the rest of the document. When more than one appendix is used, label each individually, such as *Appendix A* and *Appendix B*. The title of an appendix can also be descriptive, such as *Temperature Conversion Chart*.

An **index** is an alphabetical list of important topics, key terms, and proper nouns used in the manual with the page numbers on which each is located. An index is usually only needed for a lengthy manual.

Technical Descriptions

A **description** is detailed written and visual information about an item or process. A description may provide readers with information to help form a mental picture of what is being described. The two types of technical descriptions are object descriptions and process descriptions.

Object Descriptions

An **object description** provides detailed information about an object or a mechanism. An **object** is something that is not living and can be seen or touched, such as a pencil. A **mechanism** is a type of object that has working parts. An example of a mechanism is a seat belt.

When the reader looks at an object or mechanism, he or she may not understand what it is. It may not be obvious what the parts are or how they work together. A written description can help bring understanding to the item. An object description should include these parts:

- title
- introduction
- part-by-part description
- conclusion

Title

As with other technical documents, the title should clearly communicate the information that follows. If there is a model number or an important reference number, it should be noted. A picture of the entire item may be shown immediately following the title.

Introduction

The introduction begins with identification of the object and its purpose. Give information regarding the intended use of the object and identify the audience that will use it. State whether the reader needs a specific skill set or prior knowledge in order to understand the description.

If an object contains multiple parts, each part should be identified. An illustration might be included to show each part individually.

 **Green** Cleaning Products

Products used to clean buildings and workstations can have an impact on the environment. Toxic chemicals in many traditional cleaning products can pollute water sources and other business assets. They are also hazardous for employees to use, as the chemicals are poisonous. Instead, many businesses use green cleaning products in their facilities. Employees who clean the building can do just as good of a job with nontoxic green cleaners as they can with hazardous chemical cleaners.

Chemical cleaners should also be avoided when cleaning computer screens and work areas. These chemicals are hard on the equipment. If used improperly, chemical cleaners can damage computer equipment. On the other hand, green cleaning products are safe to use on almost any surface and are also safer for the employee using them.

Part-by-Part Description

The part-by-part description includes the dimensions of the object, including the length, width, height, and weight. The appearance of each individual part or component of the object should be described separately, in logical order. For example, each part may be identified starting left to right. Explain the purpose of each part as well.

Illustrations or photographs of the object or mechanism being described can be included in this section of the document. The entire object should be illustrated, as shown in Figure 10-3. Callouts on the illustration to name each part described can add clarity. Separate images can be included that provide a closer look at one part or group of parts.

Conclusion

A conclusion serves as a summary. It also provides an opportunity to remind readers of the purpose of the object as a whole.

Process Descriptions

A **process description** helps the reader understand the actions taken to reach a specific goal. A **process** is a series of actions taken to achieve a stated goal. Process descriptions often include these parts:

- title
- introduction
- step-by-step description
- conclusion

Title and Introduction

Similar to other titles and introductions, the information should be specific and concise. The reader should understand what will be included and how it applies to the situation.

Step-by-Step Description

The description should be in the order in which the process takes place. Each step should be numbered and begin with a verb unless a condition exists. If a condition must be met before completing a step, it should be written first. Processes are well illustrated using a flowchart, as shown in Figure 10-4. A *flowchart* is a visual representation of the actions taken in a process. The flowchart shows conditions and the cause and effect of each step in the process.

Conclusion

A conclusion that summarizes the key points can be included. If the description is short, a conclusion can serve as the last paragraph in the document.

Title

Introduction

8-Inch Garden Clippers

These garden clippers are designed to be used to trim and prune bushes, shrubs, grasses, and other foliage. This product is intended for personal or commercial use. The dimensions of the product are 9 1/4 inches wide by 2 1/4 inches deep by 21 2/3 inches high. The weight of the product is 3 pounds. These garden clippers have a maximum cutting thickness of 1/8 inches.

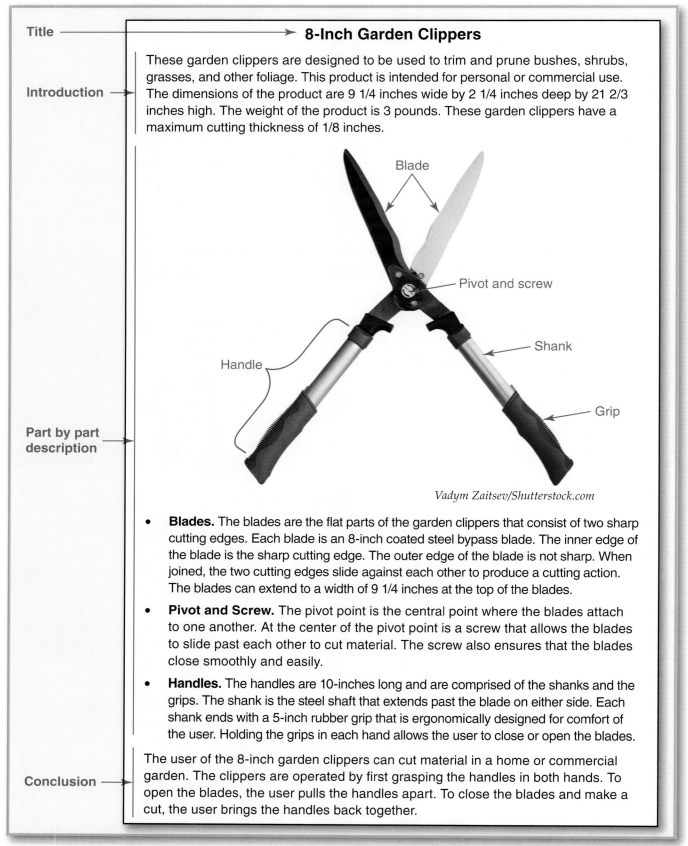

Part by part description

Vadym Zaitsev/Shutterstock.com

- **Blades.** The blades are the flat parts of the garden clippers that consist of two sharp cutting edges. Each blade is an 8-inch coated steel bypass blade. The inner edge of the blade is the sharp cutting edge. The outer edge of the blade is not sharp. When joined, the two cutting edges slide against each other to produce a cutting action. The blades can extend to a width of 9 1/4 inches at the top of the blades.

- **Pivot and Screw.** The pivot point is the central point where the blades attach to one another. At the center of the pivot point is a screw that allows the blades to slide past each other to cut material. The screw also ensures that the blades close smoothly and easily.

- **Handles.** The handles are 10-inches long and are comprised of the shanks and the grips. The shank is the steel shaft that extends past the blade on either side. Each shank ends with a 5-inch rubber grip that is ergonomically designed for comfort of the user. Holding the grips in each hand allows the user to close or open the blades.

Conclusion

The user of the 8-inch garden clippers can cut material in a home or commercial garden. The clippers are operated by first grasping the handles in both hands. To open the blades, the user pulls the handles apart. To close the blades and make a cut, the user brings the handles back together.

Goodheart-Willcox Publisher

Figure 10-3   An object description along with an illustration or photo can help bring understanding to an item.

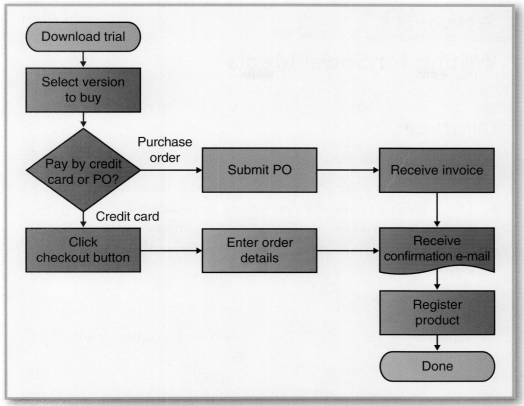

Goodheart-Willcox Publisher

Figure 10-4 A flowchart is a visual description of a process.

Section 10.1 Review

Check Your Understanding

1. Name two common types of technical documents.
2. List the five elements included in effective instructions.
3. Describe the purpose of an introduction to a set of instructions.
4. Explain the difference between a single set of instructions and a manual.
5. What are the two common types of technical descriptions?

Build Your Vocabulary

As you progress through this course, develop a personal glossary of key terms. This will help you build your vocabulary and prepare you for a career. Write a definition for each of the following terms and add it to your personal glossary.

technical document   description
manual   object description
troubleshooting guide   object
glossary   mechanism
appendix   process description
index   process

Section 10.2

Writing for Social Media

Objectives

After completing this section, you will be able to:

- **Describe** the writing process as it is applied to social media.
- **List** guidelines to use when prewriting for social media.
- **Explain** how to write copy for social media posts.
- **Identify** ways to publish professional communication on social media platforms.

Key Terms

social media
copy
keyword

search engine optimization (SEO)
blog
hashtag

Essential Question

Why is writing for social media a unique task?

Social Media

Social media refers to the websites and apps that allow individual users to network online by creating and sharing content with one another. For many individuals, social media is an important part of everyday life. People use it to build their personal brand, to develop a community, and to communicate with others. Unlike other forms of media, such as television, radio, and newspapers, social media allows for interaction between people.

Businesses and governments also have learned the many advantages that social media can provide. Platforms such as Facebook, Twitter, and LinkedIn are no longer just for personal use. This awareness brings the need for writers who are capable of presenting information in an appropriate format for the medium.

Social media writing calls for a specific tone and method. However, all professional writing should apply the prewriting, writing, postwriting, and publishing steps of the writing process. Following the four-step writing process will help you create content for social media that adheres to the four Cs of communication. Content is also known as copy. **Copy** is written information intended for publication.

Prewriting

Prewriting is the planning stage of the writing process and is an important step. Use the journalistic approach of asking *who, what, when, where, why*, and *how* questions.

254

Start with defining the purpose of the communication. Social media is generally used to inform, instruct, request, or persuade. The goal may be to achieve one or all of the following.

- Build the brand of the business.
- Manage the reputation of the business.
- Deliver customer service.
- Obtain customer feedback.
- Reach out to customers.
- Increase website traffic.

Once the purpose is established, the subject area on which you will be writing must be defined. Social media posts typically have length restrictions. It will be necessary to narrow the subject to one manageable topic. After the topic is defined, you can gather and research the information.

The next step is to analyze the audience. Who will be interested in your post? Recall that analyzing the audience is an important step of the writing process. Social media engages audiences in different ways than other media. Studying the demographics will help define the audience for your copy.

Writers of social media must be aware of the importance of time. Social media is timely. Messages must be published when they are relevant. Consider when the message must be available to an audience. For example, if the business is responding to news reports of a product recall, the message must be posted at a time when customers need the information.

Also important in the planning process is determining the approach of the content. The direct approach works well when delivering information. The *topic* is introduced first and then followed by descriptive details. The indirect approach works well for persuasive messages. *Details* are given first and are then followed by the main idea. Begin with information that prepares the reader to respond how you want him or her to respond.

Out of Office Notice

If you are going to be out of the office for a significant period of time, such as for an afternoon off or a week of vacation, notify coworkers in advance. Remind others of your absence by setting up an automatic e-mail reply and a voicemail greeting that states you are out of the office and when you will return. Doing so helps people remember you are unavailable rather than simply avoiding them.

Writing and Postwriting

Once the prewriting tasks are completed, you are ready to begin the writing stage. This starts with creating a draft of the message. Writing social media copy for professional purposes is not the same as writing for personal use. Professional communication requires that the rules of writing apply. An active voice should be used. Industry jargon, slang, and acronyms should be limited or avoided.

In general, use short words and short sentences. Contractions and common abbreviations are acceptable due to the length restrictions for messages on most platforms. However, do not use text messaging abbreviations. In addition, avoid using extra spaces because every character counts. If the message is longer than a few paragraphs, headlines and bulleted lists can save space and draw attention to the message.

As you write, think in terms of digital devices. Many social media messages are read on a smartphone or tablet. Long words and sentences can be hard to read on a small screen. A message that is lengthy may not be read by the audience in its entirety.

Consider the needs of the audience and focus on the customer by using "you" statements. The reader must see how or why the information will benefit him or her. The message must immediately convey its importance. People are busy, and their attention span for social media is short. Keep in mind that the reader will be sifting through many online communications. If the reason for reading is not obvious, the message may be overlooked or deleted.

A **keyword** is a word that specifically relates to the subject matter in the social media post. Using strategic keywords will yield better results when readers search for the topic on which you are writing. **Search engine optimization (SEO)** is the process of indexing a website so that it will rank higher on the list of returned results when a search is conducted.

As you will recall, persuasive messages close with a call to action. Close the message by inviting the reader to do something, such as view a video. You can also engage readers by inviting them to comment on the post or reply to the message.

Once you have your draft complete, improve the quality of the message by revising it. The length of the copy will probably be short, but do not overlook the importance of revision. Do a final edit and ask someone to read your finished product and give feedback.

Proofread the copy to make sure there are no errors. Errors in social media copy destroy credibility, since the message is public and read by a large number of people. Also because the message is public, it is very important to get all of the facts correct. Always double check names, dates, times, and website URLs for accuracy during proofreading.

Exploring Communication Careers

Technical Writer

A technical writer makes complex topics easier to understand. Textbooks, instruction manuals, articles, and online help systems are examples of the types of documents prepared by technical writers. People in these positions must gather information, conduct research, and explore products and processes in order to successfully write the documentation. Information gathering often includes communicating with the engineers or programmers who built the mechanism or software program. Another typical job title for this position is *technical communicator*.

Some examples of tasks that technical writers perform include:

- Determine the purpose of the technical communication.
- Study product samples and talk with their developers.
- Use the writing process to write clear and easy-to-use documents.
- Select or create drawings, charts, or photos to accompany documents.
- Revise technical writings to reflect changes in product or user feedback.

Technical writer jobs often require a bachelor degree in English, journalism, or communication. Courses in a technical subject such as engineering, computer science, or medicine can be helpful. These positions require the ability to take a complex or technical subject and translate it so it is understandable to nontechnical readers. Communication skills, attention to detail, and imagination, along with strong writing skills, are essential.

Publishing

Social media writing should be tailored to the chosen platform. Specific platforms have unique posting requirements that can greatly impact a message. There are many choices of social media that can be used for business. Popular platforms used are blogs, Facebook, Twitter, and LinkedIn.

Pressmaster/Shutterstock.com

There are many social media platforms to use for professional communication.

Blogs

A **blog** is an informational or discussion-based website that consists of a series of dated posts in reverse chronological order. The word blog is short for *web log*. Many businesses use blogs to write narrative updates about their products and services. Blogs also provide information about a company. There are many blog platforms available, such as Wordpress and Blogger. Often companies have blogs built into their own website.

Customers can follow a blog, which means they will receive an e-mail when a new blog post is published. Bloggers should aim to highlight the strengths of the business for which they are writing. This can be accomplished by using narratives and pictures. Featuring success stories on a blog is one way to connect with customers.

Social media writers can maximize the impact of a blog post in several ways. When writing a company blog post, consider the following.

- Focus on writing short posts, as shorter is better. Blog posts do not have a character limit like other social media platforms. It is common to keep blog posts between 300 and 1,000 words to maintain the reader's attention. An ideal length is 500 words.

- Use a professional tone, avoid abbreviations, and apply the basics of professional communication.

- Use creative titles that will catch a potential reader's attention. Getting a reader to click on the blog is the first step, and a good title will help.

- Use multimedia elements to break up the text, such as video clips, photos, illustrations, and links.

Facebook

With more than one billion users, Facebook is becoming a must for most businesses, both large and small. Businesses and organizations create pages to share their stories and to connect with people. These pages can be customized by posting stories, sharing photos, hosting events and contests, and more. People who follow the page using the **Like** button will have access to updates from the business.

When writing copy to be posted on Facebook, consider the following.

- Write posts within the 420-character limit.

- Link to a website or video by including a URL.

- Encourage readers to like the Facebook page and share posts.

- Post topics that encourage readers to participate in a conversation.

Twitter

Twitter is a useful tool for real-time conversations with customers. Businesses can connect with customers who may be using their product or

PiXXart/Shutterstock.com

Twitter is a unique way for businesses to connect with customers.

visiting their booth at a convention. Customers can instantly find information about the company, a product, or some other announcement the business makes. In turn, the company can gather feedback and opinions about their products. They can also learn about the competition or the industry. Twitter is useful for networking and expanding the customer base of a business.

Businesses using Twitter can optimize their tweets by using hashtags. A **hashtag** is a searchable keyword on Twitter marked by the hashtag symbol (#) that links users to all Tweets marked with the same hashtag keyword. Anyone searching Twitter for a topic can find all Tweets containing that hashtag in a single location. Hashtags increase the likelihood of a Tweet being seen. They can also help a business gain followers. When writing copy to be posted on Twitter, consider the following.

- A twitter post, called a *Tweet*, is limited to 140 characters.

- Headline-style messages work well.

- A glossary is available on the Twitter website to confirm appropriate vocabulary to use in your tweets.

- Pictures may be posted with your Twitter message.

- A translations center is available on the Twitter website if you need to translate your tweet into another language.

LinkedIn

LinkedIn is a social media website designed for professional networking. Businesses can create a LinkedIn profile at no charge and invite others to follow their company. LinkedIn also offers professional groups comprised of people representing different companies or industries. These groups allow companies and employees to network with others in their industry. The site offers solutions and tips to help employers make the most of this social media platform.

LinkedIn provides a vehicle for businesses to promote themselves as an employer of choice. Creating a professional network gives businesses the opportunity to recruit candidates and obtain referrals for job applicants. For a fee, businesses can post job openings on the website and invite members to apply. By using keywords to target certain skills, qualified candidate profiles can be reviewed. Candidates can even be contacted directly.

When writing copy to be posted on LinkedIn, consider the following.

- LinkedIn messages are generally company descriptions, marketing copy, or classified ads for open positions that are written professionally.

- A professional tone should be used, abbreviations avoided, and the other basics of professional communication should be applied.

- LinkedIn messages are limited to a certain number of characters, which varies depending on the type of post. These are explained on the LinkedIn website.

Section 10.2 Review

 Check Your Understanding

1. List the steps of the writing process that should be used when writing for social media.

2. State one of the goals that a business may achieve with social media.

3. Summarize how to write the first draft of a social media post.

4. Why should digital devices be considered when writing for social media?

5. List examples of social media platforms.

 Build Your Vocabulary

As you progress through this course, develop a personal glossary of key terms. This will help you build your vocabulary and prepare you for a career. Write a definition for each of the following terms and add it to your personal glossary.

social media
copy
keyword

search engine optimization (SEO)
blog
hashtag

Chapter Summary

Section 10.1 Writing Technical Documents

- A technical document is one that informs or instructs the reader how to use mechanical, technological, or scientific information. Two examples of technical documents are instructions and manuals.

- The ultimate goal of instructions is to guide the reader through completing a task as effectively and efficiently as possible. Use the writing process when developing instructions. Effective instructions typically include a title, an introduction, a list of needed items, numbered steps, and a conclusion.

- When a single set of instructions cannot provide readers with all of the information they need, a manual can be written. A manual is a comprehensive, multisection document covering a technical topic that often includes a combination of instructions and descriptions. The content of a manual should be well organized. An effective manual may include a title, table of contents, introduction, instructions, glossary, appendix, and index.

- A description is detailed information in words, and usually a visual, about an object, mechanism, or process. There are two types of technical descriptions: an object description and a process description. An object description should include a title, introduction, part-by-part description, and a conclusion. While a process description also includes a title, introduction, and conclusion, the core of it is the step-by-step description.

Section 10.2 Writing for Social Media

- Social media writing calls for writers to use the writing process just as with any other professional communication. The four steps of the writing process are prewriting, writing, postwriting, and publishing.

- Prewriting is the planning stage of the writing process and is an important step. Use the journalistic approach of asking *who, what, when, where, why,* and *how* questions.

- When writing for social media for professional purposes, the rules of writing apply. Social media writing should always use an active voice and avoid jargon, slang, and other industry or unprofessional terms. Messages should be kept short for reading on a digital device. Keywords can be used in social media posts to enhance search engine optimization.

- Social media writing should be tailored to the chosen platform. Popular platforms used are blogs, Facebook, Twitter, and LinkedIn. Each social media platform comes with a unique set of rules, such as character limits, that can impact the message.

Online Activities

Complete the following activities which will help you learn, practice, and expand your knowledge and skills.

- **Posttest.** Now that you have finished the chapter, see what you learned by taking the chapter posttest.

- **Vocabulary.** Practice vocabulary for this chapter using the e-flash cards, matching activity, and vocabulary game until you are able to recognize their meanings.

- **English/Language Arts.** Visit www.g-wlearning.com to download each data file for this chapter. Follow the instructions to complete an English/language arts activity to practice what you have learned in this chapter.

  Activity File 10-1: Improving Your Editing Skills

  Activity File 10-2: Improving Your Reading Skills

Review Your Knowledge

1. Describe the purpose of technical documents.

2. Describe the main goal of instructions.

3. Name the eight parts of an effective manual.

4. What is the purpose of a technical description?

5. How does an object description differ from a process description?

6. Why are writers of social media needed?

7. Contractions and abbreviations are not generally acceptable in professional writing. Why are they acceptable when writing for social media?

8. What importance do keywords serve in a post?

9. Why do businesses use blogs for communication?

10. Which social media platform enables real-time conversation with customers?

Apply Your Knowledge

1. Technical documents are typically used for reference purposes to learn how to complete a task or process. Locate a technical document in your home, classroom, or online. Read through the document. Why would the reader use this document as a reference? Summarize your opinion.

2. Identify a task you know how to do well, such as make mashed potatoes or build a bookcase. Develop a technical document in the form of instructions that explains how to complete the task you identified. Include a title, introduction, needed items, steps, and conclusion.

3. Identify an object that has at least four distinct parts. Write an object description so your classmates will understand the item you selected. First, identify the order in which the parts should be described. Next, decide which words you could use that would provide a mental picture of the object. Consider the features such as color, size, or other descriptors. Using the writing guidelines in this chapter, write the object description. Include a title, introduction, part-by-part description, and conclusion. After you have finished, ask for feedback from your classmates. Was your object description clear?

4. Consider a process with which you are familiar, such as ironing a button-down shirt or feeding a pet. Write a process description. First, identify the order in which the steps should be completed. Next, decide which words could you use that would help the reader understand the process. Using the writing guidelines in this chapter, write a process description. Include a title, introduction, step-by-step description, and conclusion. After you have finished, ask for feedback from your classmates. Was your process description clear?

5. Locate a manual in your home, classroom, or online. Review the table of contents of the manual. Does it include all of the sections mentioned in this chapter? Read the instructions section. Does it include all of the parts mentioned in this chapter? Are there illustrations included? If so, are they helpful to the reader? Using your answers to these questions, write an evaluation of the manual.

6. You have been invited by the principal of your school to start a blog for the student body. This blog can be about school sports activities, CTSOs, community service, or any other topic that may be relevant to students. Select a topic and write the first post that will introduce the blog and explain its purpose. Use the steps of the writing process to create the copy for your first post.

Communication Skills

College and Career Readiness

Reading. Using independent research, write a report in which you describe and analyze the use of aptitude tests, such as SAT, ACT, ACCUPLACER, and ASVAB. Why do these tests play such an important role in the post–high school plans of students? Cite specific evidence to support your understanding of this issue.

Writing. Standard English means that word choice, sentence structure, paragraphs, and the format of communication follow standard conventions used by those who speak English. Research the topic of college access. Write an informative report, consisting of several paragraphs to describe your findings. Edit the writing for proper syntax, tense, and voice.

Speaking. Social media is an important tool for professional communication. Answer the following questions, and prepare for a productive group discussion with your classmates. What are the benefits of using social media to enhance productivity? What are some disadvantages or risks of using social media? What actions could you take to mitigate the disadvantages or risks? In your opinion, for what applications will social media most likely be used?

Internet Research

Social Media Writers. Using the Internet, research the demand for social media writer jobs. Locate two to three job postings for each. What skills are required for each type of job? In what ways are they similar? In what ways are they different?

Teamwork

A person who is called *a professional* is an individual who is considered an expert at his or her career. To be *professional* is to act in a certain manner that is acceptable in the workplace.

Working with your team, discuss the behaviors that are considered as acting professionally. Share your opinions with the class.

Portfolio Development

College and Career Readiness

Schoolwork. Academic information is important to include in a portfolio in order to show your accomplishments in school. Include items related to your schoolwork that support your portfolio objective. These items might be report cards, transcripts, or honor roll reports. Diplomas or certificates that show courses or programs you completed should also be included. Other information can be included as a list, such as relevant classes you have taken.

1. Create a Microsoft Word document that lists notable classes you have taken and activities you have completed. Use the heading "Schoolwork" on the document along with your name.

2. Scan hard-copy documents related to your schoolwork, such as report cards, to serve as samples. Place each document in an appropriate folder.

3. Place the hard copy documents in the container for future reference.

4. Update your spreadsheet.

CTSOs

Digital Media. The *Digital Media* competitive event may consist of a pre-judged promotional video project and a live presentation that will be given by the contestant in front of judges. The video must be designed using specified software, time requirements, and other guidelines as listed on the organization's website. The project should display participants' knowledge of digital media and design as well as appeal to the target audience.

To prepare for the digital media event, complete the following activities.

1. Read the guidelines provided by your organization.

2. Visit the organization's website and look for this year's digital media topic. Because you must submit the video before the event, the topic will be posted. Rules and regulations for the event must be met or the submission will be disqualified.

3. Look for the evaluation criteria or rubric for the event. This will help you determine what the judges will be looking for in your video.

4. For the live presentation of the project, appropriate video equipment will be required. Confirm if the equipment will be provided by the CTSO or if you will have to supply your own digital equipment.

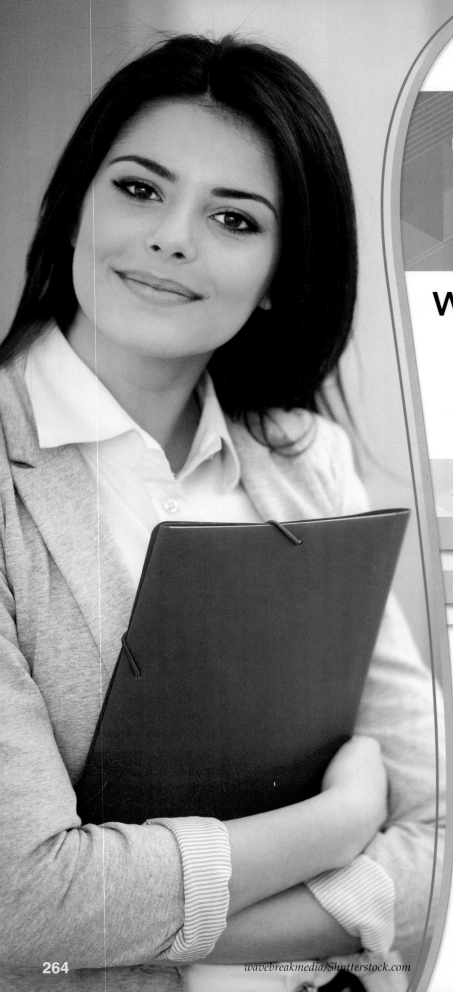

11

Writing Reports

Sections

| 11.1 | Planning and Research |
| 11.2 | Formal and Informal Reports |

College and Career Readiness

Reading Prep. Arrange a study session to read the chapter with a classmate. After you read each section independently, stop and tell each other what you think the main points are in the section. Continue with each section until you finish the chapter.

wavebreakmedia/Shutterstock.com

Check Your Communication IQ 📤

Before you begin the chapter, see what you already know about communication by taking the chapter pretest. The pretest is available at www.g-wlearning.com.

Case Study

Adequate Research

Jeffrey Magee is on the operations committee of GreenHomes Corporation. The committee is examining the feasibility of establishing an additional day off for employees in the form of a floating holiday. The committee chairperson asked Jeffrey to study the matter and present a brief report. The report was to include specific recommendations that could be presented to the president of the company.

Jeffrey decided to survey employees. Pressed for time, he selected ten people he has lunch with every day. Jeffrey's survey asked:

- Would you be in favor of a floating holiday?

- Why or why not?

Jeffrey tallied the responses and tried to write a report. However, he struggled with it. So, he went to the chairperson and gave his report verbally. When asked for a copy of the report, Jeffrey said there was not enough information to put into a written report. The chairperson said his findings were inadequate and told him to start the project over.

Goodluz/Shutterstock.com

Critical Thinking

1. Was Jeffrey's survey adequate? Why or why not?

2. How could he have gathered more information so that a detailed report could be written?

Planning and Research

Objectives

After completing this section, you will be able to:

- **Identify** the purpose for writing a report.
- **Explain** the importance of the prewriting process when planning a report.

Key Terms ➦

report
formal report
informal report
data
qualitative data
quantitative data

primary research
focus group
survey
representative sampling
secondary research

Essential Question

How are reports dependent on professional communication skills?

Reports

Reports are documents used to present information in a structured format to a specific audience for a defined purpose. In the workplace, they are often used to convey information that is the basis for making business decisions. Reports provide facts and information from which conclusions are drawn. They also discuss problems and recommend solutions. Reports may be developed for use inside of an organization. They may also be sent to people outside of the organization, such as government agencies, stockholders, and customers.

A **formal report** is a document that focuses on a broad main topic which is divided into subtopics for complete and clear coverage. These reports are often supported by formal research or gathering of information. They are usually longer than an informal report and may require formal components, such as a table of contents and a bibliography. Formal reports are often created by teams. Individuals assume responsibility for designated sections and then work collaboratively to create the final document.

An **informal report** is a document that does not require formal research or documentation. Informal reports are typically short, no more than a few pages long. They are commonly a part of the regular work routine. Informal reports may be written in the first person when the writer is reporting his or her own actions, conclusions, or ideas.

By following the steps in the writing process, you will be able to complete a well-written, professional-looking document. The steps of the writing process are shown in Figure 11-1.

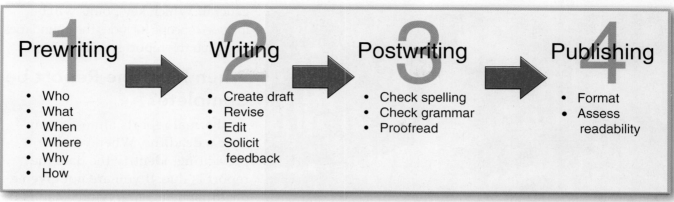

Goodheart-Willcox Publisher

Figure 11-1   There are four stages in the writing process.

Prewriting

Prewriting is the planning stage of the writing process. As you learned in Chapter 6, this is the most important stage of writing a document. Taking time to plan thoroughly will help make the writing process go smoothly.

Who Is the Audience?

Analyzing the audience will help you make decisions about the approach, style, tone, and level of formality of a report. The first question to ask is will the audience be internal, external, or both? This will help to determine the depth of information they already possess about the company, business, or topic. They may have biases and prior knowledge that may need to be considered.

Will there be a primary audience, secondary audience, or both? This will influence how you present the content in the report. It will also affect how the report is published.

Reviewing the demographics can help note preferences for language and style. Background information, vocabulary, and other data may need to be provided in the report.

Analyzing the audience is an important step in the prewriting process. Be certain to give it full attention.

What Do You Want to Communicate?

Knowing what ideas you want to communicate helps focus on the purpose of the message. What do you want the reader to do as a result of reading the report? Answering this question will help narrow the subject area so that you can select the specific topic that will be covered.

After the topic has been decided, a *statement of purpose* can then be written to define why you are writing the report. An example of a statement of purpose is "To update the management team on reasons why management positions have been difficult to fill." This statement will help guide you in reaching the goal of the report.

Next, consider the scope of the content. The *scope* of the report is the guideline of how much information will be included. Is it detailed or

Orange Line Media/Shutterstock.com

The calendar in a PIM system can be used to schedule report-writing tasks.

general? Which key points will be included? Scope includes the boundaries in which the report should be kept.

When Must the Report be Complete?

Formal reports almost always have a deadline. When you begin prewriting, identify the date the report is due. If you are not given a deadline by a supervisor, establish one for yourself. Schedule enough time to finish the writing process. Use the calendar in your PIM system to schedule your report-writing tasks.

Where Is the Information?

Collecting data is an important step in preparing to write a report. **Data** are the pieces of information gathered through research. Information usually falls into one of two categories: qualitative or quantitative data. **Qualitative data** are the information that provide insight into how people think about a particular topic. An example of qualitative data is a customer's feelings after speaking with a customer service agent. **Quantitative data** are the facts and figures from which conclusions can be drawn. An example of quantitative data is the number of customers who requested to speak with a customer service agent after using a certain product.

Research might include collaboration with other departments, consulting outside experts, or convening a taskforce. The topic dictates where to look for source material. Whatever the length or purpose of the formal report, the goal is to prepare a valid, useful, and informative document.

Primary Research

Primary research is first-hand research conducted by the writer in preparation for writing a report. The most common methods of primary research for a business report are interviews, surveys, and observations.

Interviews. Interviews are an effective method of getting information about people's opinions on topics. Some reports can benefit from qualitative information, such as individual's attitudes, behaviors, motivations, or cultural backgrounds. In these cases, interviews are a good means for primary research.

Interviews may be conducted in groups or individually. One type of group interview is a focus group. A **focus group** is a small group of people with which the interviewer leads a discussion to gather answers to a set of questions. Focus groups are a good way to evaluate services or test new ideas. Typically, participants are asked about their perceptions, opinions, beliefs, and attitudes. Focus groups may include asking questions, demonstrations, or presentations for products and services. The focus group leader encourages input from all of the participants. The leader or another appointed person records the comments made by the participants. It is crucial to the success of the interview to have detailed and accurate notes. Some focus groups use video equipment or sound recorders to capture the actual discussions.

One-on-one interviews may be used to gather the same type of information collected in a focus group. Depending on the topic, individual interviews might yield better information. For example, you wish to know whether a group of workers is getting adequate on-the-job training. The workers may be more likely to give straightforward answers in a one-on-one interview.

Surveys. A **survey** is a set of questions posed to a group of people to determine how the members of that group think, feel, or act. A questionnaire is given to each person to answer without discussion with another person in the group. Surveys are often used to obtain quantitative data. This data can be collected through personal interviews, over the telephone, by mail, or electronically.

A written survey is highly structured and contains multiple items for response. Questions should be developed in a format that encourages responses. Some items to consider before deciding to use a written survey include the following.

- What is the best method for getting the information?

- Who is the target audience?

- How many people should receive the survey in order to get an adequate number of responses?

- How will you select a representative sampling?

Survey participants must be informed of its purpose and how their responses will be used.

eurobanks/Shutterstock.com

Figure 11-2 provides guidelines for creating an effective survey.

After the survey is written and ready to distribute, a representative sample must be selected. A **representative sample** is a group that includes a cross-section of the entire population that will be targeted. Surveys conducted by professionals, such as political polls, use complex formulas and methods to identify a representative sample. In a business setting, groups that represent a subset of respondents, such as customers or employees, can be identified through the use of company data.

When distributing a survey, it is important to state its purpose and how the responses will be used. If the participant understands why his

Ethics

Ethical Messages

Sometimes it is necessary to write a sales message or other type of document for your organization. Embellishing a message about a product or service or intentionally misrepresenting a product or service is unethical and may be illegal. There are truth-in-advertising laws that must be followed. Focus on the truths of the message and use your communication skills in a positive manner to create interest or demand for the product or service.

or her input is important, then the chance for response will be greater. The participant should be assured that the survey is anonymous. He or she needs to know that personal contact information is confidential. If a survey is conducted via e-mail, the document should be created in a format that is easy to return. If an online survey tool is used, a hyperlink should be included for participants to easily click and complete. The online survey service provider will specify steps in creating the form.

A deadline for returning the form should be clearly stated. Participants must be made aware that timely responses are valuable to the success of the survey. In some cases, an incentive is used to increase the number of responses. Common incentives include a gift, a copy of the final report, or some other motivational item.

Observations. Observations can provide support for the topic of a business report. *Observation* involves watching people interact with their surroundings or others with whom they come in contact. The key to collecting good data is to make sure the subjects do not know they are being observed.

An example of observation is a retailer that employs secret shoppers. A *secret shopper* is a person hired by a business to observe store operations and evaluate service quality. Retailers often use secret shoppers to report on the behavior of sales staff. The secret shoppers record their experience, and the retailers use the information to identify whether employees need additional training.

When collecting data by observation, objectivity is important. The observer needs to accurately record data and remain unbiased. When enlisting the assistance of others to be observers, a checklist should be developed so each observer records consistent data.

Creating a Survey

Make the questions easy to answer. Write questions that have a choice of answers, such as yes/no, multiple choice, or agree/disagree/strongly agree/strongly disagree. These are known as closed-ended questions. They make it easy for the responder to give an answer. Open-ended questions that are subjective take more time to answer and evaluate.

Write objective questions. Write questions that do not lead respondents to a particular answer. Biased questions produce biased data.

Put the questions in a logical sequence. Group items and, when possible, give them headings.

Keep the survey short. If you ask too many questions, the respondent may not want to take the time to complete the survey.

Include space for comments. Often the best information comes from unstructured responses.

Goodheart-Willcox Publisher

Figure 11-2   Follow these guidelines when creating a survey.

Secondary Research

Secondary research is data and information already assembled and recorded by someone else. This might include published materials or resources available at school or work. In many cases, media literacy skills should be used when conducting secondary research to find credible information. Primary research is conducted only if data are not found.

Collecting the Data. There are many sources available as you research, so take advantage of the opportunities to gather information. A wealth of information is available in print and online.

When conducting research online, search engines are useful to find reliable statistics and reports related to your topic. These are often published by major publications, trade and industry organizations, and government agencies. Educational institutions, private industry organizations, and news outlets are also generally reliable Internet sources. Since there are many websites available, it is important to start by narrowing the search. Decide what specific information is needed. Then, determine keywords to use in the search. It is usually best to be very specific at first. Expand the search by being less specific if the search does not turn up enough hits.

Another way to search is to look for a source of information. Sources may be familiar to you because they are well-known or well-respected publications, authors, organizations, journalists, bloggers, or news sources. These sources publish information by writers whose credentials can be checked. It is important to use information that is accurate and complete.

When conducting secondary research, the reliability and credibility of the sources should be considered. The following questions should be asked.

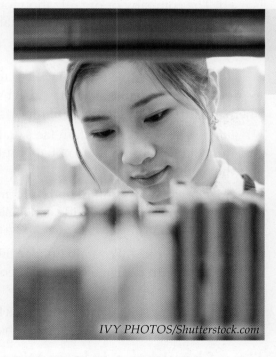

Well-known publications are a good place to start when conducting secondary research.

- What are the author's credentials?

- What is the reputation of the publication in which the source material appears?

- Is the source a mainstream publication or unknown?

- Is the information current?

- What is the copyright date?

- If data are presented, how were they collected and what is the source?

- Can the information be validated through other sources?

IVY PHOTOS/Shutterstock.com

Analyzing the Data. Once the data has been collected, it must be analyzed and interpreted so that it can be used effectively. *Analyze* means to study or examine. If the data gathered is quantitative, facts and figures can be determined and analyzed based on participant responses. If the data is qualitative, individual responses can be summarized and compared. In order for the findings to be relevant, both primary and secondary data should be accurate and valid. Sources used must be reputable and without bias.

After the data is analyzed, it can be interpreted and used to create a report. Conclusions can be drawn and recommendations can be made. A *conclusion* is the researcher's opinion based on the interpretation of the data. A *recommendation* is a course of action suggested to be taken based on the findings.

Crediting Sources. Writers can reference material from other writers provided proper credit is given. This is done by summarizing the work in your own words or by directly quoting part of it. Recall that *plagiarism* is use of another's work without permission and is illegal. A *copyright* legally protects the material's owner from the distribution of his or her work without permission. It is necessary to credit sources when referencing or paraphrasing someone else's work. The following information is needed for creating footnotes or a list of sources at the end of a report:

- author's name

- publication title

- name and location of the publisher

- publication year

- website name, URL, and date of retrieval

Footnotes should appear at the bottom of the page where the information is used. The company or organization for which you are writing the report may have preferences as to how information is documented.

Why Are You Writing?

Reports are written for a specific purpose. Sometimes they are written to provide information. They may also be used to persuade the audience. There are three common types of reports.

- *Informational reports* contain facts, data, or other types of information. Informational reports do not attempt to analyze the data or persuade the reader.

- *Analytical reports* contain both information and analysis of the data. These reports often provide conclusions or recommendations drawn from the analysis.

- *Proposals* typically contain an idea and attempt to persuade the reader to take a certain course of action. Extensive research and analysis often go into a proposal.

Most reports state why the report is being written in the introduction. This helps the audience focus on why they are reading the report.

How Should the Information Be Organized?

As you prepare to write, select an approach that supports your material. The direct or indirect approach must be decided in order to achieve the desired outcome. When using the direct approach, start with a general statement of purpose. Follow this with supporting details. The direct approach is desirable when the reader is expecting a straightforward message. When using the indirect approach, discuss supporting details up front. This will prepare the reader for a general statement of purpose or conclusions.

After the approach has been decided, the next step is to create an outline. As you create the outline for the report, consider the best order in which to present the material. Think ahead and plan the introduction and conclusions that will be made. Note the main points that need to be covered. Once you have all of the information, arrange it in the order that will make the report most effective.

There are several approaches to organization that can be applied to reports. Reports can be organized by chronological or sequential order, order of importance, cause and effect, or problem-solution. A combination of two or more may be used to accomplish a goal.

- *Chronological or sequential order.* When reporting events or discussing a process, the chronological or sequential order is a good choice. *Chronological* means in order of time. *Sequential* means in order of sequence. In this order, start with the earliest events and proceed to the most recent. A variation is to use the reverse order, where the most recent events are presented first.

- *Order of importance.* When organizing by order of importance, present information from most to least important. Readers can easily follow this logic. In some cases, it is better to present information in the reverse order, from least to most important.

- *Cause-and-effect order.* The cause-and-effect organization is useful when a report reflects an investigation. This approach lists facts or ideas followed by conclusions. Opinions should be reported only after careful research and fact finding.

- *Problem-solution order.* This organization type works well when the report will describe a problem and offer a solution or multiple solutions.

 Light Bulbs

Switching from traditional 60-watt incandescent light bulbs to new energy-efficient light bulbs can save a business a lot of money. Two light bulbs commonly used in place of the traditional incandescent light bulb are the 15-watt compact fluorescent lamp (CFL) and the 12-watt light emitting diode (LED).

CFLs can save up to 75 percent of the energy used by an incandescent light bulb. Regular light bulbs last around 1,000 hours, while CFLs can last up to 10,000 hours—ten times longer. LEDs can save up to 80 percent of the energy used by a regular light bulb, and last up to 25,000 hours. Using one of these alternative light bulbs can save a lot of money over time. Not only will there be money saved on energy costs, but because they last longer they do not need to be replaced as often. However, CFLs can contain mercury, so always take care to recycle light bulbs properly.

Presenting the problem helps the reader know why an action is needed. The reader then has options for solving the problem. This approach is common in the professional world when writing a report to a superior.

Figure 11-3 shows a basic outline for a short report. For a long report, the outline might consist of key points with details.

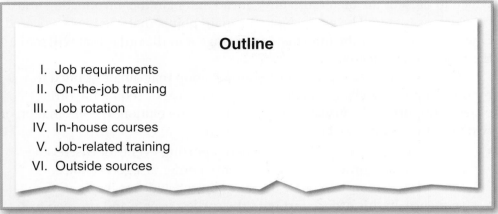

Outline

I. Job requirements
II. On-the-job training
III. Job rotation
IV. In-house courses
V. Job-related training
VI. Outside sources

Goodheart-Willcox Publisher

Figure 11-3 This is an outline for a report.

Section 11.1 Review

 Check Your Understanding

1. Describe how a formal report is different from an informal report.
2. What is accomplished during the prewriting stage when writing a report?
3. List and describe the three types of reports.
4. Name the most common methods of primary research used for a business report.
5. Explain how a writer can make sure a report is completed on time.

 Build Your Vocabulary

As you progress through this course, develop a personal glossary of key terms. This will help you build your vocabulary and prepare you for a career. Write a definition for each of the following terms and add it to your personal glossary.

report
formal report
informal report
data
qualitative data
quantitative data

primary research
focus group
survey
representative sampling
secondary research

Formal and Informal Reports

Objectives

After completing this section, you will be able to:

- **Explain** how to write a formal report.
- **Describe** the steps necessary to complete and publish a report.
- **Explain** how to write an informal report.

Key Terms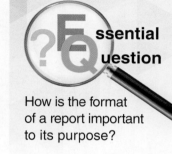

table of contents
executive summary
conclusion
recommendation
citation

heading
periodic report
progress report
informal study report

?ssential Question

How is the format of a report important to its purpose?

Writing Formal Reports

Once your research is finished and your sources are organized, you are ready to continue the writing process and compose the report. The writing stage includes creating the first draft. You will complete the first draft and revise as many times as necessary to create the final product. Once you have finished revising the report, it will be necessary to edit the document. Where revising focuses on constructing the content, editing is polishing the document until it is in finished form.

When you prepare a report, ask if there are standards that must be followed. Formal reports are written in the third person. They follow a structured format that adheres to standards used by most businesses. There may be templates that you need to use to create a new report. A company template may include text fields or a letterhead, for example. If there are no standards to follow, you may use the templates provided in your word processing software. You can also look for examples online.

The parts of a formal report vary according to the purpose and topic. There are several common parts that may appear in a formal report.

Title Page

All formal reports should have a title page designed for readability and visual appeal. These elements belong on the title page, as shown in Figure 11-4:

- name of the report
- name of the person or group for whom the report was written

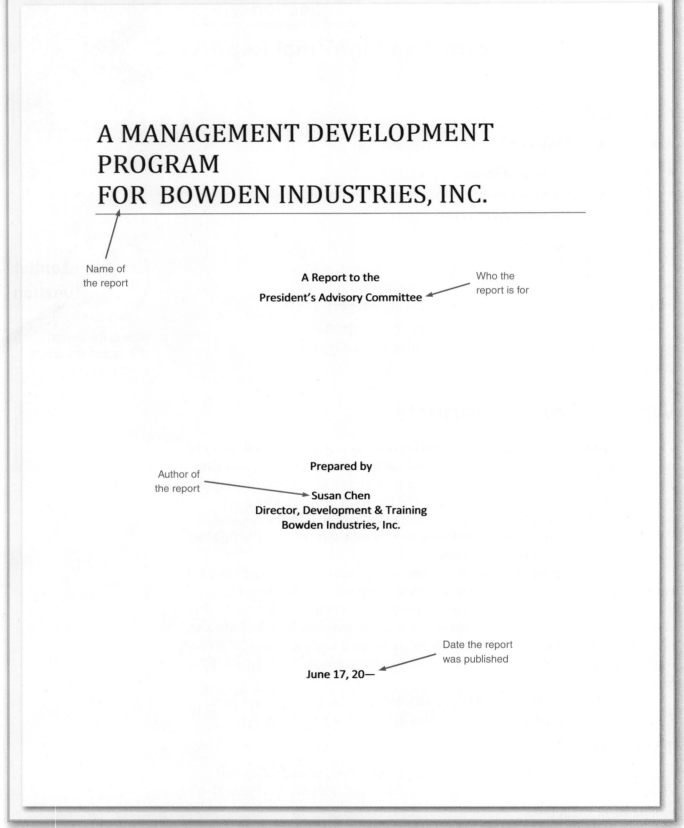

A MANAGEMENT DEVELOPMENT
PROGRAM
FOR BOWDEN INDUSTRIES, INC.

Name of
the report

A Report to the

President's Advisory Committee

Who the
report is for

Prepared by

Author of
the report

Susan Chen
Director, Development & Training
Bowden Industries, Inc.

Date the report
was published

June 17, 20—

Figure 11-4   This is an example of a title page.

- name of the author of the report
- date the report is published

Sometimes other information, such as the location of the company, may also be needed.

Table of Contents

A table of contents is necessary so the reader knows what is included in the report. The **table of contents** lists the major sections and subsections within the report with page numbers, as shown in Figure 11-5. This page may be referred to as *table of contents* or *contents*.

Executive Summary

The **executive summary** summarizes the main points in the report, as shown in Figure 11-6. It is sometimes referred to as a *summary* or *abstract*. This summary should be an overview for some recipients who may not read the entire report. It appears at the beginning of the report, before the introduction.

Introduction

The reader's attention should be captured by giving an overview of the content of the report. An introduction usually discusses the purpose of the report and the benefits of the ideas or recommendations you are presenting. The introduction of the report often covers this information.

- History or background that led to the preparation of the report.
- Purpose for which the report was written, including the need or justification for the report.
- Scope of the report, including what is covered and, if necessary, what is not covered.
- Definitions of terms that may present problems for certain readers.
- Method of gathering information, facts, and figures for the report.

An example of an introduction is shown in Figure 11-7. However, the order of information in an introduction may differ based on the requirements for the report you are writing.

Body

The body of the report contains all of the information, data, and statistics you assemble. Your outline will help you organize ideas and information in a logical manner. Providing supporting facts and figures from reliable sources will help the audience understand the content.

If the topic you are writing about is very high level, formal tone is more likely to achieve this goal. You want to convince the reader you have thoroughly studied the matter and that your facts and figures are highly trustworthy. If, on the other hand, you are writing a report on employee activities that boost morale and create a sense of team, a conversational tone would be appropriate. This friendlier tone will help set the stage for the theme of the report.

Your place in the organization will influence the tone of the content. A report addressed to the company president is likely to be formal in tone. If you have a friendly relationship with your supervisor, a report you write for her or him may be more conversational.

Begin introduction on page 1 and use Roman numerals for preceding pages

CONTENTS

Executive Summary iii
  Introduction 1
Job Requirements 5
  Senior Executives 5
  Vice Presidents 6
  Managers 6
  Supervisors 7
  Employees 8
On-the-Job Training 8
  Establishing Objectives 10
  Organization Planning 12
  Delegation of Authority 12
  Job Counseling 13
Company Training Programs 14
Company Structure and Objectives 14
  Basic Management Techniques 15
  Professional Development Courses 15
  Job-Specific Training 16
  Job Rotation 17
Career Paths 18
  Career Ladders at Bowden 22
  Studies on Promotion and Retention 24
  Succession Planning 25
Recommendations 27
Conclusion 29
Works Cited 30
Appendix 31

ii

Goodheart-Willcox Publisher

Figure 11-5 This is an example of a table of contents.

EXECUTIVE SUMMARY

The President's Advisory Committee of Bowden Industries, Inc., requested a study to determine the reasons the company has had difficulty filling management positions and to find solutions to the problem. If Bowden is to continue on a path to future expansion, a concerted effort must be made to hire and develop the necessary managerial expertise.

Research

A thorough examination of hiring, training and development, management, and promotion practices was conducted. The research looked at why vacancies occurred, how they were filled, and the success rate of these hirings. The data suggest that management positions at Bowden require a high level of training, experience, and education and that there is no established route to provide this combination of preparedness for those entering management.

Findings

Findings showed that the majority of openings had to be filled from the outside because current staff had not been prepared to accept the greater responsibilities of management. The studies also revealed that those hired from outside required extensive training once they came onboard. The lack of inside promotions had a negative impact on morale and the on-the-job adjustment period for employees recruited from outside was very expensive.

Recommendations

The attached report recommends that the company create a formal, well-rounded training program under the guidance of an appointed director and a Management Education Committee for the purpose of training candidates for managerial positions.

iii

Goodheart-Willcox Publisher

Figure 11-6   An executive summary provides a brief overview of the main points and, when used, appears at the beginning of the report.

INTRODUCTION

Bowden Industries, Inc., is often referred to as "a family that keeps outgrowing its home." This implies little planning, innovation, and management leadership in the company's twelve years of existence, which is simply not true. Product diversification, innovative marketing and manufacturing, and sound financial management all attest to the effective leadership with which the company has been blessed.

At the May 9 meeting of the President's Advisory Committee, the question was asked, "where will the managerial expertise needed for future growth and expansion come from?" The purpose of this report is to provide possible answers to that vital question.

History

In the past, Bowden has depended largely on universities and executive placement agencies for sources of managerial talent—and, of course, on its own promotion-from-within policy. By and large, these have been good sources of talent and, no doubt, will continue to be used. However, training and developing those new management hires has been through hit-or-miss, largely unstructured, on-the-job supervision. The results are mixed. Some people were well trained and quickly moved up when positions became available. Others languished and, seeing no opportunity for growth, left the company.

Scope

The term "management" in this report refers to all positions from first-line supervisors (classified as Levels 13 and 14 by the Human Resources Department) right on up to the top executive positions. No attention has been given to lower-level jobs in this report, although this is obviously a subject that deserves full exploration later.

Statement of Problem

During the past year, 44 vacancies occurred in management positions. Of that number, 22 were the result of retirement because of age or health, 13 resigned to accept positions in other companies, and the remaining nine were the result of newly created positions within the company.

It is interesting to find that 27 of the 44 openings had to be filled from the outside. In other words, only 17 employees were considered ready to accept the greater responsibilities of management. Actually, few of the people recruited from the outside were actually ready either (the unknown often looks better than the known); many required a long break-in period. Besides having a negative effect on employees who were denied promotion, outside recruiting and on-the-job adjustment are very expensive.

Goodheart-Willcox Publisher

Figure 11-7   An introduction states the purpose of the report. A page number does not appear on the first page of the introduction.

Bias

Sometimes bias on the part of the reader will influence your handling of the topic. Consider biases the reader might bring to the subject matter, and develop content to address them. For example, your reader may be known to be very timid about innovations. In this case, recommendations for new product designs should concentrate on facts rather than appealing to trends.

Knowledge

Assess the level of knowledge the audience will bring and if there is variation within the audience. The amount of background information and the need to define terms depends on your assessment of the audience's prior knowledge. The higher the reader knowledge in the area covered by the report, the less explanation needed.

Readability

Another aspect of preparing the body of your report is readability. Remember that readability is a measure of how easy it is for the audience to understand your writing and locate information.

Conclusions and Recommendations

Your closing should summarize the key points. In some cases, you will want to close with conclusions and recommendations based on your study or analysis. **Conclusions** are the writer's summary of what the audience should take away from the report. **Recommendations** are actions the writer believes the reader should take. Both of these should follow logically from the information presented in the body of the report, as shown in Figure 11-8. If you make a leap in logic, you risk losing credibility with the audience.

RECOMMENDATIONS

On the basis of this study, there would appear to be a definite need for a well-rounded education program at Bowden Industries, Inc. There are numerous possible methods of operating and conducting it. The following recommendations are offered.

1. Appoint a Director of Management Development, preferably a person with sound academic credentials (possibly a Ph.D.), teaching experience in management at the undergraduate and graduate levels, and broad business experience in supervision and management. The appointed person would report directly to the Executive Vice President or to the President.

2. Appoint a Management Education Committee, consisting of the top executive of each of the six divisions in the company and the Executive Vice President (ex officio). This committee would advise the Director of Management Development in planning and operating the program, using as many of the sources described in this report as feasible.

Goodheart-Willcox Publisher

Figure 11-8   Recommendations provide the writer's suggestions for a course of action.

Citations

If your report contains information from sources you have researched, these sources should be acknowledged. A **citation** lists the author, title, and publisher of the source, date of publication, and location of the publisher or online address. Citations may be listed in footnotes on the page where the reference occurs or in a bibliography at the end of the report. Examples of citations are shown in Figure 11-9. It is necessary to provide citations for both print and electronic sources.

Optional Elements

Complex reports may contain other elements that help the reader find information and understand the contents.

- *List of visuals.* A report can be greatly enhanced with the use of visuals in the form of tables and figures. Enhancing reports with visuals is covered in Chapter 12. If visuals are used, include a list at the front of the report with page references. This will aid readers in quickly finding information.

- *Glossary.* If terminology used in the report may be unfamiliar to some readers, include a list at the end of the report to define important terms.

- *Appendices.* Information that users might want to refer to, but is not integral to the body, may be included at the back of the report in an appendix. For example, if your report includes survey results, you might provide the survey questionnaire in an appendix.

These optional elements are opportunities to include extra information that may not fit into the scope of the report body.

Preparing the Report

The writing process also includes soliciting feedback. If there is someone available to read the report, have that person give it a final review. Ask for feedback and suggestions that will make the report more effective.

The next step in the writing process is postwriting. In the postwriting stage, the report is proofread one final time. Errors distract from the

WORKS CITED

Arbor, Jonathan Cole, "Training That Works." *Train the Trainer* (March 20—) pp. 23–25.

Coletta, Nicole, *The Essentials of Performance Management.* New York: Future Publishing, 2010.

Newberg, Alexis, "Formal Training Programs at Bowden Industries," Report Submitted to the Executive Board, Bowden Training Department, 2009.

Goodheart-Willcox Publisher

Figure 11-9   Always cite works that are referenced in the report.

message and suggest you were careless in preparing the communication. Your written work will be judged by its correctness and appearance.

Completing Formal Reports

The final step in the writing process is publishing. Formatting is a part of the publishing step. It is important to carefully format your report so the report appears polished and professional. Publishing a report in the correct format ensures it will be read by its audience, either inside or outside the organization.

Formatting

The appearance of the document is important. Many organizations have formatting guidelines for reports. Other organizations use templates provided in Microsoft Word or other word processing software.

When the topic covers more than one key point or important issue, consider using headings as a design element. **Headings** are words and phrases that introduce sections of text. Headings are leveled, beginning with the section opener title and continuing with the main heading and subheadings. They organize blocks of information in a document and serve as guideposts to alert the reader to what is coming. Most narrative text can be divided into main topics and subtopics with no more than three levels of headings. Figure 11-10 shows examples of how to display these levels using the heading styles in Microsoft Word.

Exploring Communication Careers

Fashion Designer

The size and shape of the buttons on your shirt and the style of pants in your closet are examples of some of the decisions made by fashion designers. Fashion designers bring their artistic ability and knowledge of garment construction together to create clothing and accessories. Understanding the target audience for the clothing they design is an important responsibility of the job. Typical job titles for this position include *fashion coordinator*, *technical designer*, *costume designer*, and *apparel designer*.

Some examples of tasks that fashion designers perform include:

- Sketch both rough and detailed drawings of clothing and accessories.
- Discuss designs with sales team and management or clients.
- Revise designs based on feedback.
- Adapt designs for target audiences.
- Select textiles, materials, and production techniques to achieve the intended design.
- Keep current regarding fashion trends by attending fashion shows and reviewing publications about fashion.

Fashion designers need a high school diploma and some college. Many jobs require an associate degree or bachelor degree in fashion design or a related field. Knowledge of image editing or graphics software and knowledge of garment construction are needed as well.

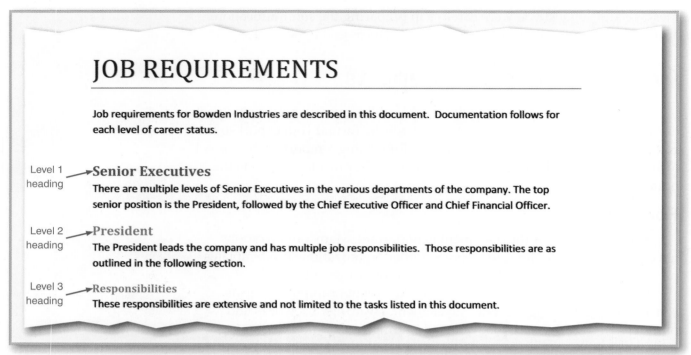

JOB REQUIREMENTS

Job requirements for Bowden Industries are described in this document. Documentation follows for each level of career status.

Level 1
heading → **Senior Executives**

There are multiple levels of Senior Executives in the various departments of the company. The top senior position is the President, followed by the Chief Executive Officer and Chief Financial Officer.

Level 2
heading → **President**

The President leads the company and has multiple job responsibilities. Those responsibilities are as outlined in the following section.

Level 3
heading → **Responsibilities**

These responsibilities are extensive and not limited to the tasks listed in this document.

Goodheart-Willcox Publisher

Figure 11-10   Levels of headings within the body of the report help to organize information and guide the reader.

The use of white space for readability is important. This includes margins, space between paragraphs, and other blank space on the page. Style manuals like *The Chicago Manual of Style* and the Modern Language Association *MLA Handbook* include formatting guidelines. You may also opt to use the default spacing in Microsoft Word. Use the formatting preferred by your organization.

Publishing

Publishing is preparing a document for distribution. Formal reports are often published on the intranet site of an organization. This makes it convenient for those within the organization who need to read the report to have access at their convenience. Alternatively, reports intended for the public may be posted on the organization's website.

The electronic file containing the report should be in PDF format so that no unauthorized changes can be made. The audience can read the report online or print a copy.

If the report will be presented at a meeting, it may be bound to make the presentation polished and highly professional. Binding may be handled through a company's graphics department or an outside service.

Writing Informal Reports

An informal report does not require the research that a formal report requires. It is generally used internally and uses a casual tone and personal pronouns. An informal report does not have a table of contents, appendices, or other components of a formal report. Generally, it has an introduction, body, and conclusion and will be only a few pages long.

Introduction

The introduction states the purpose of the report. If the report is being written at the request of someone, you might mention that in the introduction. For example:

> Following is a report on my visit to the new conference facility we are considering for next month's meeting on digital media and advertising.

Body

The body contains the information of the report. Decide whether or not the content has subtopics that will help the reader scan and skim for information. A short report on a site visit to view a facility might be divided into these sections: location, facility description, and cost. The body of the report should be of sufficient length to communicate the purpose of the document.

Conclusion

Reports should end with a brief summary of main points from the writer's point of view. If you use headings, this section might be labeled *Conclusion*, *Recommendations*, or *Summary*. If your report does not have headings, the conclusion is the last paragraph. In the above example, the writer would likely conclude with a recommendation about whether to use the facility.

Types of Informal Reports

It is not possible to list the many types of informal reports used in the workplace. Some of the types of informal reports used in business are described as follows.

Periodic Reports

Periodic reports are written according to a specified schedule: daily, weekly, monthly, quarterly, etc. A periodic report generally provides the status of a project, reports facts and figures over a specified period, or summarizes an ongoing activity. Such reports usually can be presented in a standard format.

An example of a periodic report is a progress report. A **progress report** is written in a specified format and periodically submitted to track the status of a project. Progress reports are also known as *status reports*. These types of reports can be as simple as a monthly one-page update using a template. They can also be as complex as an annual report from a corporation written for its stockholders.

An informal report can be incorporated as part of an e-mail or as an e-mail attachment. In Figure 11-11, the report is incorporated in the body of the e-mail. While this format is not difficult to read, the layout makes it hard to make comparisons. Additionally, each quarter the report will have to be created from scratch. Another option is to send the report as an e-mail attachment. When attaching a report, use the report file name as the e-mail subject line. This helps the receiver manage his or her e-mail more efficiently.

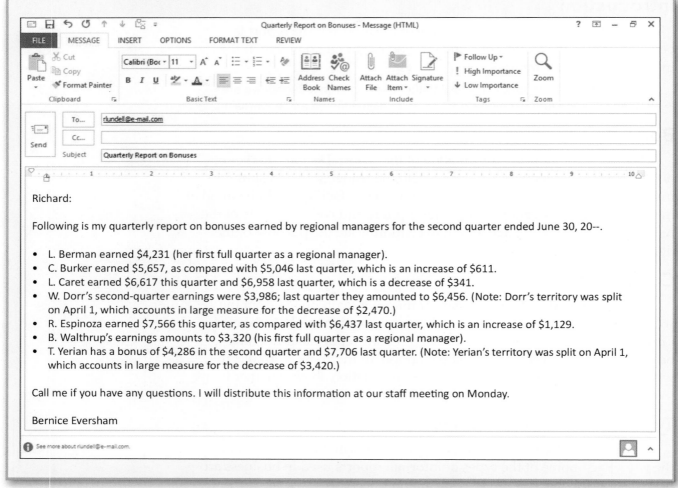

Figure 11-11   This is an example of a quarterly report sent in the body of an e-mail.

Informal Study Reports

An **informal study report** provides information that is gathered by the writer through methods other than formal research. These methods of research may include reading documents, conducting informal interviews, reviewing competitive products, or attending a meeting. Informal study reports may be initiated by the writer or prepared at the request of someone higher up in the organization. Informal reports on activities are sometimes written in the first person to state your own actions, conclusions, and ideas.

Informal study reports can be incorporated into a memo or e-mail or created as a separate document. Figure 11-12 is an example of a report based on an informal study. Note that this report uses appropriate headings to guide the reader.

Method (describing the method used to obtain the data)

Findings and Conclusions (including the procedure used)

Recommendations

Review of Customer Correspondence

I have completed the review of customer correspondence you requested on December 16 for the period of November 1 through December 15, 20--. As you suggested, I read all outgoing letters and e-mails written by the six Customer Care Specialists. During this period, 64 pieces of communication (18 letters and 46 e-mails) were written and mailed to customers on issues not covered by our form letters.

Method

As I read each letter, I assigned a grade to it:

- A (excellent)
- B (good)
- C (passable)
- D (poor)

The elements considered in assigning these grades were: tone (friendliness), helpfulness, accuracy of information, organization, and correct mechanics (grammar, spelling, and punctuation).

Findings and Conclusions

Number of Letters and E-mails	Grade Assigned
14	A
13	B
25	C
12	D

My evaluations were subjective; however, the distribution of grades I assigned supports the types of criticisms we have been hearing from the sales staff. As they mentioned to us at the last meeting, there are many examples of indifference, carelessness with facts, lack of clarity, and negativism. It seems apparent, based on the 64 pieces of correspondence that were examined, that the standard of customer correspondence is much lower than it should be.

Recommendations

Based on this informal study, I recommend we set up a written communications course for all Customer Care Specialists. I have contacted Dorothy Fairchild in Human Resources Training about setting up and teaching the course. Last year, she organized and taught a course for the Credit Department and, according to the credit manager, Clark Pinson, it was a great success. I will be happy to assist in setting up the course and will help the instructor in any way I can, if you think this is a feasible solution.

Goodheart-Willcox Publisher

Figure 11-12   This is an example of a report based on an informal study.

Idea and Suggestion Reports

Idea or suggestion reports are written when employees are asked for ideas and suggestions for making improvements. Some of the areas where input is often requested include improving employee morale, saving time, and cutting costs. In responding to such requests, follow these guidelines.

- Be assertive in offering your opinion. You would not have received an invitation to contribute your ideas if they were not considered valuable.

- Try to begin with positive remarks about the present situation and tactfully proceed with your suggestions for change.

- Be specific in your recommendations. The reader should not have to guess what you have in mind.

- When appropriate, group your ideas according to subject. Prominently display the subjects.

Section 11.2 Review

 Check Your Understanding

1. What are the standard elements of a formal report?

2. Summarize the importance of a report's introduction.

3. After writing and preparing a formal report, what two steps need to be completed before a report is finished?

4. Name the standard elements of an informal report.

5. Name, and briefly describe, an example of an informal report.

 Build Your Vocabulary

As you progress through this course, develop a personal glossary of key terms. This will help you build your vocabulary and prepare you for a career. Write a definition for each of the following terms and add it to your personal glossary.

table of contents	heading
executive summary	periodic report
conclusion	progress report
recommendation	informal study report
citation	

Chapter Summary

Section 11.1 Planning and Research

- A report is a document that presents information in a structured format. Examples of reports are informational reports, analytical reports, or proposals. They can be formal or informal.

- Prewriting helps identify the purpose and audience of the report by answering the questions of who, what, when, where, why, and how. Reports often require research. Primary research is conducted by the writer in preparation for writing a report. Secondary research is data and information already assembled and recorded by someone else. When using secondary research, always credit your sources.

Section 11.2 Formal and Informal Reports

- Formal reports are written in the third person and follow a structured format. The parts of a formal report vary according to the purpose and topic. Common parts that may appear in a formal report are the title page, table of contents, executive summary, introduction, body, conclusions or recommendations, and citations.

- Formal reports must be appropriately formatted and published. Carefully format a report so it appears polished and professional. Select a method of publishing that meets the needs of the audience.

- Informal reports are generally used internally, project a casual tone, and use personal pronouns. They typically have an introduction, body, and conclusion and will be only a few pages long. Types of informal reports include periodic reports, informal study reports, and idea or suggestion reports.

Online Activities

Complete the following activities which will help you learn, practice, and expand your knowledge and skills.

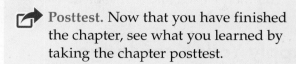

Posttest. Now that you have finished the chapter, see what you learned by taking the chapter posttest.

Vocabulary. Practice vocabulary for this chapter using the e-flash cards, matching activity, and vocabulary game until you are able to recognize their meanings.

English/Language Arts. Visit www.g-wlearning.com to download each data file for this chapter. Follow the instructions to complete an English/language arts activity to practice what you have learned in this chapter.

Activity File 11-1: Creating a Survey

Activity File 11-2: Improving Your Formatting Skills

Review Your Knowledge

1. How are reports used in the workplace?
2. Summarize the three common methods of primary research for a business report.
3. What is the role of a representative sampling when conducting a survey?
4. How can the credibility of a secondary source be evaluated?
5. What information is needed to create a footnote?
6. Why is it important to keep reader bias, reader knowledge, and readability in mind when writing the body of a formal report?
7. What are some optional elements that enhance the understanding of a report?

8. Describe how headings can be applied when formatting a report.

9. What is the benefit of publishing a report in PDF format?

10. Explain how informal study reports are commonly used and distributed.

Apply Your Knowledge

1. Identify a research topic. The topic of your report might be informational, analytical, or persuasive. After you have chosen your topic, begin prewriting by answering these questions: Why are you writing? Who is the audience? What do you want to communicate? Where is the information? How should the information be organized? When must the report be finished?

2. Create an instrument to use for conducting primary research. Depending on your report topic, you might develop a survey to distribute, write questions for interviewing people, or prepare an observation checklist.

3. Next, begin researching your topic. Select the representative sampling for your research. Create a spreadsheet listing the people in the survey and their information such as name, age, gender, or other important data that will influence the research.

4. Utilize a software application such as a spreadsheet program to record the data you gathered. Analyze and interpret he data and describe your observations. What did you uncover? You will create graphics to illustrate the data in the next chapter.

5. Next, conduct secondary research on your project. Use the guidelines in a style guide, such as *The Chicago Manual of Style* or the *MLA Handbook*, to cite a book, newspaper article, or copy on a website. How is the citation for each type of source unique?

6. Write a formal report of your findings using word processing or publishing software. Address reader bias, reader knowledge, and readability. Use the formatting guidelines provided in this chapter. Save the report that you just completed. You will use this report for the Apply Your Knowledge activities in the next chapter.

Communication Skills

College and Career Readiness

Writing. Rhetoric is the study of writing or speaking as a way of communicating information or persuading someone. Describe a rhetorical technique that can be used to provide information or persuade someone when writing a formal report.

Speaking. Select three classmates to participate in a discussion panel. Acting as the team leader, assign each person to a specific task such as time-keeper, recorder, etc. Discuss the difference between qualitative and quantitative data and how to interpret each type. What techniques should be used to communicate the data after it has been interpreted?

Internet Research

Finding Credible Sources. Research 529 plans using various Internet resources. Apply your secondary research skills to find the information in a variety of formats such as reports, graphs, or articles. Define the 529 plan and its purpose. What methods did you use to extract information from the resources? Write a short informal report on your findings. Cite each source that you use.

Teamwork

Work with your team to develop a checklist that could be used to observe reactions of people passing by a retail window display. The checklist should provide information for the observers so that each observes, interprets, and communicates the same data. The observation technique is successful only when the same criteria are used by everyone on the research team.

Portfolio Development

College and Career Readiness

Talents. You have collected documents that show your skills and talents. Select a book report, essay, or poem that you have written that demonstrates your writing talents. If you are an artist, include copies of your completed works. If you are a musician, create a video with segments from your performances.

1. Create a Microsoft Word document that lists your talents. Use the heading "Talents" along with your name. Next to each talent listed, write a description of an assignment or performance and explain how your talent is shown in it. If there is a video, state that it will be made available upon request or identify where it can be viewed online. Indicate that sample screenshots are attached.

2. Scan hard-copy documents related to your talents to serve as samples. Save screenshots from a video, if appropriate, in an appropriate file format. Place hard copies in a container for future reference.

3. Place the video file in an appropriate subfolder for your digital portfolio.

4. Update your master spreadsheet.

CTSOs

Ethics. Many competitive CTSO events include an ethics component that covers multiple topics. The ethics component of an event may be part of an objective test. However, ethics may also be a part of the competition in which teams participate to defend a given position on an ethical dilemma or topic.

To prepare for an ethics event, complete the following activities.

1. Read the guidelines provided by your organization.

2. Make notes on index cards about important points to remember. Use these notes to study.

3. To get an overview of various ethical situations that individuals encounter, read each of the Ethics features that appear throughout this text.

4. Ask someone to practice role-playing with you by asking questions or taking the other side of an argument.

5. Use the Internet to find more information about ethical issues. Find and review ethics cases that involve business situations.

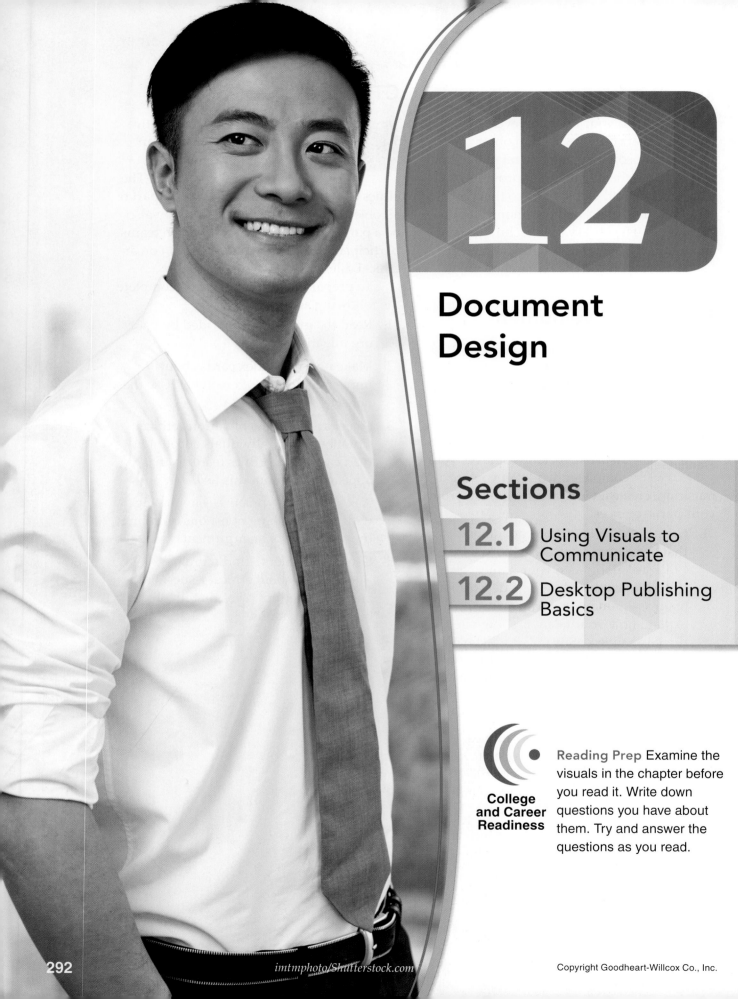

12

Document Design

Sections

12.1 Using Visuals to Communicate

12.2 Desktop Publishing Basics

imtmphoto/Shutterstock.com

Check Your Communication IQ

Before you begin the chapter, see what you already know about communication by taking the chapter pretest. The pretest is available at www.g-wlearning.com.

Case Study

Visual Communication

Macy Bertram works at a marketing firm. She wants to propose a new brochure for a client's large chain of fitness centers. She thinks a large brochure with high-quality colorful photos featuring the luxurious spa, pool, and racquetball courts, as well as the gym and classes, would attract new customers for the client.

Macy's research supports her idea that users of fitness centers are looking for more than just a place to exercise. They want a place to socialize, network, and relax. Macy believes the target market will respond if the company changes its promotion strategy to include the new, glossy brochure. She must convince both her manager and the client that the new brochure is a good idea.

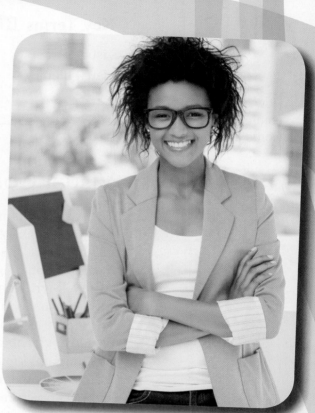

wavebreakmedia/Shutterstock.com

Critical Thinking

1. Why should Macy include other types of visuals in her presentation or just photos?

2. Are there any ethical issues that need to be considered when creating a brochure for a client that includes photos?

Using Visuals to Communicate

Objectives

After completing this section, you will be able to:

- **Identify** different types of visuals.
- **Explain** how to use visuals appropriately in a professional document.

Key Terms 📤

visual

visual literacy

table

legend

figure

infographic

illustration

caption

figure number

Essential Question

How can visuals communicate what words cannot?

Visual Communication

An important component of professional communication is visual communication. As you recall, visual communication is using visuals to communicate an idea or concept. A **visual** is any image that represents an idea, concept, or information. An example of a visual is a map or chart.

Well-written professional documents are necessary in the business world. Visuals can be used to enhance the power of written communication. They serve as a tool to complement, and sometimes communicate, a message. Visuals are used to attract attention and provide interest. They can illustrate, entertain, or inform. Visuals are typically used in printed reports, letters, and other documents to add clarity or interest. Readers appreciate looking at pictures or charts that help them understand the message of a document.

Visual literacy is the ability to create or interpret the meaning of a visual message. A visually literate writer understands that clear images help the reader interpret a message. It *does not* require that the writer be an expert designer. It *does* require following certain guidelines to produce the desired results.

Before creating visuals for a document, consult a style guide, such as the *Publication Manual of the American Psychological Association*, for specific guidelines. The American Psychological Association (APA) offers guidance on developing well-designed elements that can be easily interpreted by the reader.

The APA simplifies the choice of visuals by classifying them as tables or figures. This aids the writing process to select which type of image will be used.

Tables

A **table** is a visual that displays information in columns and rows and is often used to compare data, as shown in Figure 12-1. The information that is displayed should be clear to the reader without additional explanation. A well-designed table helps the reader interpret what is being displayed.

Table 1: Game Downloads

Game Title	Number of Downloads	Number of Returns	Total Units Sold
Age of Aces	68,249	9,861	58,388
Alien Encounter	73,017	15,637	57,380
Badge of Courage	105,225	2,385	102,840
Gridiron	97,531	4,976	92,555
Soldier's Quest	22,753	12,874	9,879
Sparta	85,021	1,115	83,906
Total	451,796	46,848	404,948

Goodheart-Willcox Publisher

Figure 12-1   Tables are used to compare data.

Exploring
Communication Careers

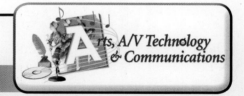

Editor

Editors work at publishing houses and other producers of print and online material. Editors write content, revise manuscript, and guide authors to create the best product possible. They verify facts and improve grammar, sentence structure, and punctuation in manuscript.

An editor may work with copy editors and proofreaders to polish final manuscript before it goes to press. Typical job titles for an editor include *developmental editor* and *print editor*.

Some examples of tasks that editors perform include:

- Plan the scope and subject matter of content to be published.

- Prepare, write, and edit copy to improve readability.

- Verify facts, statistics, and other elements to ensure accuracy and that plagiarism has not occurred.

- Oversee copy editors, proofreaders, and others to finalize materials.

- Work with the publisher's art department or director to develop visuals.

Editors must have an excellent knowledge of English and understand how to use language to convey ideas in a clear, concise manner. They must have good communication skills to work with authors and other editorial personnel. Most editor jobs require a bachelor degree. Those in higher-level editing jobs may be required to have a master degree. Previous experience in editing or writing is preferred.

The reader should focus on the information rather than the design elements. A well-designed table includes:

- a title that includes the word "table"
- clearly labeled columns and rows
- a balanced number of columns and rows
- a caption that describes the information it contains
- left-aligned text
- numbers aligned by decimal point
- credit or source lines, if applicable

If symbols, colors, or abbreviations are used, explanations should be given. Providing a legend may be helpful to interpret the information. A **legend** is a list that explains the set of symbols used.

Figures

Visuals that are not tables are called figures. A **figure** is a visual such as a graph, chart, or illustration.

Graphs

A *graph* depicts information through the use of lines, bars, or other symbols. There are several different types of graphs. Each type of graph has a specific purpose to which it is well-suited.

- *Circle graphs* show the relationship of the parts to a whole. Figure 12-2 illustrates the impact a circle can make in a document.

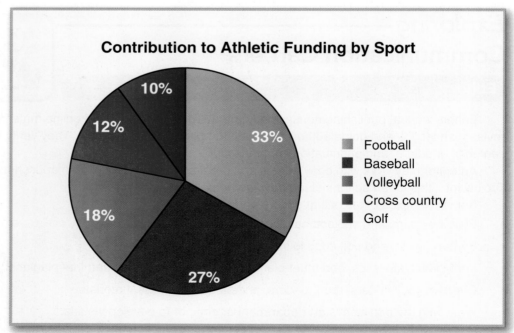

Goodheart-Willcox Publisher

Figure 12-2   A circle graph illustrates the relationship of parts to a whole.

- *Line graphs* illustrate changes in data over a period of time, as shown in Figure 12-3. The horizontal axis shows time or quantity. The vertical axis shows amounts.

- *Bar graphs* show comparison of data. The bars may be vertical, as in Figure 12-4, or horizontal, as shown in Figure 12-5.

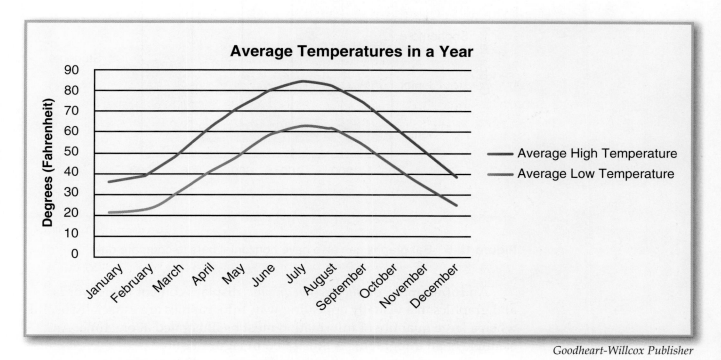

Goodheart-Willcox Publisher

Figure 12-3   A line graph illustrates changes over time.

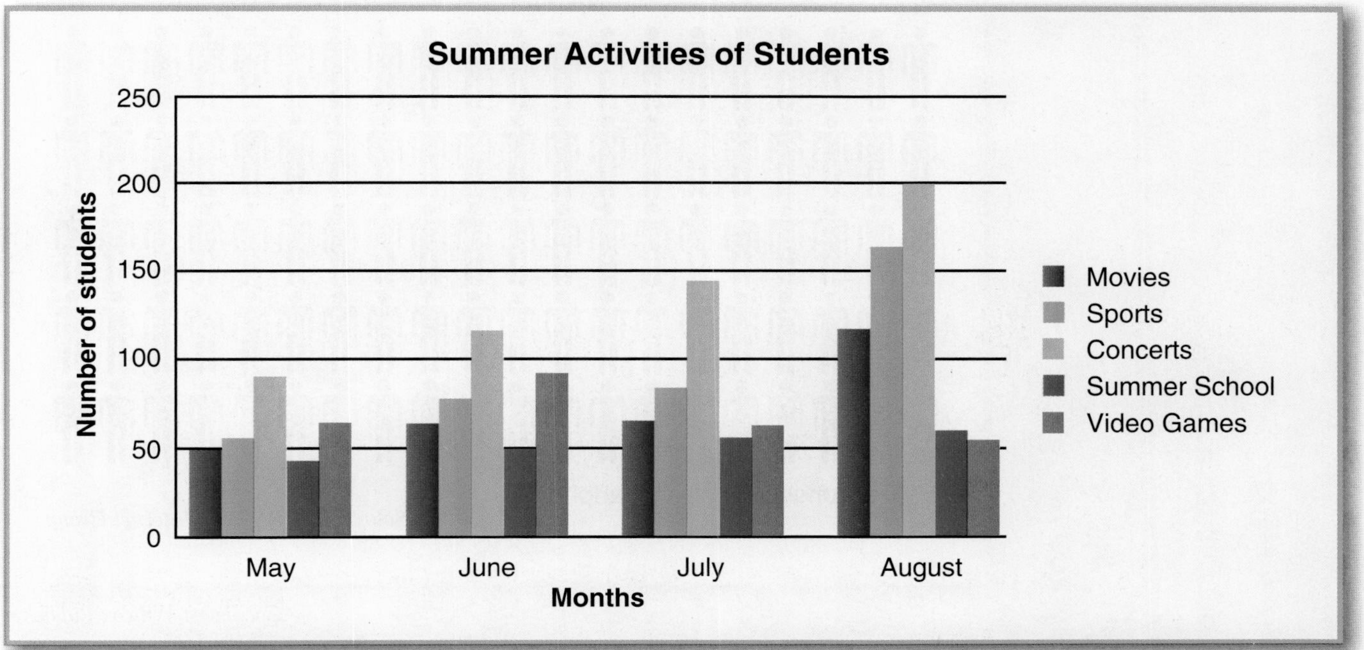

Goodheart-Willcox Publisher

Figure 12-4   Bar graphs used to compare data often have vertical bars.

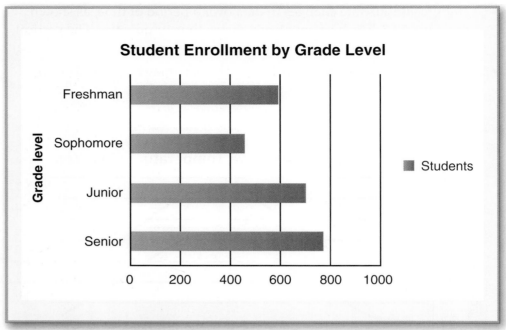

Figure 12-5   Bar graphs can also have horizontal bars to compare data.

An **infographic**, or *information graphic*, displays content using words and graphics in a visually appealing way. Infographics are especially useful when a large quantity of information must be illustrated at one time. An example of an infographic is illustrated in Figure 12-6.

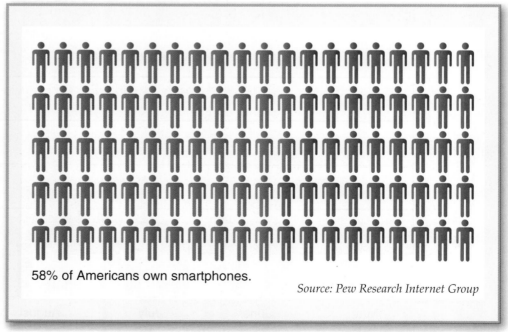

Figure 12-6   Infographics illustrate data in a visually appealing way.

Charts

A *chart* shows a process or hierarchy. A *flowchart* depicts steps in a process, illustrated in Figure 12-7. Directional lines may be used to show the order in which steps should be completed. The shape of each symbol used represents an action.

An *organization chart* shows channels of authority in an organization, as shown in Figure 12-8. Lines are used to show who reports to whom in the organization.

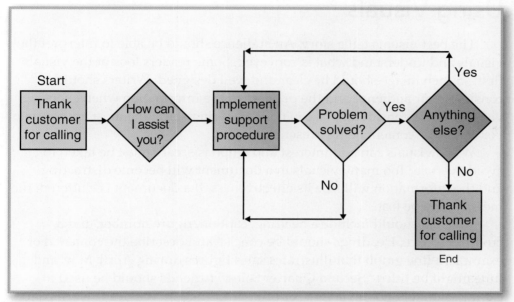

Goodheart-Willcox Publisher

Figure 12-7   Flowcharts illustrate the steps in a process.

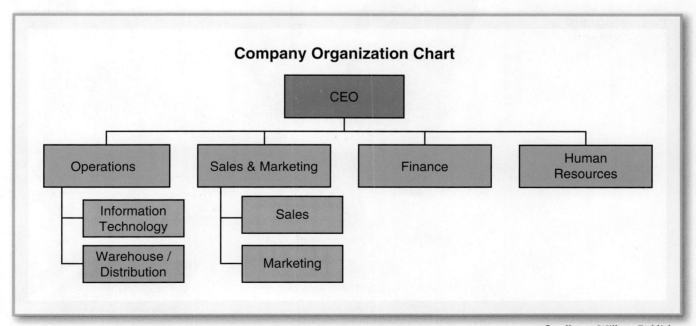

Goodheart-Willcox Publisher

Figure 12-8   Organization charts show channels of authority and reporting.

Illustrations

Maps, drawings, or photographs are types of figures called **illustrations**. Illustrations add interest and provide a realistic view of the information being presented.

- *Maps* show geographic regions.
- *Drawings* are clip art or line art.
- *Photographs* are real-life pictures.

Using Visuals

The best visuals tell a story. An audience should be able to interpret the visuals and understand what is conveyed. Some readers look at the visuals first, so each image should be clear and well designed. Writers should consider their audience and the purpose of the information when choosing visuals. These considerations can help the writer select the most appropriate visual for the content being presented.

While visuals can add interest and emphasis, care must be taken to avoid overuse. Too many visuals in a document will become distracting, and the information will lose its effectiveness. If a document is cluttered, the message can be lost.

A visual should include a heading, caption, figure number, and a credit or source. Headings should be concise and describe the content. For example, a line graph that illustrates sales figures during April, May, and June might be titled "Second Quarter Sales." Legends should be used to explain symbols, abbreviations, or other information that needs clarification.

Using well-designed visuals can complement the message that is being conveyed.

wavebreakmedia/Shutterstock.com

Visuals should always be labeled with both a caption and a figure number. A **caption** is text that appears next to or below a visual that explains the image itself or its purpose in the document. The caption for the Second Quarter Sales graph might read, "Sales during the second quarter were positive overall."

The **figure number** is the unique identifier within a numbering system that is used to identify each visual. It may be alphabetic or numeric, such as *Figure C* or *Figure 3*. If the document has chapters or sections, include the chapter number and the sequence number of the figures. For example, *Figure 4-1* would be the first figure in chapter four. Figure numbers can be used for both figures and tables. In specialized documents, tables may be labeled separately with *table numbers*.

The placement of each item should be carefully considered. Insert visuals as close to the relevant content in the document as possible. The document's layout will not always allow them to appear in the exact locations where they are mentioned. For clarity, use words to refer to the visual in the content with a reference phrase, such as "see Figure 4-1."

Ethical communication practices apply when using visuals. Do not be tempted to misrepresent information or data or let visuals skew the message. The goal is to attract the attention of the audience with facts rather than with flash.

It is unethical to plagiarize someone else's material. If a source or credit line is needed, it should be inserted at the end of the information. Even if the source is yourself or your company, it may be necessary to include the information.

Section 12.1 Review

Check Your Understanding

1. Describe the purpose of using visuals in a professional document.
2. Explain what is meant by *visual literacy*.
3. List three elements that a well-designed table includes.
4. Summarize the guidelines for using figure numbers within a document.
5. Explain the importance of using visuals in an ethical manner.

Build Your Vocabulary

As you progress through this course, develop a personal glossary of key terms. This will help you build your vocabulary and prepare you for a career. Write a definition for each of the following terms and add it to your personal glossary.

visual	infographic
visual literacy	illustration
table	caption
legend	figure number
figure	

Desktop Publishing Basics

Objectives

After completing this section, you will be able to:

- **Explain** important concepts in desktop publishing.
- **Describe** how to create a document using desktop publishing software.

Key Terms

desktop publishing	symmetry
visual design	typography
contrast	typeface
alignment	font
repetition	kerning
proximity	leading
balance	master page
emphasis	style sheet
harmony	widow
variety	orphan
proportion	

Essential Question

How can the design of a document enhance communication?

Desktop Publishing

Effective writers follow the steps in the writing process, as shown in Figure 12-9. Once the presentation is defined and the audience is identified, the final document is created.

Most reports and documents are formatted using word processing software. However, if a document is being created for a formal purpose or large audience, consider using software that is intended to produce a professional appearance.

Desktop publishing is using software on the computer to lay out text and graphics for professional-looking documents, such as newspapers or brochures. Desktop publishing software often includes writing and publishing features. Microsoft Publisher and Adobe InDesign are examples of desktop publishing software that are fairly easy to use with training. The finished document may be printed or electronically distributed.

When creating a document using desktop publishing software, visual design is as important as the content. The **visual design** is the arrangement of the visual and artistic elements used to accomplish a goal or communicate an idea. The term *graphic design* is sometimes used interchangeably with visual design.

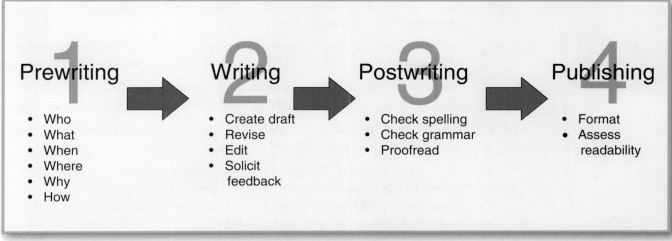

Goodheart-Willcox Publisher

Figure 12-9   There are four steps in the writing process.

Desktop publishing requires using the elements of art, which are shape, form, line, color, value, space, and texture. The elements of art are "building blocks" that are used to create a design. However, to use these elements effectively, the principles of design must be applied. The *principles of design* are concepts that suggest how to arrange the elements of art to produce a visually appealing overall effect.

- **Contrast** is having two dissimilar elements next to one another.
- **Alignment** is how items line up with one another, such as on the left side or the right side and horizontally or vertically.
- **Repetition** creates consistency and pattern.
- **Proximity** is how near or far two design elements are from each other.
- **Balance** is an arrangement of elements to create a feeling of equality across the document.
- **Emphasis** creates a focal point and draws attention.

 Green   Efficient Computer Equipment

Advances in computer technology have improved hardware capabilities and performance. The equipment commonly used in offices today is much more energy-efficient than even just ten years ago.

By upgrading to new equipment, businesses not only save the environment but save money on operating expenses. Some businesses are replacing desktop computers with laptops, which are 30 percent more energy efficient. Often, terminals can be set up at several workstations and connected to a single server where the programs and applications actually run. Sharing the computing power of a single server reduces the need for multiple computers, which reduces the amount of power used by a business.

To get the most out of office equipment, turn off any equipment that is not in use. Make sure to keep everything maintained and operating efficiently, as broken or malfunctioning equipment can use more power than is necessary.

- **Harmony** is using like elements such as color, pattern, or shapes to create unity in a presentation.

- **Variety** is using differing elements such as color, pattern, or shapes to create interest or emphasis. Variety and harmony must be in balance.

- **Proportion** is the relationship of the size of elements to the whole and to each other. In general, if an item needs to be emphasized, it is made larger.

- **Symmetry** is used to create formal balance so that what appears on one side of the page is mirrored on the other.

By applying principles of design, the message becomes more clear and memorable to the reader.

Concepts of desktop publishing that lead to a successfully designed document include typography and readability.

Typography

Desktop publishing applies the concepts of typography to create professional-looking documents. **Typography** is the style and arrangement of type. Typography includes the **typeface**, which is the definition of the characters that make up a set of letters, numbers, and symbols. The typography helps to create the tone of the document.

There are different styles of type. Examples are shown in Figure 12-10. Type may be serif or sans serif. A *serif* is a small line at the end of a stroke of a letter. *Sans serif* is a letter without the stroke at the end. A *script* typeface has a distinguished calligraphy-style look, such as Monotype Corsiva. Many *decorative* typefaces exist to give certain types of documents a thematic look or feel. For example, Comic Sans is a decorative font that is fun and casual. Script and decorative fonts should be used sparingly in the workplace.

The typeface, size, and style of characters make up the **font**. The size of the typeface is measured in *points*. One point measures 1/72 of an inch. The *font style* is the variation of the appearance of the font, such as bold, italic, or regular. For example, while the typeface may be Times New Roman, the font might be 10-point Times New Roman italic.

Serif versus Sans-Serif Fonts	
Serif font	The quick brown fox jumped over the lazy dog.
Sans-serif font	The quick brown fox jumped over the lazy dog.
Script font	*The quick brown fox jumped over the lazy dog.*
Decorative font	The quick brown fox jumped over the lazy dog.

Goodheart-Willcox Publisher

Figure 12-10   Styles of type are classified as either serif or sans serif. Type can also be script or decorative.

Readability

Readability is a measure of how easy it is for the reader to understand and locate information within a document. Recall that the arrangement of information in relation to the white space on the page contributes to readability. White space includes margins, space between paragraphs, and any other blank space on the page.

Kerning is the amount of space between two letters. Letters in words that have little space between them creates a crowded look. Letters in words with too much space between them can be hard to read.

Leading is the amount of space between two lines of type. Similar to kerning, lines of text that have little space between them creates a crowded look. Lines with too much space between them can be difficult to read.

The pages of the document can have several different alignments that effect readability. The pages may be left aligned, right aligned, or centered. Text may be *ragged*, meaning there are uneven end points for each line. Text can also be *justified*, meaning the spaces between words are adjusted to make each line the same length.

Business Protocol

Prompt Response

Business requires prompt responses to customers or coworkers. When people try to reach you via phone or e-mail, respond as soon as possible. If you are not able to do what the person is asking you right away, acknowledge that you have received the call and will follow up at a later time. It is important that the sender knows that the call was received and not lost in transmission.

Using Desktop Publishing Software

Most desktop publishing software is easy to learn with some training or tutorials. Certain aspects of desktop publishing software make designing documents fast and easy. Using templates and text controls speeds up the process of laying out a document and applying a visual design across several pages. It is important to always review and edit a desktop publishing project.

Using Templates

When creating documents in desktop publishing software, it can be a time-consuming challenge to get everything just right. In order to make it easier and faster to lay out documents, templates are used to automate much of the process. The purpose of creating a template is so repeated elements such as headings, page numbers, font choices, or graphic elements do not have to be created for each new page. It takes time to create a template, but the amount of time saved is generally much greater. Pre-made templates can also be downloaded from the Internet. The two most useful portions of a template are the master page and the style sheet.

The **master page** defines the page size, recurring areas for type and graphics, and placement of recurring elements, such as page numbers. Sometimes the master page is simply called the *master*. Depending on the needs of the document, multiple master pages can be created within a single template. For example, one template may have a master for the section opener, a master for the pages of the body, and a master for the works cited and index pages.

Using master pages and style sheets can make a desktop publishing project go smoothly.

wavebreakmedia/Shutterstock.com

A style sheet is a part of a template that deals only with font characteristics. A **style sheet** is a desktop publishing file that saves the attributes of every font that will be used in a project. The style sheet defines the typography used in the document. Point size, typeface, leading, kerning, alignment, color, and other special customizations can be set in a style sheet. A unique name is created for each font in the style sheet. Each individual named font is called a *style*.

Style sheets allow an individual style to be applied to text so you do not have to select the typeface, point size, and other characteristics of the font every time you want to use it. For example, if every heading in a report will be in 14-point Cambria bold, a style can be created with these characteristics. The style is applied with one click rather than the several clicks necessary to select these characteristics for each heading.

Styles can be set up for use on individual characters, words, or whole paragraphs. Refer to your specific software and available reference materials and training for more instruction.

Text Controls

When the template is created, you are ready to begin laying out your document. *Layout* is arranging the text and graphics to create an appealing document. Desktop publishing software typically has several tools that make this process very simple.

A basic text control feature controls how pages break for increased readability. In desktop publishing, a **widow** is the last line of a paragraph that falls immediately *after* a page break, making it appear as though it is not part of the previous paragraph. The opposite of a widow is an orphan. An **orphan** is the first line of a paragraph that falls immediately *before* a page break, making it appear as though it is not part of the paragraph on the next page. *Widow and orphan control* can be switched on to automatically prevent widows and orphans from happening. Widows and orphans are always undesirable because they can cause confusion and reduce readability.

Another tool is *automatic text flow*. This allows you to place text into controlled portions of the layout known as text boxes. For example, you may need to flow text into column-shaped text boxes across several pages. Once the columns are created, you can insert the entirety of the text. The software automatically places enough text to fit into one column. The next column will pick up where the text previously left off.

Another option when pasting text into the layout is automatic text wrap. *Automatic text wrap* allows you to surround visuals with text so the text does not have to be broken up. For example, if you need to run text around photographs from a company event, automatic text wrap will allow you to do this easily.

Editing the Final Project

Once the desktop publishing project is complete, review the document for any errors. It is necessary to review both the content and the layout. Read through the final product. Spelling and grammatical errors should have been fixed in the word processing program and should be minimal. However, do not depend on software to "think" for you. Read for spelling errors that the spell-checker may not find.

Successful document design requires attention to detail.

scyther5/Shutterstock.com

Review the layout and visual design. When editing a desktop publishing project, check these aspects of the design.

- Every item appears as intended.
- Font styles are applied appropriately.
- Correct templates were used for each page.
- Graphics are labeled appropriately.
- Headings are accurate.
- There is consistency in font, spacing, and other important elements.

As you become more proficient at desktop publishing, add additional criteria to this list. This will help to ensure your final projects look as professional as possible.

Section 12.2 Review

 Check Your Understanding

1. Describe the purpose of desktop publishing in professional communication.
2. List three of the principles of design.
3. Differentiate between kerning and leading.
4. What is the advantage of using templates?
5. Explain the purpose of widow and orphan control.

 Build Your Vocabulary

As you progress through this course, develop a personal glossary of key terms. This will help you build your vocabulary and prepare you for a career. Write a definition for each of the following terms and add it to your personal glossary.

desktop publishing	symmetry
visual design	typography
contrast	typeface
alignment	font
repetition	kerning
proximity	leading
balance	master page
emphasis	style sheet
harmony	widow
variety	orphan
proportion	

Chapter Summary

Section 12.1 Using Visuals to Communicate

- Visual communication is using images to represent an idea, concept, or information. Visual literacy is the ability to create or interpret the meaning of a visual message. Two types of visuals commonly used to enhance documents are tables and figures.

- Well-designed visuals tell a story. Visuals that are overused or poorly designed will distract the reader. Following the guidelines of creation and placement of visuals will result in a professional-looking document. Remember to apply ethical rules of communication and cite any sources that are used for visuals.

Section 12.2 Desktop Publishing Basics

- When creating a formal document, it is preferable to use desktop publishing software to produce an appealing visual design. Concepts of desktop publishing that lead to a successfully designed document include typography and readability.

- Desktop publishing software can make designing documents fast and easy. Through the use of templates and style sheets, the layout process can be quick and efficient. As with other documents, always remember to edit the final product one last time.

Online Activities

Complete the following activities which will help you learn, practice, and expand your knowledge and skills.

Posttest. Now that you have finished the chapter, see what you learned by taking the chapter posttest.

Vocabulary. Practice vocabulary for this chapter using the e-flash cards, matching activity, and vocabulary game until you are able to recognize their meanings.

English/Language Arts. Visit www.g-wlearning.com to download each data file for this chapter. Follow the instructions to complete an English/language arts activity to practice what you have learned in this chapter.

Activity File 12-1: Improving Your Editing Skills

Activity File 12-2: Improving Your Speaking Skills

Review Your Knowledge

1. Differentiate between a table and a figure.
2. Explain the difference between a circle graph and a flowchart.
3. List three types of illustrations.
4. How should visuals be placed within a document?
5. How can plagiarism be avoided when using visuals?
6. List the basic elements of art.
7. Explain the difference between serif and sans serif type.
8. What is the measurement of a point?
9. How do style sheets differ from master pages?
10. Explain the difference between a widow and an orphan.

Apply Your Knowledge

1. In the Apply Your Knowledge activities in the last chapter, you identified a topic and created a formal report. One part of the assignment was to perform primary research and place the data in a spreadsheet. Using that spreadsheet, create three visuals to interpret the information in a way the reader can understand: a table, a chart, and another figure of your choosing. Add the visuals to your report and interpret the data in a narrative to explain your findings. Label each visual with a figure number and include a heading, caption, and credit. Refer to the figures in the report.

2. The type of formatting used for your report depends on the purpose and the intended audience. Define the purpose of your report and identify your intended audience. How will this information impact your formatting decisions?

3. Using the desktop publishing software of your choice, create a template that includes a master page for each type of page and a style sheet. Address each item in the list that follows as you develop the template.

   - Set margins, kerning, and leading to establish white space.
   - Select layout options.
   - Select a color palette.
   - Choose font attributes for headings and body text, such as typeface, point size, and style.
   - Identify graphics to be used.

4. Using the desktop publishing software of your choice, begin laying out your report. Use the principles of page design to guide your decisions about the product's visual design. As you place the text, use text control such as automatic text flow, text wrap, and widow and orphan control tools. Apply graphic design concepts such as contrast, alignment, repetition, and proximity to place the graphics you created in the previous activities.

5. When your desktop publishing project is finished, edit the final product. What needed to be changed or adjusted? When you are finished, publish the document for your class. Check for these items.

   - Every item appears as intended.
   - Font styles are applied appropriately.
   - Correct templates were used for each page.
   - Graphics are labeled appropriately.
   - Headings are accurate.

Communication Skills

College and Career Readiness

Reading. Analyze the quality of the information about using visuals that you found in this chapter. Is the information coherent? Is concrete evidence presented? Report your findings to the class.

Listening. Passive listening is casually listening to someone speak. Passive listening is appropriate when you do not have to interact with the speaker. Active listening is fully participating as you process what others are saying. Listen actively to a classmate as he or she is having a conversation with you. Focus your attention on the message. Ask for clarification for anything that you do not understand. Provide verbal and nonverbal feedback while the person is talking.

Writing. Everyone has a stake in protecting the environment. Taking steps as an individual to become more environmentally conscious is a behavior of responsible citizens. From a business standpoint, it may also help a company be more profitable. What things can businesses do in the workplace to save energy or other resources? Use visuals to convey your opinion.

Internet Research

Typeface Anatomy. Research typeface anatomy using various Internet resources. What does the term mean? Create a list of some of the common terms used to describe a typeface. Illustrate your examples.

Teamwork

Working with your team, select a topic for a brochure, newsletter, or announcement. For example, the topic could be about an upcoming sporting or social event. First, write the content. Next, design the document applying the concepts presented in this chapter. Ask your classmates to review the finished project. Which team created the project that got the most positive reviews?

Portfolio Development

College and Career Readiness

Diversity Skills. As part of an interview with an organization, you may be asked about your travels or experiences with people from other cultures. Many different organizations serve people from a variety of geographic locations and cultures. Some companies have offices or other types of facilities in more than one region or country. You may need to interact with people from diverse cultures. Your work may involve travel to facilities in different countries. Speaking more than one language and having traveled, studied, or worked in other countries can be valuable assets. You may be able to help an organization understand the needs and wants of diverse people. You may also be better able to communicate and get along with others.

1. Identify travel or other educational experiences that have helped you learn about another culture, such as foreign languages studied or trips taken.

2. Create a Microsoft Word document that describes the experience. Use the heading "Diversity Experience" and your name. Explain how the information

you learned might help you better understand classmates, customers, or coworkers from this culture. Save the document in an appropriate folder.

3. Place a printed copy in the container for future reference.

4. Update your checklist to reflect the file format and location of the document.

CTSOs

Desktop Publishing. The *Desktop Publishing* competitive event may be either a team or individual event. An objective test may be administered that will be evaluated and included in the overall team score. The majority of the overall score will be based on a desktop publishing project that will be completed according to specifications provided by the organization. The desktop publishing event judges for creativity, desktop publishing skills, and decision making.

To prepare for the desktop publishing event, complete the following activities.

1. Read the guidelines provided by your organization.

2. Visit the organization's website and look for this year's desktop publishing topic. Confirm if the project is to be completed before the competition or completed during the competition.

3. If the project is completed and submitted before the competition, make sure to allow yourself adequate time to meet the submission deadline. Read all the rules and inquire if any are unclear. Submission guidelines must be followed as stated or the project will be disqualified.

4. If the project is completed at the competition, prepare any documents or other information that will be needed once the event begins. Make sure you are familiar with the desktop publishing software that will be available and that you are comfortable using it.

Unit 4

Speaking and Presenting

Professional Communication

Why It Matters

Making a presentation in front of an audience can generate feelings of nervousness for many people. It is not uncommon to feel some apprehension in the minutes before standing in front of a group of strangers. However, this uncomfortable feeling can be minimized through preparation and practice.

The first step is to allow enough time to research and write the presentation. Once the draft is complete, consider using multimedia to complement the words you will say. Enhancing your content with visuals helps guide you and your audience through the material and adds interest to the information. The final step is to practice. The more you practice, the more comfortable you will be when the time comes to stand up in front of an audience.

Chapters

While studying, look for the activity icon for:

- Pretests and posttests
- Vocabulary terms with e-flash cards and matching activities
- Videos
- Self-assessment

Video

Before you begin this unit, scan the QR code to view a video about professional communication. If you do not have a smartphone, visit www.g-wlearning.com.

Comstock/Stockbyte/Thinkstock.com **313**

13

Informal and Formal Presentations

Sections

13.1 Speaking in the Workplace

13.2 Formal Presentations

College and Career Readiness

Reading Prep Skim the chapter by reading the first sentence of each paragraph. Use this information to create an outline for the chapter before you read it.

Halfpoint/Shutterstock

Check Your Communication IQ ➦

Before you begin the chapter, see what you already know about communication by taking the chapter pretest. The pretest is available at www.g-wlearning.com.

Case Study

Audience Attention

Ray Haley just finished up his monthly meeting with the five sales representatives he manages. The reps were packing up their notes and discussing dinner plans when Ray interrupted: "Oh, one last thing before we go. Pauline sent me an e-mail about a change in the order form. The box for the distributor code number has been moved to the top-right corner of the screen. See you next month."

Pauline Chan, vice president of sales, called Ray two weeks later. "Remember that e-mail I sent you about the new order form? I am told that your region is the only one in which the reps have not been correctly coding their orders."

"That's funny," Ray replied. "I told them about it at our last meeting."

g-stockstudio/Shutterstock.com

Critical Thinking

1. Why do you think Ray's reps were not correctly coding the orders?

2. What could he have done to avoid this problem?

Speaking in the Workplace

Objectives

After completing this section, you will be able to:

- **Explain** verbal communication.
- **Describe** how to make appropriate introductions in the workplace.
- **Explain** proper telephone techniques that should be used in the workplace.

Key Terms 📲

oral language
impromptu speaking
group discussion

introduction
telephone etiquette

?Essential **Q**uestion

How can verbal communication lead to workplace success?

Verbal Communication

Verbal communication is speaking words to communicate. It is also known as *oral communication*. It enables us to share information, make requests from others, give direction, and persuade when action is needed. Verbal communication can be *interpersonal*, which is communication that occurs between the sender and one other person. It can also be *public communication*, which is speaking to a large group. The primary communication happens on the part of the speaker.

Verbal communication requires oral language. **Oral language** is a system in which words are spoken to express ideas or emotions. Similar to communicating through writing, oral language reflects an individual's tone and style. When we speak, we use oral language. The characteristics of oral language are as follows.

- *Phonemes* are the smallest units of sound in speech that differentiate one word from another. For example, the sounds of a *v* and an *f* are very similar, but there is a distinct difference between the two sounds. This difference is what changes the word *vault* to the word *fault*. Understanding word sounds allows you to identify the words that are being spoken. Phonemes are the foundation of oral language. When phonemes are written, they are called *graphemes*.

- *Semantics* are the meaning of a word or phrase. Knowing what a word means allows you to understand what is being said when you hear the word spoken in a particular context. For example, "litter" can mean either garbage scattered about or a group of newborn animals. It is important to recognize the difference between the two to ensure you are using the word correctly.

- *Morphemes* are the smallest meaningful units of speech. The word *unlike*, for example, has two morphemes: *un* and *like*. Recognizing morphemes helps you understand parts of language and the relationships between words.

- *Grammar* is a set of rules that dictates how words and their components come together to form sentences. Understanding grammar will help you know how root words and parts of speech work together in a meaningful way.

- *Syntax* is the order or arrangement of words in a sentence, phrase, or clause. Understanding syntax will help you determine the meaning of the sentence. For example, syntax explains how "I had sculpted that statue" is different from "I had that statue sculpted."

- *Pragmatics* are social communication rules. Knowing and implementing these rules will help you know when it is best to speak, how to speak in different situations, and when it is best to listen.

There are many instances during a typical day when you will be required to communicate verbally. The situation may be *formal*, such as presenting to a group of people. A *formal presentation* is one that is planned and carefully composed. An example of a formal presentation is speaking from a podium to an audience.

Alternatively, the situation may be *informal* and take place in the lunchroom or on a phone call. Many informal situations call for impromptu speaking. **Impromptu speaking** is talking without advance notice to plan what will be said. For example, a coworker may stop you in the hall and ask an unexpected question. A person from another department may call you on the phone to ask a question for which you are not prepared. It is important not to react hastily to these unexpected conversations. In impromptu situations, take a moment to think about what you are going to say. If someone is asking

Monkey Business Images/Shutterstock.com

An impromptu speaking situation is an informal presentation.

for complex information, you can say, "I will get back to you." Or, courteously direct the person to another source for the information. The goal is to always respond in a positive and intelligent manner.

Sometimes you will be faced with impromptu speaking situations that affect you emotionally. A manager might be critical, a colleague might be demanding, or a customer might be rude. It is important to maintain professionalism and poise no matter what feelings are evoked. If you have a positive attitude, you are more likely to speak appropriately. This will help avoid conflict or misunderstanding.

You may find yourself as a participant in a group discussion. A **group discussion** is a situation in which three or more individuals share their ideas about a subject. Group discussions are often informative or persuasive. Similar to brainstorming, ideas are given without any judgment. When speaking freely and sharing ideas, choose your words carefully and follow professional protocol.

In every situation and conversation, confident verbal communication conveys who you are as a professional. Your voice and wording should be clear and concise, just as when you are writing. If you have to cover more than one topic of conversation, pause and ask for feedback before changing the subject. Look for visual cues that a listener wants to respond, such as opening his or her mouth to speak. Always be courteous, and do not talk over or interrupt others. Give your audience the opportunity to respond to what you are saying.

Making Introductions

You may be called upon to make introductions in the workplace. An **introduction** is making a person known to someone else by sharing the person's name and other relevant information. The way in which the introduction is made can create a positive or negative first impression. This can impact the success of the situation.

> Making introductions is a situation for which all professionals should be prepared.

Andrey_Popov/Shutterstock.com

There will be business events at which you will have to make introductions. You may have to introduce coworkers, managers, or customers to each other or to people in your company. On occasion, you will make formal introductions of a person who is the speaker at an event. Or, you may be the speaker and be required to make your own introduction. For these introductions, you may be required to approach a stage and use a microphone.

It is important to understand the professional etiquette for each situation. When making introductions, the *situation* might be informal, but the *language* should always be formal and appropriate for the workplace.

Introducing Yourself

In both social and professional settings, you will need to introduce yourself to new people. Introducing yourself exhibits friendliness and confidence. A firm handshake is customary when meeting both men and women for the first time. In a business setting, tell the person your full name and your role in the company. For example, a person might introduce herself by saying, "Hello, my name is Madison Gomez. I am the multimedia artist."

If the person is in rank above you, use professional protocol. Using a title like "Mr." or "Ms." may be appropriate. When the other party gives his or her name, repeat the person's name as you greet him or her. "It is great to meet you, Mr. Alexander," is a polite way to respond when being introduced to someone in rank above you. Saying a person's name after being introduced will help you remember it. Remembering a person's name is important to business success. A person generally responds well to the use of his or her name.

When you approach someone whom you may have met before but do not know well, introduce yourself again. This saves embarrassment for all parties if names have been forgotten. Doing so puts everyone at ease and shows your professionalism.

Introducing Others

When introducing two people to each other, say each person's full name clearly. It is professional protocol to introduce the lower-ranking person to the higher-ranking person. If you are introducing a new intern to an executive, you would say, "Tyler, this is Ms. Anita Ogawa, vice president. Anita, this is Tyler Lombard. Tyler is working as our marketing intern this summer." Try to offer more information to help the two people easily make conversation. For example, you might say, "Clark Morgan, I would like to introduce you to Olivia Price. Olivia is a set designer for the local theater. She has a great idea about how we can improve our merchandise displays."

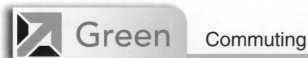 **Green** Commuting

Employees must get to work using some form of transportation. According to the United States Census Bureau, over 75 percent of American workers drive to work alone on a commute that is an average of 25 minutes. This adds up to billions of gallons of gas burned and billions of hours wasted driving each year.

Much of this time and fuel can be saved when workers consider commuting in other ways. By sharing a carpool or using public transportation, fuel is conserved and time spent commuting can be used in other ways. Many metropolitan areas also have car sharing services. Some employers give bonuses or perks to employees who commute to work in an environmentally-friendly way.

Ethics

Ethical Communication

Distorting information for a business' gain is an unethical practice. Honesty, accuracy, and truthfulness should guide all communications. Ethically, communication must be presented in an unbiased manner. Facts should be given without distortion. If the information is an opinion, it should be labeled as such.

Introducing Speakers

Many individuals become nervous when called on a stage to make introductions using a microphone. As a professional communicator, you will learn how to remain calm, project your voice, and show enthusiasm. If you are introducing yourself, give a brief background of who you are and why you are making a presentation. Keep it short and interesting. Do not use the time as a bragging session.

If you are introducing another person as a speaker, request information in advance from the person. Be specific with what you would like to convey to the audience. For example, you might say what city the person is from or where he or she went to college. Select information from the speaker's notes that will complement the presentation to be made. Write the points that you wish to express so that you do not forget the important ones.

Handling Telephone Calls

Telephone calls are an important part of communication in the workplace. Whether you are making or receiving a telephone call, remember that you are a professional and representing your company.

Etiquette is the art of using good manners in any situation. **Telephone etiquette** is using good manners on the telephone. When you make and receive telephone calls on the job, it is important to use good telephone etiquette. Learn the guidelines that your organization has in place for using the telephone.

It will be necessary to record a *voice mail greeting* for those times when you cannot answer a call. State the company name, your name, and a specific message that lets the caller know when he or she can expect a

Handling telephone calls is an important responsibility in the workplace.

michaeljung/Shutterstock.com

return call. Your voice mail greeting might be the first impression the caller will have of you and the company. Speak clearly with a positive, pleasant attitude. You will be setting the tone for future conversations. The company will probably have guidelines for recording a voice mail greeting.

Making Telephone Calls

Making telephone calls for business purposes is a common task for most employees. You can improve your effectiveness and the productivity of a telephone call by planning. Any time you have a number of issues to discuss, questions to ask, or items of information to provide, develop a list ahead of time. Written notes will help you clearly express yourself and stay organized. They will also help you remember everything you intend to cover during the call. The goal is to be friendly and achieve your purpose in an efficient amount of time. Guidelines for making telephone calls are shown in Figure 13-1.

Leaving Voice Mail Messages

Voice mail is an important part of professional communication. Before you make a call, think about what you will say if you reach a person's voice mail. Determine how much you need to explain about the purpose of the call. Also, plan what you will ask the recipient of the call to do. If you want the call returned, specify a time you will be available. The guidelines in Figure 13-2 will help you prepare to leave a voice mail message.

Receiving Telephone Calls

As an employee, you will receive calls from colleagues and customers. Try to answer the telephone on the first or second ring. Always be courteous to the caller. It is important to identify yourself when you answer the phone. Practices vary, but you might say the name of the company first and then your own name. For example, "Horton and Associates, Celeste Burrell speaking."

Making Telephone Calls

- Prepare notes to use for the call.
- If the call will be lengthy, make an appointment in advance.
- When the telephone is answered, state your name, job title, and company.
- Speak clearly and in a normal tone of voice.
- Avoid using the speakerphone feature unless other people are in the room with you.
- At the end of the call, summarize any important points or decisions.
- If follow-up action is required, summarize what each person will do and when.
- Thank the person you called for his or her time, information, or assistance.

Goodheart-Willcox Publisher

Figure 13-1 Follow these guidelines when placing telephone calls.

Leaving Voice Mail Messages

- Speak clearly and at a pace that can be easily understood.
- State your name, company, your position or department and your telephone number.
- If your name is unfamiliar or difficult to understand, clearly spell it.
- Leave a brief message stating the purpose of the call and when you will be available to receive a return call.
- If your call is urgent, say when you need a response.

Goodheart-Willcox Publisher

Figure 13-2   These are guidelines for leaving voice mail messages.

Have a plan for answering the telephone just as you should for making calls. Most businesses have a script to follow if you are taking customer calls. The script can guide you in conducting a productive conversation and help you follow the expected company protocol. If you are working in customer service, you will receive training on how to interact with customers.

Section 13.1 Review

 Check Your Understanding

1. Identify the characteristics of oral language.
2. List reasons people speak in the workplace.
3. What is the goal of impromptu speaking?
4. Give three examples of situations that may call for a person to make introductions.
5. Name three telephone situations for which employees should be prepared to handle.

 Build Your Vocabulary

As you progress through this course, develop a personal glossary of key terms. This will help you build your vocabulary and prepare you for a career. Write a definition for each of the following terms and add it to your personal glossary.

oral language   introduction
impromptu speaking   telephone etiquette
group discussion

Formal Presentations

Objectives

After completing this section, you will be able to:

- **Summarize** the steps for planning a formal oral presentation.
- **Discuss** how to prepare content for a presentation.

Key Terms ↱

presentation   subjective

analogy

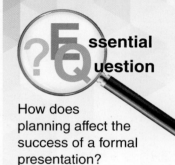

? essential Question

How does planning affect the success of a formal presentation?

Planning a Formal Presentation

A **presentation** is a speech, address, or demonstration given to a group. This type of presentation is sometimes called *public speaking*. Formal presentations vary greatly in length, topic, and level of formality. In some situations, the speaker does the majority of the presentation. In other situations, there may be a panel discussion in which two or more of the presenters share responsibility. Formal presentations generally include a question-and-answer session that encourages participation from the audience. The audience may be coworkers or customers. Alternatively, it may be professionals from other companies or some other group with a shared interest in the topic.

Who Is the Audience?

It is important to identify who will be attending your presentation. First, note whether the individuals are internal or external to the organization. An *internal audience* has a specific background and experience. It can be assumed they have a basis for and can relate to at least some of the information that is being conveyed. An *external audience* will probably need more background information about your topic.

Analyze the audience to evaluate their interest in what you have to say. You can then determine the best way to gain their attention. What is the occasion for the speech? The *occasion* is why a speech is needed. If the occasion is a wedding, families may be in attendance. If it is a conference for people who collect coins, people with very specific interests would be in attendance.

Demographics can help with the evaluation process. Characteristics such as gender, age, and level of education of the audience may influence their interest level. For example, a highly educated audience may be more interested in statements of facts and data. In this situation, a presentation could be more effective using visuals.

An important element of preparing a speech is to research the audience who will attend the presentation.

Monkey Business Images/Shutterstock.com

Ask yourself what the audience needs from you. A more mature audience may prefer bright lighting, while a younger audience may opt for subtle light. Lighting affects the tone of the message.

Continue asking questions about who will be present for your speech. What is the age range of the attendees? Are they local or will they travel to your location? A speaker who does not meet the needs of the audience will probably not achieve the intent of the presentation.

What Is the Topic?

A speech is typically given because an audience has gathered for an occasion. An occasion for a public speech could be a conference, business meeting, or a communication class. It could also be a family reunion or a high school graduation.

Before writing a speech, the subject must be selected. The subject is a broad idea of what the presentation will be about. Many times, the subject will be assigned to you. There may be other times when it is necessary for you to select an idea for a speech. If you must identify a subject, start with activities you enjoy, areas in which you excel, or some other idea with which you are comfortable. For example, sports may be a subject in which you are interested.

After the subject is selected, narrow the larger idea to a specific topic. Subject areas can be very broad. Focusing your speech on a topic within the subject makes it more manageable. For example, if the subject you choose is sports, it could be narrowed down to a specific topic, such as tennis. It could be further refined to be about a specific age group that plays tennis, such as teens. The refining process can continue until you have a topic that works for your presentation. Talking about one aspect of a subject rather than the entire subject itself makes for a more focused, interesting speech.

Next, consider the scope of the content for the presentation. It will be necessary to narrow the topic so that the content is manageable as well as meaningful. The *scope* of the presentation is the guideline of how much information will be included. Will the information be detailed or general? Scope defines what should be included and what should be left out of the presentation.

When Is the Presentation?

Most often, formal presentations must be given on a certain date, at a certain place, and for a specific occasion. Time is an important element when preparing for a speech. When you begin prewriting, identify the date of the presentation. If you are not given a date by a supervisor, select a date of your own to have the presentation finished.

Writing a presentation takes time, so do not underestimate the effort that will be required. Schedule your writing or preparation time just as you would schedule meetings or appointments. Allow appropriate time to research, write, and practice your presentation. Use your personal information management (PIM) system to schedule enough time for these tasks. Rushing through the writing process could result in an unprofessional presentation. It may also lead to apprehension as you feel unprepared.

Where Is the Information?

Once you have decided the topic of your speech, you may need to conduct primary research, secondary research, or both. Researching for a speech is similar to researching for a written report. The same steps are applied to gathering information for a speech.

Research will be necessary to support the points you make in your presentation. For example, you might interview coworkers about their experiences selling a new product. This would be primary research. Alternatively, you may need to consult sales figures, compare prices to competitors, or obtain product information from manufacturers. This would be secondary research.

Researching requires the application of media literacy skills. When reviewing print or digital materials, it is necessary to access, analyze, and evaluate what is being read. Each source should be reviewed for bias and credibility. Keep in mind that what appears in the media may not always be truthful or accurate. It is the responsibility of the presenter to decide which sources are accurate and which ones have been driven by profit or politics. When delivering a presentation, your credibility is at stake. It is important to thoroughly research sources that are used.

Remember the importance of crediting secondary sources. Mention the source during the presentation when you discuss your research findings. Source citations add to speaker credibility and the overall believability or acceptance of the presentation. Formally cite the sources in any handouts or printed reports accompanying the presentation.

Why Are You Presenting?

Public speeches are formal presentations that are made to an audience. When writing a formal presentation, first determine the purpose. Speeches are generally made for the purpose of informing or persuading the listener.

Take time to write an introduction that will capture the attention of the audience.

Warren Goldswain/Shutterstock.com

Speaking to inform usually includes sharing descriptions or definitions about a topic. The content is structured and may sound like the speaker is telling a story. If a process is being explained, a demonstration may be useful to convey the ideas. After you have relayed the information, ask if

Exploring
Communication Careers

Video Editor

Often when a video is shot, the result is many hours of video content. To create a single, seamless video, a video editor is often involved. A video editor takes the video content along with music, audio effects, and visual effects, to create a final seamless video. Typical job titles for this position include *film editor*, *news video editor*, and *online video editor*.

Some examples of tasks that video editors perform include:

• Create a single video from raw footage.

• Work with directors and producers to ensure understanding of the desired final video.

• Organize raw video footage based on scripts and information from the director.

• Determine appropriate use and placement of audio and visual effects.

• Review and revise video for length or other changes based on feedback.

Many video editor jobs require a bachelor degree in film production or a related field. Related experience is usually required. People skills are important, as a video editor needs to be able to work with onscreen talent as well as film directors and producers.

you were clear and if there are any questions. Be patient if you are asked to repeat yourself or explain something in more detail.

Many business situations require you to persuade others. Recall that when you *persuade* someone, you convince that person to take a course of action you propose. Persuasion is one of the most challenging forms of communication. Each situation requires a different approach or, in some cases, several different approaches.

A *persuasive speech* requires that the presenter be clear about what is needed from the audience. It has the goal of trying to convince the listeners to agree with the information that is being shared. The topic must be inviting, and the speaker must be convincing and passionate about what he or she is saying. A well-executed persuasive speech will have the audience agreeing with the speaker.

How Should the Presentation Be Organized?

As you prepare to write your speech, select an approach that supports the message you want to convey. Then you will prepare an outline.

Determine Approach

The *approach* of the document is how the information is presented. The direct approach works well when delivering an informative speech. The topic is introduced first and then followed by descriptive details. The indirect approach works well for persuasive messages. Details are given first and are then followed by the main idea. Begin with information that prepares the reader to respond in the manner you want him or her to respond.

Develop an Outline

The outline will serve as a guideline to identify the information to be presented and its proper sequence. As you will recall from Chapter 6, one way to create an outline is to make a numbered list of the key points. These are the main ideas you will be sharing about the topic. If you are using the direct approach, start with the main ideas followed by the details, as shown in Figure 13-3. If using the indirect approach, do the reverse. These will be considered as the headings in the outline. Start recording the main ideas in the order in which you think of them. Then, reorder the points until they reflect the order in which the information will best be presented.

As you compose the outline, keep in mind how much time has been allotted for your speech. The presentation must fit into the available time. This may mean adjusting the amount of detail in certain parts of the presentation. Or, facts and figures might need to be provided to the audience as handouts instead of being explained during the presentation.

The outline will also be influenced by the medium you are using to make your presentation. If your speech is delivered in real time or via web seminar, your outline might include time for audience participation. A speech that is being prerecorded for YouTube might be more streamlined because there will be no audience in the room.

Presentation Outline

I. First main point
- a. Subpoint
- b. Subpoint

II. Second main point
- a. Subpoint
- b. Subpoint

III. Third main point
- a. Subpoint
- b. Subpoint

Goodheart-Willcox Publisher

Figure 13-3 Developing an outline helps organize a presentation.

Preparing Content for a Presentation

When the outline is completed, it is time to begin the writing stage for the presentation. To begin drafting the presentation, follow the outline you created. Write sentences, words, or phrases next to each topic on the outline to act as cues for what you want to say. If you are a speaker with little presentation experience, you might decide to draft the presentation word for word. Keep in mind that when words are written, they may sound more formal than when they are spoken. As you write each word on paper, think about how each word will sound when you say them aloud. Aim for a less formal, more conversational delivery. Be sure to identify any words that might be unfamiliar to your audience and plan to explain them.

Audiences expect a speaker to be credible and present accurate information.

g-stockstudio/Shutterstock.com

Introduction

The introduction of the presentation serves several purposes. It should introduce the topic of the presentation and preview the main points. In other words, "tell them what you are going to tell them."

The introduction should also draw the listener into the presentation. Drawing the listener into the presentation is an important step that is often overlooked. Include something to grab the attention of those listening to the presentation. This is often called an *attention-getting device*.

Common attention-getting devices include asking a question, citing a surprising statistic, reciting a relevant quote, and telling a story. If you are giving a speech to your coworkers about team-building methods, your attention-getting device might be to ask, "What do you think you know about teamwork?"

Body

The body of the presentation is where the main points are made and supported. Remember, you have introduced the audience to the main points in the introduction. These points should be presented using the direct or indirect approach. After you finish each main point, briefly summarize it. Having too many main points can lead to a long, drawn-out presentation. This usually loses the attention of the audience. Remember, one of the four Cs of communication is to be concise. Keep the number of main points manageable.

Two techniques that can enhance a presentation are the use of facts and humor. Using reliable, informative facts is an important part of any good presentation. Humor can also be a way to win over an audience, provided you use it correctly.

Facts

It is important to back up generalizations or opinions with facts and figures. Audiences want specifics, and you want to be perceived as credible. Throughout your presentation, be clear about whether you are stating a fact or an opinion. A fact is true information, while an opinion is a personal belief or judgment.

> **Opinion**
>
> Our competitors are using advertising and it is working. I believe that if we invest more dollars in print and online advertising, our sales will grow over the next six months. This opinion is based on recent studies by Reliable Data Today, our standard source for consumer studies.

This speaker is clearly providing an opinion because it is stated as such. In addition, the speaker uses the phrase "I believe" which also clearly indicates the information that follows is not fact.

> **Fact**
>
> I have some statistics from Reliable Data Today, our standard source for consumer studies. Their numbers indicate that people who purchased new electronics over the past six months relied on print and online advertising 50 percent of the time. My conclusion is that advertising would be the best way to increase sales over the next six months.

This speaker is clearly presenting facts. The source of the facts is provided, and specific data are presented from the source. The conclusion, which is an opinion, is drawn from the facts.

Because statistics are likely to influence opinion, they must be used responsibly. Consider this example.

> Sales of exercise equipment rose almost 6 percent in March—that's up 18 percent over last year's sales during the same period.

At first glance, this may seem like a simple statement of fact. However, important information may not be included. What if the percentage of sales in March included purchases by fitness centers, when previous figures did not? Would the statistics cited reflect an actual difference in overall sales or just more accurate reporting? This important information may change how the listener perceives the facts that have been presented.

It is helpful for the audience to know how data were gathered and analyzed when they are used to make a point. Cite only data that come from reliable sources. Never alter data to support your position. Altering data is unethical, and in many cases, may be illegal.

If you use statistics in a presentation, keep in mind that numbers and facts can be dry and boring. Nothing puts an audience to sleep faster than a long list of data. Make the facts interesting by relating them to everyday experiences or ideas. An **analogy** is a comparison of two unlike things based on a particular aspect each have in common. Consider how the following analogy aids the listener to understand the facts.

> Fitness experts recommend walking at least 10,000 steps per day in your daily routine. Is that really possible for the average person who works behind a desk? Does anyone know or want to guess how that translates to distance? [Let audience members answer/guess.] It's the equivalent of walking from here to downtown—about five miles.

The speaker not only used an example the audience could easily grasp, the audience was asked for participation. Doing this at the beginning of a talk is a good way to lock-in audience interest.

Humor

A short, funny story is often a good way to open a talk or provide comic relief during a presentation. However, some topics are very serious and using humor would be inappropriate. Take into consideration the occasion and the makeup of the audience. When the topic will not be diminished by humor, consider how you might use a joke or anecdote related to your topic in the presentation.

It is important to use facts to support the main points in a presentation.

Dragon Images/Shutterstock.com

Do not feel pressured to use humor in your presentation. But if you do use humor, remember it is extremely subjective. **Subjective** means that how something is interpreted depends on personal views, experience, and background. What is funny to one person may be offensive to another. Never use a joke or anecdote that could offend someone. A joke in poor taste or at the expense of someone else will ruin your connection with the audience.

Conclusion

The conclusion summarizes the entire presentation. In other words, "tell them what you said." Conclude the presentation by restating the main points. As you restate each point, relate it back to the purpose of the presentation. This will help the audience more easily retain the information.

The conclusion is often where the presenter will answer audience questions. Many presenters invite audience questions by announcing that the time has come for them. Having time for questions helps engage the audience with the presentation. It also allows the audience to get clarification on any points they did not understand.

If the audience is expected to act on any information presented in the speech, explain what steps should be taken. For example, if you are making handouts available on a website, give the URL and state when the materials will be available.

After you have adequately concluded the speech and answered any audience questions, close with a clincher. A *clincher* is a statement to finish the presentation that will make an impact on the audience. It is similar to the attention-getting device in the introduction. You may make a lasting positive impression on the audience if you close with a comment or anecdote with which they will remember you.

Section 13.2 Review

 Check Your Understanding

1. What questions should be asked during the prewriting stage?

2. How can demographics be used to analyze an audience?

3. What factors affect the organization of a presentation?

4. What are the three basic parts of a presentation that need to be drafted?

5. Explain how to conclude a presentation.

 Build Your Vocabulary

As you progress through this course, develop a personal glossary of key terms. This will help you build your vocabulary and prepare you for a career. Write a definition for each of the following terms and add it to your personal glossary.

presentation   subjective

analogy

13 Review and Assessment

Chapter Summary

Section 13.1 Speaking in the Workplace

- Verbal communication is speaking words to communicate. It is also known as *oral communication*. To be an effective communicator, it is important to identify and understand the characteristics of oral language. Speaking can be formal, such as a presentation, or informal, such as impromptu speaking or a group discussion.

- You will need to make introductions for yourself and for others in a variety of situations. When making introductions, the language should always be formal and appropriate for the workplace.

- Telephone calls are an important part of professional communication. It is important to use good telephone etiquette when making telephone calls, leaving voice mail messages, and receiving telephone calls.

Section 13.2 Formal Presentations

- A presentation is a speech, address, or demonstration given to a group. It is also known as public speaking. The steps for planning a presentation follow the steps in the writing process. Begin with the prewriting stage.

- Once the prewriting stage is complete, you are ready for the writing stage. Begin with the introduction and "tell them what you are going to tell them." Then write the conclusion and "tell them what you said."

Online Activities

Complete the following activities which will help you learn, practice, and expand your knowledge and skills.

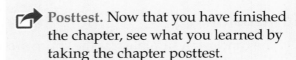 **Posttest.** Now that you have finished the chapter, see what you learned by taking the chapter posttest.

Vocabulary. Practice vocabulary for this chapter using the e-flash cards, matching activity, and vocabulary game until you are able to recognize their meanings.

English/Language Arts. Visit www.g-wlearning.com to download each data file for this chapter. Follow the instructions to complete an English/language arts activity to practice what you have learned in this chapter.

Activity File 13-1: Improving Your Speaking Skills

Activity File 13-2: Using Analogies

Review Your Knowledge

1. Explain verbal communication.
2. Give an example of how to respond to someone asking for complex information in an impromptu situation.
3. Summarize how to introduce yourself to others.
4. Explain what is meant by telephone etiquette.
5. What is a presentation?
6. Why is persuasion one of the most challenging communication processes?
7. Explain why it is important to know if your audience is internal or external to the organization.
8. In the preparation process for a speech, what does occasion mean?

9. What are the two major tasks that will help a presenter decide how a presentation will be organized?

10. Give some examples of common attention-getting devices.

Apply Your Knowledge

1. As you prepare for school or a career after graduation, there will be times when you will be required to introduce yourself to others. Assume you are visiting the campus of a local university. You have been instructed to go to the admissions office when you arrive on campus. For this visit, you will introduce yourself to the admissions counselor. In addition, you will discuss your career goals and talk about classes in which to enroll. Prepare an informal presentation about your career goals that you will make to the counselor.

2. In the previous activity, you wrote an informal presentation about your career goals. How would you approach this situation if the formal appointment was cancelled and you had an impromptu meeting in the student lounge? Which specific points about your career goals would you make in a casual conversation with the counselor? How can you be prepared for such an impromptu meeting?

3. You have been asked to introduce the principal of your school at a formal presentation to members of the community. You will step to the podium and make the introduction using a microphone. What steps will you take to research the information about the principal to make the introduction? Explain how professional protocol will influence how you make the introduction.

4. You have been requested to write a script that the school's office staff will use when answering the telephone.

Write the script that applies appropriate telephone etiquette. Practice reading the message aloud until it has an appropriate professional tone.

5. Your assignment is to write a speech. First, identify the occasion. Potential occasions could be a sports event, graduation, or presenting to the student body. Next, determine the purpose of the speech. Will you be providing information or persuading the audience to take some type of action? After you have determined the occasion and purpose, identify the subject and narrow down the topic. What topic did you choose?

6. In the previous activity, you determined the occasion for the speech, the purpose, and the topic. The next step is to identify the audience for this presentation and analyze the demographics. Write the description of your audience.

7. The topic for your speech will require research using primary research, secondary research, or both, depending on information that is needed. Apply media literacy skills to determine the type of research necessary and perform the task. Remember to cite your sources.

8. Decide how your speech will be organized. First, determine if you will use the direct or indirect approach. Next, develop an outline. Write down at least three main points and three supporting details for each.

Communication Skills

College and Career Readiness

Speaking. The way you communicate with others will have a lot to do with the success of the relationships you build with them. Create a speech that will introduce you to a counselor at a local college. The counselor should be a person you have never met. Deliver the speech to your class. How did the style, words, phrases, and tone you used influence the way the audience responded to the speech?

Listening. Active listeners know when to comment and when to remain silent. Practice your listening skills while your instructor presents this chapter. Participate when appropriate and build on his or her ideas. Respond appropriately to the presentation.

Writing. Conduct research on desirable workplace skills. Pick five from the list. Beside each of the five you selected, indicate an academic skill that directly relates to the workplace skill.

Internet Research

Speaking Occasion. Research the term *public speech occasion* using various Internet resources. Make a list of occasions for which public speaking is needed. Select one occasion from your list. Analyze how the tone, topic, and other aspects of the speech are influenced by the occasion.

Famous Speeches. Research *famous speeches* and select one that captures your attention. The speech can be about politics, sports, or another realm of life. Note the speaker and the year the speech was given. Analyze the purpose of the speech. Was it to inform, persuade, request, or entertain? Why is the speech valuable today? What visual imagery was produced by the speech?

Teamwork

Working with your team, select a topic for an informative or persuasive group discussion. You might decide to discuss your future career goals (informative) or whether your school should have a dress code (persuasive). Openly share at least three of your ideas with your team. Be receptive of others' ideas. Share your experiences with the class.

Portfolio Development

College and Career Readiness

Hard and Soft Skills. Employers evaluate candidates for open positions, and colleges are always looking for qualified applicants. When listing your qualifications, illustrate both hard and soft skills. For example, you might discuss software programs you know or machines you can operate. These abilities are often called *hard skills*. The abilities to communicate effectively, to get along with customers or coworkers, and to solve problems are examples of *soft skills*. These are also important skills for many jobs. Make an effort to learn about and develop the hard and soft skills needed for your chosen career field.

1. Conduct research about hard and soft skills and their value in helping people succeed.

2. Create a Microsoft Word document and list the hard skills you possess that are important for a job or career that interests you. Use the heading "Hard Skills" and your name. Next to each skill, write a paragraph that describes the skill and give examples to illustrate it. Save the document.

3. Create a Microsoft Word document and list the soft skills you possess that are important for a job or career that interests you. Use the heading "Soft Skills" and your name. Next to each skill, write a paragraph that describes the skill and give examples to illustrate it. Save the document.

4. Update your master spreadsheet.

CTSOs

Case Study. A case study presentation may be part of a CTSO competitive event. The activity may be a decision-making scenario for which your team will provide a solution. The presentation will be interactive with the judges.

To prepare for a case study event, complete the following activities.

1. Conduct an Internet search for *case studies*. Your team should select a case that seems appropriate to use as a practice activity. Look for a case that is no more than a page long. Read the case and discuss it with your team members. What are the important points of the case?

2. Make notes on index cards about important points to remember. Team members should exchange note cards so that each evaluates another person's notes. Use these notes to study. You may also be able to use these notes during the event.

3. Assign each team member a role for the presentation. Ask your instructor to play the role of competition judge as your team reviews the case.

4. Each team member should introduce him- or herself, review the case, make suggestions for the case, and conclude with a summary.

5. After the presentation is complete, ask for feedback from your instructor. You may also consider having a student audience to listen and give feedback.

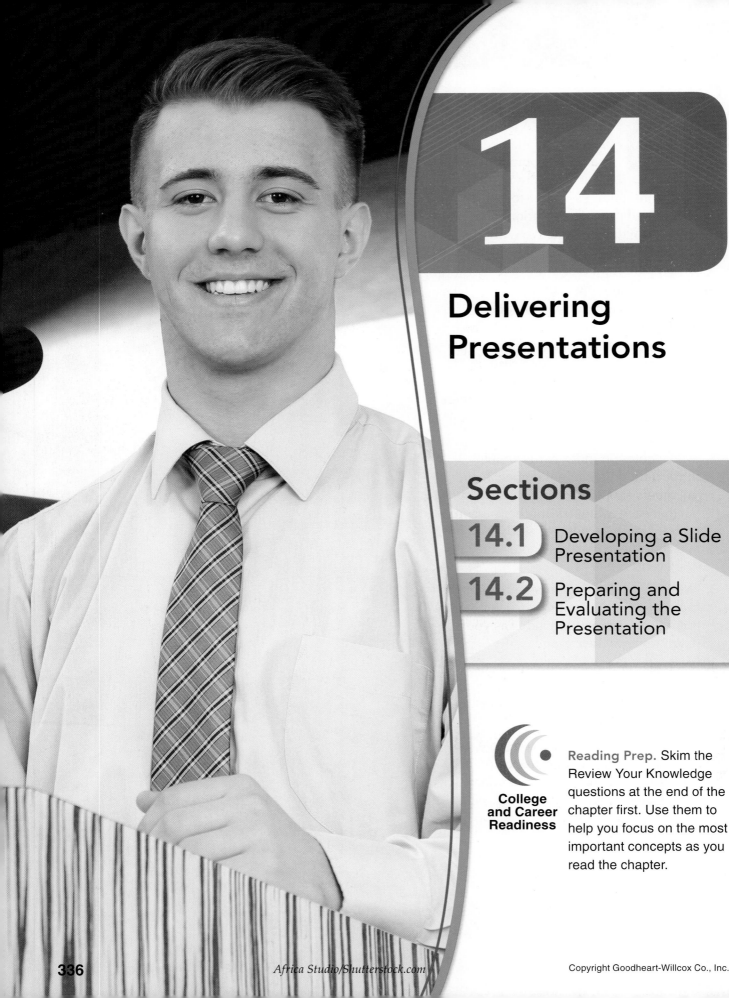

14

Delivering Presentations

Sections

14.1 Developing a Slide Presentation

14.2 Preparing and Evaluating the Presentation

College and Career Readiness

Reading Prep. Skim the Review Your Knowledge questions at the end of the chapter first. Use them to help you focus on the most important concepts as you read the chapter.

Africa Studio/Shutterstock.com

Check Your Communication IQ

Before you begin the chapter, see what you already know about communication by taking the chapter pretest. The pretest is available at www.g-wlearning.com.

Case Study

Target Audience

Teresa Espada is a scientist in the environmental lab of a chemical processing plant, ChemRite. She was asked by the town council to explain the company's pollution reduction activities and how these efforts conform to regulations. She is comfortable with this topic, so she readily outlined the information she would cover in her talk. Because she is rarely asked to speak publicly, she wrote the presentation in full. Here is an excerpt:

> With regard to regulations, I will expound upon the exemplary record of ChemRite. No other company of similar size or stature has maintained the stringent regulatory standards that are the hallmark of ChemRite's environmental policy. The polemic of certain environmental groups aside, we at ChemRite care deeply about preserving the earth and our future on this planet.

A and N photography/Shutterstock.com

Critical Thinking

1. How will Teresa's choice of words and language be received by the audience?

2. What constructive criticism would you give her regarding her choice of wording and language?

Developing a Slide Presentation

Objectives

After completing this section, you will be able to:

- **Explain** the steps for creating an effective slide presentation.
- **Describe** the importance of supporting visual aids for a presentation.
- **Identify** ways to create presentation notes.

Key Terms

visual aid

master slide

animation

auditory aid

handout

demonstration

presentation notes

Essential Question

What do successful slide presentations have in common?

Effective Presentations

The business world expects polished and well-put-together presentations. An effective presentation not only delivers a message but impacts and influences the audience. A speech that is presented with appropriate use of visual aids will be appealing and memorable for the listener.

Visual aids are useful tools for delivering an effective presentation.

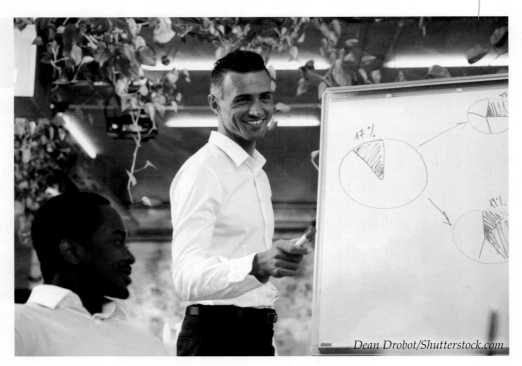

Dean Drobot/Shutterstock.com

A **visual aid** is an object that is used to clarify an idea, concept, or process. Tasteful and appropriate visual aids can be used to emphasize key points and add variety and interest to a presentation. A *slide presentation* is an effective visual aid that is commonly used when presenting to an audience.

A professional-looking slide presentation can easily be created by using software such as Microsoft PowerPoint, Google Slides, and Prezi. If the end product is a presentation with text and some visuals, a slideshow will adequately meet the needs of the audience. Three important elements of a slide presentation are the master slides, content, and visuals.

Master Slides

When creating a digital slide presentation, a master slide should be created to add consistency. A **master slide** is one containing design elements that are applied to a particular set of slides or all slides in a presentation. If you need to make a design change, simply change the master slide and it is reapplied to all associated slides.

Master slides typically contain a background design, image, or text, as shown in Figure 14-1. The master slides might also include headers and footers. Often there is a master slide for title slides and another for all other slides.

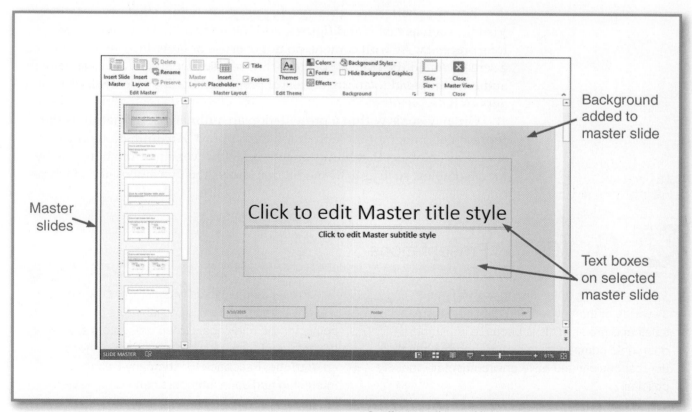

Goodheart-Willcox Publisher

Figure 14-1   Master slides are an easy way to ensure each slide in a presentation looks the same.

It is important to keep the design elements simple and consistent. A basic presentation design will make it easier for the audience to read the slide content and follow the presentation. The number of fonts on a screen should be limited, and script fonts should be avoided. The size of the font should be appropriate so that people in the back of the room can read the screen. It is suggested to use fonts that are 18-point or larger in slide presentations. Color should be used for emphasis and interest but not overused.

Content

The most important feature of a presentation is the content. When creating slides, focus on the important points of your speech. The slides are not intended for you to read each line to the audience. Instead, they should be talking points to help you stay on track with the presentation. Slides also help the audience stay on track with what you are saying.

Keep the sentences short and do not crowd the space with too many words. A common rule of thumb is the *4 × 5 rule*, which states no more than four points per slide each with no more than five words per point. Copying and pasting content from a document is not a good practice. This can easily lead to bullet points that are too long for the audience to read. Additionally, copying material from a source that is not your own can be plagiarism.

Visuals

Visuals are effective when used appropriately in a slide presentation. Visuals, such as tables and figures, add interest and help the audience interpret data. As with content, do not overuse or crowd too many items on a screen. Avoid the overuse of clip art. Overuse of visuals can disengage the audience and lead to an unsuccessful presentation. The rule of "less is more" applies here.

Often, visuals within a presentation are animated. **Animation** is the representation of motion with graphics or in text. An animation may be as simple as an object that blinks on and off. However, an animation may be more complex, such as a 3D model that shows the movement of a machine.

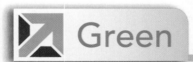 Green   Presentations

Many companies find that being good stewards of the environment can help increase sales and profits. This is because consumers often hold companies in higher regard when they act responsibly and have environmentally friendly policies.

When making presentations to customers and other audiences, many companies are requesting presenters to make green presentations. Green presentations avoid waste of paper, supplies, and energy.

Presentations typically consist of slide shows, website demonstrations, and handouts of important points for the audience. Green presenters are taking advantage of technology to post presentations on YouTube, Facebook, or company websites. Interested audience members can visit to review information about the presentation, download or view the presentation itself, and download electronic handouts. This saves resources such as paper for handouts and energy to run the presentation with lights and audio equipment.

Movement can be used to transition from one slide in a presentation to the next. Transitions make the movement from slide to slide far less static. For example, a slide can appear to spin off of the screen while another slide spins into place. However, transitions can be distracting if they are overused.

Sound can also be used in a slide presentation. An **auditory aid** is a sound element used to add interest or clarify information. Sound can be used to indicate transitions of slides, play background music, or any other special effect you would like to add. If you choose, your voice can be recorded into the slide show as you make the presentation. The slide show can then be made available to the audience to listen to and watch your presentation at their convenience.

Supporting Visual Aids

In addition to slide presentations, there are additional visual aids that can be used when speaking to an audience. **Handouts**, also called *leave-behinds*, are printed materials that are distributed to the audience. Generally, handouts are used to help the listener understand the information in the presentation, provide additional information about the topic, or both. They are useful for providing an outline of key points or supplemental information that is not covered in the presentation. However, do not overload people with a large amount of reading material. The audience should be paying attention to the key points of the presenter, not trying to read material. If listeners need the information during the presentation, distribute the materials before you begin. Place handouts on a table at the front or hand them out as people enter. For distribution after the presentation, pass them out while people are still seated. Figure 14-2 provides some guidelines for using handouts.

Is there a way to show your audience exactly what you are describing? If so, work a demonstration into your presentation. A **demonstration** is an act of showing how something is done. For example, if you are explaining how to operate a piece of equipment, demonstrate its operation for your audience.

Using Handouts

- Do not assume audience members will read your handouts.
- Keep handouts as short as possible; be concise.
- Use a format that presents the information in a way that is visually appealing and professional.
- Include your contact information and the date of the presentation.
- If the handout or presentation is available on a Website, include the appropriate URL.
- Before the presentation, plan when and how you will use handouts.
- Have a plan for quickly distributing materials without distraction.
- Before referring to a handout during your presentation, be sure each person has a copy.

Goodheart-Willcox Publisher

Figure 14-2   Follow these tips when using handouts with a presentation.

The equipment becomes a great visual aid. If possible, involve the audience in the demonstration. Audience participation makes an impact on listeners and adds interest to your talk. It is a way to engage the audience with the topic of your presentation.

Flip charts or white boards are common visual aids used by presenters. These are especially helpful for presentations in which audience participation is requested. As individuals make comments or suggestions, they can be written on the charts or board so everyone can see.

Developing Presentation Notes

Once you have the presentation completely planned and written, you can then convert the script to an outline with notes. **Presentation notes** are notes used to keep the speaker on topic. They are used during the presentation to help you keep your place and to remind yourself of points should you forget anything.

To create the notes, begin with the outline for the presentation. A well-developed and well-written outline simplifies the process of creating notes. Write down a few words for each point. Choose words that remind you of what you want to say, but be brief. Note any transitions you want to use between points.

If you are using Microsoft PowerPoint to create a slideshow for your presentation, you can make use of the notes feature. Add a few words in the notes area of each slide. Then, when you print the slides, you can choose to print the notes. These pages can serve as your presentation notes.

Some presenters prefer to use index cards over the notes feature in the software for important points. The small size is easier to handle than full sheets of paper but limits the number of words that can be added as notes. Use whichever method works for you. However, remember to maintain eye contact with the audience and do not read from notes.

Section 14.1 Review

 Check Your Understanding

1. Explain the purpose of a slide presentation.
2. What are the three important elements of a slide presentation?
3. Give several examples of how sound can be used in a slide presentation.
4. What purpose do handouts serve for the audience?
5. Name two common ways to create presentation notes.

 Build Your Vocabulary

As you progress through this course, develop a personal glossary of key terms. This will help you build your vocabulary and prepare you for a career. Write a definition for each of the following terms and add it to your personal glossary.

visual aid   handout
master slide   demonstration
animation   presentation notes
auditory aid

Preparing and Evaluating the Presentation

Objectives

After completing this section, you will be able to:

- **Describe** how to prepare to speak to an audience.
- **Explain** the importance of practicing before a presentation.
- **Describe** how to evaluate the effectiveness of your presentation and performance.

Key Terms ⤵

communication apprehension

modulation

pitch

intonation

monotone

enunciation

Essential Question

How can practice lead to a speaker's success?

Preparing to Speak

Some people enjoy giving presentations while others approach them with fear. The average person often feels nervous about speaking in front of an audience. Fear of speaking in public is known as **communication apprehension.** Through planning and preparation, much of the apprehension can be eliminated.

Presentation skills are important when assuming the role of a speaker. These skills include speaking ability, which is voice quality, tone, and enunciation. Another skill is using body language effectively, which includes eye contact, hand gestures, and body movements. These are all delivery skills that can add to a presentation if mastered. By analyzing and adjusting how you use your voice, words, and body language, you can improve the delivery of your message. It will also help you with your confidence level when you step up to the podium. The benefits of sharpening your skills extend beyond formal speaking situations. You will also become more effective in the daily interactions that require you to speak.

Control Your Voice

Naturally, your voice is your most important tool in speaking situations. The first step toward improving your voice is to become aware of how you sound to others. Only then will you know what, if anything, needs improvement. Fortunately, you can significantly improve your voice quality by concentrating on a few simple techniques.

Evaluate Your Voice

Evaluate your voice by listening to yourself speak. Record yourself reading a few paragraphs using your normal speaking voice. Then, play

Inside Voice

Be aware of the volume
of your voice when
speaking to a coworker
or on the phone. Often,
others are within earshot
of your conversation.
Talking in the hallways,
outside an office, or in a
cubicle can be disturbing
to those around you. If
a conversation requires
more than a few words,
move into a conference
room or other space where
a door can be closed.

back the recording. Try to listen to the voice you hear as if it were someone else speaking. Ask yourself questions to determine how that voice sounds.

- Is the volume appropriate?
- Is the rate of speaking too fast or too slow?
- Are words correctly pronounced?
- Do words run together, are word endings dropped, or are syllables added?
- Are phrases such as "um," "you know," or "like" used frequently?
- Is emphasis used enough, too much, or too little?

If you cannot be objective in evaluating yourself, ask someone for help. Select someone who has excellent speaking skills, understands your objectives, and can give you constructive criticism.

Volume and Rate

When you speak too loudly or too softly, listeners will be distracted from the content of your message. The audience will quickly tune out what you are saying. Be aware that you must adjust your volume to the room and the audience.

To determine if your volume is appropriate, ask a friend or coworker to sit in the back of the room where you will be presenting and provide cues. Or, during the presentation, you can ask the audience if everybody can hear you. If not, you need to speak louder.

If the room is set up for a microphone, practice using it before the presentation. Make sure you can use the microphone with comfort. Also, make sure the amplification is the right volume for the audience.

Be aware of the rate, or speed, at which you speak. In general, maintain a consistent, normal rate. This should be a speed at which the listeners can comfortably stay with you. If you are usually a very fast or very slow speaker, practice your rate of speech with someone.

However, you can vary your rate of speech for emphasis. Slow down when you present something technical or something the audience will write down. This is where handouts can be helpful. Repeat the information if necessary or ask if everyone is ready for you to move on.

Voice Modulation

When speaking, it is important to vary your voice modulation. **Modulation** is changing the emphasis of words by raising and lowering your voice. You can stress a word to make it stand out from the others by simply raising the volume of your voice. You can also provide emphasis by raising or lowering the pitch of your voice. **Pitch** describes the highness or lowness of a sound. **Intonation** is the rise and fall in the pitch of your voice.

Another effective technique is simply to pause so that the word or phrase following the pause receives extra emphasis. You can also introduce the words you want to emphasize. The words preceding the pause prepare listeners for the important information to follow.

> Now, here is the key to increasing profits. [pause] We must all sell 10 percent more product each quarter.

The pause lets the listener know that what is to follow is related to increasing profits.

When speaking, you cannot emphasize everything you say. The opposite, emphasizing nothing, is equally ineffective. Speech that is **monotone** is delivered with the same intonation, pitch, and volume. A monotone speech offers no variety and no emphasis. Most audiences will find a monotone delivery boring and will likely tune out the speaker.

Pronunciation and Enunciation

Mispronounced words are a distraction and may even affect your credibility with the audience. Make sure you have the correct pronunciation of any technical or unfamiliar terms. In some cases, you might be more familiar with a word in writing than you are with saying it aloud. Regional differences in speech or English as a second language might also contribute to different pronunciation. Your goal is to have the audience clearly understand your words. Refer to Figure 14-3 for examples of common pronunciation errors. **Enunciation**, which is clearly and distinctly pronouncing syllables and sounds, is also a factor in the audience understanding what you say.

Common Errors in Pronunciation

Dropping Sounds at the End of Words
For example, do you drop the *g* in *ing* words and say *runnin', eatin',* or *workin'*? Do you drop the final *t* when you say words such as list and tourist? Do you drop the final *d* in words such as field and build?

Omitting Letters and Sounds
For example, consider the word introduce. The correct pronunciation is IN-tro-duce, not IN-ter-duce.

Adding Sounds
For example, do you say ATH-a-lete? The correct pronunciation is ATH-lete.

Altering Vowel Sounds
For example, do you say GEN-you-in (correct) or GEN-you-ine (incorrect)?

Stressing the Wrong Syllable
For example, you should say in-COM-pa-ra-ble, not in-com-PAR-a-ble, and in-SUR-ance, not IN-sur-ance.

Mispronouncing Words
Many people make the mistake of pronouncing words just as they appear in writing. For example, do you pronounce the word epitome as i-PIT-i-me (correct) or I-pi-tome (incorrect)? Another common mispronunciation is aks (incorrect) instead of ask (correct).

Using Incorrect Words
For example, for the verb form of orientation, do you say orient (correct) or orientate (incorrect)?

Goodheart-Willcox Publisher

Figure 14-3 Presenters must be careful to avoid pronunciation errors.

You can heighten your awareness of appropriate pronunciation and enunciation by paying attention to the speech patterns of public speakers you admire. Consult a dictionary when a question of pronunciation arises.

Control Your Body Language

Effective communicators control their body language to coincide with and complement their messages. When preparing for your presentation, close your eyes and visualize yourself making the presentation. See yourself as a confident presenter in front of a friendly, receptive audience. Visualize how you would handle problems, such as a difficult question. In most cases, the audience is rooting for you. They want you to succeed as much as you want to succeed.

Important methods for controlling body language include making eye contact, avoiding unnecessary movement, standing up straight, smiling, and dressing appropriately.

Make Eye Contact

It is important to make eye contact with the audience. It adds a personal touch and makes the audience feel connected to you. As you begin to speak, make eye contact with someone in front, then someone to the left, someone to the right, and so on. This engages the audience and makes them feel as if you are talking directly to each person. Eye contact is one of the best ways of establishing a rapport with the audience.

Connecting with the friendly face of a colleague or a listener who gives you a look of interest or a nod of agreement will bolster your confidence. This can help you settle in and feel comfortable in front of the group.

Exploring Communication Careers

Interior Designer

Interior designers are responsible for how the inside of a home or office is laid out, furnished, and decorated. People in this career plan, design, and furnish the inside of residential, commercial, or industrial buildings. They work with clients to understand their needs for the space along with their budget. Then, the designer analyzes the building to determine layout and use of furnishings or equipment and color coordination. Typical job titles for this position include *decorating consultant*, *director of interiors*, and *interior design consultant*.

Some examples of tasks that interior designers perform include:

- Meet and discuss with clients the purpose of the space.
- Create and present design plans that meets the client's purpose.
- Depict design ideas using computer-aided drafting (CAD) software or sketches and models.
- Coordinate contractors, architects, engineers, and plumbers to complete design plans.
- Select, purchase, and oversee the placement of furnishings and artwork.

Most interior designer jobs require a bachelor degree in interior design or a related field. Interior designers must be proficient using CAD software for most positions.

Avoid Unnecessary Movement

Any movements outside of normal hand gestures, facial expressions, and motioning toward your visuals could distract the audience. If you have water, do not drink excessively. Do not play with materials, such as a pen, your papers, or a pointer. Do not play with jewelry, clothing, or hair. Avoid tapping the podium or walking around a great deal. Too much unnecessary movement will distract the audience from the message.

Stand Up Straight

You should stand upright, not slouched, with your feet comfortably apart. Slouching is distracting, and good posture heightens your professionalism and can add to your confidence as a speaker. Avoid shifting your weight from foot to foot as this shows discomfort and nervousness. Maintain good posture but do not lock your knees.

Smile

Unless the topic is too serious, display a friendly, at-ease smile as you introduce your topic. Show some enthusiasm for what you have to say and it is likely to be contagious. The audience is more likely to be receptive to a message when the speaker shows interest and confidence.

Dress Appropriately

Clothing can be a loud communicator to the audience. An appropriate appearance for the situation will go a long way in establishing your confidence. If you look good, you feel good. The audience will pick up on that, and share your positive outlook. Avoid wearing clothes that are too dressy or too casual. Business attire that is understated, yet flattering, is the best choice.

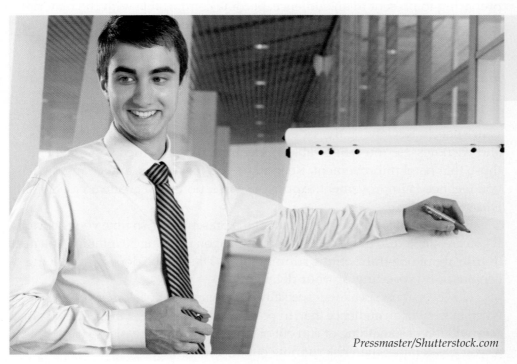

When preparing for a presentation, practice controlling your voice and body language.

Pressmaster/Shutterstock.com

Prepare for Questions

One important part of an oral presentation is feedback in the form of questions from the audience. Preparing for questions will help your confidence level so you can maintain composure and professionalism. Speakers who are not prepared may become flustered and lose creditability with the audience.

Before presenting, decide if you are willing to answer questions as they arise. You may prefer to have a question-and-answer session following the presentation. Some speakers announce in the introduction that it would be appreciated if questions are held until the conclusion of the presentation.

Some speakers are comfortable with answering questions as they arise. Audience members sometimes ask questions that interrupt the flow of a presentation. If someone interrupts with a question that is on topic, you might choose to answer briefly and move on. If the question is off topic, ask the person to see you at the end of your talk. If you do not know the answer, just say so. Offer to find the information later and get back to the individual. Keep in mind that it is not possible to anticipate all questions from an audience.

Be prepared to use critical listening strategies when audience members ask questions. If you note confusion, anger, or other emotion from the audience, it will be necessary to evaluate the cause. Alternatively, if the audience seems receptive, note what you did well. Both negative and positive feedback will help you be a better presenter.

Practice the Presentation

Effective presentations are the result of careful planning, preparation, and plenty of practice. Many beginning presenters overlook this step, but practice is important if you want to deliver a successful speech. When preparing to present to an audience, become comfortable with the material you will be covering and visuals that will be used. Memorize the sequence of topics and use transitions between key points. Control your voice and body movements. Experiment with pausing, emphasizing a word, and lowering or raising your voice. When using visual aids and handouts, look at the audience and stand up straight.

One effective method of preparation is to create a video while practicing your speech. Reviewing the video will help you recognize your strengths and weaknesses. You will be able to identify areas in which you excel and those that need improvement. Keep what you feel works, and change what you feel needs improvement. Apply the corrections and create a video again. Did you improve?

It is essential to control the length of the presentation, so time your delivery. If you are allotted 20 minutes, but the presentation is taking 30 minutes, you need to trim about one-third off the running time. This can be done by removing content or by speeding up your delivery.

However, most speakers, especially beginners, will speak more quickly when in front of an audience than in practice. Many speakers' biggest fear is that they will forget something or run out of material. It may be easier to trim content as you speak rather than risk running out of or forgetting key material.

Conduct a dress rehearsal in the clothes you will wear for the presentation. Practice in front of a mirror or recruit friends or family to listen to your speech. Ask them for feedback about every aspect of your presentation. Review the suggestions and criticisms and use them to improve your talk.

Do not read your presentation word-for-word even when you are practicing. Commit important points to memory so you can look at your audience and move with ease. If you try to recall the presentation entirely from memory without using any notes, you run the risk of forgetting part of the presentation. Use the presentation notes as reference to keep you on topic. Starting with a well-written, concise outline for the presentation greatly improves the ability to keep track of content and reduces reliance on notes.

If possible, visit the room where the speech will be given so you can make adjustments if necessary. For example, you may decide you do not want a podium. If using equipment, make certain that you know how to operate it. Do not take it for granted as equipment can be difficult to use. You want the audience to stay focused on what you are saying, not what you are doing.

Use your personal information management (PIM) system to schedule adequate time to practice your speech before the day comes. This will help you feel prepared and confident on the day of your formal presentation.

Deliver and Evaluate the Presentation

Arrive early for your presentation. Make one final check of the room arrangement and equipment. Set up the computer and launch your presentation to make sure everything is working. Confirm your presentation notes are in order. Place handouts in a convenient place for distribution. Put a bottle of water on the podium.

When it is time to present, take a deep breath. Smile and try to look relaxed. If you have prepared and practiced, you will be surprised how well your presentation will flow.

After giving the presentation, evaluate your performance as soon as possible. Post-presentation evaluation will help you assess what you did well and what could be improved for the next occasion.

Evaluate the effectiveness of a presentation after it is given.

Audience Feedback

A formal presentation presents an opportunity for written feedback from the audience. This can be obtained by asking the audience to complete an evaluation form or questionnaire.

kataijudit/Shutterstock.com

If you are creating an evaluation form, develop this document using strategies similar to those used for developing a survey discussed in Chapter 11. Write questions that honestly evaluate the content of the presentation and your delivery of the material. Feedback documents can help you assess the effectiveness of your presentation and improve your presenting skills in the future.

Self-Evaluation

To conduct a self-evaluation on the effectiveness of the presentation, start by asking yourself what you did well. These questions can help you begin your self-evaluation.

- Was I adequately prepared?
- Did I stay within my allotted time?
- Were the visuals appropriate?
- Were the handouts clear and effective?
- Was I in control of my body language and my voice?
- Did I interact well with the audience?
- Was I prepared for audience questions?

Next, be honest about where the presentation could have been improved. If your answer to any of these questions was "no," evaluate why it was no. Think about what you could have done differently in the days and weeks leading up to the next presentation. Remember that no one is perfect. Every presentation is a learning experience that will make you a better presenter next time.

Finally, set a goal for your next speaking occasion. For example, you might have gone over your allotted time. Your goal for next time might be to time yourself while practicing to make sure you do not make the same mistakes again.

Section 14.2 Review

Check Your Understanding

1. How can you improve the delivery of your message?
2. Explain how to evaluate your voice.
3. Why should a presenter avoid delivering a monotone presentation?
4. Describe the elements a presenter should pay attention to when practicing his or her presentation.
5. How should a presenter prepare for questions that might be asked?

Build Your Vocabulary

As you progress through this course, develop a personal glossary of key terms. This will help you build your vocabulary and prepare you for a career. Write a definition for each of the following terms and add it to your personal glossary.

intonation

monotone

enunciation

communication apprehension

modulation

pitch

Chapter Summary

Section 14.1 Developing a Slide Presentation

- A visual aid is used to clarify an idea, concept, or process. A slide presentation is an effective visual aid commonly used in formal presentations. When creating a slideshow, a master slide adds consistency to the presentation. The most important feature of your presentation is the content. Visuals add interest and help the audience interpret data.

- Supporting visual aids make a presentation more interesting and informative. Tasteful and appropriate visual displays, demonstrations, and handouts can be used to emphasize key points and add variety and interest to a presentation.

- Presentation notes are used during the presentation to keep your place and to remind of talking points. To create the notes, begin with the outline for the presentation. Write down a few words for each point. Remember to maintain eye contact with the audience and do not read from notes.

Section 14.2 Preparing and Evaluating the Presentation

- Presentation skills include speaking ability, which is voice quality, tone, and enunciation. Another skill is using body language effectively, which includes eye contact and hand gestures. By analyzing and adjusting how you use your voice, words, and body language, you can improve the delivery of your message.

- It is important to practice your presentation. Become familiar with the topics and key points. Practice using your voice, body movements, and visual aids. Be sure to time yourself. Commit important points to memory to avoid reading the presentation aloud.

- A question-and-answer session typically follows a formal presentation. Often, audience members will ask questions during the presentation. Be prepared to handle questions in either situation. Use critical listening skills when an audience member asks you a question.

Online Activities

Complete the following activities which will help you learn, practice, and expand your knowledge and skills.

Posttest. Now that you have finished the chapter, see what you learned by taking the chapter posttest.

Vocabulary. Practice vocabulary for this chapter using the e-flash cards, matching activity, and vocabulary game until you are able to recognize their meanings.

English/Language Arts. Visit www.g-wlearning.com to download each data file for this chapter. Follow the instructions to complete an English/language arts activity to practice what you have learned in this chapter.

Activity File 14-1: Improving Your Speaking Skills

Activity File 14-2: Improving Your Reading Skills

Review Your Knowledge

1. Describe the advantage gained when using visual aids in a presentation.
2. What is the 4 x 5 rule?
3. Explain why master slides should be used in a slide presentation.
4. How is animation commonly used in slide presentations?
5. Summarize how to create presentation notes.

6. What is the purpose of presentation notes?

7. Describe how to heighten awareness of appropriate pronunciation and enunciation.

8. What is the difference between pitch and intonation?

9. Give examples of methods for controlling body language.

10. Why should you have a plan for handling audience questions during your presentation?

Apply Your Knowledge

1. Explore the slide presentation software of your choice, such as Microsoft PowerPoint, Google Slides, or Prezi. Create a master slide template that is personalized for your use. Include a logo, your name, or other elements that will identify this template as yours. Create a master title slide and a master content slide. You will use this template for presentations that you will create.

2. In Chapter 13, you prepared a persuasive speech. Using the master slides you created in the last activity, insert the content for your speech. Use appropriate visuals and cite them as necessary. Vary the type fonts and colors appropriately. Embed auditory aids for impact.

3. Presentation notes will help you stay on track when you are presenting. Create presentation notes for your speech using the note feature in the presentation software or on index cards.

4. Next, create a feedback form for the presentation. At the top of the form, insert your name, the name of the presentation, its date, and its location. Write 10 questions that relate directly to your presentation. Use correct grammar, sentence structure, and vocabulary.

5. Practice the presentation. Walk through each slide of the presentation to make sure the content is exactly as you

planned. Use your presentation notes and rehearse what you are going to say. Make sure the equipment works and that you are comfortable with the surroundings. As you practice, focus on voice control and your body language. By practicing your presentation, you will gain command of the information and build confidence. It will also help you overcome communication apprehension.

6. Deliver the presentation to your class. Apply the concepts for making a presentation that you learned in this chapter. Use appropriate verbal and non-verbal strategies as you present the speech.

7. Conclude the presentation with a question-and-answer session. Listen carefully to the feedback you receive. What did you learn from your audience that will help you be better prepared to give a speech in the future?

8. After giving your presentation, conduct a self-evaluation. Ask yourself the questions listed in this chapter to evaluate your performance. Then, write several paragraphs summarizing what you did well and what you can improve for next time.

Communication Skills

College and Career Readiness

Writing. To become career ready, it is important to learn how to communicate clearly and effectively by using reason. Create an outline that includes information about trade-offs and opportunity costs. Consider your audience as you prepare the information. Using the outline, make a presentation to your class.

Speaking. Rhetoric is the study of writing or speaking as a way of communicating information or persuading someone. It is important to be prepared when you are speaking to an individual or to an audience. Style and content influences how the listener understands your message. Make an informal presentation to your class about the importance of a positive attitude. Adjust your presentation length to fit the attention of the audience.

Reading. Read a magazine, newspaper, or online article about hemispheric dominance. Take notes to identify the purpose of the article and the intended audience. Determine the central ideas of the article and review the conclusions made by the author. Demonstrate your understanding of the information by summarizing what you read, making sure to distinguish fact from opinion.

Internet Research

Valedictorian Speech. Research *valedictorian speeches* using various Internet resources. What are common suggestions given for preparing this type of speech? Using the suggestions you found, create an outline you might use for preparing a valedictorian speech.

Teamwork

Record yourself for 10 to 15 minutes giving a presentation or reading a passage from an article, essay, or from this textbook. Trade recordings with at least two other classmates and evaluate each other's speaking skills. Discuss the comments and make sure you understand them. Use this feedback to improve your speaking skills.

Portfolio Development

College and Career Readiness

Technical Skills. Your portfolio must also showcase the technical skills you have. Are you exceptionally good working with computers? Do you have a talent for creating videos? Technical skills are very important for succeeding in school or at work.

1. Create a Microsoft Word document that describes the technical skills you have acquired. Use the heading "Technical Skills" and your name. Describe the skill, your level of competence, and any other information that will showcase your skill level. Save the document file.

2. Update your master spreadsheet.

CTSOs

Role-Play and Interview. Some competitive events for CTSOs require that entrants complete a role-play or interview. Those who participate will be provided information about a situation and given time to practice. A judge or panel of judges will review the presentations or conduct the interview.

To prepare for the role-play or interview event, complete the following activities.

1. Read the guidelines provided by your organization.

2. Visit the organization's website and look for role-play and interview events that were used in previous years. Many organizations post these events for students to use as practice for future competitions. Also, look for the evaluation criteria or rubric for the event. This will help you determine what the judge will be looking for in your presentation.

3. Practice in front of a mirror. Are you comfortable speaking without reading directly from your notes?

4. Ask a friend or an instructor to listen to your presentation or conduct an interview. Give special attention to your posture and how you present yourself. Concentrate on the tone of voice. Be pleasant and loud enough to hear, but do not shout. Make eye contact with the listener. Do not stare, but engage the person's attention.

5. After you have made your presentation, ask for constructive feedback.

15

Enhancing a Presentation with Digital Media

Sections

15.1 Digital Media Basics

15.2 Creating Digital Media Presentations

College and Career Readiness

Reading Prep Write all of the chapter terms on a sheet of paper. Highlight the words that you don't know. Before you begin reading, look up the highlighted words in the glossary and write the definitions.

Check Your Communication IQ

Before you begin the chapter, see what you already know about communication by taking the chapter pretest. The pretest is available at www.g-wlearning.com.

Case Study

Copyrights

Josh Hanneken is an employee of a nationwide hardware store chain. He has been placed in charge of creating a presentation about a new set of health care benefits that will take effect in the coming year. Once it is ready, employees across the nation will log into the corporate intranet and view the presentation.

Josh has started planning the presentation and has done some preliminary research as well. He has found some media on the Internet that he would like to use, including sounds, graphics, and photographs. He thinks that copyright laws would not be in effect since he is using the media for educational purposes: educating the employees.

Dmitry Kalinovsky/Shutterstock.com

Critical Thinking

1. Do you think that Josh has a clear understanding of copyright law? Why or why not?

2. Are there any other considerations? Explain your answer.

Digital Media Basics

Objectives

After completing this section, you will be able to:

- **Explain** the role of digital media in presentations.
- **Discuss** licensing agreements that accompany software programs.

Key Terms

digital media
end user license agreement (EULA)
site license

?Essential Question

How can technology make a presentation more effective?

Digital Media Presentations

When a slide presentation is not quite adequate for the purpose or audience, digital media can add a professional touch. **Digital media** refers to visuals, animation, video, audio, or other media created in a format that can be read by computers. This includes applications for creating and editing all types of digital media.

Digital media puts the power to create an engaging presentation at your fingertips. A *digital media presentation* is a presentation that uses the components of digital media to inform or persuade an audience. They generally include narrative, animation, and other elements. Digital media presentations may be delivered as a live presentation or may be prerecorded.

Businesses use digital media to advertise and sell their products. Individuals use digital media to present themselves for employment opportunities or to share events with family. These are just two examples of their purpose.

In order for the presentation to convey a message and engage the audience, the message must not be lost in the technology. Professional images, narrative, and other elements must be considered and planned. The process starts by selecting the right tools for the project.

Hardware

All digital media presentations are developed and presented using hardware, such as a desktop computer system. The basic components of a computer system are the computer, monitor, and *input devices* such as a mouse, keyboard, or touch screen. These components may be separate, as with a desktop unit, or integrated, as with a laptop or tablet computer. There are a number of other input devices that are used to produce a digital media presentation.

- A digital camera or digital video recorder is used to capture photos and videos.

- A digital sound recorder is used to capture speech, music, or other sounds.

- A synthesizer or music keyboard is used to create music.

There are many options for *output devices* to display a digital media presentation. The presentation could be displayed on anything from a smartphone to a theater-size screen. Other possibilities for display include a touch screen, interactive whiteboard, and a video or home theater projector.

If you intend to do high-end digital media work, check the system requirements of the software against the computer system you plan to use for the presentation. The software may require an advanced graphics card, increased RAM, or other computer enhancements in order to run on your system.

Software

When considering which software to use, assess the project as a whole. Determine the desired result and which digital media elements the project will need to incorporate. Powerful software is used to combine various elements into a digital media presentation.

Digital media–development software can be divided into five main types: text, audio, video, graphics, and website development.

- *Word processing software* is used to write and edit documents or other text-based files. A common use in digital media would be keying XHTML commands into a document that can then be imported or copied and pasted into a website development application. Examples of text editors include Microsoft Word, Google Docs, and OpenOffice Writer.

- *Audio software* is used to create and edit audio files. Audio software

Exploring Communication Careers

Arts, A/V Technology & Communications

Multimedia Artist

The animated images found in movies, on television, in computer games, and online are the work of multimedia artists. Multimedia artists create special effects, animation, or other two-or three-dimensional images using computer animation or modeling programs. Typical job titles for this position include *animator*, *3D animator*, *multimedia creative director*, and *multimedia art director*.

Some examples of tasks that multimedia artists perform include:

- Work with a team of animators to create multimedia effects.

- Research live versions of subjects to be depicted in an animation.

- Create sketches of characters and settings to be rendered on a computer.

- Create original graphics and animations using a computer.

- Meet with clients to understand project requirements and receive feedback on completed work.

Most multimedia artist jobs require a bachelor degree in art, animation, or a related field. People in this career must have artistic ability and a strong portfolio. Knowledge of computer programs or writing of programming code may be required.

allows you to filter out background noise, increase or decrease the volume, and change the speed at which the audio is played. You can also trim the audio to just the portion you need to use. Adobe Audition, Apple GarageBand, and Avid Pro Tools are a few examples of audio applications.

- *Video software* is used to create, edit, and manipulate video files. Commonly used applications are Adobe Premiere, Microsoft Windows Movie Maker, and Apple Final Cut Pro.

- *Graphics software* is used to resize, crop, and change the color of existing images. Additionally, the software can be used to alter images as well as create original artwork from scratch. Examples of graphics application software include Adobe Photoshop, Adobe Illustrator, and Corel Paint Shop Pro.

- *Website development software* is used to create the pages on a website. Several commonly used applications are WebEasy Professional and Adobe Muse. Many people use online website development in place of application software, particularly for simpler websites.

Some software works with multiple file types and allows the different digital media elements to be integrated, such as Adobe Fireworks. Other application software is part of a suite of applications designed to be used together. These programs, like Adobe Creative Suite, allow for the seamless transfer of content from one application to another.

Licensing Agreements

Some projects will require the use of copyrighted digital media. Copyright laws apply in all situations when using intellectual property that does not belong to you. The specifics of digital citizenship are explained in Chapter 3.

When buying software, the purchaser is agreeing to follow the terms of a license. A *license* is the legal permission to use a software program. A *licensing agreement* is a contract that gives one party permission to use, market, or produce a product or service owned by another party. A licensing agreement may be personal or commercial. It may be *nonexclusive*, meaning the owner may sell licenses to many people. On the other hand, the license may be *exclusive*, meaning that only one entity has the right to use the product for a specified

Ammentorp Photography/Shutterstock.com

Selecting the right hardware and software is an important part of enhancing a presentation.

amount of time. All software has terms of use that explain how and when the software may be used.

Software programs are governed by an end user license agreement. The **end user license agreement (EULA)** is the set of rules that every user must agree to before using the software. Some allow the software to be installed only once on one machine. Other agreements may allow the software to be installed multiple times on the same machine to allow for reinstallation after a hard drive failure. A **site license** allows the software to be installed on any machine owned by the company that purchased the software.

Audio and video files are also controlled with EULAs that define how the material can be used. These licenses usually grant the purchaser the right to use the audio or video file on a personal or corporate website, in television and radio broadcasts, in films and videos, on compact discs and DVDs, in software, as ringtones, and in podcasts.

Licenses to use digital media presentations, which may incorporate video, animations, and audio, can also be purchased. Depending on the content, there may be more restrictions on the use of a digital media presentation than what is typically found for individual audio or video files. For example, you may purchase the license for a ready-made digital media presentation on proper netiquette. The license may allow you to use the presentation within your company for viewing by all employees. However, that license may not allow you to place the presentation on your corporate website for anyone to view for free.

EULAs for electronic communication software or applications typically provide rights for the user. These rights permit the user to download, install, and use the software to communicate electronically using either a computer or other digital device. These agreements are usually personal, noncommercial, and nonexclusive, though you are usually permitted to use the devices for business correspondence. As with any legal agreement, it is important to read the EULA to clearly understand what you are and are not permitted to do.

Section 15.1 Review

Check Your Understanding

1. What is a digital media presentation?
2. What are two important tools that are used to create a digital media presentation?
3. Name the five main types of digital media–development software.
4. What is a license?
5. What is a licensing agreement?

Build Your Vocabulary

As you progress through this course, develop a personal glossary of key terms. This will help you build your vocabulary and prepare you for a career. Write a definition for each of the following terms and add it to your personal glossary.

digital media

end user license
  agreement (EULA)

site license

Creating Digital Media Presentations

Objectives

After completing this section, you will be able to:

- **Describe** media elements used in a digital media presentation.
- **Explain** the steps involved in creating a digital presentation.

Key Terms

pixel	movement
resolution	rhythm
filtering	perspective
layering	milestone
footage	production
canvas size	storyboard

Essential Question

Why is planning the use of digital media important?

Digital Media Elements

Digital media may be created and used solely within a software application or saved as separate files for use in other applications. These files can be inserted into a presentation or linked to from within the presentation. *Object linking and embedding (OLE)* is a way to reference the source file from within another file, such as a presentation. The audio and video must be synchronized and all part of a single source file. An application that integrates the various

When planning the use of digital media, only include media that adds interest and emphasis.

MR. LIGHTMAN/Shutterstock.com

components of a digital media presentation, such as Adobe Creative Suite, would be a preferred tool for such a job.

In a general sense, a *medium* is any means of conveying information. *Media*, the plural of medium, has the same purpose: to convey information. Careful placement of digital media in the presentation is important. Media typically used are animation, digital photography, video, and audio.

Animation

Often, visuals within a presentation are animated. An animation may be as simple as an object that blinks on and off. However, an animation may be more complex, such as a 3D model that shows the movement of a machine. Animations are often saved as an animated GIF, AVI, or MPEG file.

The illusion of motion is created in an animation by displaying still frames that each contain a small difference in rapid succession. The small differences are interpreted by the brain as motion. Think of the stick figure cartoons you can create on notebook paper. By fanning the pages, you can see motion in the animation.

Digital Photography

Despite the vast resources available on the Internet, there will be times when the image that is needed cannot be found. In these situations, you may need to take a photograph. If a digital camera or smartphone is used, the photograph can then be directly uploaded to the computer where the digital media presentation is being created.

The quality and sophistication of digital cameras can vary greatly. Which camera you use depends on your needs and the funds available for the camera's purchase. Every camera has its own set of features, so review the user's guide. However, some features are common to most cameras. There are usually options for automatic or manual flash operation and a way to zoom in and out. Usually, you will have the ability to preview the image before you take it and review it afterward.

Photo Resolution

Most cameras allow the user to select the number of pixels with which the image will be recorded. **Pixel** is short for *picture element* and refers to the tiny dots of color that make up a digital image, such as a digital photograph or a computer screen display. The number of pixels that make up an image is referred to as the **resolution** of the image. The greater the number of pixels, or the higher the resolution, the crisper and clearer the picture will be. Higher resolution also means a larger file. Be aware, an image can easily be adjusted to a lower resolution, but adjusting an image to a higher resolution causes problems.

Photo Editing

Rarely is a photograph perfect. An image that may work well in one circumstance may need to be altered to be appropriate in another. Fortunately, there are many software applications with photo editing features. Some photo-editing software includes Adobe Photoshop, Corel Paint Shop Pro, Apple iPhoto, and Serif PhotoPlus.

Photo-editing software allows the manipulation of an image in many ways. An image can be cropped, rotated, or resized. The contrast of the image, along with the brightness and the color, can be altered. The image itself can also be altered.

Filtering is a technique by which a special effect is applied to an image. The concept comes from film photography. A photographer may place a special lens called a *filter* over the camera lens to alter the look of the scene being photographed. In photo-editing software, the filter is applied during the editing stage instead of the creation stage. There are hundreds of filters from which to choose. Common filters include blur, feather, sharpen, mosaic, watercolor, and pastel.

Layering is the process of building an image by putting different parts of the image on different levels. Think of each layer as a sheet of tracing paper that is stacked on the other layers. By using layers, you can compose a scene in the photo-editing software. The background can be one layer. Another layer can be created for each object or person in the scene. Different layers can be turned on and off to make editing easier. Then, the layers can be rearranged to bring one object in front of another, for example. The final composition can be flattened and saved in a common image file format, such as JPEG or TIFF.

Video

Video refers to live-action movies. As with other digital media, videos can be files that you capture, create, or obtain through online resources. While a video can quickly and sometimes more accurately convey what might otherwise take many slides in a presentation, it is still important to make sure that the video being used is appropriate for the situation, Figure 15-1.

The creation of a video for a digital media presentation has a specific purpose and specific requirements. The best way to make sure a video contains all of the elements needed for your presentation is to write a script. A *script* provides the outline and structure for the video. It details what will happen and when, what the scenes will look like, what will be said by any individuals, and what the actions of the individuals will be. It also makes clear the sequence of events. Following a detailed script helps ensure the finished video will meet the needs of the presentation.

 Green   Environmentally Friendly Electronics

A variety of electronic equipment is necessary to communicate efficiently. It is important to purchase environmentally friendly devices as older equipment is replaced. Lead-free and mercury-free computers that are built using reduced amounts of chemicals are available. Many manufacturers phased out the use of arsenic in the production of glass display screens. Some manufacturers use recycled materials in the construction of their products. Additionally, many electronics retailers offer electronics recycling services. These retailers often partner with responsible recyclers who use the best practices available to repair, repurpose, or recycle the equipment.

Many businesses focus on purchasing equipment that respects the environment. Various organizations, such as *Green Seal*, use rigid criteria to evaluate products for sustainability. If a product meets all of the requirements, it earns an official green seal of approval. A product with a seal of approval sends the message that a business values preserving the environment.

Evaluating Video
• Does the video support the goals of the project?   • Will the video be distracting or helpful?   • Are there too many videos in the presentation?   • Are the videos an appropriate size for use in this type of project?   • Have necessary permissions been obtained for any people appearing in the video?

Goodheart-Willcox Publisher

Figure 15-1   Evaluate each video clip before using it in a digital media presentation.

Video Cameras

Video can be recorded with several types of cameras. However, including a high-quality video in a digital media presentation requires high-quality equipment and careful planning.

The features of video cameras vary by model and manufacturer. In general, there are usually options to zoom in and zoom out. There will be a way to view the video as you are recording it and usually an option to review it afterward. Studio cameras and professional camcorders allow for adjustment and fine-tuning of numerous settings. Consumer camcorders usually have settings that provide options for recording in different scenarios.

There are essentially three types of cameras used for recording digital videos: studio camera, camcorder, and webcam. Digital video cameras are connected to a computer using a high-speed interface, such as FireWire (IEEE 1394) or USB.

A *studio camera* is a large piece of equipment, as you may have seen on a television news set. The camera picks up video feed that is sent to a recording device for storage or broadcast. The audio is picked up by a system of microphones placed in strategic locations. The audio feed is sent to the same recording device for storage or broadcast. Later, the audio and video are mixed and synchronized.

A *camcorder* is smaller than a studio camera. Camcorders can usually be held in the hand or rested on the shoulder. Professional camcorders record audio and video on separate tracks that must be mixed later. The consumer version records audio and video and mixes them automatically.

A *webcam* is a low-resolution digital video camera, usually combined with a microphone for recording audio. Many computers and tablets now come with a built-in webcam. Webcams are used to broadcast live, real-time video for video conferencing and live chatting, among other things. The content from webcams can be recorded and saved as a file, but be aware that the quality is not very high. Additionally, the video recording function of most smartphones is webcam resolution.

The basics of using a video camera are straightforward. Hold the camera steady; a tripod helps with this. Point the camera in the direction of the scene you are shooting. Frame the scene using the viewfinder. Then, activate the recording function. **Footage** is the video content recorded by the camera.

Ethics

Information

Don't believe everything you read. Just because you read an article in a magazine or newspaper, don't assume it is correct, legal, or ethical. Ethical communication is based on an individual's perception, either on the part of the writer or the reader. Analyze the information based on your own personal ethics.

Video Quality

The quality of a video is determined by resolution, canvas size, and color depth. *Resolution* is determined by the pixel dimensions of the frame, just like a photograph. The number of *frames per second (fps)* is also important to the quality of the video. Smoother and sharper videos are created with greater fps, but the file size also increases. Be aware, there are standard frame rates for playback devices. For example, a computer plays video at 30 fps.

The **canvas size** is the area in which the video will be displayed. Another way to refer to this is *frame size*. The canvas size should match the output device for delivering the digital media presentation.

Color depth is the number of distinct colors that can be represented and is based on the number of bits used to define a color, such as 24-bit color or 32-bit color. Color depth is important for the realistic appearance of a video. The greater the color depth, the more lifelike the images will appear, but the larger the file will be. However, the number of colors that can be seen in the video delivered is determined by the hardware in use. It is important, therefore, to consider the delivery method when determining the color depth setting.

Videography Basics

When creating a video, you will apply visual design basics to the scene, just as you would to any visual element. The choices you make are dictated by the information you want to convey, the tone you want to set, and the limitations of the setting. The basic choices when recording a video are camera shots, camera moves, and lighting.

Camera shots are wide shot, medium-wide shot, medium shot, bust or head shot, medium close-up, and close-up. Each of these types of shots has a different purpose in videography, such as establishing the scene or connecting to a character.

When creating a video, the camera does not have to keep still as the scene unfolds. There are basic options for moving the camera while recording, which creates effects unique to videography. You can *pan* the scene, showing what is to the left or the right of the current view, or *tilt* the camera to show what is above or below. The entire camera can also move in a circle around the scene, which is known as *trucking*, or it can *dolly* to move toward or away from the scene.

The four basic elements of lighting are direction, quality, ratio, and control. Each of these elements contributes to the overall effect of the lighting and needs to be considered when selecting the lighting for a video or a specific scene within a video. These qualities are described in Figure 15-2.

Editing Video Footage

Once you have recorded the footage, it will need to be edited before it is ready to be included in the digital media presentation. Depending on the editing software, there are several modifications that can be made.

- Create *clips*, or short segments, from the video.
- Cut clips of video from one location and paste them in another.

Four Basic Elements of Video Lighting

Element	Description
Direction	**Light direction** is related to the height and angle of the light source. *Height* is the location of the light source relative to the subject. Is it above, below, or even with the subject? *Angle* refers to the slope of the light's beam. Together, height and angle dictate where the shadows and highlights fall on the subject of the video.
Quality	**Light quality** refers to the hardness or softness of the light on the subject. Hard light is created by strong beams of light, which cause sharp edges between light and shadow. Soft light is created with diffused light. Consequently, the transition from light to shadow is soft, not sharp.
Ratio	**Lighting ratio** is the difference in brightness between the lightest and darkest areas of the shot. This is quantified by a numerical ratio. The brightest area is compared to the darkest area in terms of how many times brighter it is. How great of a ratio can be captured in a video depends on the sensitivity of the video camera. The commonly used lighting ratios for videos are 2:1, 3:1, and 4:1. A ratio of 2:1 is probably most frequently used.
Control	**Light control** refers to any action that alters the shape or color of the light. For example, a piece of colored, translucent material may be placed in front of a beam of light to change the color of the light. Or, part of the beam could be blocked in order to create a shadow or reduce a highlight in a specific area of the scene.

Goodheart-Willcox Publisher

Figure 15-2   When creating video, pay attention to these lighting elements to achieve the desired effect.

- Overlay and synchronize audio, text, and narration.
- Add transitions between segments of video.
- Change the canvas size, color depth, and frame rate.
- Add informational graphics, illustrations, and animations.
- Save the video in different file formats for DVD, podcast, or the Internet.

There are several video-editing programs available, including Adobe Premiere Pro, Apple Final Cut Pro, Apple iMovie, Avid Media Composer, and Microsoft Windows Movie Maker, among others. Some video-editing programs must be purchased, but there are shareware and freeware options. Before purchasing software, you may wish to download a trial version to be sure the software contains the features that are needed.

Audio

Audio in a digital media project can take many forms. A presentation can be enhanced by sound effects, music, or voice-overs. As with photography and videos, audio should not be overused in a digital media project. Figure 15-3 shows questions to ask when evaluating audio.

Sounds may be recorded, created with a computer or musical instrument, or obtained through online resources. Be sure to read and follow the terms and conditions for using any downloaded files. Sometimes a fee must be paid to use the files, and others may be obtained free of royalty. Others simply require a permission to use the files.

Evaluating Audio
•   Does the audio support the goals of the project? •   Is the sound quality appropriate for this project? •   Will the audio be distracting? •   Are there too many sounds in the presentation? •   Are the audio files an appropriate size for using in this type of project? •   Have necessary permissions been obtained to use the audio? Are the sources appropriately cited?

Goodheart-Willcox Publisher

Figure 15-3   Evaluate each audio clip before using it in a digital media presentation.

Creating a Digital Media Presentation

Knowing what to do and how to do it is a good first step in creating a digital media presentation. Before you begin, make sure you have the necessary funding to complete the project. Then it will be necessary to create the visual design, develop a schedule, and complete the production process.

Visual Design

Digital media projects almost always contain visuals because the medium is visual by nature. While planning a presentation, the quality of visuals should be carefully considered. Only include media that is clear and adds interest and emphasis. Care must be taken also to avoid overuse. Too many visuals in a presentation will become distracting and the presentation will lose its effectiveness. If a presentation is cluttered with images, your message can be lost.

When creating a digital media presentation, the visual design is as important as the content. *Visual design* is the arrangement of the visual and artistic elements used to accomplish a goal or communicate an idea. An effective presentation will follow the principles of design along with what you learned about writing a presentation. The *principles of design* are concepts that suggest how to arrange the elements of art to produce a visually appealing overall effect. These concepts were covered in Chapter 12.

In addition to the basic principles of design, digital media is governed by additional design concepts that are used when a visual design is not static, as in a digital media presentation. These concepts are movement, rhythm, and perspective.

- **Movement** in a digital media presentation may be real action, such as in a video clip, or it can be the *appearance* of action, such as wavy lines in a presentation about the ocean. Movement creates action and a sense of perspective within space.

- **Rhythm** is the regular repetition of objects or sound to show movement or activity. Rhythm can also be used to create a sense of energy or urgency. Rhythm creates a visual or auditory tempo or pace.

- **Perspective** is an artistic technique that creates the illusion of depth on a two-dimensional surface. It is created by varying the sizes of objects within a field and overlapping them. The objects to be viewed as closer are made larger and placed in front of the objects that are to be viewed as farther away.

Schedule

A crucial component of any project is developing the schedule. A schedule identifies all required tasks for building, testing, and producing the project. **Milestones** are important dates that need to be met to keep the project moving forward. For each task, milestones are set so that progress can be checked. Milestone dates can be determined in one of two ways.

- Set milestone dates moving forward from the current date based on experience and an estimate of how long a given task will take.

- Set milestone dates starting with the final due date and working backward, known as *backdating* or *timeline*.

Project management applications, such as Microsoft Project, Gantt Project, or Basecamp, are used to develop and maintain a schedule for the work to be done. These applications provide the basic tools needed to develop a schedule for a digital media presentation or to assist in its development.

Production Process

There are many elements involved in creating a digital media presentation. **Production** is the process of creating a digital media presentation. The three main stages of production are preproduction, production, and postproduction.

Preproduction

Preproduction is the planning, scripting, and storyboarding of the presentation. It is the work done before any video is recorded, pictures are taken, or sound is recorded. Planning includes following the steps in the writing process to create the content. Once the content is finalized, the script is then written. The script represents the words and actions that will be played out in the presentation. A **storyboard** illustrates the content of the digital media presentation with a sketch of each important scene or event along with a brief description of what will happen, as shown in Figure 15-4. The storyboard provides a visual representation for ideas. The storyboard gives the team an opportunity to verify that everyone has the same understanding of what the presentation will look like.

Production

Production is the creation of the graphic, video, and audio elements. The production phase of creating a video is the actual creation of the product. Whether you are creating a slideshow, website, DVD, or streaming video, consider the overall design of the presentation. It must be visually pleasing, not distracting, and be the right vehicle to promote your message. The

Goodheart-Willcox Publisher

Figure 15-4   A storyboard contains a sketch of the scene and a brief description of what will happen.

principles that apply to creating artwork or taking photographs are the same ones that apply to the layout and design of a digital media presentation.

Postproduction

Postproduction is everything that occurs after production to create the final master copy. It includes the editing of images and video. It can take as long, or longer, than creating the actual graphic, video, and audio elements.

Section 15.2 Review

 Check Your Understanding

1. What media are typically used in a digital media presentation?
2. What is OLE?
3. What does photo-editing software allow a user to do?
4. List four basic options for moving a video camera when recording.
5. What are the three stages of production?

 Build Your Vocabulary

As you progress through this course, develop a personal glossary of key terms. This will help you build your vocabulary and prepare you for a career. Write a definition for each of the following terms and add it to your personal glossary.

pixel	movement
resolution	rhythm
filtering	perspective
layering	milestone
footage	production
canvas size	storyboard

Chapter Summary

Section 15.1 Digital Media Basics

- When a slide presentation is not quite adequate for the purpose or audience, consider using digital media. A digital media presentation can be very effective if you remember to focus on the message and use the media to enhance, rather than dominate, the content. With proper planning and right hardware and software, you can create an effective presentation.

- Licensing agreements should be taken very seriously when purchasing and using software. Software programs are governed by an end user license agreement. The end user license agreement (EULA) is the set of rules that every user must agree to before using the software. Ignoring these rules is copyright infringement.

Section 15.2 Creating Digital Media Presentations

- Media typically used in a digital media presentation are animation, digital photography, video, and audio. Remember to use the media wisely in your presentation. As in other presentations, too many visuals will become distracting and the information will lose its effectiveness.

- The first step in creating a digital media presentation is planning. Planning includes creating the visual design, deciding a schedule, and taking the project through the production process.

Online Activities

Complete the following activities which will help you learn, practice, and expand your knowledge and skills.

Posttest. Now that you have finished the chapter, see what you learned by taking the chapter posttest.

Vocabulary. Practice vocabulary for this chapter using the e-flash cards, matching activity, and vocabulary game until you are able to recognize their meanings.

English/Language Arts. Visit www.g-wlearning.com to download each data file for this chapter. Follow the instructions to complete an English/language arts activity to practice what you have learned in this chapter.

Activity File 15-1: Improving Your Editing Skills

Activity File 15-2: Improving Your Reading Skills

Review Your Knowledge

1. Explain the difference between nonexclusive and exclusive licensing agreements.

2. What permissions does an end user license agreement (EULA) for audio and video files grant the user?

3. What elements determine the quality of a video?

4. List the four basic elements of lighting.

5. Describe the purpose of a script.

6. List the three types of cameras used for recording digital videos.

7. Give three examples of modifications that can be made with video editing software.

8. What is visual design?

9. Describe the two ways in which milestones can be set.

10. How can a storyboard aid the preproduction stage?

Apply Your Knowledge

1. In Chapter 14, you created a slideshow as a visual aid to present a speech. Next, you will create a video from the slideshow presentation. For your presentation, include audio in the form of narration or a voice-over as well as music or other audio effects to add interest. Begin planning your video by writing a script. Then, create storyboards, if needed.

2. Next, schedule the production of the video. Include all milestones that are necessary to create the final product. If others will be helping you with this project, include their names, responsibilities, and deadlines for their tasks.

3. Identify the hardware and software that you will need to create and deliver the finished product. Make a list of what is available in the school computer lab, at the local library, or at home.

4. Ask your teacher for a copy of an end user's license agreement (EULA) for software that is used in your class. What are the main points covered in this agreement? Explain the end user's rights.

5. Once you have finished planning, create your video. Edit the footage until you are satisfied with the final product. Use the information in this chapter to guide you. When the video is complete, post it where your instructor can view it, such as on the school's network or on social media.

6. Reflect on the quality of the video presentation you created. Summarize the techniques used. List what you did well and what you could have done better.

How do you feel about your performance on this assignment? How can you use this assignment in the future?

Communication Skills

College and Career Readiness

Listening. Communication is an important part of the job for any employee. Individuals who are career ready understand the importance of communicating clearly using verbal skills. They listen carefully and consider their audience when sending a message. Create a script that you could use for a one-minute public service announcement about the importance of clean water.

Writing. Identity theft is a serious problem for businesses as well as consumers. Conduct research on how much money businesses lost in the past year due to identity theft. Write an informative report consisting of several paragraphs to describe your findings of the implications for consumers. Edit and revise your work until the ideas are refined and clear to the reader.

Speaking. Select three of your classmates to participate in a group discussion. Acting as the team leader, name each person to a specific task such as timekeeper, recorder, etc. Discuss software for digital media presentations. Gain consensus from the group on which software is the better one to use for a basic presentation. Keep the panel on task and promote democratic discussion.

Internet Research

Fair Use and Copyright Laws. Using the Internet, research the laws that relate to fair use. When were they created? What is their purpose? Next, research copyright laws. Summarize what you learned about duplication of materials that are copyrighted and ethical conduct.

While studying, look for the activity icon **for:**

- Pretests and posttests
- Vocabulary terms with e-flash cards and matching activities
- Videos
- Self-assessment

G-WLEARNING.com

Video

Before you begin this unit, scan the QR code to view a video about professional communication. If you do not have a smartphone, visit www.g-wlearning.com.

Rido/Shutterstock.com

Listening with a Purpose

Sections

16.1 Listening Is a Skill

16.2 Active Listeners

College and Career Readiness

Reading Prep. Before reading this chapter, review the highlighted key terms within the body. Determine the meaning of each key term.

Check Your Communication IQ ↱

Before you begin the chapter, see what you already know about communication by taking the chapter pretest. The pretest is available at www.g-wlearning.com.

Case Study

Careful Listening

Samantha Pelzer was recently assigned to manage all promotional materials for Classic Works Theater Company. She still has much to learn about this new area, but a coworker, Roland Varnas, provided some helpful information. Yesterday, a representative from Allied Printing stopped by Samantha's office to talk about his company's services. The rep told Samantha, "Allied Printing is an agent for independent printers. We guarantee you the lowest cost and the fastest deliveries. For example, we would charge you only 29 cents a copy for this brochure. Other printers would charge you more."

As Samantha listened, she thought, "Roland said you get the best prices when you deal directly with the printer. When you deal with an agent, the agent gets a commission. That must cost more. But I know we paid more than 29 cents a copy for the University Ballet brochure. I'd better ask Roland about that."

Charlotte Purdy/Shutterstock.com

Critical Thinking

1. How did prior knowledge help Samantha evaluate what the representative said?

2. How can Samantha's active listening help her save the company money?

Listening Is a Skill

Objectives

When you complete this section, you will be able to:

- **Differentiate** between hearing and listening.
- **Explain** how to listen with a purpose.

Key Terms

hearing
listening
passive listening
active listening
prior knowledge
evaluate
appreciative listening

critical listening
empathetic listening
reflective listening
deliberative listening
evasive
literal
inferential

Listening Process

Think about how much time you spend listening. In any given week, you may listen to your favorite music, get directions from someone, or receive feedback from others. But are you really listening?

?**E**ssential **Q**uestion

Why is listening important in professional communication?

Developing good listening skills is important for success.

Monkey Business Images/Shutterstock.com

Hearing is a physical process. **Listening** is an intellectual process that combines hearing with evaluating. In addition, listening often leads to follow-up. Just because you can hear a person speak does not mean you are listening to what is said. When you *listen*, you make an effort to process what you *hear*. To process what you hear, consider why the person is speaking, relate what you already know, and show attention.

Few people would argue against the importance of listening, yet listening skills are often ignored. To develop listening skills takes time, patience, and practice. Children are expected to listen, but are not always taught to listen as they are taught to read, write, or speak. Listening skills are difficult to observe and measure. In most cases, listening is assumed. How effectively someone is listening is often unknown.

Effective listening is achieved by using the listening process. The steps in the *listening process*, as shown in Figure 16-1, are similar to the steps in the communication process.

- *Receive.* Focus on the sender and hear the message.

- *Decode.* Assign meaning to words and sounds so the message can be understood.

- *Remember.* Take time to remember what is being said so that the information can be used.

- *Evaluate.* Apply critical thinking skills to evaluate what was said.

- *Respond.* Give feedback to show that you received the message.

Following the steps in the listening process can improve your listening skills. There are two types of listening: passive listening and active listening.

Passive Listening

Passive listening is casually listening to someone talk. You may or may not hear everything that is said, and you are not actively trying to understand. When you are watching a movie, you are a passive listener. Passive listening is appropriate when you do not need to interact with the person speaking. Passive listeners are more interested in *hearing* and less interested in *listening*.

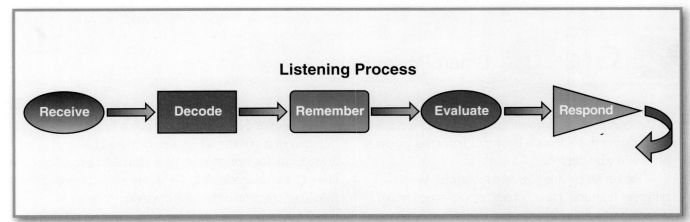

Goodheart-Willcox Publisher

Figure 16-1   The listening process is similar to the communication process.

Active Listening

Active listening is fully participating as you process what a person says. Active listening is used to get information, respond to requests, receive instructions, and evaluate persuasive speech. Active listeners consider the purpose of what is being said and show attention through body language and words. Active listeners know when to take notes, follow directions, comment, or remain quiet.

Prior knowledge is important to active listening. **Prior knowledge** is experience and information a person already possesses. Active listeners relate what they know to what they hear and continuously evaluate the information. To **evaluate** is to judge the accuracy and truthfulness of the spoken words. Evaluation can also keep you focused on the topic and can aid your memory.

There are several types of active listening. Each type serves a specific purpose. You may engage in more than one type of active listening at a time.

- **Appreciative listening** is the process of listening for enjoyment. Listening to music is an example of appreciative listening.

- **Critical listening** occurs when specific information or instructions are needed. For example, a customer service representative must use critical listening to determine what a customer needs.

- **Empathetic listening** occurs when you attempt to put yourself in the speaker's place and understand how he or she feels. Customer service representatives very frequently must use empathetic listening to understand why a customer is upset. By understanding the issue, the customer service representative may be better able to assist the customer.

- **Reflective listening** occurs when the listener demonstrates an understanding of the message by restating what was said. The listener does not try to change the meaning of the message, but may paraphrase to show understanding. All active listening involves reflective listening.

- **Deliberative listening** is the process of determining the quality or validity of what is being said. For example, if a salesperson tells you that by purchasing a piece of equipment you will save thousands of dollars each year, you must evaluate this statement to determine if it is valid.

 Green Smart Power Strips

Computer workstations should be set up so all of the computer equipment is plugged into a power strip. Doing this allows a user to control the power to an entire workstation.

Power strips are now available with several different features. New "smart" power strips make it easy and convenient to save power each day. A power strip with a timer feature can be set to automatically turn the power strip off at a designated time. Occupancy power strips have a motion detector that senses when a person has been away from the workstation for a specified period of time. Once time elapses, the power strip turns off. Because electronic devices draw power even in sleep mode, a power-sensing strip can turn off the power supply when sleep mode is detected.

Listen with Purpose

Your purpose for listening varies greatly depending on whether you are listening in a one-on-one conversation, in a group discussion, or as a member of a large audience. You will be a more effective listener if you can identify your purpose and adapt your listening behavior accordingly.

Listen for Specific Information

Before you go to a meeting, attend a conference, or make a telephone call, decide what information you hope to gain. If you initiate a conversation with someone, develop a list of notes or questions before the conversation occurs. If someone contacts you, be prepared to take notes as he or she talks.

An active listener asks questions to clarify information.

When someone is responding to your question or request, listen carefully. In some cases, a response can be very long, or the person may use language that is not clear. Always make sure you understand all parts of the response and its details. Write notes and ask questions to clarify any points that are confusing.

In some situations, people may be **evasive**, which means to avoid giving a direct

Monkey Business Images/Shutterstock.com

answer. Perhaps the person may not know the answer and try to hide the uncertainty. In other situations, the person may be uncomfortable giving an answer because the issue may be sensitive or not appropriate for all members of the audience. If you recognize that a person does not know an answer, be gracious. Pressing people for information they do not have can result in embarrassment for everyone.

Listen to Instructions

When others are instructing you, help them out by actively listening to what they are saying. Find out as much as you can about what you are to hear before you attend the meeting or presentation. Bring the catalog, report, budget, or any other materials that will be discussed. Having this prior knowledge will give you something to which you can relate your new knowledge.

At the meeting or presentation, take notes. Ask questions and make comments to clarify and confirm the information. If necessary, politely ask the speaker to slow down or repeat a point. As you listen, try to anticipate your future needs. Will you need any additional information after the meeting? Find out when and where you can get help if a problem should arise and make note of it.

Shared Workspace

Whether you are in an office, a cubicle, or an open room, chances are you will have to share your workspace with others. Always allow your neighbors their privacy. Knock before entering a room or speaking to someone. Walk around walls or partitions to communicate; do not shout over or around them. Wait to be invited into a conversation rather than jumping in just because it is within earshot.

Make sure you have all of the information before leaving. Write a brief summary of the information you learned. *Summarizing* is an active listening technique that can help to ensure you omit nothing. When you summarize, you write or think through all of the main points you just heard.

When possible, give feedback to the speaker to show you understand the information that is being presented. Sometimes, simply making eye contact tells the person you are listening. If there is an opportunity to give comments or ask questions, your feedback will be appreciated by the speaker.

Listen to Requests

Requests come in all shapes and sizes. Some are simple and need only a brief response. Others are tedious and time-consuming. In many cases, your first decision must be whether you can or should perform whatever is being asked. Your second decision may be whether you can do so in the allotted time. When you receive a request, consider the following.

- Determine whether the request is one of your assigned job tasks.
- Listen to be sure you understand the *who, what, where, when, why,* and *how* of the request.
- Ask follow-up questions to clarify complex issues.
- Make comments that summarize what you are to do.
- Do not rely on your memory. Take notes, especially for numbers, dates, and other details.

It is wise to always question and evaluate the requests you receive. You must decide whether the request is reasonable.

Listen to Persuasive Talk

When someone is trying to persuade you, that person has a purpose: to influence your attitude or behavior. When you know what he or she wants, you will be better able to analyze what is being said. When you recognize persuasive talk, determine the purpose of being persuaded by asking yourself questions.

- What is in it for the person speaking?
- Whom does he or she represent?
- What does he or she want me to do or believe?
- What are the pros and cons of this issue?

Persuasive statements may be interpreted as literal or inferential. **Literal** means the person speaking means exactly what the words indicate. **Inferential** means you are to draw a conclusion from what is said. For example, consider the following statement from a salesperson trying to sell a maintenance-service contract for a laptop computer.

| With the contract, complete computer repair is a telephone call away!

Is this a literal or inferential statement? Since the process of repairing the defect begins with a telephone call to request that your computer be serviced, the statement is inferential. If the statement were literal, the telephone call would repair the computer, which is not correct.

When a person is trying to persuade you, he or she attempts to predict your objections and argue against them in advance. A savvy person might

Effective listeners identify a purpose for listening.

Vitchanan Photography/Shutterstock.com

direct arguments using prior knowledge of any weaknesses you may have. Do not make the mistake of being a passive listener. Recognize that effective persuasive talk is carefully prepared and is adjusted to obtain the desired results. As a listener, you should prepare to analyze incoming information. Take into consideration the purpose of the persuasive talk and your own needs and motivations.

Active listeners recognize when their own needs and motivations get in the way of making a good decision. Active listeners try to listen *above* their preferences to make rational, rather than emotional, decisions. Use silent self-talk to question incoming information. If you doubt the accuracy of what you hear, you may politely ask the speaker to support questionable statements.

Section 16.1 Review

 Check Your Understanding

1. What is the difference between passive listening and active listening?
2. Identify the steps in the listening process.
3. When listening to directions, what responsibility does the listener have?
4. What is the difference between a literal and inferential statement?
5. What purpose does a persuasive speaker have?

 Build Your Vocabulary

As you progress through this course, develop a personal glossary of key terms. This will help you build your vocabulary and prepare you for a career. Write a definition for each of the following terms and add it to your personal glossary.

hearing	critical listening
listening	empathetic listening
passive listening	reflective listening
active listening	deliberative listening
prior knowledge	evasive
evaluate	literal
appreciative listening	inferential

Active Listeners

Objectives

After completing this section, you will be able to:

- **Describe** how an individual can become an active listener.
- **Explain** how to demonstrate to a speaker that you are listening.

Key Terms 📷

skepticism   rapport

?**E**ssential **Q**uestion

What does it mean to you to be an active listener?

Become an Active Listener

In any listening situation, active listening requires your complete engagement. Two things you can do to become an active listener are focus on the message and evaluate the message.

Focus on the Message

When you speak, you have a purpose or reason for delivering the message. Likewise, when you listen, you are listening to someone who has a purpose or reason for delivering the message. Your job as a listener starts by recognizing the purpose of the person speaking. Concentrate on what the speaker is saying. Take notes when necessary.

Does the message match the nonverbal cues given by the speaker? Body language and other nonverbal cues will help you interpret a speaker's message. When you watch as well as listen to someone speak, you often understand more than when you only listen. Seeing someone speak provides more information about the meaning of the words than simply hearing the person speak. Other nonverbal cues, such as tone of voice, also help you assign meaning to a speaker's words.

Evaluate the Message

When listening, you must evaluate and assign meaning to what you hear. Relate the new information to your prior knowledge. Evaluating messages based on prior knowledge has three general benefits:

- improved memory
- improved focus
- improved understanding

If new and old information match or agree, you may choose to believe what you hear. However, when new and old information contradict each other, you must question what you hear. Does the message make sense?

Can you think of any reason not to believe it? Skepticism can help you interpret the real meaning of a message. **Skepticism** means having a degree of doubt. It is not useful to doubt everyone all of the time, but balancing belief with skepticism is smart. A time for skepticism is when you know the speaker stands to benefit from what is being said. Be skeptical if a person's statements seem exaggerated.

The better you know the person and the situation, the better you can detect his or her real purpose for speaking. For example, if you know someone has a history of being honest and following through on promises, then you are probably safe to assume the speaker will be forthright in speaking to you. In contrast, if you know someone frequently hides information, you should be more careful when determining his or her intentions.

Show You Are Listening

Listening requires discipline. Companies lose millions of dollars every year because employees are not listening to what is being said by customers, managers, or peers. Paying attention is important in the workplace. Not learning effective listening skills can cost you your job.

When listening, show that you are receptive to the message that is being conveyed. An essential element of being receptive to messages is having an open mind. To have an *open mind* means you are willing to respectfully listen to the sender without letting negative feelings, emotions, or biases get in the way. Making assumptions about what someone is going to say before he or she speaks might cause you to ignore words that send a different message.

Exploring Communication Careers

Producer

Producers prepare and supervise the making of a film, television show, play, or other performing arts production. This job is responsible for overseeing the development from beginning to end and arranging for funding of the project. The producer interprets the script to tell a story or inform the audience. They also hire the performing staff, such as the actors and musicians, as well as the functional staff, such as accountants and caterers. Typical job titles for this position include *director* and *executive producer*.

Some examples of tasks that producers perform include:

- Read, research, and assess ideas and finished scripts.

- Raise funds for film, television shows, or other performing arts projects.

- Hire key staff for projects.

- Keep the project on budget and on schedule.

Producer positions require a bachelor degree and experience working in various roles in film, television, or other performing arts productions. Leadership and management skills are required as these people lead teams. Producers can be employed by a production company or be an independent worker.

Many people take listening for granted. Listening is not something people often think about. However, there is no question that good listening is a critical skill for career success. Routine business situations require that you listen carefully and evaluate what you hear. Actively listening to a supervisor or client can make the difference between successful and unsuccessful performance at work. Your attention and understanding in meetings, as well as your ability to carry out instructions, can influence your success in significant ways. Through your actions, you must show that you are listening carefully.

More formal situations require extra listening effort. A job interview, a meeting with a manager, a business lunch with clients, or listening to a presentation are situations that require special attention. If you are attending a formal presentation, you can show you are listening in the following ways.

Arrive Early

Arriving early is not merely a courtesy to the speaker and other meeting participants, but it is also an aid to your listening. By arriving early, you have time to settle in, familiarize yourself with your surroundings, and greet people you know.

The beginning and end of any speaking event are often crucial. Speakers often introduce and summarize main points both at the beginning and the end. By missing the first few minutes of a presentation, you cannot benefit from the speaker's attempt to focus the discussion and introduce main ideas. Finally, arriving late is disruptive and disrespectful to others in the audience.

Sit in the Front

The front of the room usually provides fewer distractions. You are less likely to be distracted by those sitting between you and the speaker. From the front, you can hear the speaker better and see any visuals with less effort. By sitting in the front of the room, you will more easily be able to participate in the listening process.

Pressmaster/Shutterstock.com

Sitting in the front of a room is one way a listener can show he or she is listening.

Show Attention

Convey through body language that you are paying attention. This is necessary in all situations, but can be especially important to your career in formal situations. Here are some key ways to show attention.

- Face the speaker and give your full attention.

- Engage in eye contact to signal that you are focused. Avoid staring, which can be intimidating and distracting.

- Lean toward the speaker to indicate you are paying attention.

- Be appropriately responsive. Smile or laugh at a joke and frown at bad news.

- Nod your head when you understand a point. If you are puzzled by something, let the speaker know by furrowing your brow or asking a question.

Apply these suggestions as they fit the circumstances. Be mindful that the speaker will be evaluating your body language. Nonverbal cues, such as roving eyes and inappropriate facial expressions, communicate indifference and even rudeness.

In order to show attention, you need to pay attention to the message. Your attention builds positive rapport with the speaker. **Rapport** is a feeling of harmony and accord in a relationship that encourages further communication. The discipline of showing attention makes it easier to ignore distractions. By committing yourself physically to the task of listening, you are less likely to be distracted.

Take Notes

Effective note-taking requires careful, active listening. Jot down the speaker's points that are meaningful to your purpose for listening, as shown in Figure 16-2. You must not only hear what is said, but you must also comprehend, evaluate, and translate or summarize the information. Then, determine if the information is important enough to write down. Next, you must quickly record it. Continue listening unless the speaker stops while you write. Do not use note-taking as a substitute for active listening.

Taking Good Notes

- Be selective. Write down only what is important or what you may not remember.
- Organize your notes as you write, if possible. Let the format of your notes correspond to the speaker's message.
- Use abbreviations and symbols. If the notes are for you only, cut as many corners as you like as long as the notes remain useful.
- Avoid noting information that appears in a handout. Highlight or put a check mark in the margin of the handout to remind yourself of key points.
- Write down the main point of a visual aid. If it contains data you need later, write down the source or ask the speaker afterward for a copy of the visual.
- Often speakers summarize the most important points in the closing. This is a good time to be listening carefully with pen ready, if necessary.

Goodheart-Willcox Publisher

Figure 16-2   Consider these tips for taking good notes.

It is important to write down things you must do following a discussion or meeting. Relying on memory is not a good idea. Carefully listen for any instructions, whether directly stated or implied, and write them down. You will often leave meetings with many things on your mind, some of which you will forget if you do not take notes.

Fight Barriers

Good listeners fight external distractions and barriers so they can give all of their attention to the task of listening. As you will recall, a barrier is anything that prevents clear, effective communication. Be aware of the barriers, both internal and external, that might interfere with good listening. Concentration helps to keep internal distractions created by one's own mind in check. There are several strategies that fight barriers to listening.

- *Be attentive.* Attentive listeners become involved in what the speaker is saying. Inattentive listeners become distracted because they are bored or are multitasking. Turn off your cell phone. Follow along with the speaker. Resist the temptation to daydream.

- *Be flexible.* Flexible listeners are open to new ideas. Inflexible listeners refuse to listen to a speaker who has said or implied something they disagree with. They tune out a speaker and are not interested in learning.

- *Be unbiased.* Unbiased listeners do not make judgments. Being biased will interfere with your ability to listen. Do not decide in advance that a speaker lacks credibility or does not deserve your attention.

- *Be empathetic.* To *empathize* with the speaker is to put yourself in his or her shoes. Imagine how you would feel as the speaker.

Provide Feedback

When possible, provide feedback by asking questions and making comments. Be aware that the tone of questions and comments can influence the communication process. Friendly questions that ask for clarification or further information are welcomed by a speaker. Such feedback will put the speaker at ease and provide an opportunity to repeat or elaborate on a point. By asking friendly questions and making friendly comments, you show that you are listening and interested. You also demonstrate that you have enough confidence in the speaker to seek more information. See Figure 16-3 for examples of questions.

If spoken in an unfriendly tone, questions and comments can put a speaker on the defensive and create communication barriers, as shown in Figure 16-4. Challenging questions or comments are not a form of constructive feedback. Even if the speaker has a good response to an unfriendly question or comment, the challenge may create an uncomfortable atmosphere.

Avoid the pitfalls of being friendly versus unfriendly by carefully phrasing your question or comment. Pay attention to these points.

- *Ask questions at the appropriate time.* Avoid interrupting a speaker in group meetings or a presentation. Instead, write down questions or comments and wait until the speaker invites them. A presenter may

Friendly Questions

These questions can be considered friendly questions. Friendly questions are usually welcomed by the speaker.

- Did your marketing questionnaire elicit any information on family income?
- This summary sheet says the year's sales goal is 10 percent higher than last year's. Is that 10 percent over last year's actual sales or 10 percent over budgeted sales?
- How expensive is this new technology for fuel conservation?
- I agree we must get our budget back on track, but do we have some specific ways to get around the higher prices in the marketplace?
- If we give them a copy of the appendix, will it answer all of their questions?

Goodheart-Willcox Publisher

Figure 16-3   Friendly questions can help establish a rapport with the speaker.

Unfriendly Questions

These questions may be considered unfriendly questions. Unfriendly questions can put up a barrier between you and the speaker.

- Last week you said last month's sales were up 10 percent, but today you say they were down five percent. Which is it?
- You claim there are no problems with clear-cutting forests, but how do you account for the article in last week's *Forestry Magazine*, which listed several problems with clear-cutting?
- That sounds like a very high number. Do you have empirical evidence to support that claim?
- You always talk about participative management, but have you really implemented it in this department?

Goodheart-Willcox Publisher

Figure 16-4   Unfriendly questions can damage the relationship between you and the speaker.

welcome questions during a presentation or indicate that questions and comments will be taken at the end. If you have more than one question or comment, pause between them to give others a chance to participate.

- *Be sure the question is relevant.* Avoid questions or comments that do not relate to the topic. The speaker may not be able to answer and other listeners will probably become impatient. If you need to discuss an unrelated topic, approach the speaker after the formal session concludes.

- *Limit the length of your question.* Keep your questions and comments short. Avoid getting into a long, one-on-one discussion. This is inconsiderate to the group. If you need to pursue a discussion beyond a follow-up question or comment, do so after the formal session.

- *Observe good diplomacy.* No matter how much you disagree, always maintain a professional tone. If you ask a good question or make a good comment in an unprofessional manner, your lack of professionalism is what people will remember. If the speaker appears to have given incorrect information, give the speaker the benefit of the doubt and carefully phrase your question or comment.

- *Avoid nitpicking.* Do not allow a small detail to become a distraction. Sometimes a speaker makes a general point with which you agree, but supports it with a detail with which you disagree. Do not challenge the detail unless you foresee it being misused later. In most cases, the general point is the more important aspect and the rest can be disregarded.

- *Never get personal.* If a speaker says something with which you disagree on principle or that you find offensive, consider letting it go. As a listener, it is not your role to challenge a speaker on behalf of your beliefs. If your disagreement is intense, approach the speaker in private. However, your goal should be to share a different perspective with the speaker, not to embarrass or to argue with him or her.

Section 16.2 Review

Check Your Understanding

1. Name two ways an individual can become an active listener.
2. What is meant by evaluating the message?
3. List ways a person can show he or she is listening to the speaker.
4. What does it mean to have an open mind?
5. Explain why it is beneficial to arrive early to a presentation.

Build Your Vocabulary

As you progress through this course, develop a personal glossary of key terms. This will help you build your vocabulary and prepare you for a career. Write a definition for each of the following terms and add it to your personal glossary.

skepticism

rapport

Chapter Summary

Section 16.1 Listening Is a Skill

- Hearing is a physical process, while listening involves evaluating what you hear. The steps of the listening process are receive, decode, remember, evaluate, and respond. Listening can be passive or active. The types of active listening include appreciative, critical, empathetic, reflective, and deliberative.

- You will be a more effective listener if you can identify your purpose and adapt your listening behavior accordingly. The different purposes for listening include listening for information, to directions, to requests, and to persuasive talk.

Section 16.2 Active Listeners

- To become an active listener, first focus on the message. Next, evaluate the message.

- A listener can show that he or she is listening in many ways. You can arrive early and sit in the front of the room. Show your attention and take notes on what is being said. Fight any distractions and barriers to communication. Provide friendly feedback when appropriate.

Online Activities

Complete the following activities which will help you learn, practice, and expand your knowledge and skills.

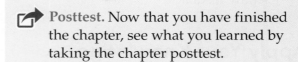

Posttest. Now that you have finished the chapter, see what you learned by taking the chapter posttest.

Vocabulary. Practice vocabulary for this chapter using the e-flash cards, matching activity, and vocabulary game until you are able to recognize their meanings.

English/Language Arts. Visit www.g-wlearning.com to download each data file for this chapter. Follow the instructions to complete an English/language arts activity to practice what you have learned in this chapter.

Activity File 16-1: Improving Your Listening Skills

Activity File 16-2: Improving Your Reading Skills

Review Your Knowledge

1. Explain the difference between hearing and listening.
2. Explain the components of the listening process.
3. Name five types of active listening.
4. What are some purposes for which we listen?
5. When listening to a request, how can you evaluate if it is reasonable?
6. How can the speaker's body language help a listener evaluate a message?
7. Evaluating messages based on prior knowledge has at least three general benefits. What are they?

8. Explain what is meant by personalizing information.

9. List three ways a listener can fight distractions and barriers.

10. Describe the importance of offering friendly feedback.

Apply Your Knowledge

1. Observe two speeches. The speeches can be seen live or recorded, such as on video, YouTube, or television. For one, be a passive listener. For the other, be an active listener. The day after observing each speech, write down as much as you can recall. Which one could you better recall? Write several paragraphs describing what you did differently when listening to each speech.

2. Create a table with two columns. In the first column, list the five types of active listening: appreciative, critical, empathetic, reflective, and deliberative. In the second column, describe a situation in which each could be used in an appropriate manner. Next, evaluate your listening skills. Which type of active listening is the one that you do the best? How did you make that choice?

3. As your instructor presents to the class, apply the active listening skills you have learned in this chapter. One part of active listening skills is to focus on the message. Make a list of actions you took that demonstrated you were actively listening to the message.

4. Applying the steps of the listening process in Figure 16-1 will help you become an active listener. List examples of critical-listening strategies effective communicators use in the workplace. How can you apply these strategies when evaluating a presentation?

5. Create a grid to record your daily listening habits. On the X axis, enter the five types of active listening. On the Y axis, list each person to whom you listen in a day's time. Check the appropriate type of listening that you did each time.

Communication Skills

College and Career Readiness

Listening. Practice active-listening skills while your teacher presents a lesson. Focus on the message and monitor it for understanding. Were there any barriers to effective listening? How did you use prior experiences to help you understand what was being said? Share your ideas in the group discussion.

Reading. Figurative language is used to describe something by comparing it with something else. Locate an advertisement for a product. Scan the information for figurative language about the product. Compare this with a description using literal language. Did the use of literal or figurative language influence your opinion of the products?

Writing. The workplace requires that employees adapt to diversity of the many individuals with whom they will come in contact. The interaction can be in formal or informal situations. Make a list of potential listening barriers that can evolve within a diverse group of coworkers and solutions to eliminate those barriers.

Internet Research

Communication Errors. Research examples of communication errors in the workplace. Cite an example of a business that lost money, lost productivity, or had another implications resulting from an employee not applying active listening skills.

Teamwork

Working with your team, make a list of good listening skills versus bad listening skills. After you have completed the list, prepare a short skit that demonstrates both types of listening skills. Incorporate both verbal and nonverbal communication tools to show active listening, such as body language, asking questions, or note-taking. Perform your skit in front of the class. Afterward, ask the audience to give feedback on the information you provided them.

Portfolio Development

College and Career Readiness

Networking. *Networking* means talking with others and establishing relationships with people who can help you achieve career, educational, or personal goals. You have probably already begun to build one, even if you have not thought of it in these terms. People in your network include your instructors, employers, coworkers, or counselors who know about your skills and interests. Those who participate with you in volunteer efforts, clubs, or other organizations can also be part of your network. These people may help you learn about open positions and may be able to give you information that will help you get a position.

1. Identify people who are part of your network.

2. Create a spreadsheet that includes information about each person. Include each person's name, contact information, and relationship to you. For example, the person might be a coworker, employer, or fellow club member. Save the file. This will be used for your personal use and not included in your portfolio.

CTSOs

Careers. Many competitive events for CTSOs competitions offer events that include various careers. This competitive event may include an objective test that covers multiple topics. Participants are usually allowed one hour to complete the event.

To prepare for the careers component of an event, complete the following activities.

1. Read the careers features in each chapter of the text. As you read about each career, note an important fact or two that you would like to remember.

2. Do an Internet search for *careers*. Review careers that may be a choice for the event. Make notes on important facts about each.

17

Reading with a Purpose

Sections

17.1 Reading Skills

17.2 Reading Techniques

College and Career Readiness

Reading Prep. Before reading this chapter, preview the section heads and key terms lists. Make a list of questions that you have before reading the chapter. Search for answers to your questions as you continue reading the chapter.

Phil Date/Shutterstock.com

Check Your Communication IQ 📑

Before you begin the chapter, see what you already know about communication by taking the chapter pretest. The pretest is available at www.g-wlearning.com.

Case Study

Careful Reading

Mark Brandenberg is a new marketing manager for a magazine publishing company. A coworker gave him a news article with the following paragraph flagged.

> The current status of the paper pulp industry, affected by developments in environmental protection and the scarcity of natural resources worldwide, leads to the conclusion that paper prices must rise by up to 32 percent next year alone.

Mark's company purchases millions of dollars worth of paper each year. The increase would be a financial disaster for the magazine. Mark rushed to see Elena Mateo, Director of Purchasing.

Looking worried, Elena reached for the clipping and scanned the article. Then, her face relaxed. She said, "The source is a spokesperson for the Federal Lumber Association. When environmental protection groups talk about stopping a logging operation, lumber companies and paper manufacturers have to react. They consider the worst, and that often gets presented in the scariest terms possible."

Santiago Cornejo/Shutterstock.com

Critical Thinking

1. Was this article for persuasion or information? Explain your answer.

2. In what ways could Mark be a more active reader?

Reading Skills

Objectives

After completing this section, you will be able to:

- **Describe** the importance of reading skills.
- **Explain** techniques that will enable you to master the skill of active reading.

Key Terms

active reading	read for detail
skim	presumption
scan	prioritize

Essential Question

How do you actively read?

Active Reading

Reading is something many people take for granted. Just like speaking and listening, reading is a skill. When *reading skillfully*, you get meaning from written words and symbols and evaluate their accuracy and validity. **Active reading** is processing the words, phrases, and sentences you read. Active reading is a complex task that involves concentration. You must be involved and do something in response to the words. To actively read, you must:

- consider the writer's purpose for writing
- consider your purpose for reading
- relate what you read to your prior knowledge
- evaluate information both as you read and after you read to ensure understanding and form judgments

Consider the Writer's Purpose

Before reading, identify the writer's purpose. This helps to absorb the message and understand how and when to

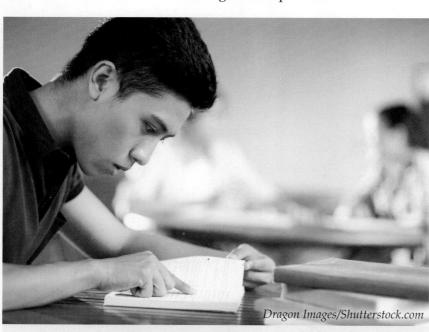

Dragon Images/Shutterstock.com

Active readers concentrate on the words and sentences that are being read.

respond. For example, an e-mail with a subject line of "Horizon Industries Estimate" tells you the purpose at a glance. To determine the purpose, ask yourself these questions.

- Who is the writer? What do I know about him or her?

- Does the writer expect something from me? If so, what is it?

- Is the writer trying to persuade me to do something? If so, what?

- Does the writer have a bias regarding the subject? If so, how might it have influenced what was written?

These questions are almost automatic when you read marketing propaganda such as a sales e-mail, advertisement, or marketing brochure.

The more you know about the writer, the better you will be able to identify a bias and assess motive. A *bias* is a prejudice that influences someone's thinking. Biases may be purposeful or accidental, conscious or unconscious. Whenever the writer has a financial motive, remember that the goal is to persuade the reader to make a purchase. In other situations, a motive may be less obvious. As with listening, it helps to have a touch of skepticism as you interpret a message.

Consider Your Purpose for Reading

After you have identified the writer's purpose, determine your purpose for reading. It is important to know why you are reading. Concentrate to be sure you read what is actually on the page and not just what you expect to see. Be aware that the writer's purpose for writing is not necessarily the same as the reader's purpose for reading. The four primary reasons for reading are reading for information, reading to follow instructions, reading persuasive writing, and reading requests.

Reading for Information

When reading for specific information, combine the reading approaches of skimming, scanning, and reading for detail. First, skim until you find the portion of the document that is likely to contain the information you seek. To **skim** is to quickly glance through an entire document to get an overview. It is also known as *prereading*. Then, scan to locate the specific piece of information. To **scan** means to quickly glance through a message to find specific information. When you find the information you are looking for, read for detail. To **read for detail** is reading all words and phrases, considering their meaning, and determining how they combine with other elements to convey ideas.

Reading to Follow Instructions

Reading to follow instructions is a common workplace reading task. This often calls for reading for detail. When reading to follow instructions, you might:

- complete forms, such as a job application

- follow a general process or procedure, such as using a style guide when writing

- follow numbered steps, such as for assembling a piece of furniture

When reading to follow instructions, pay attention to the sequence of the steps. It is also necessary to combine reading approaches of skimming, scanning, and reading for detail.

Reading Persuasive Writing

Persuasive reading materials try to convince the reader to take some course of action. Reading persuasive materials has a direct impact on the reader's decision-making process. Some examples of persuasive reading materials include a:

- text message from a colleague asking you to be on a committee to plan a company event

- form letter from a charitable organization asking you to volunteer

- marketing brochure or e-mail blast from a supplier

Evaluating the merit of persuasive writing usually requires reading for detail. Often persuasive writing requires the highest degree of detailed reading because of the need to constantly evaluate as you read. A wise reader does not presume the writer's information is accurate or the opinions valid. A **presumption** is something believed based on probable or assumed reliability.

Reading Requests

You will most likely need to read messages that make a request. Someone may need very specific information from you. Other times, a coworker may need to ask you a quick question via e-mail. Other times the request may be in the form of a persuasive message that urges you to change your behavior. When someone makes a written request, read for detail. This will help you understand exactly what is being asked and how to respond.

When reading for information, combine skimming, scanning, and reading for detail.

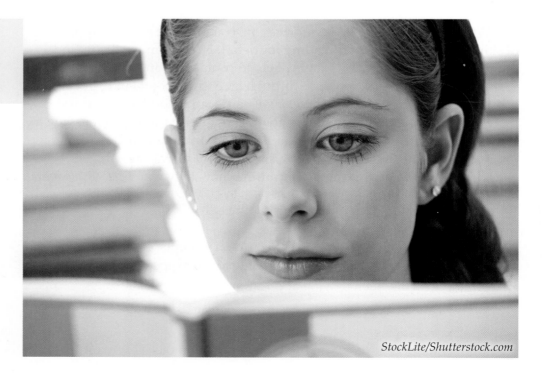

StockLite/Shutterstock.com

Use Prior Knowledge

Your prior knowledge of a situation allows you to quickly make sense of new information. Consciously or unconsciously, you answer these questions in your mind as you read.

- What do I already know about the writer, the situation, and the subject in general?

- Did I request this information?

- Have I said or done something recently that prompted this information?

- Am I receiving this information because it relates to my job?

- How can I use this information?

Recalling prior knowledge to aid reading works at all levels of the thought process. As you think about the situation, attach new knowledge to prior knowledge and act accordingly.

A similar use of prior knowledge in reading takes place at the word or concept level. If you come across words or groups of words that are unfamiliar, you can often figure out a meaning by recalling usage in other contexts. The ability to apply prior knowledge to new words and concepts is important to your success as a reader.

Evaluate What You Read

Evaluation should take place both as you read and after you read. The need to evaluate *after* you read should come as no surprise. To evaluate something *as* you read is also natural even though you might not be aware you are doing so most of the time. Consider the questions and comments that you think about as you read. These are likely to be an evaluation

Exploring Communication Careers

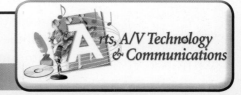

Set Designer

The background on a television show, movie, or play is considered the set. The set designer designs and creates these sets. A set can be as simple as arranging props in a room or on a stage. On the other hand, an entire building can be erected as part of a set. Set design work often begins by reading a script and meeting with the production's director. This foundational work must be done before sketches of a set are created. After having the sketches reviewed and approved, the set can be built. Typical job titles for this position include *art director* and *production designer*.

Some examples of tasks that set designers perform include:

- Read the script and meet with the director or producer.

- Sketch set designs and revise as needed.

- Conduct research to create realistic sets, such as finding and reviewing old photographs to create a realistic historical set.

- Participate in the building of the sets.

A bachelor degree in fine arts is often needed for set designer jobs. Courses in set design can lead to hands-on work experience, as well.

Ethics

Gossip

As an employee of a company, you may hear confidential information about employees or the company business. It is unethical to share any confidential information you learn and doing so may cost you your job. Repeating information is sometimes known as gossiping and some people find it harmless. However, depending on the confidentiality of the topic, sharing information may be considered slander. Always protect any confidential information you learn and respect the situation in which you learned it.

of either the message or your own understanding of the information. Evaluation is one of the most important parts of being an active reader. Evaluate after reading by asking these questions.

- Do the facts support what I already know?
- Do the facts support the writer's conclusions?
- Do I accept what the writer is saying or do I need to find another source?
- Does the writer's tone match the words?
- Are there unwritten messages here that I should think about?
- Are there questions I need to have answered before I act?

The evaluation process is simple in the course of everyday reading related to routine job tasks. Just as you would analyze and critique the content of your own written drafts, you will often need to analyze and critique what others have written.

Reading Approaches

All reading tasks do not require the same level of focus. How you approach a given task is determined by the type of communication, the writer's purpose, your purpose for reading, and your prior knowledge of the topic or situation. The approaches of skimming, scanning, and reading for detail will help you become a more efficient reader. The more you read on the job and understand your purpose for reading, the more you will be able to easily select and sometimes combine these approaches.

Skim to Get an Overview

Skimming, or prereading, is quickly glancing through an entire document to get an overview. When skimming a document, notice headings, key words, phrases, and visual elements. The goal of skimming is to get a sense of the main ideas and scope of the content. When you skim, you combine new information with prior knowledge to determine the next step. Skimming is especially useful when you want to:

- read for general information
- read simple responses and requests
- review the general coverage or content
- preview something you must read in greater detail
- locate a specific section of a long document

Skimming is a fast process. For busy people, it is a good skill to have. However, be aware of when it is appropriate to skim and when it is not. Many times, business communication contains standard words, phrases, or entire paragraphs. This standard language is also known as *boilerplate* wording or paragraphs. They appear the same way in every document where they are used. When reading documents containing boilerplate material, it is likely you will skim the words.

Be especially careful in the workplace when skimming e-mails and letters. Many busy workers make the mistake of skimming only the beginning and drawing conclusions without further reading. This can create problems because business writers often place important information at the end of a document. The intent is to have the reader read the most important information last. Miscommunication and problems can occur when readers do not skim each paragraph.

One of the most important reasons for skimming is to help you prioritize your work. To **prioritize** means to rank items in order from most to least important. Prioritizing is an important skill that will help you manage and organize your work. Workers who receive a lot of reading material use skimming to determine how to prioritize further detailed reading and writing responses. Tips for skimming are given in Figure 17-1.

Scan for Specific Information

Scanning means to quickly glance through a message to find something specific. Skimming is done when you are not sure what is in the communication. Scanning is done when you know the information you need is in the communication, you just have to find it. You might scan when you want to find a:

- phone number in contact list
- word in a dictionary or index
- date for an event in an e-mail you previously read

However, if you scan too quickly, you are likely to miss what you are looking for. Tips for scanning are shown in Figure 17-2.

Skimming
E-mails and Letters
• Read the subject line to identify the purpose of the message.
• Check the letterhead, e-mail address, or signature block to identify the sender.
• Glance to see if others were copied.
• Check for attachments.
• Identify words in the body that are underlined, italicized, boldfaced, or in all capital letters.
• Look for information that is called out, such as a bulleted list.
Reports, Proposals, Brochures, Articles, and Online Information
• Read the title.
• Read section titles and headings. Use the table of contents if there is one.
• Note sections that are boxed, bulleted, numbered, or set in different typefaces.
• Flip through pages, spending no more than 10 to 15 seconds on each page.
• Look at visuals and their captions.
• Review summaries if included.

Goodheart-Willcox Publisher

Figure 17-1 Follow these tips for skimming a document to get an overview of the information.

Scanning
• Determine the specific information for which you are looking.
• Determine clues or characteristics that will help locate the information.
• Look briefly each time there is an item with characteristics that match the search. If it is not what you need, continue scanning.
• It may be necessary to quickly read surrounding material to determine whether it is the exact information for which you are scanning.

Goodheart-Willcox Publisher

Figure 17-2   Follow these tips for scanning a document for specific information.

Read for Detail

Reading for detail is reading all words and phrases, considering their meaning, and determining how they combine with other elements to convey ideas. Other elements may include sentences, paragraphs, headings, or graphics. Reading for detail helps you comprehend what you have read. It is also known as *reading for comprehension.*

Reading for detail is what most people think of when they hear the word "reading." Reading for detail is necessary in many situations, such as when you read a textbook chapter to learn the concepts being taught. This process can be complex and may be different for each reader. Consider the words and the way they are used by the writer to encourage a response from the reader. This involves many factors, including:

- prior knowledge of words and other language symbols, such as spacing and punctuation

- interpretation of aspects of the text, such as the purpose, tone, and truthfulness

- prior knowledge of the situation or topic and what this knowledge suggests to the reader, including related emotions and biases

- general prior knowledge which includes the life experiences the reader brings to the situation or topic

Generally, the process of reading for detail involves using the approaches shown in Figure 17-3. Notice how this process incorporates elements of active reading.

Reading for Detail

- Anticipate content and the purpose for reading based on prior knowledge.
- Read phrase by phrase, connecting smaller concepts to form larger ideas.
- Question and comment on the writer's statements, while checking your understanding and comprehension of the material.
- Reread until you understand, or read ahead to see if later text provides clarity.
- If you get stuck on words or concepts, use prior knowledge to work through the problem areas, or seek help from a coworker or reference materials.
- When you finish reading for detail, evaluate and analyze what was read, considering the purpose of the information.
- Draw conclusions about the reading based on the purpose and situation, putting biases and emotions aside.

Goodheart-Willcox Publisher

Figure 17-3   Follow these tips for reading a document for detail.

Section 17.1 Review

 Check Your Understanding

1. What happens when you read skillfully?
2. Why is it important to identify the writer's purpose?
3. List four primary reasons for reading.
4. When should reading evaluation take place?
5. Name the three approaches to reading.

 Build Your Vocabulary

As you progress through this course, develop a personal glossary of key terms. This will help you build your vocabulary and prepare you for a career. Write a definition for each of the following terms and add it to your personal glossary.

active reading	read for detail
skim	presumption
scan	prioritize

Reading Techniques

Objectives

After completing this section, you will be able to:

- **Explain** general reading techniques.
- **Describe** ways to improve your reading skills.
- **Discuss** techniques for reading on the screen of a digital device.

Key Terms

annotation   ergonomics

General Reading Techniques

Your reading skills and habits were probably set years ago. If your skills are good, you should have no problem applying them on the job. If your reading skills are weak, you can strengthen them by practicing. Read as much as you can and challenge yourself to apply the principles of active reading. If you strive to actively read, the more you read, the better you will become.

Prioritize Your Reading

One of the first orders of business is to prioritize documents that you must read. For each document, decide if you need to read it immediately, if you can wait and read it later, or if you need to read it at all. Separate the material into three groups.

- Read now: important to your job duties and current priorities; read as soon as possible.

- Read later: material you do not have to read today.

- File or discard: information you do not need now (file) or will never need (discard).

Prioritizing ensures you do not take time away from other important tasks. Most business e-mail systems have automated features that help with prioritizing. Learn to use these tools to make your task easier.

Prioritizing reading assignments is an effective reading technique.

?Essential **Q**uestion

How is the importance of reading demonstrated in the workplace?

Making a daily "to do" list in order of importance is also a good habit to form. Use your personal information management (PIM) system to keep your to-do list updated. Assign due dates for reading materials and other tasks, including items that do not have a formal deadline. Schedule these dates in your personal calendar. This will help avoid having low-level items stay on the list too long as new, more important ones are added.

Read Phrases, Not Words

Active readers read groups of words, rather than individual words. Reading word by word is slow, reduces concentration, and reduces the ability to connect concepts to form meaning. Words combine to make meaningful phrases. Many words have significant meaning only when combined with other words to form phrases. Some words acquire new meaning when attached to other words.

Read the following sentence one word at a time.

> One of the companies that submitted a bid for this project is Dean & Brown Contracting.

Now read the same sentence in meaningful phrases:

> One of the companies / that submitted a bid / for this project / is Dean & Brown Contracting.

Reading in phrases requires concentration and steady practice. If you find that you do not already read in phrases, practice this technique. This change in the way you read will help you read faster and improve understanding at the same time.

Mark Reading Materials

Making annotations or highlighting material is an effective reading technique. An **annotation** is a note or comment added to a document to help explain its contents. Annotations will help you better understand and remember what you have read. You will also be able to identify questions that come up as you read.

Always have a pen ready to use when you read printed documents. Write annotations in the margins in the form of notes, questions, or comments. If you need to write notes but do not want to mark directly on the material, use self-stick notes instead. Use stick-on tabs to mark pages you will use repeatedly.

Highlight or underline important text. *Highlighting* information helps you focus while reading and also helps you remember what you read. When you need to refer back to the materials in the future, you can scan for the highlighted information and find it easily.

Build Your Vocabulary

To build your vocabulary, make a point of looking up words you do not understand. If it is inconvenient to check a dictionary while reading, write down unknown words and look them up later. Then, reread the document once you learn the meanings of the words. Work especially hard at understanding words and terms that are commonly used in your industry or business. Consider buying a vocabulary-building book, either in print or electronic form.

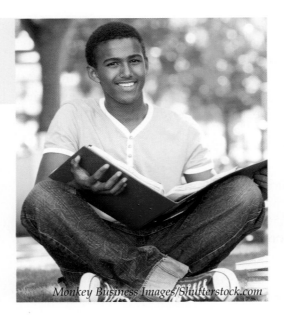

Control the reading environment to reduce or eliminate interruptions.

A large vocabulary not only makes your reading easier and your writing more exact, it also makes you a better thinker. Reading on your own is a form of self-education. Develop the habit of supplementing the information you receive in school or on the job with reading selections of your own. By expanding your knowledge through reading, you will increase your self-confidence and become more comfortable with new challenges.

Control Your Reading Environment

Is your place of work or school a noisy environment? Are you interrupted often as you read? If your answer to either question is yes, consider what you can do to reduce or eliminate these interruptions. It is important that you are comfortable and able to focus so that you are able to retain what you read and can use your time efficiently.

You may need to take reading home so you can have quiet time to catch up on your reading materials. Some people who work in very busy or noisy environments form the habit of arriving early at work so they can address the day's reading before the distractions begin. It is also possible to form the habit of blocking out distractions.

Be Ready to Read

If you have a job where it is hard to find the time to read, plan your reading time. For example, you might choose to read important documents while everyone else is at lunch. Put it on your daily schedule. Print reading materials and organize them in a folder so they can easily be accessed. This way, you will be able to take the materials with you to read during your commute or while waiting for a meeting to start.

Improving Your Reading Skills

The average student reads 250 words per minute. If you are a slow reader or have insufficient reading skills in general, now is the time to correct this. Reading more and using a dictionary are the best ways to improve your reading skills. By reviewing your reading habits, you can look for those areas where your skills need improvement. Here are tips for improving how effectively you read.

- Time yourself. How long does it take you to read and understand a section of text or a chapter of a book? If it takes you longer than average, read more to practice.

- Pay attention to how often you interrupt yourself before finishing reading something. If frequent, look for the factors that might be the cause and work on staying focused.

- Assess your reading environment. Find ways to make it quiet and comfortable.

- Pay attention to your thoughts as you read. If you think about something other than what you are reading, you will not remember what you have just read.

- Consider whether you use different reading approaches for different kinds of reading. If not, review the techniques discussed here and practice using them to suit various reading needs.

- Recognize whether you read word by word or phrase by phrase. Practice reading in phrases.

- Keep track of the number of times you read a page and find that you do not really know what you just read. Analyze why this is happening, and use the information in this chapter to try to correct it.

If you feel that you need professional help, a class on reading comprehension or time management might be the answer for you. Libraries and schools offer classes for reading improvement.

Reading on a Digital Device

Reading words on the screen of a digital device is somewhat different than reading from printed documents. Many individuals read a large percentage of information each day on a digital device rather than printing the material. The same rules for improving reading skills apply. However, reading on the screen requires certain adjustments. For example, most screens allow users to *zoom in* and *zoom out* to make material appear larger or smaller. Adjusting the zoom of the screen may make it easier to see words and comprehend meaning. Marking reading materials may require using a comment feature since you cannot physically mark the information.

Ergonomics can help making reading on a screen more comfortable. **Ergonomics** is the science concerned with designing and arranging things people use so that they can interact with them both efficiently and safely. In the workplace, it can include designing workstations to fit the unique needs

 Green   Carbon Footprints

A *carbon footprint* is a measurement of how much the everyday behaviors of an individual, company, or community impact the environment. This includes the amount of carbon dioxide put into the air from the consumption of energy and fuel used in homes, for travel, and for business operations.

Online carbon footprint calculators can be used to determine areas and practices that need to change. Companies can reduce their carbon footprints by recycling, reducing waste, and using responsible energy options. For example, video communication can be used to hold business meetings across the country. This reduces the fossil fuel emissions for travel by automobile, train, or airplane.

of the worker and the equipment used. Applying ergonomic principles results in a comfortable, efficient, and safe working environment.

There are many types of ergonomic accessories that may improve the comfort of reading on a screen, including wrist rests, specially designed chairs, and back supports. In addition, Figure 17-4 identifies actions that can be taken to create a comfortable environment for reading on a screen and help prevent injury or strain to the worker's body.

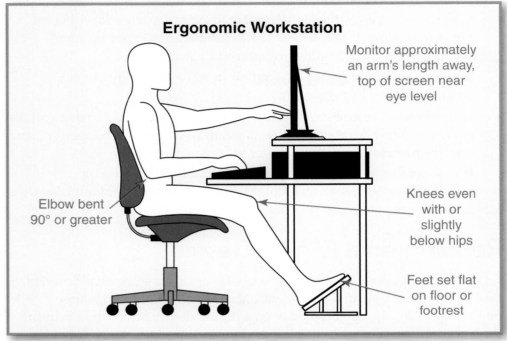

Goodheart-Willcox Publisher

Figure 17-4   Ergonomics help prevent muscle pain, eyestrain, and headaches caused by improper placement of monitors, desks, and chairs.

Section 17.2 Review

 Check Your Understanding

1. List several examples of general reading techniques that can improve your reading skills.
2. Reading material can be categorized into three groups when prioritizing. What are they?
3. Why should you mark notes on reading materials?
4. What is the best way to improve your reading skills?
5. Describe the adjustments required for reading on a digital screen.

 Build Your Vocabulary

As you progress through this course, develop a personal glossary of key terms. This will help you build your vocabulary and prepare you for a career. Write a definition for each of the following terms and add it to your personal glossary.

annotation   ergonomics

Chapter Summary

Section 17.1 Reading Skills

- Active reading is a skill that can be learned and improved, even if you are already a good reader. Active reading requires the reader to concentrate, be involved, and do something in response to the words.

- To engage in active reading, consider the writer's purpose, consider your purpose, relate what you read to prior knowledge, and evaluate the reading material. Applying these steps will help you focus on what you are reading.

- The three basic approaches to reading are skimming, scanning, and reading for detail. To skim is to quickly glance through the document to get an overview of the information. To scan means to quickly glance through the document in search of specific information. Reading for detail involves reading all of the words and phrases, considering their meaning.

Section 17.2 Reading Techniques

- It is a good practice to prioritize your reading material. Once you decide what is important to read, mark the content to help you focus on key information. If you find words you do not understand, look them up to help build your vocabulary. Select a comfortable environment in which to read to help you focus.

- Reading more and using a dictionary are the surest ways to improve your reading skills. By reviewing your reading habits, you can look for areas where your skills are weakest and then work to improve them.

- Many individuals read a large percentage of their reading materials on a computer screen. Reading on the screen requires certain adjustments. Applying ergonomics can help make reading on a screen more comfortable.

Online Activities

Complete the following activities which will help you learn, practice, and expand your knowledge and skills.

- **Posttest.** Now that you have finished the chapter, see what you learned by taking the chapter posttest.

- **Vocabulary.** Practice vocabulary for this chapter using the e-flash cards, matching activity, and vocabulary game until you are able to recognize their meanings.

- **English/Language Arts.** Visit www.g-wlearning.com to download each data file for this chapter. Follow the instructions to complete an English/language arts activity to practice what you have learned in this chapter.

  Activity File 17-1: Improving Your Reading Skills

  Activity File 17-2: Improving Your Listening Skills

Review Your Knowledge

1. What is required in active reading?
2. What are four things you must do when actively reading?
3. What is a bias?
4. Explain how presumptions relate to reading persuasive writing.
5. What is the difference between skimming and scanning?
6. When is skimming especially useful?
7. Why should you prioritize your reading?

8. Why is it important to read phrases rather than individual words?

9. What are the advantages of highlighting when reading?

10. Explain how ergonomics can make reading on a screen more comfortable.

Apply Your Knowledge

1. Read a newspaper article beginning to end. Answer the following questions.
   A. What is the main point of the article? Identify the author's purpose.
   B. Why are you reading the article? Identify your purpose for reading.
   C. What knowledge did you already possess that can help you better understand the article? Apply prior knowledge.
   D. Evaluate what you read. Write several paragraphs to summarize your findings.

2. It is necessary to prioritize reading materials. Make a checklist that you will use to classify materials that you will read now, read later, or discard. Use this list to sort through your printed reading materials as well as e-mail.

3. Select an article from a magazine or journal on a topic that is unfamiliar to you. For example, if you do not know much about science, you may select an article from *Scientific American* or *Science*. You will use this article to help build your vocabulary. As you read, annotate the material. Use a highlighter or self-adhesive notes to mark information you want to remember. Complete the following.
   A. Read the article, making note of any words you do not understand.
   B. For each word you did not understand, look up a definition in a dictionary.
   C. Write one sentence for each word you looked up.

4. Create a chart to record everything you read in one week. On the X axis, enter the labels *Item Read*, *Purpose*, *Time*, *Approach Used (Skim, Scan, Read for Detail)*, and *Purpose Achieved (Yes or No)*. On the Y axis, list each reading activity that you have for the week. As you finish each activity, check the appropriate columns to see how you did for each assignment. At the end of the week, analyze your grid and check whether your purpose for each reading assignment was achieved.

5. Based on your findings in the last activity, write several paragraphs analyzing your reading habits. Identify what you did well, where you could improve, and what your goals are to become a better reader.

Communication Skills

College and Career Readiness

Reading. Read a magazine, newspaper, or online article about the importance of professional communication. Take notes to identify the purpose of the article and the intended audience. Determine the central ideas of the article and review the conclusions made by the author. Demonstrate your understanding of the information by summarizing what you read, making sure to analyze the audience, purpose, and message of the article.

Listening. Hearing is a physical process. Listening combines hearing with evaluation. Effective leaders learn how to listen to their team members. Listen to your instructor as he or she presents a lesson. Analyze the effectiveness of the presentation. Listen carefully and take notes about the main points. Then organize the key information that you heard.

Writing. A successful employee demonstrates creativity and innovation. Whether you see problems as challenges or opportunities, solving them often requires creative thinking. Many new inventions are the result of attempting to solve a problem. Describe a problem you faced that led you to the creation of a new way of doing things or a new invention.

Internet Research

Annotation Techniques. Using the Internet, research different ways to annotate and take notes as you read. Which techniques are commonly used? Did you learn about any new ones? Write a brief summary of the techniques you researched. Then, create a system for annotating works, such as color coding, a symbol system, or listing topics of interest.

Teamwork

Collaborating with your team, make a list of the various types of reading materials that you regularly use to find specific information. Examples include a bus schedule, onscreen TV guide, blogs, text messages, newspapers, and magazines. For each type of medium, list the information you are reading to find and discuss strategies for finding it quickly.

Portfolio Development

College and Career Readiness

References. An important part of any portfolio is a list of references. A *reference* is a person who knows your skills, talents, or personal traits and is willing to recommend you. References will probably be someone from your network. These individuals can be someone for whom you worked or with whom you provided community service. Someone you know from your personal life, such a youth group leader, can also be a reference. However, you should not list relatives as references. Consider which references can best recommend you for the position for which you are applying. Always get permission from the person before using his or her name as a reference.

1. Ask several people from your network if they are willing to serve as a reference for you.

2. Create a Microsoft Word document with the names and contact information for your references. Use the heading "References" and your name. Save the document.

3. Update your master spreadsheet.

CTSOs

Job Interview. Job interviewing is an event you might enter with your CTSO. By participating in the job interview, you will be able to showcase your presentation skills, communication talents, and ability to actively listen to the questions asked by the interviewers. For this event, you will be expected to write a letter of application, create a résumé, and complete a job application. You will also be interviewed by an individual or panel.

To prepare for a job interview event, complete the following activities.

1. Use the Internet or textbooks to research the job application process and interviewing techniques.

2. Write your letter of application and résumé, and complete the application form (if provided for this event). You may be required to submit this before the event or present the information at the event.

3. Make certain that each piece of communication is complete and free of errors.

Unit

6

Career Success

Professional Communication

Why It Matters

Most of us will start working at a job and then pursue a career. Creating a career plan can help define career goals and what is required to reach those goals, such as education requirements and professional experience.

When looking for your first job, your résumé must persuade the employer that your skills and experience fit the position. The cover message you write must complement the résumé and show you are the right person for the job.

Once your application documents have been accepted and you are considered for a position, you will start the interviewing process. An interview is your opportunity to sell yourself in person. Being prepared is the key to a successful interview experience.

When you are hired for a position, the employer will conduct an official employment process. This will include the completion of forms as well as the background checks on who you are. The employment process can take a substantial amount of time, but may result in a great start to a successful career.

Chapters

Chapter **18** Career Planning

Chapter **19** Writing for Employment

While studying, look for the activity icon for:

- Pretests and posttests
- Vocabulary terms with e-flash cards and matching activities
- Videos
- Self-assessment

Video

Before you begin this unit, scan the QR code to view a video about professional communication. If you do not have a smartphone, visit www.g-wlearning.com.

Monkey Business Images/Shutterstock.com

18

Career Planning

Sections

18.1 Choosing a Career

18.2 Planning for Your Education

College and Career Readiness

Reading Prep. The summary at the end of the chapter highlights the most important concepts. Read the chapter and write a summary of it in your own words. Then, compare your summary to the summary in the text.

Viorel Sima/Shutterstock.com

Check Your Communication IQ

Before you begin the chapter, see what you already know about communication by taking the chapter pretest. The pretest is available at www.g-wlearning.com.

Case Study

Networking

Krista Gomez, a new college graduate, attended an alumni event at her university. She met and talked with several local professionals at the event. She asked each person she met for his or her business card. When she returned home, Krista e-mailed them to say that she was glad to meet them.

Krista received the following e-mail response from Marjorie Rivers, the vice president of a local company in Krista's chosen field.

Thank you for your e-mail. It was great to meet you at the State University alumni event last weekend. I am interested in hearing more about your volunteer work with the city. My company is looking to become more community-minded.

I would like to meet you for lunch to discuss your experiences. Please call my office to schedule an appointment.

patpitchaya/Shutterstock.com

Critical Thinking

1. How did Krista use her connection with her university for future opportunities?

2. Explain the role Krista's e-mail played in helping her get the chance to meet with a professional in her industry.

Choosing a Career

Objectives

After completing this section, you will be able to:

- **Determine** the skills needed for the workplace.
- **Describe** how to create a career plan.
- **Explore** sources of career information.
- **Summarize** how CTSOs can prepare a student for a career.

Key Terms ↪

?Essential Question

How do a person's skills relate to career success?

Skills for the Workplace

A **job** is the work a person does regularly in order to earn money. A **career** is a series of related jobs in the same profession. A job may be a part-time position you go to after school. A career is a position for which you prepare by attending school or completing specialized training. Over time, a job can turn into a career.

All employment opportunities require skills. A **skill** is something an individual does well. Skills are the foundational elements of all career fields. **Job-specific skills** are critical skills necessary to perform the required work-related tasks of a position. Job-specific skills are acquired through work experience and education or training. Without them, the individual would be unlikely to perform the job successfully.

Employability skills are applicable skills used to help an individual find a job, perform in the workplace, and gain success in a job or career. Employability skills are known as *foundation skills*. They are also known as *transferrable skills*. You have already acquired many of these skills. However, some of them are gained through life experience. Others may be gained from working at a job. Some of these may be gained in social situations. These skills are not specific to one career but are transferrable to many different jobs and professional positions. Examples of employability skills are in Figure 18-1.

Career Clusters

Studying the career clusters is a good way to begin analyzing the principles of career fields. The **career clusters**, shown in Figure 18-2, are 16 groups of occupational and career specialties. Career clusters are centered around related career fields.

Within each of the 16 career clusters are multiple career pathways. **Career pathways** are subgroups that reflect occupations requiring similar knowledge and skills. These pathways include careers ranging from entry-level to those that require advanced college degrees and many years of experience. All of the careers within the pathways share a foundation of common knowledge and skills.

Employability Skills	
Basic skills	Reading Writing Speaking Listening Technology Mathematics
Thinking skills	Decision making Creative thinking Problem solving Visualization Reasoning
People skills	Social perceptiveness Leadership Teamwork Cultural competence
Personal qualities	Self-management Integrity Honesty Sociability responsibility

Goodheart-Willcox Publisher

Figure 18-1   Employability skills will help lead to success in the workplace.

The 16 Career Clusters

Careers involving the production, processing, marketing, distribution, financing, and development of agricultural commodities and resources.

Careers involving management, marketing, and operations of foodservice, lodging, and recreational businesses.

Careers involving the design, planning managing, building, and maintaining of buildings and structures.

Careers involving family and human needs.

Careers involving the design, production, exhibition, performance, writing, and publishing of visual and performing arts.

Careers involving the design, development, support, and management of software, hardware, and other technology-related materials.

Careers involving the planning, organizing, directing, and evaluation of functions essential to business operations.

Careers involving the planning, management, and providing of legal services, public safety, protective services, and homeland security.

Careers involving the planning, management, and providing of training services.

Careers involving the planning, management, and processing of materials to create completed products.

Careers involving the planning and providing of banking, insurance, and other financial-business services.

Careers involving the planning, management, and performance of marketing and sales activities.

Careers involving governance, national security, foreign service, revenue and taxation, regulation, and management and administration.

Careers involving the planning, management, and providing of scientific research and technical services.

Careers involving planning, managing, and providing health services, health information, and research and development.

Careers involving the planning, management, and movement of people, materials, and goods.

States' Career Clusters Initiative 2008

Figure 18-2 Each of the 16 career clusters contains several career pathways.

Levels of Careers

In each career area, there are many opportunities for employment. Positions are generally grouped by skill level or education. There are five levels of careers that make up a career ladder, shown in Figure 18-3.

- An *entry-level* position is usually a person's first or beginning job. It requires very little training.

- A *career-level* position requires an employee to have the skills and knowledge for continued employment and advancement in the field.

- A *specialist-level* position requires specialized knowledge and skills in a specific field of study. However, someone in this position does not supervise other employees.

- A *supervisory-level* position requires specialized knowledge and skills. It also has management responsibility over other employees.

- An *executive-level* position is the highest level. This position is responsible for the planning, organization, and management of a company.

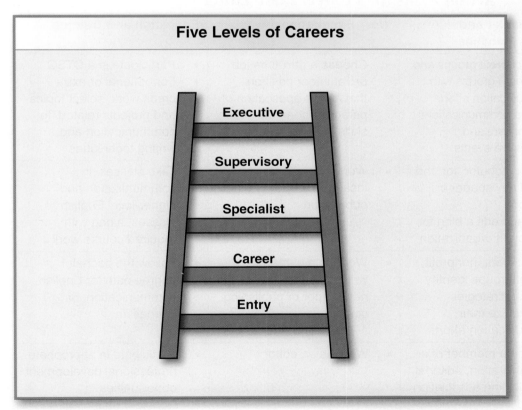

Goodheart-Willcox Publisher

Figure 18-3 Most careers have different positions based on years of experience, education, and technical skills.

Career Planning

Planning for your career can be exciting. Your career choice will direct many other decisions in life. It will affect decisions about your education and even where you will live. To determine the careers that will be enjoyable for you, you must first learn about yourself.

A **career plan** is a list of steps on a timeline to reach each of your career goals. It is also known as a *postsecondary plan*. A career plan should include education options. Education options include four-year colleges, two-year colleges, or technical schools. It should also address current job opportunities in your career of interest.

There is no set format for writing a career plan. Many free career plan templates can be found on the Internet. Figure 18-4 illustrates action items for a career plan. To create a plan, you should first conduct a self-assessment and then set SMART goals. You will continue revising the career plan as you achieve your goals and set new ones.

Action Items for a Career Plan: Editor			
	Extracurricular and Volunteer Activities	**Work Experience**	**Education and Training**
During Junior High School	• Help nonprofit groups and local youth groups with communication efforts • Prepare communications tools for fairs and competitive events	• Choose a part-time job or volunteer position that allows application of personal communication skills	• Participate in a CTSO • For optional or extra credit work, select topics and projects related to communication and writing techniques
During High School	• Be a contributor for the school newspaper or yearbook • Write and edit a blog for a nonprofit organization	• Work as an intern at a local newspaper or other publication	• Take classes in communication and higher-level English classes, along with required course work
During College	• Help student, nonprofit, or local groups identify the best strategies to maximize their communication efforts	• Work as a part-time writer or editor for a local newspaper or publishing company	• Follow the bachelor degree path for English, communication, or journalism
After College	• Become a member of a communication, editorial, or publishing association • Attend local communication professionals and chamber of commerce events	• Work as an editor	• Participate in appropriate professional development opportunities • Consider obtaining master degree in communication

Goodheart-Willcox Publisher

Figure 18-4   This table illustrates action items to use for a potential career plan in the Arts, A/V Technology & Communications career cluster.

Conducting a Self-Assessment

A *self-assessment* is the first step in evaluating your aptitudes, abilities, values, and interests. By conducting a self-assessment, you can focus your energy on what is necessary for you to become successful in a career. Some self-assessment techniques are thinking or writing exercises. Others are in the form of tests, such as a personality test. Your career counselor can help you conduct a self-assessment.

Consider what you like to do and what you do well. This can give you clues to aid your self-assessment. If you always do well in math class, you may find success in a career that requires you to work with numbers. On the other hand, if you do not do well in English class, a career that requires writing may not be your best match. Identifying a career that you will enjoy and excel in begins with finding out what you like to do.

What is your *work style*? Some individuals prefer to work independently. Others need constant direction to accomplish a task. Mornings are more productive for some workers, where as others perform better in the afternoons. Casual dress influences one person to perform well. Business dress makes others more effective on the job.

When taking a self-assessment, you strive to identify your aptitudes, abilities, values, and interests. Learning this information can reveal careers for which you are well suited.

Aptitudes

An **aptitude** is a characteristic that an individual has developed naturally. Aptitudes are also called *talents*. When a person naturally excels at a task without practicing or studying, he or she has an aptitude for it. For example, a person with an aptitude for music may be very good at accurately humming a tune or keeping a beat, even if he or she has never studied music.

Knowing your aptitudes can lead to job success. Some examples of aptitudes are:

- mathematics
- drawing
- writing
- sports

Abilities

Ability is a mastery of a skill or the capacity to do something. Having aptitudes and skills are supported or limited by your abilities. For instance, a student who has musical aptitude and skill might not have the ability to perform under pressure in musical concerts.

While aptitudes are something a person is born with, abilities can be acquired. Often, it is easier to develop abilities that match your natural aptitudes. For example, someone with an aptitude for acquiring languages may have the ability to speak French. A person without an aptitude for acquiring language can also learn to speak French. However, it may be more difficult.

Aptitudes and abilities do not always match. Someone with an aptitude for repairing machines may not enjoy doing this type of work and never develop the ability. Examples of abilities include the following.

- teaching others
- multitasking
- thinking logically
- speaking multiple languages

Values

The principles and beliefs that you consider important are your **values**. They are beliefs about the things that matter most to an individual. Values are developed as you mature and learn. Your values will affect your life in many ways. They influence how you relate to other people and make decisions about your education and career.

Your work values can provide great insight into what kind of career will appeal to you. For some individuals, work values include job security. For others, the number of vacation days is important. Everyone has a set of work values that are taken into consideration when choosing a career path. For example, a person who values the environment may want to pursue a career in green energy or conservation. Examples of values include:

- perfection
- equality
- harmony
- status

Closely related to values are family responsibilities and personal priorities. These can have a direct impact on career choice. For example, if you expect to have a large family, you may decide that time is a family responsibility. You may want to spend as much time as possible with your children as they grow. This may mean choosing a career that does not typically require travel or working long hours. On the other hand, it may be important to you to live in an expensive house and drive an expensive car. This personal priority will require you to enter a career with an income level that will support these choices.

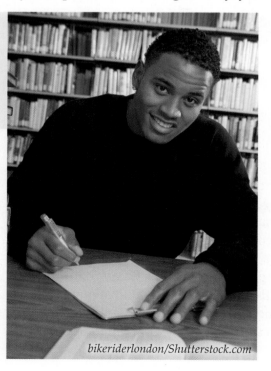

By conducting a self-assessment, an individual can focus on what is necessary to become successful in a desired career.

bikeriderlondon/Shutterstock.com

Interests

An **interest** is a feeling of wanting to learn more about a topic or to be involved in an activity. Your interests might include a subject, such as history.

You may be interested in local politics or cars. Your interests can also include hobbies, such as biking or cooking. There is a good chance there is a career that would allow you to do what you enjoy as a profession.

Your interests may change over time. You may find new hobbies or topics that interest you. Try to determine if there is a uniting theme to your interests. When considering your interests, look at the "big picture." For example, you may enjoy being on the cross country team right now. In a few years, a career as an arborist might suit you because you enjoy physical activity and being outdoors. Examples of interests include:

- art and creativity
- technology
- sports and adventure
- collecting

Setting SMART Goals

Another step in the career-planning process is to set goals. A **goal** is something a person wants to achieve in a specified time period. There are two types of goals: short term and long term. A *short-term goal* is one that can be achieved in less than one year. An example of a short-term goal may be getting an after-school job for the fall semester. A *long-term goal* is one that will take a longer period of time to achieve, usually more than one year. An example of a long-term goal is to attend college to earn a four-year degree.

Goal setting is the process of deciding what a person wants to achieve. Your goals must be based on what you want for your life. Well-defined career goals follow the SMART goal model. **SMART goals** are specific, measurable, attainable, realistic, and timely, as illustrated in Figure 18-5.

SMART Goals

S — Are my short- and long-term goals **specific**? Exactly what do I want to achieve?

M — Are my goals **measurable**? How will I know when a goal is achieved?

A — Are my goals **attainable**? Am I setting goals that can be achieved?

R — Are my goals **realistic**? Have I set goals that are practical?

T — Are my goals **timely**? Are the dates for achieving my goals appropriate?

Goodheart-Willcox Publisher

Figure 18-5   Well-defined career goals follow the SMART goal model.

Specific

A career goal should be specific and straightforward. For example, "I want to have a career" is not a specific goal. Instead, you might say, "I want to have a career in writing." When the goal is specific, it is easier to track your progress.

Measurable

It is important to be able to measure progress so you know when you have reached your goal. For example, "I want to earn a bachelor degree in journalism." This goal can be measured. When you earn the degree, you will know your goal has been reached.

Attainable

Goals need to be attainable. For example, "I want to be editor-in-chief at a newspaper when I graduate from college." This is not reasonable for that point in a person's career. Gaining work experience is necessary before obtaining an executive position. This goal becomes more attainable when coupled with a plan to gain the necessary aptitudes, skills, and experience.

Realistic

Goals must be realistic. Obtaining a position as editor-in-chief at a newspaper may be practical with proper planning. It is not realistic for a new college graduate. Finding an entry-level position as a reporter and working your way up to editor-in-chief over a period of years makes this a realistic goal.

Timely

A goal should have a starting point and an ending point. Setting a time frame to achieve a goal is the step most often overlooked. An end date can help you stay on track. For example, you may want to be editor-in-chief by the time you are 35 years old. Aiming to get the experience and education to achieve this position by a specific age will help you remain motivated to reach your goal on time.

Finding Career Information

There are many career research resources to help you evaluate which careers would make the most of your talents, skills, and interests.

Internet Research

The Internet is a good place to start when you begin researching your future career. Researching various professions, employment trends, industries, and prospective employers provides insight to careers that may interest you. Many postsecondary schools have websites that provide career information.

The Occupational Information Network (O*NET) is a valuable resource for career information. The most comprehensive database of occupational information, O*NET Online, was created by the US Department of Labor

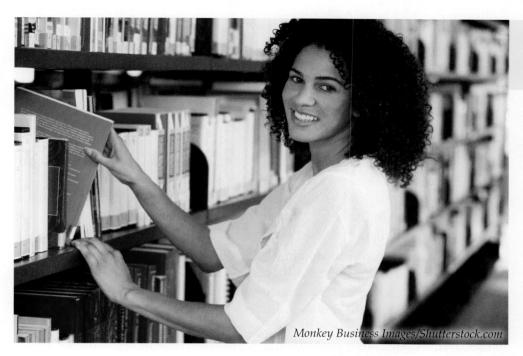

There are many resources for career information.

and is updated regularly. This website contains data on salary, growth, openings, education requirements, skills and abilities, work tasks, and related occupations for more than 1,000 careers. The database can be searched by career cluster.

The Internet is also a great tool to use when you begin applying for jobs. You can search for available jobs in almost any career field. When you find a job that interests you, you can submit a résumé, job application, and cover letter via the Internet.

Career Handbooks

Career handbooks offer a great place to begin researching specific careers, their industries, and the areas of the country or world in which these industries thrive. The US Bureau of Labor Statistics publishes the *Occupational Outlook Handbook* and the *Career Guide to Industries*. An *industry* is a group of businesses that produce the same type of goods or services. These handbooks describe the training and education needed for various jobs. They provide up-to-date information about careers, industries, employment trends, and even salary outlooks. The average person spends 30 percent of his or her time working every day. Understanding the industry of a chosen career is an important step to take.

The communication industry is a broad area that includes many aspects of the Arts, A/V Technology & Communications industries. It includes designing, producing, exhibiting, performing, writing, and publishing multimedia content. Also included are visual and performing arts and design, journalism, and entertainment services.

The communication industry is considered a nature of business. **Nature of business** is a general category of operations that generate profit. These businesses can be organized as proprietorships, partnerships, or corporations.

- A **proprietorship** is a business that has a sole owner. This person is responsible for every aspect of the business including making money or losing money.

- A **partnership** is comprised of two or more people working toward a joint purpose. Individual partners bring many attributes to a business, such as money, talent, and time. All are responsible for the business, including making money or losing money.

- A **corporation** is a type of business that is recognized as a separate legal entity from its owners. A corporation is defined by the US Supreme Court as "an artificial being, invisible, intangible, and existing only in contemplation of the law." It is a form of ownership in which owners are not personally liable for the business.

Because the communication industry generates profit, it provides an economic base for many communities. An **economic base** is an industry that provides employment that is necessary for a community to survive. For example, consider the movie industry. It provides employment for hundreds of people to work in Los Angeles and contribute to its economy. Actors, writers, and other professionals gain employment opportunities and pay taxes. But the economic opportunities do not end there. When a movie is complete, there is a need for theatres. Theatres hire workers. Digital distribution of the movie becomes necessary. It creates jobs for marketers, sales people, and other professionals. The economic factors of employment and tax revenue multiply. Without the movie industry, the community would not be able to support itself.

Networking

Networking means talking with people you know and making new contacts. Networking with family and friends can lead to job opportunities. The more contacts you make, the greater your opportunities for finding career ideas. Talking with people you know can help you evaluate career opportunities. It also may lead to potential jobs.

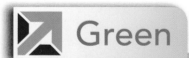 Green   Job Search

Technology has made finding and applying for jobs more eco-friendly than ever before. Before the widespread availability of the Internet, job seekers read through the want ads in piles of newspapers. They needed to either mail their résumés or travel to multiple business locations to complete job applications. This required a lot of resources, such as paper and fuel.

Using the Internet, job seekers can now locate and apply for open job positions online by electronically uploading and e-mailing their résumés in response to a job posting. Many websites allow job seekers to complete and submit their applications online. Some companies even conduct online interviews, using Skype or similar technology. This saves on travel costs. Searching and applying for jobs electronically saves employers and job seekers time and money.

Informational Interviews

Informational interviews can give you unique insight into a career. **Informational interviewing** is a strategy used to interview a professional to ask for advice and direction, rather than for a job opportunity. This type of interview will help you get a sense of what it is like to work in that profession.

It can also be a valuable networking opportunity. By talking with someone in the field, you can learn more about what is expected. You can also learn what types of jobs are available and other information about an industry.

At informational interviews, be as professional and polite as you would in any other interview situation. Follow up with your contact after an interview. Send a thank-you message to show appreciation for his or her time.

Career and Technical Student Organizations

Career and technical student organizations (CTSOs) are national student organizations with local school chapters that are related to career and technical education (CTE) courses. CTSO programs are tied to various course areas. Internships and other cooperative work experiences may be a part of the CTSO experience. CTSOs can help prepare high school graduates for their next step, whether it is college or a job.

CTSO Goals

The goal of CTSOs is to help students acquire knowledge and skills in different career and technical areas. They also help students develop leadership skills and gain work experience important for professional development. These organizations guide student members to become competent, successful members of the workforce.

Support for local CTSO chapters is often coordinated through each state's education department. Local chapters elect officers and establish a program of work. The CTSO advisors help students run the organization and identify the best programs that meet the goals of the educational area.

CTSO Opportunities

Competitive events are a main feature of most CTSOs. Competing in various events enables students to show mastery of specific content. Events also measure the use of decision-making, problem-solving, and leadership skills. Students may receive recognition awards for participation in events. In some cases, scholarships may be awarded if they win at state and national-level competitions.

Participating in a CTSO program and its activities can promote a lifelong interest in community service and professional development. Student achievement in specific areas, such as leadership or patriotism, is recognized with certificates or through award ceremonies. Other professional development opportunities may include:

- completing a school or community project related to the field of study
- training in the field
- supporting a local or national philanthropic organization
- attending CTSO state meetings
- participating in leadership conferences

Your participation in a CTSO can help you learn more about a profession. These organizations give students firsthand experience with the demands of a career.

Section 18.1 Review

Check Your Understanding

1. Explain the difference between a job and a career.
2. Describe the relationship between career clusters and career pathways.
3. Explain the importance of setting SMART goals.
4. Name and describe three types of organizations of business.
5. Summarize how CTSOs can prepare you for a career.

Build Your Vocabulary

As you progress through this course, develop a personal glossary of key terms. This will help you build your vocabulary and prepare you for a career. Write a definition for each of the following terms and add it to your personal glossary.

job
career
skill
job-specific skills
employability skills
career clusters
career pathways
career plan
aptitude
ability
values
interest

goal
SMART goal
nature of business
proprietorship
partnership
corporation
economic base
networking
informational interviewing
career and technical student organization (CTSO)

Planning for Your Education

Objectives

After completing this section, you will be able to:

- **Describe** the role of education, training, and certification on career choices.
- **Explain** the term college access.
- **Identify** sources of funding for pursuing an education.

Key Terms

formal education
postsecondary education
not-for-profit school
for-profit school
occupational training
internship
apprenticeship

certification
college access
529 plan
scholarship
work-study program
need-based award

Essential Question

Why is planning for education, training, or certification worthwhile?

Education, Training, and Certification

There are many steps you will take as you plan your career. Your educational needs will depend on your career interests and goals. Some careers require a high school diploma followed by technical training or a bachelor degree. Others require a master degree, as well. Still others require professional certification. Early career planning can help you make decisions about your education.

Robert Kneschke/Shutterstock.com

A person's education, training, and certification needs depend on his or her career goals.

Education

Formal education is the education received in a school, college, or university. Most careers require a college degree. However, for an entry-level position, a high school diploma may get you in the door. Jobs higher on the career ladder often require additional formal education.

High School

During high school, a variety of subjects are covered. This gives students a well-rounded education to serve as a foundation for life-long learning. English, history, and science are some of the subjects all students study in high school. At the end of four years, students graduate and receive a *high school diploma*.

Postsecondary Education

Postsecondary education is any education achieved after high school. This includes all two- and four-year colleges and universities. Common postsecondary degrees are an associate degree and a bachelor degree. An associate degree is a two-year degree. A bachelor degree is a four-year degree.

Area of Study. Students in postsecondary schools choose an area of study that suits an interest or meets a career goal. This is referred to as a *major*. For example, a student who wants to become an elementary school teacher may major in education.

When considering a major, research the income potential of the career. Some careers start at a low salary and steadily increase over the course of the career. Other careers may start high and continue to increase. In addition to earnings potential, look into the number of jobs that are available in the area, both for new graduates and for those with experience.

In addition to major area of studies, postsecondary students are typically required to take a wide variety of classes in other subjects. These courses are referred to as *general education courses*. They cover many of the same subject areas as high school courses. They also cover subjects not often offered at the high-school level, such as political science and psychology.

Not-for-Profit and For-Profit Schools. A postsecondary school may be either a not-for-profit school or a for-profit school. A **not-for-profit school** is one that returns the money it earns back into the school. These schools receive funding from student tuition and fees, donations, and governmental programs. A not-for-profit school is what most people think of in terms of "college." It may be public, such as a state university. Others may be private, such as a private college or a community college. Not-for-profit schools tend to encourage academic exploration and personal growth beyond the specific requirements of a student's major.

A **for-profit school** is one that is set up to earn money for investors. It provides a product, which is education. In return for providing education, for-profit schools receive money from their customers, who are students. For-profit schools are also known as *proprietary schools*. They tend to focus on specific skills and do not require general education courses. A trade school is an example of a for-profit school. They typically offer a two-year degree specialized in a field of trade, such as automotive repair or cosmetology. Some for-profit schools offer bachelor degree programs.

Requirements and Costs. When considering a college or university, be aware of what is needed to apply. Requirements may include:

- official transcripts
- college exam test scores

- essays

- interviews

For all requirements, be sure to know the deadlines for completing and submitting the information. Missing a deadline can mean not being accepted to the school.

The costs of a postsecondary education must be considered. In addition to tuition, there are fees for many classes. Some majors include many laboratory classes. These classes can have more fees than other courses. Living expenses must also be considered as part of the cost of a postsecondary education.

Graduate and Postgraduate Education

Education received after an individual has earned a bachelor degree is *graduate education*. Master degrees are graduate degrees. Education beyond a master degree is called *postgraduate education*. Doctorate degrees are postgraduate degrees.

Graduate study often builds on the same subject area or a closely related subject in which the bachelor degree was earned. For example, a student who earned a Bachelor of Science in computer programming may pursue a Master of Science degree in information technology.

Continuing Education

Some careers that have professional licenses require *continuing education* classes. These classes are completed to maintain the license. Completing these classes earns the student *continuing education units (CEUs)*. If you are a teacher, for example, your school system may require that you earn a specified number of CEUs every year.

Exploring Communication Careers

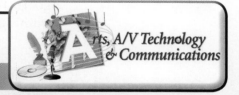

Agent

Agents represent the business interests of clients who are typically performing artists, authors, or athletes. They negotiation salary, credits, and many other business issues for the people they represent. Potential employers, such as movie studios, publishers, or sports teams, deal with the agent when wanting to hire his or her client. Typical job titles for this position also include *business manager*, *artist manager*, and *talent agent*.

Some examples of tasks that agents perform include:

- Conduct interviews to evaluate potential clients.

- Communicate with clients about business decisions.

- Negotiate client's contracts with current or potential employers.

- Arrange appearances for clients to forward their careers.

- Manage general finances along with business matters for clients.

Agent jobs often require a bachelor degree in arts and entertainment or business. This job requires customer-service skills to maintain positive relationships with clients.

Many careers require a college degree.

bikeriderlondon/Shutterstock.com

Another form of continuing education is more commonly called *adult education* or *adult ed*. These classes are for people age 18 or older and have traditionally focused on basic skills. Classes are offered in a wide variety of topics. They can range from learning computer skills or the English language.

Training

A college degree is not necessary for all career paths. Before taking on the expense of college classes, decide if college is right for you and your goals. There are many options for career training, including occupational training, internships, apprenticeships, and military service.

Occupational Training

Training for a specific career can be an option for many technical, trade, and technology fields. **Occupational training** is education that prepares you for a specific type of work. This type of training typically costs less than a traditional college education. It can also be completed in less time.

Internships

An **internship** is a short-term position with a sponsoring organization that gives the intern an opportunity to gain on-the-job experience in a certain field of study or occupation. Internships can be paid or unpaid. Often, high schools, colleges, and universities offer school credit for completing internships. Internships are an opportunity to gain work experience while working on an education.

Apprenticeships

An **apprenticeship** is a combination of on-the-job training, work experience, and classroom instruction. Apprenticeships are typically available to those who want to learn a trade or a technical skill. The apprentice works on mastering the skills required to work in the trade or field under the supervision of a skilled tradesperson.

Military Service

Service in the military can provide opportunities to receive skilled training, often in highly specialized technical areas. In addition to receiving this training, often it can be translated into college credit or professional credentials. After completing military service, there are many benefits available to veterans. For example, the *GI Bill* is a law that provides financial assistance for veterans pursuing education or training. Other forms of tuition assistance are also available.

Some people choose to enter the armed forces through the *Reserve Officers Training Corp (ROTC)*. Each branch of the military has an ROTC program at selected colleges and universities. Some high schools have Junior ROTC programs. The purpose of the ROTC program is to train commissioned officers for the armed forces. It can provide tuition assistance in exchange for a commitment to military service. Students enrolled in this program take classes just like other college students. The program is considered an elective. However, students also receive basic military and officer training. Information is available on the *Military Career Guide Online* at www.todaysmilitary.com. Also, opportunities available in the armed forces are outlined in the *Occupational Outlook Handbook*.

Professional Certification

Some professional organizations offer certifications. **Certification** is a professional status earned by an individual after passing an exam focused on a specific body of knowledge. The individual usually prepares for the exam by taking classes and studying content that will be tested.

Some jobs require a professional certification. There are many types of certifications in most industries and trades, as shown in Figure 18-6. For example, a financial planning agency might require a financial planner to be certified as a qualification for the job. Other employers may prefer, but not require, certification.

There are certifications that must be renewed on a regular basis. For example, many certifications sponsored by Microsoft are only valid for the specific version of software. When the next version is released, another exam must be taken to be certified for the update. Other certifications require regular continuing education classes to ensure individuals are current with up-to-date information in the profession.

Some certifications are not subject-specific. Instead, they attest that the individual has employability skills. These certifications confirm that the person possesses the skills to be a contributing employee. The focus of these certifications is on workplace skills. Individuals who earn this type of certification have demonstrated they possess the qualities necessary to become an effective employee.

Certifications by Industry	
Administrative	Certified Professional Secretary (CPS) Certified Administrative Professional (CAP)
Automotive	ASE Certified Medium/Heavy Truck Technicians ASE Master Certified Automobile Technician
Financial Planning	Certified Financial Planner (CFP)
Health Support	Certified EKG/ECG Technician (CET) Certified Nurse Technician (CNT)
Hospitality	Certified Hospitality Accountant Executive (CHAE) Certified Hospitality Supervisor (CHS)
Human Resources	Professional in Human Resources (PHR) Senior Professional in Human Resources (SPHR)
Information Technology	Cisco Certified Network Professional Microsoft Certified Systems Administrator Sun Certified Java Programmer
Internal Auditing	Certified Internal Auditor (CIA) Certification in Control Self-Assessment (CCSA)
Manufacturing	Certified Manufacturing Technologist (CMfgT) Certified Engineering Manager (CEM)
Project Management	Project Management Professional (PMP) Certified Associate in Project Management (CAPM)
Real Estate	Certified Commercial Real Estate Appraiser (CCRA) Certified Residential Specialist (CRS)
Workplace Safety	Certified Environmental Health and Safety Management Specialist (EHS) Certified Safety Auditor (SAC)
Workplace Skills	National Career Readiness Certificate (NCRC)

Goodheart-Willcox Publisher

Figure 18-6   Certifications are available in many different industries.

College Access

College access refers to building awareness about college opportunities, providing guidance regarding college admissions, and identifying ways to pay for college. College access includes access to many types of postsecondary institutions. This includes colleges, universities, and trade schools. Attending a postsecondary school to further your education can be a critical step in your career plan. However, preparing to go to college can present challenges to students and families both academically and financially. The sooner you begin planning, the better. It is never too early.

Academic preparation includes taking the right classes and doing your best. If you have always been a good student, keep up the good work. If you have not been performing to your potential, demonstrate your abilities and commitment by showing improvement. Along with strong academics, involvement in organizations at your high school or in your community will also provide greater access to college. Most schools are looking for well-rounded individuals. As you plan for your education, learn as much as possible about what it takes to be admitted to the college of your choice.

Many websites provide information to help you gain access to college. You can begin by searching the Internet for resources offered in your state. Search using the term *college access* plus the name of your state. If you have already been thinking about a specific school, check its official website to learn about admission requirements and to find out what financial help might be available to you. The US Department of Education, the College Board, and the National College Access Program Directory have websites that include a wealth of information about college access. Topics include applying to college and paying for college. If you have not already done so, talk to your family, friends, and your guidance counselor today for information to begin planning for college.

Funding Your Education

As you are making decisions on your education, you will need to create a financial plan for paying for your education. Whether you attend a trade school, community college, or university, someone has to pay the cost of the education. Funds to pay for education can come from a variety of sources. Each student's financial situation is different. You will need to figure out which sources are available to you and which ones fit your needs.

Many online college cost calculators can help you estimate how much money you will need to fund your education. Once you have an idea of how much it will cost to go to college, you need to figure out how you will pay for it.

Some families can afford to pay for college with current income or savings. If your parents or other family members are able and willing to pay for a college education for you, take advantage of their generosity. Thank them by studying hard and earning your degree.

Someone in your family may have established a 529 plan to fund your college education. A **529 plan** is a savings plan for education operated by a state or educational institution. These plans are tax-advantaged savings plans and encourage families to set aside college funds for their children. These funds may be used for qualified colleges across the nation. Each state now has at least one 529 plan available. Plans vary from state to state because every state sets up its own plan. There are restrictions on how this money can be used, so make sure you understand how the plan works. You will be penalized if you use money invested in a 529 plan for anything other than college expenses.

Even if your family has a 529 plan, the amount saved might not be enough to pay for all your college expenses. Many families pay for college using savings, current income, and loans. Parents, other family members, and students often work together to cover the cost of college. You might contribute money you have saved, money you earn if you work while attending school, and money for loans you will have to repay. More

Business Protocol

Dress Code

The workplace requires appropriate dress. Most businesses have a dress code that employees are required to follow. Some jobs require uniforms or protective clothing. If your company requires business attire, clarify with your manager what is expected. Remember that business casual does not typically mean jeans or shorts. Always dress appropriately and do not push the limits on the appearance that is expected from you.

than half the students attending college get some form of financial aid. Figure 18-7 shows potential sources of funding for your education.

Financial aid is available from the federal government as well as from nonfederal agencies. There is more than $100 billion in grants, scholarships, work-study, need-based awards, and loans available each year. Some states also offer college money to attend a state school if you have good grades in high school.

A *grant* is a financial award that does not have to be repaid and is typically provided by a nonprofit organization. Grants are generally need based, and are usually tax exempt. A Federal Pell Grant is an example of a government grant.

Potential Sources of Funding a College Education

Source	Brief Description	Repayment
529 Plan	Tax-advantage savings plan designed to encourage saving for future college costs. Plans are sponsored by states, state agencies, and educational institutions.	No repayment.
Grants	Money to pay for college provided by government agencies, corporations, states, and other organizations. Most grants are based on need and some have other requirements.	No repayment.
Scholarships	Money to pay for college based on specific qualifications including academics, sports, music, leadership, and service. Criteria for scholarships vary widely.	No repayment.
Work-study	Paid part-time jobs for students with financial need. Work-study programs are typically backed by government agencies.	No repayment.
Need-based awards	Aid for students who demonstrate financial need.	No repayment.
Government education loans	Loans made to students to help pay for college. Interest rates are lower than bank loans.	Repayment is required. Repayment may be postponed until you begin your career.
Private education loans	Loans made to students to help pay for college. Interest rates are higher than government education loans.	Repayment is required.
Internships	Career-based work experience. Some internships are paid and some are not. In addition to experience, you will likely earn college credit.	No repayment.
Military benefits	The US Military offers several ways to help pay for education. It provides education and training opportunities while serving and also provides access to funding for veterans. The US Reserve Officers' Training Corps (ROTC) programs and the military service academies are other options to consider.	No repayment, however a service commitment is required.

Goodheart-Willcox Publisher

Figure 18-7   There are multiple alternatives for funding a college education.

A **scholarship** is financial aid that may be based on financial need or some type of merit or accomplishment. There are scholarships based on standardized test scores, grades, extra-curricular activities, athletics, and music. There are also scholarships available for leadership, service, and other interests, abilities, and talents.

It is surprising how many scholarships and grants go unused because no one has applied for them. Do not fail to apply for help just because you do not want to write the essay or fill out the application. Talk to your school counselor. Be persistent if you think you might qualify for a scholarship.

Work-study programs are part-time jobs on a college campus. They are subsidized by the government. Wages earned at a work-study job go toward paying for tuition and other college expenses.

Need-based awards are financial-aid awards available for students and families who meet certain economic requirements. Income and other demographics determine if a student qualifies for this assistance.

Section 18.2 Review

 Check Your Understanding

1. What are three ways an individual can meet his or her educational needs for a career?
2. Describe the role formal education can play in career preparation.
3. How is an apprenticeship different from an internship?
4. Explain the importance of college access.
5. Give several examples of financial aid that might be available for high school students.

 Build Your Vocabulary

As you progress through this course, develop a personal glossary of key terms. This will help you build your vocabulary and prepare you for a career. Write a definition for each of the following terms and add it to your personal glossary.

formal education
postsecondary education
not-for-profit school
for-profit school
occupational training
internship
apprenticeship

certification
college access
529 plan
scholarship
work-study program
need-based award

Chapter Summary

Section 18.1 Choosing a Career

- Employers require both job-specific skills and employability skills. Job-specific skills are those that are specific to the tasks related to a position. Employability skills are not specific to one career, but rather transferrable to any career. Studying the career clusters is a good way to learn about type and levels of careers.

- Creating a career plan will help you reach your goals. Conducting a self-assessment is the first step to discover who you are and what your interests are. Next, setting SMART goals will help you as you write your career plan.

- There are many resources for career research to help evaluate which careers would make the most of your talents, skills, and interests. The Internet is a good place to start. Career handbooks and informational interviews are also a way to gain insight into a career.

- Career and technical student organizations (CTSOs) are national student organizations that are related to career and technical education (CTE) courses. The goal of CTSOs is to help students acquire knowledge and skills in different career and technical areas, as well as related leadership skills and work experience.

Section 18.2 Planning for Your Education

- Your educational needs will depend on your career interests and goals. Most careers require a college education. However, there are many options for career training, including occupational training, internships, and apprenticeships. The military is also a career option.

- College access refers to building awareness about college opportunities, providing guidance regarding college admissions, and identifying ways to pay for college. It includes access to many types of postsecondary institutions, including colleges, universities, and trade schools.

- As you are making decisions on your education, it is important to create a financial plan for paying for your education. A 529 plan is a savings plan and is one way to pay for an education. There are also grants, scholarships, work-study, need-based awards, and loans available to help students and their families.

Online Activities

Complete the following activities which will help you learn, practice, and expand your knowledge and skills.

- **Posttest.** Now that you have finished the chapter, see what you learned by taking the chapter posttest.

- **Vocabulary.** Practice vocabulary for this chapter using the e-flash cards, matching activity, and vocabulary game until you are able to recognize their meanings.

- **English/Language Arts.** Visit www.g-wlearning.com to download each data file for this chapter. Follow the instructions to complete an English/language arts activity to practice what you have learned in this chapter.

  Activity File 18-1: Creating a Business Card

  Activity File 18-2: Improving your Editing Skills

Review Your Knowledge

1. What is the difference between job-specific skills and employability skills?

2. Describe what should be included in a career plan.

3. Why is self-assessment important when considering career choices?

4. Explain the relationship between aptitudes and abilities.

5. Explain what is meant by the nature of a business and give an example.

6. What is the goal of informational interviewing?

7. Individuals preparing for careers may seek formal education, training, and potential certification opportunities. Describe each option.

8. Describe how military service provides career training.

9. College access is important to any student considering educational opportunities. What are some sources of information for building college awareness?

10. Explain the difference between grants and scholarships.

Apply Your Knowledge

1. Skills are the foundational elements of all career fields. Two important types of skills that are foundational to your career are job specific skills and employability skills. Create a chart with two columns. In column one, list the job specific skills you currently possess. In column two, list the employability skills that you possess. Use this chart as a source of information when you create a career plan.

2. Career clusters are centered around related career fields. Analyzing the principles of various clusters will help you select a career in which you are interested. Select a career cluster to analyze. How are the different careers within the cluster related to one another?

3. Conduct an informal self assessment by defining your work style, aptitudes, abilities, values, and interests. This will help prepare you to write a career plan.

4. Creating SMART goals is important in your personal life as well as your career. Write three of your career goals as SMART goals. Specify how each of these goals is specific, measurable, attainable, realistic, and timely.

5. A career plan is a list of steps to reach a career goal. Write a list of action items for a career plan for the next five years that you might consider following. Use Figure 18-4 as an example. Include your career objectives and the strategies you will use to accomplish your goals.

6. Select a business in your community for which you would like to work. Learn all you can about the business. What is the nature of this business? What type of business is it? Analyze the economic base of the business in your community.

Communication Skills

College and Career Readiness

Speaking. Etiquette is the art of using good manners in any situation. Etiquette is especially important when making phone calls because the two parties cannot interact face-to-face. Create a script for a telephone conversation to request assistance from a loan officer asking support for a student loan. Make a list of the important facts that support why you should be granted a loan. Use "please" and "thank-you" when appropriate. Practice your presentation with a classmate.

Writing. Many postsecondary applications, such as applications to colleges, require an essay as part of the application process. Write a 500-word essay that explains why your chosen career is the perfect one for you. Identify the audience and determine an effective approach and technique that will clearly state your purpose.

Reading. Most people use technology on a daily basis. Using technology in the workplace can help employees be more productive. In other instances, technology can be a distraction. Read about five types of technology and how people can use each to be more productive in the workplace. What did you learn?

Internet Research

Career Opportunities. Using the Internet, explore a career that is of interest to you. Research the education, training, and certification requirements of the career. Next, compare this career with a career in the same career cluster. What opportunities are currently available for each career? Evaluate salaries, career paths, and demand for the careers. Does the future look promising for either pathway?

Career Match. Self-assessment tools can help decide which career opportunities might be a good fit for you. Visit the O*NET Resource Center online and select the assessment called Career Exploration Tools. After locating the tool, use it to identify a career that is matched to the skills you currently possess. Use the results from the survey to research the career using O*NET. Write several paragraphs about the career to which you were matched. Share your findings with the class.

Career Plan. As a student, you will be planning for your future career. It is important that you take ownership of a career plan that matches your interests and skills. Using the Internet, research how to create a career plan. Select a template that meets your needs. Create a career plan that aligns a career pathway to your educational goals. Using your list of SMART goals, create a career plan for the next five years.

Teamwork

By joining a CTSO, you can participate in student leadership and learn how to prepare for school and career opportunities. Working with your team, make a list of the CTSOs that are available at your school. What leadership activities are provided for students in each organization? What professional development activities are available? How can your school CTSOs help you prepare for life after graduation? Share your findings with the class.

Portfolio Development

College and Career Readiness

Introduction. As you assemble your final portfolio, compose an introduction that gives an overall snapshot of who you are. This will be the first page of the portfolio that sets the stage for your presentation, so you want to make a good impression. Tell the reader who you are, your goals, and any biographical information that is relevant. You may want to highlight information by making references to sections or page numbers. There may be a website or URL to direct the reader to examples or documents of importance.

In addition to the items you have already collected, there are some additional ones that you might include.

- *Résumé.* An updated résumé may be appropriate for the situation. If you have already submitted a résumé separately, it is not necessary to include.

- *Letters of recommendation.* If you have letters from instructors, employers, or others who have praised your performance, include these in this introductory section.

- *Photo.* Photos are not required. However, a photo will help the interviewer remember who you are after the interview and when evaluating potential candidates.

- *Table of contents.* A table of contents will give a professional appearance to your documents. Consider title pages for each section to add clarity.

CTSOs

 **How to Prepare.** No matter what competitive events you will participate in for a CTSO, you will have to be well organized and prepared. Of course, you will have studied the content exhaustively before the event, but you also have to prepare by making sure all the tools you need for the event have been secure. You must also arrange travel to the event. Confirming details well in advance of an event will decrease stress and leave you free to concentrate on the event itself.

To prepare for a competition, complete the following activities.

1. Pack appropriate clothing, including comfortable shoes and professional attire.

2. Prepare all technological resources, including anything that you might need to prepare to compete. Double check to make sure that any electronic presentation material is saved in a format that is compatible with the machines that will be available to you at the event.

3. If the event calls for visuals, make sure you have them prepared in advance, packed, and ready to take with you.

4. Bring registration materials, including a valid form of identification.

5. Bring study materials, including the flash cards and other materials you have used to study for the event. If note cards are acceptable when making a presentation, make sure your notes are complete and easy to read. Have a back-up set in case of an emergency.

6. At least two weeks before you go to the competition, create a checklist of what you need for the event. Include every detail down to a pencil or pen. Then use this checklist before you go into the presentation so that you do not forget anything.

19

Writing for Employment

Sections

19.1 Résumés

19.2 Cover Messages and Job Applications

19.3 Job Interviews and the Employment Process

College and Career Readiness

Reading Prep. Before reading the chapter, skim the photos and their captions. As you read, determine how these concepts contribute to the ideas presented in the text.

Stephen Coburn/Shutterstock.com

Check Your Communication IQ ↱

Before you begin the chapter, see what you already know about communication by taking the chapter pretest. The pretest is available at www.g-wlearning.com.

Case Study

Truthful Job Application

Omri Bowman is training for the US Olympic swim team and is looking for employment that will help support his expenses. At the mall, he saw a new sporting goods store that is hiring. Omri thought that would be a great job, so he went in to apply immediately. As he was completing the form, he noticed that the application asked for references. Omri was not prepared and had not asked permission to use several colleagues as references. He really wanted this job, so he put down their information anyway.

The HR manager said the interviewing was going to start in two days so references would be checked later in the afternoon. Omri assumed that the people he listed would be okay with him listing them as references. At least he hoped that would be the case.

Monkey Business Images/Shutterstock.com

Critical Thinking

1. Was it okay for Omri to list people as references without their permission? Explain your answer.

2. Do you think the store would consider Omri for this job if his references said they were not willing to give him a reference? Why or why not?

Résumés

Objectives

After completing this section, you will be able to:

- **Describe** a résumé.
- **List** ways to publish a résumé.

Key Terms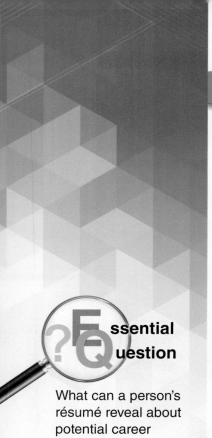

résumé
chronological résumé
keyword

reference
scannable résumé
infographic résumé

Essential Question

What can a person's résumé reveal about potential career success?

Writing a Résumé

When seeking employment, it is often necessary to compose a résumé. A **résumé** is a document that profiles a person's career goals, education, and work history. Its purpose is to prove to a potential employer that a person's experiences and skills match the qualifications of the job. Think of a résumé as a snapshot that tells the employer who you are and why you would be an asset as an employee.

The first impression most employers will have of you is your résumé. As a result, it must be well written and error free. Applying the writing process will help you create a well-written document. The writing process is shown in Figure 19-1.

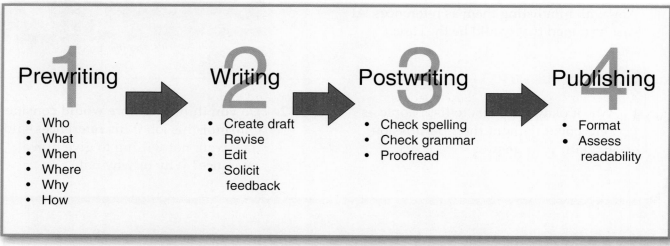

Goodheart-Willcox Publisher

Figure 19-1   Follow the steps in the writing process to ensure that your résumé is well written and error free.

After you have completed writing a final draft of your résumé, the next step is publishing. Publishing is the process of preparing a document for distribution, which includes formatting and saving the document. A general guideline is that the information should be formatted to fit on one page. A résumé is illustrated in Figure 19-2.

Contact Information

Place your contact information at the top of the résumé. Include your name, address, telephone number, and e-mail address. A professional e-mail address is necessary for the job-search process. Use one that is your full name or at least a portion of it. An e-mail address that is a nickname or screen name does not make a professional impression.

Summary and Objective

The summary section is optional. It may be labeled *Summary* or *Profile*. A summary is an opportunity to highlight qualifications as they relate to the job. Introductory summaries are valuable for people who have considerable experience and expertise in a particular field. The summary can include experience gained outside of a paying job. Skills gained through volunteer work, school activities, hobbies, or other unpaid activities can be listed. The examples that follow highlight specific information.

SUMMARY

Experienced electronics sales professional with annual sales of $100,000+.

SUMMARY

High school graduate with business major and fluency in German and Spanish.

The objective section is also optional. It may be labeled *Career Objective* or *Career Goal*. The objective can be a general or specific description of the position you are seeking.

General

CAREER OBJECTIVE

Seeking a managerial position with a publisher.

Specific

CAREER OBJECTIVE

Seeking an entry-level marketing/sales position with opportunity for training and career growth.

A summary statement and an objective can be combined and either heading may be used. Following is an example of a combined statement.

CAREER OBJECTIVE

High school graduate with business major and fluency in German and Spanish seeking entry-level position with a multinational firm.

Robert Jefferies
123 Eastwood Terrace
Saratoga Springs, NY 60123
123-555-9715
rjefferies@e-mail.edu

OBJECTIVE
A mature and responsible high school senior seeks an entry-level job as a photographer's assistant.

EXPERIENCE
Saratoga Springs City Online Newspaper, Saratoga Springs, NY
September 2016 to present
Photo Intern
- Maintain electronic photo archive for newspaper.
- Assist with the set up of photo shoots.
- Take photographs at events and for news stories as needed.
- Prepare image files for publication using Photoshop.

Hunter High School, Saratoga Springs, NY
September 2015 to September 2016
Student Volunteer Photographer
- Shot photographs of major events for student newspaper and yearbook.
- Shot photographs of faculty and facilities for promotional purposes.
- Set up and managed photograph archive for the newspaper and yearbook.
- Prepared image files for publication using Photoshop.

EDUCATION
Hunter High School, Saratoga Springs, NY
Expected graduation date: May 2017
Relevant coursework: Photography 1 and 2

HONORS
- Hunter High School Honor Roll, 8 quarters
- Student Photograph of the Year, 2014 – 2016

PUBLICATIONS
- Saratoga Springs City Online Newspaper
- Saratoga Springs City Calendar 2015

Goodheart-Willcox Publisher

Figure 19-2   This is an example of a chronological résumé with the standard sections employers expect to see.

Experience

The experience section contains details about work history. The labels *Work Experience* or *Work History* may be used instead of *Experience*. This section demonstrates to an employer the positive work behaviors and qualities that make you employable. For example, if you have been in a leadership position, you would state this and describe your experiences. Volunteer work and internships may also be included in this section. This section will be the focus for the employer. As a result, it should be given careful attention as you develop your résumé.

Work experience is listed in reverse chronological order, with the most recent employer listed first. This format is referred to as a chronological résumé. A **chronological résumé** emphasizes employers and work experience with each. List the dates of employment, position held, name of the employer, and city and state of the employer. Do not list the addresses or telephone numbers of the employer. You will provide these when you complete a job application. Include specific duties and work experience for each position held.

Employers often scan résumés for keywords. **Keywords** are words that specifically relate to the functions of the position for which the employer is hiring. They are typically nouns rather than verbs. To identify keywords to include in your résumé, review the job advertisement for the job for which you are applying. Underline the keywords. If you have the relevant experience, use the same words to describe it in your résumé. Remember, do not stretch the truth. Only use the keywords if they fit your background.

In addition to keywords, describe your work experience with words that show action or achievement. For example, action verbs such as "assisted," "sold," and "processed" help the potential employer perceive you as an

Work experience can include volunteer work as well as paid work.

mangostock/Shutterstock.com

Ethics

Applications and Résumés

When applying for a job, to a college, or for a volunteer position, it is important to be truthful in your application and résumé. Fabricating experience or education is unethical and could cost you the opportunity to be a part of that organization. This means always telling the truth about your skills, experience, and education. Do not embellish. Play up your strengths without creating the illusion of being someone you are not. Present your information in a positive light, but be honest.

achiever. A dull listing of job duties and responsibilities will not highlight your achievements. Consider the following examples.

> Part-time stock clerk during the holiday season.
>
> Maintained continuous supply of merchandise during the busy holiday season, ensuring that products were available to hundreds of additional shoppers.

These examples describe the same work experience. Draft and revise until you have statements that accurately describe what you have contributed to past employers.

Education

List your education under the heading *Education*. If you are currently in school, list the name of your high school or college and its city and state. Include your expected graduation date. Then, list courses that are relevant to the job.

- Redwood City High School, expected graduation 20--, Redwood City, CA
  Relevant Coursework: Calculus

If you are out of school, list your education beginning with the most recent diploma or degree earned. Include high school, colleges, and business or technical schools. Graduates should indicate the year a degree or diploma was earned. Postsecondary education should include the type of degree received and areas of study.

- Associate of Arts in Computer Science, 20--, College of San Mateo, San Mateo, CA

If you have earned any certifications, such as the IC3 Digital Literacy Certification, list them here. You may wish to modify the heading of this section to read *Education and Certification*. If the certification has an expiration date, note the date it expires. As an adult, you may also have licenses such as a real estate license. This is where professional licenses are listed as well.

- IC3 Digital Literacy Certification: Computing Fundamentals, Key Applications, and Living Online

Honors, Awards, and Publications

List information that shows your involvement in activities outside of work or school and the years of service. Include relevant honors, awards, or publications and the corresponding year. Employers are interested in applicants who are community oriented and volunteer their time.

- National Honor Society in high school, 20--
- Outstanding Leadership Award, 20--, received for service as chair of the student business organization, Redwood City Chapter
- Published 14 articles in the school newspaper

Memberships and Professional Affiliations

If you are a member of a CTSO, list it as a membership. You may also be a member of a professional or business association, so be certain to list each. This shows interest in your career area.

Special Skills

List any special skills you have that are relevant to the position. For example, if you are skilled using specific software programs or other technology, include that information in this section. If you have work samples, you can note in this section that they are a part of your portfolio.

References

A **reference** is a person who can comment on the qualifications, work ethic, personal qualities, and work-related aspects of a person's character. It is expected that references will be provided only when requested. References should not be included on the résumé.

Employers who require references in advance usually indicate this in the job advertisement. Otherwise, you will be told during the interview process when references are needed. To be prepared, put together a list of three or four people for whom you have worked and someone who knows you socially. Do not list relatives. Get permission from the people whom you intend to use as references. List the references on a sheet separate from your résumé. However, the format of the list should be similar to your résumé.

Publishing a Résumé

Publishing is the process of preparing a document for distribution. When you publish your résumé, you are making it available to the receiver, often a potential employer. When saving a résumé as an electronic file, use your name and the word *résumé* as the file name. For example, if your name is Shelley Jones, your file name would be ShelleyJonesResume. This makes it helpful for an employer when reviewing documents from multiple applicants.

There are multiple ways a résumé can be published.

- *Print copy.* The traditional way to publish a résumé for employment is to print a hard copy and mail or hand deliver it.

- *DOCX file.* A common way to publish a document is to save the file as a DOCX file. This format enables the creator to repurpose the document in multiple formats.

- *HTML file.* For individuals who wish to add a résumé to a personal web site, a DOCX version can also be saved as a web page. This creates a version of the document that will open in a web browser when launched. A résumé published as a web page is called a *web-based résumé*.

- *PDF file.* If you are e-mailing a résumé, it is suggested to save it in PDF format. This format prohibits any changes from being made to the content or format of the document. The document will maintain its integrity when the recipient prints or reads it.

- *TXT file.* This format strips formatting, making it easy to cut and paste information from a document into a prepublished form on the Internet. This is also referred to as a **scannable résumé**, which is a type of résumé with all typographical elements eliminated. This enables the document to be scanned and entered into a database without formatting restrictions.

Former supervisors or managers can be job references in the future.

Monkey Business Images/Shutterstock.com

- *Graphics file.* A visual résumé is one that presents information in a graphically appealing format. An **infographic résumé** is a type of visual résumé in which the content is displayed using a combination of words and visual elements to present information clearly and quickly. However, visual résumés are not appropriate for all job applications. If you choose to submit a visual résumé, confirm that this type of résumé is appropriate for the position or the industry.

Section 19.1) Review

 Check Your Understanding

1. What is the purpose of a résumé?
2. List the standard sections of a résumé.
3. Describe the type of person who should be selected as a reference.
4. What does it mean to publish a document?
5. List three ways in which a résumé can be published.

 Build Your Vocabulary

As you progress through this course, develop a personal glossary of key terms. This will help you build your vocabulary and prepare you for a career. Write a definition for each of the following terms and add it to your personal glossary.

résumé   reference
chronological résumé   scannable résumé
keyword   infographic résumé

Cover Messages and Job Applications

Objectives

After completing this section, you will be able to:

- **Describe** how to write a persuasive cover message to accompany a résumé.
- **Explain** how to apply for a job in person and online.

Key Terms 📤

cover message   job application

Writing Cover Messages

?Essential Question

Why is a cover message important to successful job searches?

A **cover message** is a letter or e-mail sent with a résumé to introduce the applicant and summarize his or her reasons for applying for a job. It is a sales message written to persuade the reader to grant an interview. A cover message provides an opportunity to focus a potential employer's attention on your background, skills, and work experience that match the job you are seeking.

It also enables you to highlight professional certifications or licenses that you have earned. Noting in a cover message that you have a professional portfolio with work samples can also capture the attention of the reader.

Writing a cover message is an important part of applying for a job. It sets the tone for the résumé that follows. A cover message should focus on your qualifications without being boastful. It does not repeat the details in the résumé. Rather, it highlights your key qualifications that are specific to the job for which you are applying.

Whether it is a printed letter or an e-mail message, follow the writing process and standard letter formatting. Figure 19-3 shows an example of a cover message that will be printed and mailed.

Introduction

The cover message should begin with an introduction that tells the employer who you are and why you are applying for the position. If responding to an advertisement, mention the position title and where you found the ad. For example, you might be responding to an online job posting. If sending a general letter of application, explain in specific terms how you identified the company and why you are interested in working there. If someone gave you the name of the employer to contact, mention the person and his or her connection to the company in your message.

Jennifer S. Fitzpatrick
204 West Pickford Road
Jefferson City, MO 65001
(Home) 573-555-1234
(Cell) 573-555-4321

April 13, 20--

Ms. Cheryl Lynn Sebastian
Director of Administration
Jefferson City Convention & Visitors Bureau, Inc.
100 E. High Street
Jefferson City, MO 65101

Dear Ms. Sebastian:

Introduction → The position you advertised in the *Network Journal* on March 14 for a customer service trainee is exactly the kind of job I am seeking. According to your ad, this position requires good business communication skills. As you can see by my résumé, my educational background and experience working at a travel agency prepared me for this position.

Body → For the past two years, I worked as a part-time receptionist at the Barcelona Travel Agency. While working there, I gained experience dealing with customers on the telephone, as well as greeting walk-in customers and handling their requests for information. I also had the opportunity to observe the full-time staff at work and attend department meetings. At these meetings, I learned the importance of satisfying customer needs and meeting the challenges of working with the general public.

As the enclosed résumé shows, I will graduate from Southeast High School in early June. While in high school, I took several business courses, including a business communication class. These classes helped me develop good English and verbal communication skills. In addition to my education and work experience, I can offer your organization a strong work ethic and the ability to fluently speak Spanish.

Conclusion → I would like very much to meet you and hope that you will contact me by phone to schedule an interview for the position. If I do not hear from you within the next couple of weeks, I hope you will not mind if I follow up with a phone call.

Sincerely yours,

Jennifer Fitzpatrick

Jennifer S. Fitzpatrick

Enclosure

Figure 19-3   This is an example of a cover message that will be sent as a letter.

Body

In the body of the cover message, demonstrate your positive work behaviors and qualities that make you employable, such as your ambition, determination, and abilities. Focus on the positive traits and skills that the employer seeks, as highlighted in the job description. Explain why you are qualified and how your skills and work experience make you the best candidate for the job. Do not expect the reader to infer why you are the right person to hire—point it out. Remember that your résumé accompanies the cover message, so it is not necessary to repeat the facts in it. Give enough information to encourage the reader to read the résumé. Show genuine interest in the business.

Conclusion

The conclusion has two purposes: to request an interview and to make it easy for the reader to grant that interview. Leave no doubt in the reader's mind about your desire to be contacted for an interview. State how and when you can be reached or indicate how and when you will follow up. Supply the employer with the information necessary to arrange an interview.

Applying For Employment

Most job applicants seeking a job will apply for one either in person or online. Employers have application guidelines that are usually stated in the job advertisement. When you connect with a potential employer, confirm the process with him or her.

Exploring Communication Careers

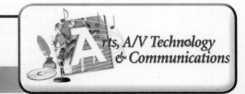
rts, A/V Technology & Communications

Printing Press Operator

Most books, magazines, and newspapers are printed on printing presses. These printers are large, complex machines with many parts. A printing press operator sets up and handles the workings of the printing press and must pay attention to detail to check the quality of print jobs, such as the way the color has printed. They must be extremely knowledgeable about the equipment in order to perform tasks needed to maintain the machinery, such as changing the ink and refilling the paper. Typical job titles for this position include *first pressman*, *offset pressman*, *press leader*, and *press operator*.

Some examples of tasks that printing press operators perform include:

- Review and understand the needs of each print job.

- Start the press and pull random tests to ensure quality.

- Change certain parts of the press, such as the plates, cylinders, or blankets.

- Communicate with supervisor about any problems with a print job.

Printing press operator positions require a high school diploma. A professional certificate is needed for some positions.

Before applying for employment, evaluate and compare employment opportunities. Are you looking for a short-term position or one that is long term? Is the job a correct fit for you in terms of hours, location, and salary? If you have taken a self assessment, you have already identified your aptitudes, abilities, values, and interests. Take the time to apply critical thinking skills to evaluate opportunities before you apply.

Some job advertisements might request candidates to submit a portfolio as part of the application process. A *portfolio* is a selection of related materials that you collect and organize to show your qualifications, skills, and talents to support a career or personal goal. It includes samples of your work as well as copies of licenses or certifications. You have been creating a portfolio throughout this course. Each chapter in this text has a Portfolio Development activity as part of the end-of-chapter exercises. Your finished portfolio can be a part of the application materials that you might need to apply for a job.

Applying in Person

The traditional way to apply for employment is to print your résumé, cover message, and portfolio and hand deliver them to a potential employer. All documents should be on the same high-quality white or off-white paper using a laser printer. Do not fold or staple the documents. Instead, use a large envelope or paper clip the pages together.

When you arrive at the employer, be prepared to complete an application. A **job application** is a form with spaces for contact information, education, and work experience. Have your personal data, information about your citizenship status, and locations and names of past employers handy. Use blue or black ink, and use your best printing. Carefully review the form before submitting it.

Applying Online

Most employers encourage job applications online. When applying online, it is acceptable to write a cover message as an e-mail. The same rules of writing apply for an e-mail cover message, but use the e-mail formatting rules in Chapter 12. Figure 19-4 is an example of a cover message sent by e-mail.

For the subject line of the e-mail, use your last name, the words "application for" and the title of the position, for example: Cortez Application for Production Assistant. It is recommended that your résumé be attached in PDF format or as a scannable résumé. If you are submitting a portfolio, name the file using the same naming convention as your résumé, for example, ShelleyJonesPortfolio.

Some employers have a website on which job applicants apply directly for open positions. The first step may be to complete an online application. Next, you may be required to upload a résumé or cut and paste information into a résumé form on the site. When cutting and pasting text, avoid any formatting and use plain text. Formatting can make the information difficult to read when the employer accesses the application.

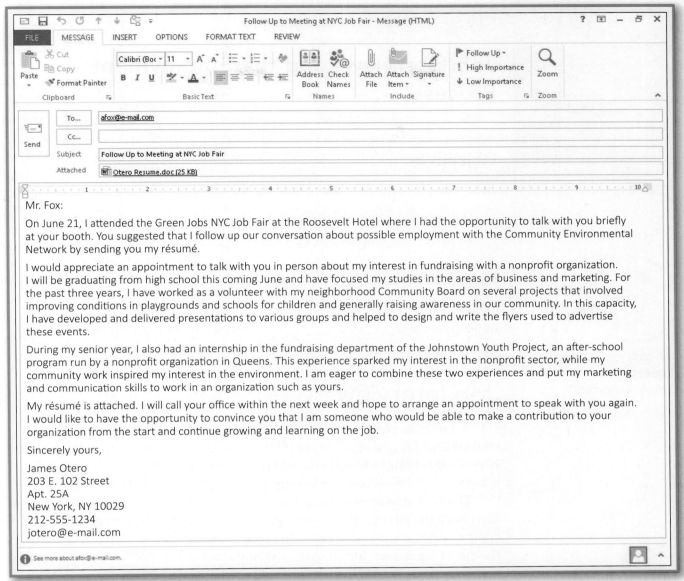

Goodheart-Willcox Publisher

Figure 19-4   This cover message is an e-mail. Notice that the résumé is included as an attachment.

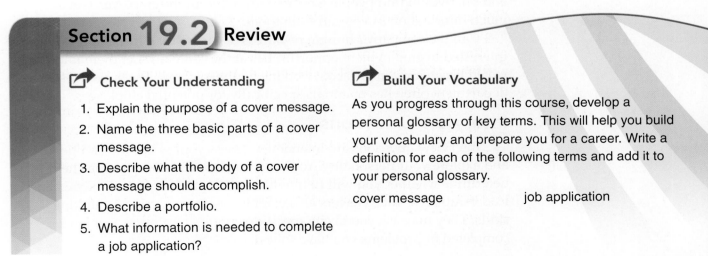

Section 19.2 Review

Check Your Understanding

1. Explain the purpose of a cover message.
2. Name the three basic parts of a cover message.
3. Describe what the body of a cover message should accomplish.
4. Describe a portfolio.
5. What information is needed to complete a job application?

Build Your Vocabulary

As you progress through this course, develop a personal glossary of key terms. This will help you build your vocabulary and prepare you for a career. Write a definition for each of the following terms and add it to your personal glossary.

cover message   job application

Job Interviews and the Employment Process

Objectives

After completing this section, you will be able to:

- **Discuss** how to prepare for a job interview.
- **Describe** the employment process.

Key Terms

job interview

mock interview

hypothetical question

behavioral question

employment verification

background check

?
ssential
uestion

Which job interview
questions are the
most important?

Job Interview

A **job interview** is the employer's opportunity to review a candidate's résumé and ask questions to see if he or she is qualified for the position. This is your opportunity to sell yourself in person. Your answers to interview questions are important in the employer's decision-making process.

The first step in preparing for a job interview is to learn as much as you can about the job and the company. There are several ways to do this. If the company has a website, thoroughly study the site. Pay special attention to the *About Us* section for an overview of the company. Look for press releases, annual reports, and information on its products or services.

While a company website can be a valuable source of information, do not limit your research to just the company site. Use your network of friends and relatives to find people who are familiar with the employer. Get as much information as you can from them.

Call the company's human resources department. Indicate that you are interested in employment opportunities at the company. Let them know you would like to know more about working for the company. The human resources department often has materials specifically for potential employees.

Interview Questions

Interview questions are intended to assess your skills and abilities and explore your personality. Your answers to interview questions help determine whether you will fit in with the company team and the manager's leadership style. Interviewers also want to assess your critical-thinking skills. They may ask you to cite specific examples of projects you have completed or problems you have solved.

A job interview is a candidate's opportunity to sell himself or herself as the best person for the job.

michaeljung/Shutterstock.com

Questions Likely to Be Asked

Before the interview, try to anticipate questions the interviewer is likely to ask you. The following are some common interview questions.

• What are your strengths?

• What are your weaknesses?

• What about this position interests you?

• What do you plan to be doing five years from now?

• Why do you want to work for this organization?

Write down your answers to these questions and practice them in front of a mirror. To prepare for an interview, conduct a mock interview with a friend or an instructor. A **mock interview** is a practice interview conducted with another person. Practice until you can give your planned responses naturally and without reading them off the page. The more prepared you are, the more relaxed, organized, competent, and professional you will appear to the interviewer.

Hypothetical Questions

Interviewers may also ask hypothetical questions. **Hypothetical questions** are questions that require you to imagine a situation and describe how you would act. Frequent topics of hypothetical questions relate to working with and getting along with coworkers. For example, "How would you handle a disagreement with a coworker?" You cannot prepare specific answers to these questions, so you need to rely on your ability to think on your feet.

For these types of questions, the interviewer is aware that you are being put on the spot. In addition to what you say, he or she considers other aspects of your answer as well. Body language is first and foremost. Avoid fidgeting and looking at the ceiling while thinking of your answer. Instead, look at the interviewer and calmly take a moment to compose your thoughts. Keep your answer brief. If your answer runs on too long, you risk losing your train of thought. Try to relate the question to something that is familiar to you and answer honestly. Do not try to figure out what the interviewer wants you to say. Showing that you can remain poised and project confidence carries a lot of weight, even if your answer is not ideal.

Behavioral Questions

Interviewers may ask behavioral questions. **Behavioral questions** are questions that draw on your previous experiences and decisions. Your answers to these types of questions indicate past behavior, which may be used to predict future behavior and success in a position. The following are some examples of behavioral questions.

- Tell me about a time when you needed to assume a leadership position in a group. What were the challenges, and how did you help the group meet its goals?

- Describe a situation where you needed to be creative in order to help a client with a problem.

- Describe a situation when you made a mistake. Tell me how you corrected the mistake and what measures you put in place to ensure it did not happen again.

Again, you cannot prepare specific answers to these questions. Remain poised, answer honestly, and keep your answers focused on the question.

Practicing answers to potential interview questions can increase confidence during an interview.

Andrey_Popov/Shutterstock.com

Questions an Employer Should Not Ask

State and federal laws prohibit employers from asking questions on certain topics. It is important to know these topics so you can be prepared if such a question comes up during an interview. It is illegal for employers to ask questions about a job candidate's religion, national origin, gender, or disability. Questions about age can only be asked if a minimum age is required by law for a job. The following are some examples of questions an employer is not permitted to ask a candidate.

- What is your religion?

- Are you married?

- What is your nationality?
- Are you disabled?
- Do you have children?
- How much do you weigh?

If you are presented with similar questions during the interview, stay professional. You are not obligated to provide an answer. You could respond, "Please explain how that relates to the job." Or you could completely avoid the question by saying, "I would rather not answer personal questions."

Questions to Ask the Employer

Write down any questions you have about the job, salary, benefits, and company policies. Keep in mind that the questions you ask reveal details about your personality. Asking questions can make a good impression. Questions show that you are interested and aware. Good questions cover the duties and responsibilities of the position. Be aware of how you word questions. Some questions are not appropriate until after you have been offered the job. In the early stages of the interview process, your questions should demonstrate that you would be a valuable employee and are interested in learning about the company.

The following are some questions you may want to ask.

- What are the specific duties of this position?
- What is company policy or criteria for employee promotions?
- Do you have a policy for providing on-the-job training?
- When do you expect to make your hiring decision?
- What is the anticipated start date?

Usually, the interviewer will tell you the hourly rate or salary for the position. Sometimes, however, an interviewer asks what salary you want or expect. Prepare for questions about salary by researching the industry. If you are unsure, you can simply tell the interviewer that the salary is negotiable.

Dressing for the Interview

An interview is a meeting in which you and the employer discuss the job and your skills. Interviews are usually in person, but initial interviews are sometimes conducted by phone. A face-to-face interview is typically the first time you are seen by a company representative. First impressions are important, so dress appropriately. You should be well groomed and on time. Your appearance communicates certain qualities about you to the interviewer. When dressing for an interview, consider what you wish to communicate about yourself.

The easiest rule to follow is to dress in a way that shows you understand the work environment and know the appropriate attire. It is better to dress more conservatively than to dress in trendy clothing. Employers understand that interviewees want to put their best foot forward. Dressing more conservatively than needed is not likely to be viewed as a disadvantage. However, dressing too casual, too trendy, or wearing inappropriate clothing is likely to cost you the job.

Evaluating the Interview

Evaluate your performance as soon as you can after the interview. Every job interview is an opportunity to practice. If you discover that you are not interested in the job, do not feel your time was wasted. Make a list of the things you feel you did right and things you would do differently next time. Asking yourself the following questions can help in evaluating your performance.

- Was I adequately prepared with knowledge about the company and the position?

- Did I remember to bring copies of my résumé, a list of references, my portfolio, and any other requested documents to the interview?

- Was I on time for the interview?

- Did I talk too much or too little?

- Did I honestly and completely answer the interviewer's questions?

- Did I dress appropriately?

- Did I display nervous behavior, such as fidgeting, or forgetting things I wanted to say?

- Did I come across as composed and confident?

- Which questions could I have handled better?

Writing Follow-Up Messages

Immediately after the interview, write a *thank-you message* to the person who interviewed you. Thank the interviewer for taking the time to talk with you about the job and your career interests. Restate any important points that were made, and reinforce your strong interest in the job, if you are still interested. A thank-you may be in the form of a printed letter sent through the mail or an e-mail. Business thank-you letters should be keyed and formatted in business style. Keep the letter brief and to the point. Remind the interviewer of your name and reiterate your enthusiasm, but do not be pushy. An example of a thank-you message is shown in Figure 19-5.

Employment decisions can take a long time. Some companies notify all applicants when a decision has been made, but some do not. If you have not heard anything after a week or two, it is appropriate to send a brief follow-up message. Be sure your tone is positive. Avoid sounding impatient

 **Green**   Sustainability Training

Green businesses lead by example and educate their employees on sustainable business practices. Through sustainability training, employees learn the importance of *going green* at work and the best practices to reduce waste and lower energy consumption.

Training employees in simple company procedures can not only help save the environment, but save the company money, too. Employees should be instructed to make small changes in their daily habits. Turning lights off when exiting a room and turning computer equipment off over the weekend can make a big difference.

Dear Ms. Cary:

Thank you for the opportunity to discuss the position of associate fashion designer.

I am very excited about the possibility of working for Clothing Design Specialists. The job is exactly the sort of challenging opportunity I had hoped to find. I believe my educational background and internship experience will enable me to make a contribution, while also learning and growing on the job.

Please contact me if you need any additional information. I look forward to hearing from you.

Sincerely,

Goodheart-Willcox Publisher

Figure 19-5   This is a standard interview follow-up message.

Dear Ms. Boswell:

I am delighted to accept the position of Assistant Telecommunication Technician at the Common Cable Company. I am excited about the opportunity of working with you and your team.

As soon as I receive the formal offer letter and additional forms you mentioned, I will complete and return them immediately. As we discussed, I will wait to hear from Mark Evans for further instructions about the medical exam and background check. I understand that there are required forms and processes that must be completed before I can start work.

Thank you again for the opportunity.

Sincerely,

Goodheart-Willcox Publisher

Figure 19-6   This is a typical message for accepting a job offer.

or demanding. Simply restate your interest in the job and politely inquire whether a decision has been made.

Accepting a job is one of the most fulfilling messages you will ever write. But, it still requires your attention and the use of the skills you have learned. Think of this as your first official act as a new employee. It remains important to present an image of intelligence, organization, courtesy, and cooperation.

In writing the acceptance message, let your natural enthusiasm show. Be positive and thank the person who has been the bearer of good news. Say that you look forward to the job. The example in Figure 19-6 is short and to the point. The writer also uses the opportunity to confirm her understanding of the employment process going forward.

Employment Process

The employment process can take a substantial amount of time. There are tasks that the employer completes to make sure a candidate is a fit for the position. In addition, there are forms that the employee must complete before starting a position.

Employment Verification

The employer will complete an employment verification using the information on your application or résumé. **Employment verification** is a process through which the information provided on an applicant's résumé is checked to verify that it is correct. Employers typically verify only the dates of employment, position title, and other objective data. Most employers will not provide opinions about employees, such as whether or not he or she was considered a good worker.

Another important part of the employment process is a background check. A **background check** is an investigation into personal data about a job applicant. This information is available from government records and other sources. This includes public information on the Internet. Sometimes employers also run a check of your credit. You must give permission for employers to conduct background and credit checks on you.

Many employers use Internet search engines, such as Google, to search for your name. Employers may also check social networking websites, such as Facebook and Twitter. Be aware of this before posting any personal information or photos. These checks might work to your advantage or against you, depending on what the employer finds. It is up to you to ensure that the image you project on social networking sites is not embarrassing or, worse, preventing you from achieving your career goals.

Employment Forms

You will spend a considerable amount of time in the human resources department completing necessary forms for your employment. Come prepared with the personal information that will be required for a multitude of forms. You will need your social security number, contact information for emergencies, and other personal information.

wavebreakmedia/Shutterstock.com

New hires will have multiple forms to complete when they start a new position.

Form I-9

A *Form I-9 Employment Eligibility Verification* is used to verify an employee's identity and that he or she is authorized to work in the United States. This form is from the Department of Homeland Security of the US Citizenship and Immigration Services. Both citizens and noncitizens are required to complete this form.

The Form I-9 must be signed in the presence of an authorized representative of the human resources department. Documentation of identity must be presented at the time the form is signed. Acceptable documentation commonly used includes a valid driver's license, a state-issued photo ID, or a passport.

Form W-4

A *Form W-4 Employee's Withholding Allowance Certificate* is used by the employer for the information necessary to withhold the appropriate amount of taxes from an employee's paycheck. Deductions are based on marital status and the number of dependents claimed, including the employee. The amounts withheld are forwarded to the appropriate government agency.

Form W-2

At the end of the year, the employer sends the employee a *Form W-2 Wage and Tax Statement* to use when filing income tax returns. This form summarizes all wages and deductions for the year for an individual employee.

Benefits Forms

The human resources department will provide a variety of forms that are specific to the compensation package offered by the employer. Be prepared to complete multiple forms on your first day.

Section 19.3 Review

 Check Your Understanding

1. Explain the purpose of a job interview for both the employer and the applicant.
2. How can you prepare for questions that an interviewer might ask?
3. What is the easiest rule to follow when dressing for an interview? Explain.
4. What should be included in a follow-up message after an interview?
5. List the forms that must be filled out by a newly hired employee.

 Build Your Vocabulary

As you progress through this course, develop a personal glossary of key terms. This will help you build your vocabulary and prepare you for a career. Write a definition for each of the following terms and add it to your personal glossary.

job interview

mock interview

hypothetical question

behavioral question

employment verification

background check

Chapter Summary

Section 19.1 Résumés

- A résumé is a document that provides potential employers with a profile of a person's career goals, work history, and job qualifications. The most important part of your résumé is the listing of your work experience and achievements. Other parts of the résumé, however, are essential to presenting your complete profile for the employer.

- After writing a résumé, the next step is to publish it. Publishing is the process of formatting, saving, and preparing a document for distribution. There are multiple ways in which to publish a document: print copy, DOCX file, HTML file, PDF file, TXT file, or graphic file.

Section 19.2 Cover Messages and Job Applications

- A cover message is a selling or persuasive message. A cover message provides an introduction to who you are and why you are the right person for the position you are seeking. Writing a cover message provides an opportunity to focus a potential employer's attention on what you want them to know—you are the best candidate for the job.

- Most job applicants apply for a job either in person or online. The traditional way to apply for employment is in person by hand delivering a printed version of your résumé, cover message, and portfolio. Applying online can vary by employer, but it typically includes uploading documents and completing forms on a company website.

Section 19.3 Job Interviews and the Employment Process

- The job interview is your opportunity to sell yourself. To prepare for the interview, prepare for questions that are typically asked. At the interview, it is important to dress appropriately. Immediately after your interview, it is important to follow up with a thank-you letter or e-mail to the person who interviewed you.

- The employment process can take a substantial amount of time. Employers must conduct employment verification and a background check to make sure the candidate is fit for the position. Employees must complete multiple forms when beginning a new job.

Online Activities

Complete the following activities which will help you learn, practice, and expand your knowledge and skills.

- **Posttest.** Now that you have finished the chapter, see what you learned by taking the chapter posttest.

- **Vocabulary.** Practice vocabulary for this chapter using the e-flash cards, matching activity, and vocabulary game until you are able to recognize their meanings.

- **English/Language Arts.** Visit www.g-wlearning.com to download each data file for this chapter. Follow the instructions to complete an English/ language arts activity to practice what you have learned in this chapter.

  Activity File 19-1: Improving Your Formatting Skills

  Activity File 19-2: Improving Your Writing Skills

  Activity File 19-3: Completing a Job Application

  Activity File 19-4: Completing Employment Forms

Review Your Knowledge

1. What should be included in the contact information section of a résumé?
2. Explain keywords and the role they play in writing the experience section of a résumé.
3. What is the advantage of submitting a résumé as a PDF file?
4. Why is the cover message important?
5. Describe the purposes of a conclusion to a cover message.
6. Describe ways a person can learn about a company when preparing for a job interview.
7. Why is it beneficial to ask questions during an interview?
8. Describe the process of interview evaluation.
9. What should be included in a message that accepts a job offer?
10. Describe what happens during employment verification.

Apply Your Knowledge

1. Prepare to write a personal résumé for a communication position. Make a list of all of your past work experiences. Write a brief description of your job responsibilities to demonstrate your positive work behaviors and qualities that make you employable. Use appropriate keywords. If you have any special licenses or certifications, note these also. Next, list your educational background and any other information you think should be included on your résumé.
2. Apply the steps in the writing process and create a draft of your résumé. After your draft is complete, format the document. Using Figure 19-2 as an example, create your final résumé. Demonstrate use of appropriate content, concepts, and vocabulary. Check the final document for grammar.

3. Practice publishing your résumé in different formats. Save your résumé as a DOCX file, TXT file, and PDF file. Which format do you prefer using? Why?
4. A résumé may be required during the application process for college or a community service position for which you are applying. How would you modify your résumé for a college application? For a volunteer position?
5. Write a cover message to submit for a communication position along with the résumé you created in the previous activities. Explain how your positive work behaviors and qualities make you employable. Mention any special licenses or certifications you have earned. Note that your professional portfolio will contain samples of your work. Demonstrate use of appropriate content, concepts, and vocabulary. Check the final document for grammar and formatting.
6. Write an answer for each of the following potential interview questions.
   - What makes you a good employee?
   - What are your strengths?
   - What are your weaknesses?
7. Create a list of five questions you might ask during the interview. Be aware of how you word questions to make the best impression.
8. You have recently been interviewed for the position of assistant manager at a local restaurant. Write the following two messages.
   A. A thank-you message to the interviewer.
   B. A follow-up letter after you have been informed that another candidate was hired.

Communication Skills

College and Career Readiness

Reading. Read a magazine, newspaper, or online article about the importance of professional communication. Take notes to identify the purpose of the article and the intended audience. Determine the central ideas of the article and review the conclusions made by the author. Demonstrate your understanding of the information by summarizing what you read, making sure to analyze the audience, purpose, and message of the article.

Speaking. Communication careers require that individuals be able to participate and contribute to one-on-one discussions. Developing intrapersonal communication skills is one way to achieve career opportunities. As your instructor lectures on this chapter, contribute thoughtful comments when participation is invited.

Writing. Conduct research for desirable workplace skills. Pick five from the list. Beside each of the five you selected, indicate an academic skill that directly relates to the workplace skill.

Reading. Read the Ethics features presented throughout this book. What role do you think ethics and integrity have at work or at school? Think of a time when you used your ideals and principles to make a decision. What process did you use to make the decision? In retrospect, do you think you made the correct decision? Did your decision have any consequences?

Internet Research

Evaluating and Comparing Employment Opportunities. Using the Internet, locate job advertisements for three communication positions that interest you. Then create a checklist of the criteria you will use to evaluate and compare the positions. Next, using the checklist, evaluate and compare what opportunities each provides. Which one would you choose and why?

Lawful Interview Questions. Research the term *lawful interview questions*. Give examples of federal laws regarding employment interviews. Write several paragraphs explaining what you learned from this research.

Infographic Résumés. Using the Internet, find examples of infographic résumés. In which career fields are they common? What information do they usually include? Create your own infographic résumé and save it in PDF format.

Teamwork

Work in pairs or teams as assigned by your teacher to conduct mock interviews. Take turns acting as the interviewer and the interviewee. Refer to the typical interview questions given in this chapter, but come up with your own questions as well. When all interviews are completed, write a brief summary evaluating how you performed in the interview. Describe what you could do better in the future.

Portfolio Development

College and Career Readiness

Presenting Your Portfolio. You have collected various items for your portfolio and tracked them in your master spreadsheet. Now is the time to organize the contents for presentation. Create a flow chart to lay out the organization for your portfolio. Your instructor may have specific guidelines for you to follow. After you have sorted through the documents that you want to include, print a copy of each. Next, prepare a table of contents for the items. This will help the person reviewing the portfolio.

Your instructor may have examples of print and digital portfolios you can review for ideas. There may be an occasion where a print portfolio is required rather than a digital one. The organization processes are similar. Search the Internet for articles about how to organize a print or digital portfolio.

1. Review the documents you have collected. Select the items you want to include in your portfolio. Do a final check of the documents you created to make sure they are high quality in form and format. Make copies of certificates, diplomas, and other important documents. Keep the originals in a safe place.

2. Create the flow chart. Revise until you have an order that is appropriate for the purpose of the portfolio.

3. Place the items in a binder, folder, or other container.

4. Present the portfolio to your instructor, counselor, or other person who can give constructive feedback.

5. Create the slide show, web pages, or other medium for presenting your e-portfolio.

6. View the completed e-portfolio to check the appearance.

7. Review the feedback you received. Make necessary adjustments and revisions.

CTSOs

 **Day of the Event.** You have practiced all year for this CTSO competition, and now you are ready. Whether it is for an objective test, written test, report, or presentation, you have done your homework and are ready to shine.

To prepare for the day of the event, complete the following activities.

1. Get plenty of sleep the night before the event so that you are rested and ready to go.

2. Use your event checklist before you go into the presentation so that you do not forget any of your materials that are needed for the event.

3. Find the room where the competition will take place and arrive early. If you are late and the door is closed, you will be disqualified.

4. If you are making a presentation before a panel of judges, practice what you are going to say when you are called on. State your name, your school, and any other information that will be requested. Be confident, smile, and make eye contact with the judges.

5. When the event is finished, thank the judges for their time.

529 plan. Savings plan for education operated by a state or educational institution. (18)

A

abbreviation. Shortened form of a word or letters used to stand for a word or term. (5)

ability. Mastery of a skill or the capacity to do something. (18)

acceptable use policy. Set of rules that explains what is and is not acceptable use of company-owned and operated equipment and networks. (3)

active listening. Fully participating as a person processes what other people say. (16)

active reading. Processing the words, phrases, and sentences a person reads. (17)

active voice. Subject of the sentence performs the action. (4)

adjective. Word that modifies a noun or pronoun. (4)

adverb. Word that describes a verb, adjective, clause, or another adverb. (4)

advertisement. Nonpersonal sales message that is paid for by a sponsor. (8)

AIDA. Acronym that stands for *attention*, *interest*, *desire*, and *action*. (8)

alignment. How items line up with one another, such as on the left side or the right side. (12)

alphabet. Consists of symbols representing basic sounds of a language. (3)

analogy. Comparison of two unlike things based on a particular aspect each have in common. (13)

animation. Representation of motion with graphics or in text. (14)

annotation. Note or comment added to a document to help explain its contents. (17)

antecedent. Word that gets replaced with a pronoun. (4)

apostrophe. Punctuation mark used to form possessive words and contractions. (5)

appreciative listening. Process of listening for enjoyment. (16)

appendix. Contains additional information that would be helpful to the reader but is not necessary to complete the numbered steps. (10)

apprenticeship. Combination of on-the-job training, work experience, and classroom instruction. (18)

aptitude. Characteristic that an individual has developed naturally; also called *talents*. (18)

article. Adjective that limits the noun or pronoun it modifies. (4)

audience. Person or group to whom a message is directed. (6)

auditory aid. A sound element used to add interest or clarify information. (14)

B

background check. Investigation into personal data about a job applicant. (19)

balance. Arrangement of elements to create a feeling of equality across the document. (12)

barrier. Anything that prevents clear, effective communication. (1)

behavioral question. Questions that draw on a person's previous experiences and decisions. (19)

bias-free words. Neutral words imparting neither a positive nor negative message. (7)

blind copy. Used when sending a copy of the memo to someone without the recipient's knowledge; noted as *bc*. (9)

block-style letter. Formatted so all lines are flush with the left margin. (9)

blog. Information or discussion-based website that consists of a series of dated posts in reverse chronological order. (10)

body language. Nonverbal messages sent through gestures, facial expressions, posture, and other body actions. (1)

C

canvas size. Area in which a video or image will be displayed. (15)

capitalization. Writing a letter in uppercase rather than lowercase. (5)

caption. Text that appears next to or below the visual that explains the image itself or its purpose in the document. (12)

career. Series of related jobs in the same profession. (18)

career and technical student organization (CTSO). National student organizations with local school chapters that are related to and technical education (CTE) courses. (18)

career cluster. Groups of occupational and career specialties. (3, 18)

career pathway. Subgroup that reflects occupations requiring similar knowledge and skills. (3, 18)

career plan. List of steps to reach a career goal; also called *postsecondary plan*. (18)

cave drawing. Murals early humans painted to relate happenings and express ideas. (3)

censorship. Practice of examining material, such as online content, and blocking or deleting anything considered inappropriate. (3)

certification. Professional status earned by an individual after passing an exam focused on a specific body of knowledge. (18)

channel. How a message is transmitted. (1)

chronological résumé. Résumé that emphasizes employers and work experience with each. (19)

citations. List of the name of the author, title, publisher of the source, date of publication, and location of the publisher or online address. (11)

clause. Group of words within a sentence that has a subject and a predicate. (4)

cliché. Overused, commonplace, or trite language. (7)

cloud computing. Using remote servers to store and access data over the Internet rather than on a personal computer or local server. (3)

code of conduct. Identifies the manner in which employees should behave while at work or when representing the company. (3)

code of ethics. Document that dictates how business should be conducted. (3)

collaboration skills. Skills that give someone the ability to work with others to achieve a common goal. (2)

collective noun. Refers to a group or unit that contains more than one person, place, or thing. (4)

college access. Building awareness about college opportunities, providing guidance regarding college admissions, and identifying ways to pay for college. (18)

colon. Internal punctuation mark that introduces an element in a sentence or paragraph. (5)

comma. Punctuation mark used to separate elements in a sentence. (5)

communication. Process of using words, sounds, signs, or actions to exchange information or express thoughts. (1)

communication apprehension. Fear of speaking in public. (14)

communication process. Series of actions on the part of the sender and the receiver of a message and the path the message follows. (1)

communicative. Willing to talk to people or share information. (2)

complimentary close. Sign-off for a letter. (9)

compromise. Give up an individual idea so that the group can come to a solution. (2)

conclusion. Writer's summary of what the audience should take away from a report. (11)

condescending. To assume an attitude of superiority. (7)

confirmation message. Message written to confirm a verbal agreement made with a customer, client, or colleague. (8)

conflict management. Process of recognizing and resolving team disputes in a balanced and effective way. (2)

conflict-resolution skills. Skills required to resolve a situation in which a disagreement could lead to hostile behavior. (2)

conjunction. Word that connects other words, phrases, or sentences. (4)

connotation. Meaning of a word apart from what it explicitly names or describes. (7)

constructive criticism. Giving well-reasoned opinions about the work of others. (6)

context. Environments or setting in which something occurs or is communicated. (1)

contraction. Shortened form of a word or term. It is formed by omitting letters from one or more words and replacing them with an apostrophe to create one word. (5)

contrast. Having two dissimilar elements next to one another. (12)

cookies. Bits of data stored on a computer that record information about the websites a person has visited. (3)

coordinating conjunction. Joins two or more sentence elements that are of equal importance. (4)

copy. Written information intended for publication. (10)

copy notation. Notation that lists names of others receiving a copy of a letter. (9)

copyright. Acknowledges ownership of a work and specifies that only the owner has the right to sell the work, use it, or give permission for someone else to sell or use it. (3)

corporation. Business that is recognized as a separate legal entity from its owners. (18)

correlative conjunction. Pairs of words or phrases that work together to connect elements in a sentence. (4)

courtesy response. Response written to confirm that a message was received and action was taken. (8)

cover message. Letter or e-mail sent with a résumé to introduce an applicant and summarize his or her reasons for applying for a job. (19)

Creative Commons (CC) license. Specialized copyright license that allows free distribution of copyrighted work. (3)

critical listening. Occurs when specific information or instructions are needed. (16)

critical-thinking skills. Skills that give a person the ability to interpret and make reasonable judgments and decisions by analyzing a situation. (2)

criticism. Comment that expresses unfavorable judgment or disapproval of a person or action. (6)

culture. Shared beliefs, customs, practices, and social behavior of a particular group or nation. (2)

cyberbullying. Using the Internet to harass or threaten an individual. (3)

D

dangling participle. Writing error in which a participle phrase modifies nothing or the wrong person or object. (4)

dash. Punctuation mark that separates elements in a sentence or signals an abrupt change in thought. (5)

data. Pieces of information gathered through research. (11)

decoding. Translation of a message into terms that the receiver can understand. (1)

definite article. Refers to a specific noun. (4)

deliberative listening. Process of determining the quality or validity of what is being said. (16)

demographics. Information about a group of people. (6)

demonstration. Act of showing how something is done. (14)

demonstrative adjective. Used before a noun to indicate number and location. (4)

dependent clause. Clause that requires the rest of the sentence to provide a complete thought. (4)

description. Detailed written and visual information about an item or process. (10)

desktop publishing. Using software on the computer to lay out text and graphics for professional-looking documents, such as newspapers or brochures. (12)

destructive criticism. Judgment given with the intention of harming or offending someone. (6)

digital citizen. Someone who regularly and skillfully engages technology such as the Internet, computers, and other digital devices. (3)

digital citizenship. Standards of behavior when using technology to communicate. (3)

digital communication. Exchange of information through electronic means. (3)

digital etiquette. See *netiquette.*

digital footprint. Data record of all of an individual's online activities. (3)

digital literacy. Ability to use technology to create, locate, evaluate, and communicate information. (3)

digital media. Visuals, animation, video, audio, or other media created in a format that can be read by computers. (15)

diplomacy. Tactful handling of a situation to avoid offending the reader or arousing hostility. (8)

direct approach. Approach in which a main idea is introduced first and then followed by descriptive details. (6)

direct object. Someone or something that receives the action of the verb. (4)

directions. Steps to get from point A to point B. (8)

diversity. People from different backgrounds, cultures, or demographics come together in a group. (2)

E

economic base. Industry that provides employment that is necessary for a community to survive. (18)

editing. More refined form of revising. (6)

empathetic listening. Occurs when a person attempts to put his or herself in the speaker's place and understand how he or she feels. (16)

emphasis. Creates a focal point and draws attention. (12)

employability skills. Applicable skills used to help an individual find a job, perform in the workplace, and gain success in a job or career. (18)

employment verification. Process through which the information provided on a résumé history is checked to verify that it is correct. (19)

enclosure notation. Alerts the reader to materials that are included in a mailing along with the letter. (9)

encoding. Process of turning the idea for a message into symbols that can be communicated. (1)

end user license agreement (EULA). Set of rules that every user must agree to before using the software. (15)

English as a second language (ESL). Use of English by those with a different native language. (2)

enunciation. Clearly and distinctly pronouncing syllables and sounds. (14)

ergonomics. Science concerned with designing and arranging things people use so that they can interact with them both efficiently and safely. (17)

ethics. Principles of what is right and wrong that help people make decisions. (3)

etiquette. Art of using good manners in any situation. (1)

euphemism. Word that expresses unpleasant ideas in more pleasant terms. (7)

evaluate. Judge the accuracy and truthfulness of the spoken words. (16)

evasive. Avoiding giving a direct answer. (16)

exclamation point. Mark used to express strong emotion. (5)

executive summary. Summarizes the main points in the report. (11)

F

fair use doctrine. Allows individuals to use copyrighted works without permission in limited situations under very strict guidelines. (3)

false advertising. Overstating the features and benefits of products or services, making false claims about them. (3)

feedback. Receiver's response to the sender that concludes the communication process. (1)

figure. Any type of visual that is not a table. (12)

figure number. Unique identifier within a numbering system that is used to identify each visual. (12)

filtering. Technique by which a special effect is applied to an image. (15)

firewall. Program that monitors information coming into a computer and helps ensure that only safe information gets through. (3)

first person. Refers to an action of someone who is speaking or writing. (4)

focus group. Small group of people with which the interviewer conducts a discussion to gather answers to a prepared set of questions. (11)

font. Typeface, size, and style of characters. (9, 12)

footage. Video content recorded by a camera. (15)

formal communication. Sharing of information that conforms to specific protocol. (1)

formal education. Education received in a school, college, or university. (18)

formal language. Language that is used in a workplace environment. (7)

formal report. Document that focuses on a broad main topic which is divided into subtopics for complete and clear coverage. (11)

format. How written information is presented on a printed page or screen. (9)

formatting. Placement and style of type in a document. (6)

for-profit school. School that is set up to earn money for investors. (18)

four Cs of communication. Qualities of clarity, conciseness, courtesy, and correctness. (6)

frequently asked question (FAQ). Website page that provides answers to common customer questions. (8)

future tense. Indicates that the action or state of being will occur at a later time. (4)

G

gerund. Verb form used as a noun. (4)

glossary. Alphabetical listing of terms used in a manual and their definitions. (10)

goal. Something a person wants to achieve in a specified time period. (18)

goodwill. Advantage an individual or an organization has due to its good reputation; it cannot be bought. (1)

grammar. Study of how words and their components come together to form sentences. (4)

graphic mark. Symbol used to indicate a trademark or service mark. (3)

group discussion. Situation in which three or more individuals share their ideas about a subject. (13)

group dynamics. Interacting forces within a group. (2)

guide word. Words *to, from, date,* and *subject* that appear at the top of the memo. (9)

H

hacking. Illegally accessing or altering digital devices, software, or networks. (3)

handout. Printed materials that are distributed to the audience; also called *leave-behinds*. (14)

harmony. The use of like elements such as color, pattern, or shapes to create unity in a presentation. (12)

hashtag. Searchable keyword on Twitter marked by the hashtag symbol (#) that links users to all Tweets marked with the same hashtag keyword. (10)

heading. Words and phrases that introduce sections of text. (11)

hearing. Physical process of sound waves reaching a person's ears, which send signals to his or her brain. (16)

homonym. Word that is pronounced *and* spelled the same as another word, but is different in meaning. (5)

hyphen. Punctuation mark used to separate parts of compound words, numbers, or ranges. (5)

hypothetical question. Questions that require a person to imagine a situation and describe how he or she would act. (19)

I

identity theft. Illegal act that involves stealing someone's personal information and using that information to commit theft or fraud. (3)

ideogram. Graphic symbol that represents an abstract idea or concept. (3)

illustration. Map, drawing, or photograph. (12)

impromptu speaking. Talking without advanced notice to plan what will be said. (13)

indefinite article. Refers to a noun in a general way. (4)

independent clause. Clause that gives a complete thought and could stand alone as a separate sentence. (4)

index. Alphabetical list of important topics, key terms, and proper nouns used in a manual with the page numbers on which each is located. (10)

indirect approach. Approach in which details are given first and are then followed by the main idea. (6)

indirect object. Names something or someone for whom the action of the verb is performed. (4)

inferential. To draw a conclusion from what is said. (16)

infinitive. The word *to* and a verb in its simple present form. (4)

infographic. Displays content using words and graphics in a visually appealing way; short for *information graphic*. (12)

infographic résumé. Résumé in which the content is displayed using a combination of words and graphics to present information clearly and quickly. (19)

informal communication. Casual sharing of information with no customs or rules of etiquette involved. (1)

informal language. Language used in a casual situation without applying the rules of grammar. (7)

informal report. Document that does not require formal research or documentation. (11)

informal study report. Provides information that is gathered by the writer through methods other than formal research, such as reading related documents, conducting informal interviews, reviewing competitive products, or making observations after visiting a site or attending a meeting. (11)

information graphic. See *infographic*.

informational interviewing. Strategy used to interview a professional to ask for advice and direction, rather than asking for a job opportunity. (18)

infringement. Any use of copyrighted material without permission. (3)

inside address. Name, title, and address of the recipient. (9)

instructions. Steps that must be followed in sequence to accomplish a task. (8)

intellectual property. Something that comes from a person's mind, such as an idea, invention, or process. (3)

intercultural communication. Process of sending and receiving messages between people of various cultures. (2)

interest. Feeling of wanting to learn more about a topic or to be involved in an activity. (18)

interjection. Word that expresses strong emotion, such as surprise, fear, anger, excitement, or shock. (4)

internal punctuation. Punctuation marks used within a sentence. (5)

Internet protocol address. Number used to identify an electronic device connected to the Internet; also known as an *IP address*. (3)

internship. Short-term position with a sponsoring organization that gives an intern an opportunity to gain on-the-job experience in a certain field of study or occupation. (18)

interpersonal communication. Communication that occurs between a sender and one other person. (1)

interpersonal skills. Skills that help people communicate and work well with each other. (2)

intonation. Rise and fall in the pitch of a person's voice. (14)

introduction. Making a person known to someone else by sharing the person's name and other relevant information. (13)

IP address. See *Internet protocol address.*

J

jargon. Language specific to a line of work or area of expertise. (7)

job. Work a person does regularly in order to earn money. (18)

job application. Form with spaces for contact information, education, and work experience. (19)

job interview. Employer's opportunity to review a person's résumé and ask questions to see if he or she is qualified for a position. (19)

job-specific skills. Critical skills necessary to perform the required work-related tasks of a position. (18)

K

kerning. Amount of space between two letters. (12)

keyword. In social media, a word that specifically relates to the subject matter in a social media post. (10) In employment documents, a word or term that specifically relates to the functions of the position for which the employer is hiring. (19)

L

layering. Process of building an image by putting different parts of the image on different levels. (15)

layout. Relationship of the text to white space. (6)

leader. Someone who guides others to a goal. (2)

leadership. The process of influencing others or making things better. (2)

leading. Amount of space between two lines of type. (12)

leave-behind. See *handout.*

legend. List that explains the set of symbols used in the chart. (12)

libel. Publishing a false statement about someone that causes others to have a bad opinion of him or her. (3)

license. Legal permission to use a software program. (3)

licensing agreement. Contract that gives one party permission to market, produce, or use the product or service owned by another party. (3)

listening. Combines hearing with evaluating. (16)

listening skills. Ability to hear what a person says as well as understand what is being said. (2)

literal. Speaker means exactly what the words indicate. (16)

M

malicious software. See *malware*.

malware. Term given to software programs that are intended to damage, destroy, or steal data; short for *malicious software*. (3)

manual. Comprehensive, multi-section document covering a technical topic that often includes a combination of instructions and other documentation. (10)

marketing. Persuasive activities that identify, anticipate, and satisfy customer needs. (8)

master page. Defines the page size, recurring areas for type and graphics, and placement of recurring elements, such as page numbers. (12)

master slide. Slide containing design elements that are applied to a particular set of slides or all slides in a presentation. (14)

mechanism. Type of object that has working parts. (10)

media literacy skills. Accessing, analyzing, evaluating, and communicating information in various formats that include print and online. (6)

mediation. Inclusion of a neutral mediator to help conflicting parties resolve their dispute and reach an agreement. (2)

medium. Form of communication; may be written, visual, oral, or digital. (6)

memo. Hardcopies used for intra-office communication; short for memorandum. (9)

milestone. Important date that needs to be met to keep a project moving forward. (15)

mixed punctuation. Style in which a colon is placed after the salutation and a comma after the complimentary close. (9)

mock interview. Practice interview conducted with another person. (19)

modified-block-style letter. A letter that positions the date, complimentary close, and signature to the right of the center point of the letter. (9)

modulation. Changing the emphasis of words by raising and lowering a person's voice. (14)

monotone. A speech delivered with the same intonation, pitch, and volume. (14)

movable type. System of printing involving individual letters or symbols that can be assembled to create words, sentences, and passages. (3)

movement. Real action or the appearance of action. (15)

N

nature of business. General category of operations that generate profit. (18)

need-based award. Financial-aid awards available for students and families who meet certain economic requirements. (18)

negotiation. When individuals involved in a conflict come together to discuss a compromise. (2)

netiquette. Etiquette used when communicating electronically; also known as *digital etiquette*. (3)

networking. Talking with people a person knows and making new contacts. (18)

nonrestrictive clause. Provides information that is not essential to the meaning of the sentence. (4)

nonverbal communication. Action, behavior, or attitude that sends a message to the receiver. (1)

notation. Found at the bottom of a memo and used to indicate specific things to the reader. (9)

not-for-profit school. A school that returns the money it earns back into the school. (18)

noun. Word that names a person, place, or thing. (4)

O

object. Something that is not living and can be seen or touched. (10)

object description. Provides detailed information about an object or a mechanism. (10)

objectivity. To be free of personal feelings, prejudices, or interpretations. (6)

occupational training. Education that prepares a person for a specific type of work. (18)

open punctuation. Style in which there is no punctuation after the salutation or complimentary close. (9)

open source. Software that has had its source code made available to the public at no charge. (3)

oral communication. See *verbal communication*. (1)

oral language. System in which words are spoken to express ideas or emotions. (13)

orphan. First line of a paragraph that falls immediately before a page break, making it appear as though it is not part of the paragraph on the next page. (12)

outline. Guideline that helps identify the information to be presented, the proper sequence, and to ensure related ideas are covered in the same section. (6)

P

paralanguage. Attitude a person projects with the tone and pitch of his or her voice. (1)

parallel structure. Method of writing in which similar elements are expressed in a consistent way or using the same pattern. (5)

parentheses. Punctuation mark used to enclose words or phrases that clarify meaning or give added information. (5)

parliamentary procedure. Process for holding meetings so they are orderly and democratic. (2)

partnership. Business that is comprised of two or more people working toward a joint purpose. (18)

passive listening. Casually listening to a speaker. (16)

passive voice. Sentence structure in which subject of the sentence is acted upon. (4)

past participle. Indicates that action has been completed. (4)

past tense. Indicates that the action or state of being has already occurred. (4)

patent. Gives a person or company the right to be the sole producer of a product for a defined period of time. (3)

peer. Persons of equal standing or work position. (1)

period. Punctuation mark used at the end of a declarative sentence. (5)

periodic report. Informal reports written according to a specified schedule: daily, weekly, monthly, quarterly, etc. (11)

permanent compound. Compound words that always have a hyphen. (5)

personal information management (PIM). System that individuals use to acquire, organize, maintain, retrieve, and use information. (2)

personal space. Physical space between two individuals. (1)

perspective. Artistic technique that creates the illusion of depth on a two-dimensional surface. (15)

persuade. Convince a person to take a proposed course of action. (8)

persuasive message. Message to convince the reader to take a certain course of action. (8)

petroglyph. Similar to a cave drawing, but is carved into rock instead of painted or drawn on rock. (3)

phishing. Use of fraudulent e-mails and copies of valid websites to trick people into providing private and confidential data. (3)

phrase. Group of words that act together to convey meaning in a sentence. (4)

pictogram. Symbol used for communication that represents what something looks like. (3)

piracy. Illegal copying or downloading of software, files, or other protected material. (3)

pitch. Describes the highness or lowness of a sound. (14)

pixel. Tiny dot of color that makes up a digital image; short for *picture element*. (15)

plagiarism. Claiming ownership of another person's material, which is both unethical and illegal. (3)

possessive noun. Indicates ownership by the noun or an attribute of the noun. (4)

postscript. Means after writing and is information included after the signature. (9)

postsecondary education. Any education achieved after high school. (18)

predicate. Describes an action or state of being for the subject. (4)

preposition. Word that connects or relates its object to the rest of the sentence. (4)

present participle. Verb form that indicates action is in progress or ongoing. (4)

present tense. Indicates an action or state of being takes place now. (4)

presentation. Speech, address, or demonstration given to a group. (13)

presentation notes. Notes used to keep a speaker on topic. (14)

press release. Sales message telling a story about and by a company. (8)

presumption. Something believed based on probable or assumed reliability. (17)

primary audience. Those directly involved in the purpose for writing. (6)

primary research. First-hand research conducted by the writer in preparation for writing a report. (11)

prior knowledge. Experience and information a person already possesses. (16)

prioritize. Rank items in order from most to least important. (17)

process. Series of actions all taken to achieve a stated goal. (10)

process description. Description that helps a reader understand the actions taken to reach a specific goal. (10)

production. Process of creating a digital media presentation. (15)

professional communication. Incorporates written, verbal, visual, and digital communication to provide factual information that is usable in the workplace. (1)

progress report. Periodic report written in a specified format and periodically submitted to track the status of a project; also known as *status report*. (11)

pronoun. Word that replaces a noun in a sentence. (4)

proofreading. Checking the final copy for correct spelling, punctuation, formatting, and typographical errors. (6)

propaganda. Messages designed to influence the audience with biased information. (8)

proportion. Relationship of the size of elements to the whole and to each other. (12)

proprietary information. Any work created by company employees on the job that is owned by that company. (3)

proprietorship. Business that has a sole owner. (18)

protocol. Set of customs or rules of etiquette. (1)

proximity. How near or far two design elements are from each other. (12)

public communication. Communicating with a group larger than 20 people. (1)

public domain. Refers to material that is not owned by anybody and can be used without permission. (3)

public relations. Applying communication skills that promote goodwill between a business and the public. (6)

publishing. Process of preparing a document for distribution. (6)

punctuation. Marks used to show the structure of sentences. (5)

Q

qualitative data. Information that provides insight into how people think about a particular topic. (11)

quantitative data. Facts and figures from which conclusions can be drawn. (11)

question mark. Punctuation used at the end of an interrogative sentence. (5)

quotation marks. Punctuation marks used to enclose short, direct quotes and titles of some artistic or written works. (5)

R

rapport. Feeling of harmony and accord in a relationship that encourages further communication. (16)

read for detail. Reading all words and phrases, considering their meaning, and determining how they combine with other elements to convey ideas. (17)

readability. Measure of whether the document is easy to read. (6)

receiver. Person who reads, hears, or sees a message. (1)

receiving barrier. Occurs when a receiver says or does something that causes the sender's message not to be received. (1)

recommendations. Actions a writer believes the reader should take. (11)

redundancy. Repeating a message or saying the same thing more than once. (7)

reference. Person who can comment on the qualifications, work ethic, personal qualities, and work-related aspects of another person's character. (19)

reference initials. Indicates the person who keyed the letter. (9)

reflective listening. Occurs when a listener demonstrates understanding of a message by restating what the speaker says. (16)

repetition. Action that creates consistency and pattern. (12)

report. Document used to present information in a structured format to a specific audience for a defined purpose. (11)

representative sampling. Group that includes a cross section of the entire population a person is targeting in a survey. (11)

request. Inquiry that asks the reader for some type of action or response. (8)

resolution. Number of pixels that make up an image. (15)

restrictive clause. Type of dependent clause that is essential to the meaning of the sentence. (4)

résumé. Document that profiles a person's career goals, education, and work history. (19)

revising. Process of rewriting paragraphs and sentences to improve organization and content. (6)

rhetoric. Study of writing or speaking as a way of communicating information or persuading an individual. (1)

rhythm. Regular repetition of objects or sounds to show movement or activity; it can also be used to create a sense of energy or urgency. (15)

routine request. Request that is expected by the receiver. (8)

S

sales message. Message used to persuade the reader to spend money for a product or service, either immediately or later. (8)

salutation. Greeting in a letter that always begins with *Dear.* (9)

scan. Quickly glancing through a message to find specific information. (17)

scannable résumé. Résumé in which typographical elements are eliminated from the document. (19)

scholarship. Financial aid that may be based on financial need or some type of merit or accomplishment. (18)

scope. Guideline of how much information will be included. (6)

search engine optimization (SEO). Process of indexing a website so that it will rank higher on the list of returned results when a search is conducted. (10)

second person. Refers to an action of someone who is being addressed. (4)

secondary audience. Those who need to know the communication took place. (6)

secondary research. Data and information already assembled and recorded by someone else. (11)

semicolon. Internal punctuation mark used to separate clauses or some items in a series. (5)

sender. Person who has a message to communicate. (1)

sending barrier. Occurs when a sender says or does something that causes the receiver to stop listening. (1)

sentence. Group of words that expresses a complete thought. (4)

service mark. Similar to a trademark, but it identifies a service rather than a product. (3)

signature block. Writer's name and title. (9)

site license. Agreements that allow software to be installed on any machine owned by the company who purchased the software. (15)

situation. All of the facts, conditions, and events that affect a message. (7)

skepticism. Having a degree of doubt. (16)

skill. Something an individual does well. (18)

skim. Quickly glancing through an entire document to get an overview. (17)

slander. Speaking a false statement about someone that causes others to have a bad opinion of him or her. (3)

slang. Words and phrases that are not considered part of Standard English. (7)

small group communication. Communication that occurs with 3 to 20 people. (1)

SMART goal. A goal that is specific, measurable, attainable, realistic, and timely. (18)

social media. Websites and apps that allow individual users to network online by creating and sharing content with one another. (10)

social responsibility. Behaving with sensitivity to social, environmental, and economic issues. (3)

software virus. Computer program designed to negatively impact a computer system by infecting other files. (3)

special request. Request that requires planning an approach that will create a positive response. (8)

speech. Expressing thought through verbal language. (3)

spyware. Software that spies on a computer. (3)

Standard English. Language usage that follows accepted rules for spelling, grammar, and punctuation. (1)

status report. See *progress report.*

stereotype. Belief or generalization about a group of people with a given set of characteristics. (2)

storyboard. Illustrates the content of a digital media presentation with a sketch of each important scene or event along with a brief description of what will happen. (15)

style sheet. Desktop publishing file that saves the attributes of every font that will be used in a project. (12)

subject. Person speaking or the person, place, or thing a sentence describes. (4)

subjective. Interpretation depends on personal views, experience, and background. (13)

subordinating clause. Joined to the rest of the sentence with a subordinating conjunction. (4)

subordinating conjunction. Connects dependent clauses to independent clauses. (4)

survey. Set of questions asked to a group of people to determine how that group thinks, feels, or acts. (11)

symbol. Object or image that represents an idea, thought, or concept. (3)

symmetry. Used to create formal balance so that what appears on one side of the page is mirrored on the other. (12)

T

table. Visual that displays information in columns and rows and is often used to compare data. (12)

table of contents. Lists the major sections and subsections within a report with page numbers. (11)

team. Group of two or more people who work together to achieve a common goal. (2)

technical document. Document that informs or instructs the reader how to use mechanical, technological, or scientific information. (10)

telecommunication. Communication over a distance. (3)

telephone etiquette. Use of good manners on the telephone. (13)

template. Predesigned forms supplied in a software program. (9)

third person. Refers to an action of someone being discussed. (4)

time management. Practice of organizing time and work assignments to increase personal efficiency. (2)

tone. Impression of the overall content of the message. (7)

trademark. Protects taglines, slogans, names, symbols, or any unique method to identify a product or company. (3)

transition. Words, phrases, and sentences that connect ideas and clarify the relationship between sentences and paragraphs. (7)

transmission. Act of sending a message. (1)

transmittal message. Routine communication accompanying documents or other materials attached to e-mails or sent by a delivery service. (8)

troubleshooting guide. Table that lists potential problems in one column and actions to correct the problem in another column. (10)

typeface. Definition of the characteristics that make up a set of letters, numbers, and symbols. (9, 12)

typography. Style and arrangement of type. (12)

V

values. Principles and beliefs that a person considers important. (18)

variety. Use of differing elements such as color, pattern, or shapes to create interest or emphasis. (12)

verb. Word that shows action or state of being. (4)

verbal communication. Speaking words to communicate; also known as *oral communication*. (1)

visual. Any image that represents an idea, concept, or information. (12)

visual aid. Object used to clarify an idea, concept, or process. (14)

visual communication. Using visual aids or graphics to communicate an idea or concept. (1)

visual design. Arrangement of the visual and artistic elements used to accomplish a goal or communicate an idea. (12)

visual literacy. Ability to create or interpret the meaning of a visual message. (12)

W

white space. Includes margins, space between paragraphs, and any other blank space on the page. (9)

widow. Last line of a paragraph that falls immediately after a page break, making it appear as though it is not part of the previous paragraph. (12)

work-study program. Part-time job on a college campus that is subsidized by the government. (18)

writer's block. Psychological condition that prevents a writer from proceeding with the writing process. (6)

writing. System of visual communication using symbols, letters, or words. (3)

writing process. Set of sequential stages for each writing task that includes prewriting, writing, postwriting, and publishing. (6)

writing style. Refers to the way in which a writer uses language to convey an idea. (7)

written communication. Recording words through writing or keying to communicate. (1)

M

N

O

direct, 82, 85, 89, 94
indirect, 82, 85, 89, 94
object linking and embedding (OLE), 360
objectivity, 157
objects and complements, 85
observations, 270
occasion, 323
Occupational Information Network
(O*NET), 422
Occupational Outlook Handbook, 431
Occupational Safety & Health
Administration (OSHA), 40
occupational training, 430
OLE. *See* object linking and embedding (OLE)
open punctuation, 225
open source, 54
oral communication, 13
oral language, 316
organization chart, 299
organize information, 272–274
orphan, 306–307
OSHA. *See* Occupational Safety & Health
Administration (OSHA)
outline, 151–153
developing, 152–153

P

pan, 364
paralanguage, 17
parallel structure, 136–138
clauses, 137–138
phrases, 136–137
words, 136–137
parenthesis, 121–122
parliamentary procedure, 37, 45
participle, 98, 102–103
dangling, 98, 103
past, 98, 103
present, 98, 102–103
partnership, 424
parts of speech, 82
passive behavior, 37
passive listening, 377
passive voice, 100, 179–180
past participle, 103
past tense, 101
patent, 52
peer, 10
period, 116–118
periodic report, 285

permanent compound, 125
personal information management (PIM), 34
personal pronouns, 103
personal space, 16
perspective, 367
persuade, 208–211
persuasive message, 208–213
anticipate questions and objections, 213
build interest, 209
create desire, 209
encourage action, 209
writing, 208–209
persuasive speech, 327
petroglyph, 65–66
phishing, 60
phoneme, 316
photo editing, 361–362
photo resolution, 361
photography, 361–362
phrase, 85
phrases and clauses, 85
pictogram, 65–66
picture element. *See* pixel
PIM. *See* personal information management
piracy, 51
pitch, 344
pixel, 361
plagiarism, 51, 150
pop-up blocker, 62
Portfolio Development
Certificates, 217
Checklist, 76
Clubs and Organizations, 371
Community Service, 241
Digital File Formats, 166
Digital Presentation Options, 143
Diversity Skills, 311
File Structure, 188
Hard and Soft Skills, 334
Hard Copy Organization, 112
Introduction, 438–439
Networking, 391
Objective, 44
Portfolio Overview, 22
Presenting Your Portfolio, 464–465
References, 409
Schoolwork, 262
Talents, 291
Technical Skills, 353
possessive noun, 91–92